HISTORY OF ENGLISH LITERATURE

NINETEENTH CENTURY

A HISTORY

OF

NINETEENTH CENTURY

LITERATURE

(1780–1895)

BY

GEORGE SAINTSBURY

PROFESSOR OF RHETORIC AND ENGLISH LITERATURE IN THE
UNIVERSITY OF EDINBURGH

New York
MACMILLAN AND CO.
AND LONDON
1896

Norwood Press
J. S. Cushing & Co. — Berwick & Smith.
Norwood Mass. U.S.A.

PREFACE

In the execution of the present task (which I took over about two years ago from hands worthier than mine, but then more occupied) some difficulties of necessity occurred which did not present themselves to myself when I undertook the volume of Elizabethan Literature, or to my immediate predecessor in grappling with the period between 1660 and 1780.

The most obvious and serious of these was the question, "What should be done with living authors?" Independently of certain perils of selection and exclusion, of proportion and of freedom of speech, I believe it will be recognised by every one who has ever attempted it, that to mix estimates of work which is done and of work which is unfinished is to the last degree unsatisfactory. I therefore resolved to include no living writer, except Mr. Ruskin, in this volume for the purpose of detailed criticism, though some may be now and then mentioned in passing.

Even with this limitation the task remained a rather formidable one. Those who are least disposed to overvalue literary work in proportion as it approaches their own time will still acknowledge that the last hundred and fifteen years are fuller furnished than either of the periods of not very dissimilar length which have been already dealt with. The proportion of names of the first, or of a very high second class, is distinctly larger than in the eighteenth century; the bulk of literary production is infinitely greater than in the Elizabethan time. Further, save in regard to the earliest subsections of this period, Time has not performed his office, beneficent to the reader but more beneficent to the historian, of sifting and riddling out writers whom it is no longer necessary to consider, save in a spirit of adventurous or affectionate antiquarianism. I must ask the reader to believe me when I say that many who do not appear here at all, or who are dismissed in a few lines, have yet been the subjects of careful reading on my part. If some exclusions (not due to mere oversight) appear arbitrary or unjust, I would urge that this is not a Dictionary of Authors, nor a Catalogue of Books, but a History of Literature; and that to mention everybody is as impossible as to say everything. As I have revised the sheets the old query has recurred to myself only too often, and sometimes in reference to very favourite books and authors of my own. Where, it may be asked, is Kenelm Digby and the *Broad Stone of Honour*? Where Sir Richard Burton (as great a contrast to Digby as can well be imagined)? Where Laurence Oliphant, who, but the other day, seemed to many clever men the cleverest man they knew? Where John Foster, who provided food for the thoughtful public two generations ago? Where Greville of the caustic diaries, and his editor (latest deceased) Mr. Reeve, and Crabb Robinson, and many others? Some of these and others are really *neiges d'antan;* some baffle the historian in miniature by being rebels to brief and exact characterisation; some, nay many, are simply crowded out.

I must also ask pardon for having exercised apparently arbitrary discretion in alternately separating the work of the same writer under different chapter-headings, and grouping it with a certain disregard of the strict limits of the chapter-heading itself.

I think I shall obtain this pardon from those who remember the advantage obtainable from a connected view of the progress of distinct literary kinds, and that, sometimes not to be foregone, of considering the whole work of certain writers together.

To provide room for the greater press of material, it was necessary to make some slight changes of omission in the scheme of the earlier volumes. The opportunity of considerable gain was suggested in the department of extract — which obviously became less necessary in the case of authors many of whom are familiar, and hardly any accessible with real difficulty. Nor did it seem necessary to take up room with the bibliographical index, the utility of which in my Elizabethan volume I was glad to find almost universally recognised. This would have had to be greatly more voluminous here ; and it was much less necessary. With a very few exceptions, all the writers here included are either kept in print, or can be obtained without much trouble at the second-hand bookshops.

To what has thus been said as to the principles of arrangement it cannot be necessary to add very much as to the principles of criticism. They are the same as those which I have always endeavoured to maintain — that is to say, I have attempted to preserve a perfectly independent, and, as far as possible, a rationally uniform judgment, taking account of none but literary characteristics, but taking account of all characteristics that are literary. It may be, and it probably is, more and more difficult to take achromatic views of literature as it becomes more and more modern ; it is certainly more difficult to get this achromatic character, even where it exists, acknowledged by contemporaries. But it has at least been my constant effort to attain it.

In the circumstances, and with a view to avoid not merely repetition but confusion and dislocation in the body of the book,

I have thought it better to make the concluding chapter one of considerably greater length than the corresponding part of the Elizabethan volume, and to reserve for it the greater part of what may be called connecting and comprehensive criticism. In this will be found what may be not improperly described from one point of view as the opening of the case, and from another as its summing up — the evidence which justifies both being contained in the earlier chapters.

It is perhaps not improper to add that the completion of this book has been made a little difficult by the incidence of new duties, not in themselves unconnected with its subject. But I have done my best to prevent or supply oversight.

CONTENTS

CHAPTER I

THE END OF THE EIGHTEENTH CENTURY

CHAPTER II

THE NEW POETRY

CHAPTER III

THE NEW FICTION

CHAPTER IV

THE DEVELOPMENT OF PERIODICALS.

CHAPTER V

THE HISTORIANS OF THE CENTURY

CHAPTER VI

THE SECOND POETICAL PERIOD

CHAPTER VII

THE NOVEL SINCE 1850

CHAPTER VIII

PHILOSOPHY AND THEOLOGY

CHAPTER IX

LATER JOURNALISM AND CRITICISM IN ART AND LETTERS

CHAPTER X

SCHOLARSHIP AND SCIENCE

CHAPTER XI

DRAMA

CHAPTER XII

CONCLUSION

CHAPTER I

THE period of English literary history which is dealt with in the opening part of the present volume includes, of necessity, among its most illustrious names, not a few whose work will not be the subject of formal discussion here, because the major part of it was done within the scope of the volume which preceded. Thus, to mention only one of these names, the most splendid displays of Burke's power — the efforts in which he at last gave to mankind what had previously been too often devoted to party — date from this time, and even from the later part of it; while Gibbon did not die till 1794, and Horace Walpole not till 1797. Even Johnson, the type and dictator at once of the eighteenth century in literary England, survived the date of 1780 by four years.

Nevertheless the beginning of the ninth decade of the century did actually correspond with a real change, a real line of demarcation. Not only did the old writers drop off one by one, not only did no new writers of utterly distinct idiosyncrasy (Burns and Blake excepted) make their appearance till quite the end of it, but it was also marked by the appearance of men of letters and of literary styles which announced, if not very distinctly, the coming of changes of the most sweeping kind. Hard as it may be to exhibit the exact contrast between, say, Goldsmith and men like Cowper on the one side and Crabbe on the other, that contrast cannot but be felt by every reader who has used himself

B   1

in the very least to the consideration of literary differences. And as with individuals, so with kinds. No special production of these twenty years may be of the highest value ; but there is a certain idiosyncrasy, if only an idiosyncrasy of transition — an unlikeness to anything that comes before, and to anything, unless directly imitated, that comes after — which is equally distinguishable in the curious succession of poetical satires from Peter Pindar to the *Anti-Jacobin*, in the terror-and-mystery novels of the school of Mrs. Radcliffe and Monk Lewis, in the large, if not from the literary point of view extremely noteworthy, department of politics and economics which in various ways employed the pens of writers so different as Moore, Young, Godwin, Priestley, Horne, Tooke, Cobbett, and Paine.

Giving poetry, as usual, the precedence even in the most unpoetical periods, we shall find in the four names already cited — those of Crabbe, Cowper, Blake, and Burns — examples of which even the most poetical period need not be ashamed. In what may be called the absolute spirit of poetry, the *nescio quid* which makes the greatest poets, no one has ever surpassed Burns and Blake at their best ; though the perfection of Burns is limited in kind, and the perfection of Blake still more limited in duration and sustained force. Cowper would have been a great poet of the second class at any time, and in some times might have attained the first. As for Crabbe, he very seldom has the absolute spirit of poetry just mentioned ; but the vigour and the distinction of his verse, as well as his wonderful faculty of observation in rendering scene and character, are undeniable. And it is not perhaps childish to point out that there is something odd and out of the way about the poetical career of all these poets of the transition. Cowper's terrible malady postpones his first efforts in song to an age when most poets are losing their voices ; Crabbe, beginning brilliantly and popularly, relapses into a silence of nearly a quarter of a century before breaking out with greater power and skill than ever ; Burns runs one of the shortest, if one of the most brilliant, Blake one of the longest, the strangest, the most intermittent, of poetical careers. Nor is it superfluous to draw attention further to the fact that when we leave this little company — at the best august, at the worst more than respectable — we drop suddenly to the flattest and most hopeless bog of poesiless verse that lies anywhere on the map of England's literature. Passing from the ethereal music of the Scottish ploughman and the English painter, from Cowper's noble or gentle thought and his accomplished versification, from Crabbe's manly vigour and his Rembrandt touch, we find nothing, unless it be the ingenious but not strictly poetical burlesque of the Wolcots and the Lawrences, till we come to the drivel of Hayley and the drought of Darwin.

Of the quartette, William Cowper was by far the oldest; the other three being contemporaries within a few years. He was born on 26th November 1731 at Great Berkhampstead. His father was a clergyman and a royal chaplain, his mother one of the Norfolk Donnes. Her early death, and that school discomfort which afterwards found vent in *Tirocinium*, appear to have aggravated a natural melancholia; though after leaving Westminster, and during his normal studies at both branches of the law, he seems to have been cheerful enough. How what should have been the making of his fortune, — his appointment as Clerk of the Journals to the House of Lords, — not unassisted by religious mania, drove him through sheer nervousness to attempt suicide, is one of the best known things in English literary biography, as indeed are most of the few events of his sad life, — owing partly to his own charming letters, partly to the biographies of Southey and others. His latest days were his unhappiest, and after years of more or less complete loss of reason he died on 27th April 1800.

It has been said that Cowper did not take to writing till late in life. He had had literary friends — Churchill, Lloyd, and others — in youth, and must always have had literary sympathies; but it was not till he was nearly fifty, nor till the greater part of twenty years after his first mental seizure, that he attempted composition at the instance of his friend Newton and the Unwins.

Beginning with hymns and trifles, he before long undertook, at
this or that person's suggestion, longer poems, such as *Truth*, *The
Progress of Error*, and *Expostulation*, which were finished by
1781 and published next year, to be followed by the still better
and more famous *Task*, suggested to him by Lady Austen. This
appeared in 1785, and was very popular. He had already begun
to translate Homer, which occupied him for the greater part of
seven years. Nothing perhaps settled him more in the public
affections than "John Gilpin," the subject of which he also owed
to Lady Austen; and he continued to write occasional pieces of
exquisite accomplishment. Almost the last, if not actually the
last, of these, written just before the final obscuration of his
faculties, was the beautiful and terrible "Castaway," an avowed
allegory of his own condition.

Cowper, even more than most writers, deserves and requites
consideration under the double aspect of matter and form. In
both he did much to alter the generally accepted conditions of
English poetry; and if his formal services have perhaps received
less attention than they merit, his material achievements have
never been denied. His disposition — in which, by a common
enough contrast, the blackest and most hopeless melancholy was
accompanied by the merriest and most playful humour — reflected
itself unequally in his verse, the lighter side chiefly being exhibited.
Except in "The Castaway," and a few — not many — of the hymns,
Cowper is the very reverse of a gloomy poet. His amiability,
however, could also pass into very strong moral indignation, and
he endeavoured to give voice to this in a somewhat novel kind of
satire, more serious and earnest than that of Pope, much less
political and personal than that of Dryden, lighter and more
restrained than that of the Elizabethans. His own unworldly
disposition, together with the excessively retired life which he had
led since early manhood, rather damaged the chances of Cowper
as a satirist. We always feel that his censure wants actuality,
that it is an exercise rather than an experience. His efforts in it,
however, no doubt assisted, and were assisted by, that alteration

of the fashionable Popian couplet which, after the example partly of Churchill and with a considerable return to Dryden, he attempted, made popular, and handed on to the next generation to dis-Pope yet further. This couplet, paralleled by a not wholly dissimilar refashioning of blank verse, in which, though not deserting Milton, he beat out for himself a scheme quite different from Thomson's, perhaps show at their best in the descriptive matter of *The Task* and similar poems. It was in these that Cowper chiefly displayed that faculty of "bringing back the eye to the object" and the object to the eye, in which he has been commonly and justly thought to be the great English restorer. Long before the end of the Elizabethan period, poetical observation of nature had ceased to be just; and, after substituting for justness the wildest eccentricities of conceit, it went for a long time into another extreme — that of copying and recopying certain academic conventionalities, instead of even attempting the natural model. It is not true, as Wordsworth and others have said, that Dryden himself could not draw from the life. He could and did; but his genius was not specially attracted to such drawing, his subjects did not usually call for it, and his readers did not want it. It is not true that Thomson could not "see"; nor is it true of all his contemporaries and immediate followers that they were blind. But the eighteenth century had slipped into a fault which was at least as fatal as that of the Idealist-Impressionists of the seventeenth, or as that of the Realist-Impressionists of our own time. The former neglected universality in their hunt after personal conceits; the latter neglect it in the endeavour to add nothing to rigidly elaborated personal sensation. The one kind outstrips nature; the other comes short of art. From Dryden to Cowper the fault was different from both of these. It neglected the personal impression and the attention to nature too much. It dared not present either without stewing them in a sauce of stock ideas, stock conventions, stock words and phrases, which equally missed the universal and the particular. Cowper and the other great men who were his contemporaries by publication if not by birth, set to work to cure this fault. Even the weakest of them could never have been guilty of such a passage as that famous one which Congreve (as clever a man as any) wrote, and which Johnson (as clever a man as any) admired. The sentiment which actuated them was, if we may trust Coleridge's account of Boyer or Bowyer, the famous tyrant of Christ's Hospital, well diffused. "' Nymph,' boy? You mean your nurse's daughter," puts in a somewhat brutal and narrow form the correction which the time needed, and which these four in their different ways applied.

We have already glanced at the way in which Cowper applied it in his larger poems : he did it equally well, and perhaps more tellingly, in his smaller. The day on which a poet of no mean pretensions, one belonging altogether to the upper classes of English society, and one whose lack of university education mattered the less because the universities were just then at their nadir, dared to write of the snake he killed

> " And taught him never to come there no more "

was an epoch-making day. Swift would have done it ; but Swift was in many ways a voice crying in the wilderness, and Swift was not, strictly speaking, a poet at all. Byrom would have done it ; but Byrom was emphatically a minor poet. Cowper could—at least in and for his day — boast the major afflatus, and Cowper did not disdain vernacular truth. He never could have been vulgar ; there is not in the whole range of English literature quite such a gentleman in his own way as Cowper. But he has escaped almost entirely from the genteel style — from the notion of things as below the dignity of literature.

His prose in this respect is at least equal to his verse, though, as it was known much later, it has greater tendency than influence. All good critics have agreed that his letters are not surpassed, perhaps not surpassable. He has more freedom than Gray ; he has none of the coxcombry of Walpole and Byron ; and there is no fifth name that can be put even into competition with him.

Ease, correctness, facility of expression, freedom from convention
within his range, harmony, truth to nature, truth to art : — these
things meet in the hapless recluse of Olney as they had not met for
a century — perhaps as they had never met — in English epistles.
The one thing that he wanted was strength : as his madness was
melancholy, not raving, so was his sanity mild but not triumphant.

George Crabbe was three and twenty years younger than
Cowper, having been born on Christmas Eve 1754. But his first
publication, *The Library*, the success of which was due to the
generous and quick-sighted patronage of Burke after the poet
had wrestled with a hard youth, coincided almost exactly with the
first appearance of Cowper, and indeed a little anticipated it.
The Village appeared in 1783, and *The Newspaper* in 1785, and
then Crabbe (who had taken orders, had been instituted to
livings in the East of England, and had married, after a long
engagement, his first love) was silent for two and twenty years.
He began again in 1807 with *The Parish Register*. *The Borough*,
his greatest work, appeared in 1810.   Shifting from the East
of England to the West in 1813, he spent the last twenty years
of his long life at Trowbridge in Wiltshire, and died in 1832 at
the age of seventy-eight.

The external (and, as will be presently remarked, something
more than the external) uniformity of his work is great, and its
external conformity to the traditions and expectations of the time
at which it first appeared is almost greater.   A hasty judgment,
and even one which, though not hasty, is not very keen-sighted,
might see little difference between Crabbe and any poet from
Pope to Goldsmith except the innovators.   He is all but constant to the heroic couplet — the Spenserian introduction to *The
Birth of Flattery*, the variously-grouped octosyllabic quatrains of
Reflections, *Sir Eustace Grey*, *The Hall of Justice*, and *Woman*,
with a few other deviations, being merely islets among a wide sea
of rhymed decasyllables constituting at least nineteen-twentieths
of the poet's outpouring.   Moreover, he was as a rule constant,
not merely to the couplet, but to what has been called the " shut "

couplet — the couplet more or less rigidly confined to itself, and not overlapping. But he did sometimes overlap, and either in fealty to Dryden, or from a secret feeling of the craving for freedom which his more lawless contemporaries expressed in other ways, he reverted to the Drydenian triplet and Alexandrine on which Pope had frowned. In Crabbe's couplet, too, there is something which distinguishes it from almost all others. This something varies very much in appeal. It is sometimes, nay, too often, a rather ludicrous something, possessing a sort of awkward prosaic "flop," which is excellently caricatured in *Rejected Addresses*. But it always shows signs of a desire to throw the emphasis with more variation than the icy uniformity of the Popian cadence admitted ; and it is sometimes curiously effective.

Crabbe's position, independently of the strange gap in his publication (which has been variously accounted for), is not a little singular. The greater and the better part of his work was composed when the Romantic revival was in full swing, but it shows little or no trace of the influence of that revival in versification or diction. His earliest attempts do indeed show the same reaction from Pope to Dryden (of whom we know that he was an eager student) which is visible in Cowper and Churchill ; and throughout his work, both earlier and later, there is a ruthless discarding of conventional imagery and a stern attention to the realities of scenery and character. But Crabbe has none of the Grace of the new dispensation, if he has some glimpses of its Law. He sails so close to the wind of poetry that he is sometimes merely prosaic and often nearly so. His conception of life is anti-idealist almost to pessimism, and he has no fancy. The "jewels five words long" are not his : indeed there clung to him a certain obscurity of expression which Johnson is said to have good-naturedly smoothed out in his first work to some extent, but from which he never got quite free. The extravagances as well as the graces of the new poetry were quite alien from him ; its exotic tastes touched him not ; its love for antiquity (though he knew old English poetry by no means ill) seems to have left him wholly cold. The anxieties and sufferings of lower and middle-class life, the "natural death of love" (which, there seems some reason to fear, he had experienced), the common English country scenery and society of his time — these were his subjects, and he dealt with them in a fashion the mastery of which is to this day a joy to all competent readers. No writer of his time had an influence which so made for truth pure and simple, yet not untouched by the necessary " disprosing " processes of art. For Crabbe is not a mere realist ; and whoso considers him as such has not apprehended him. But he was a realist to this extent, that he always went to the model and never to the pattern-drawing on the Academy walls. And that was what his time needed. His general characteristics are extremely uniform : even the external shape and internal subject-matter of his poems are almost confined to the shape and matter of the verse-tale. He need not, and indeed cannot, in a book like this, be dealt with at much length. But he is a very great writer, and a most important figure at this turning-point of English literature.

Yet, however one may sympathise with Cowper, however much one may admire Crabbe, it is difficult for any true lover of poetry not to feel the sense of a " Pisgah sight," and something more, of the promised land of poetry, in passing from these writers to William Blake and Robert Burns. Here there is no more allow-ance necessary, except in the first case for imperfection of accom-plishment, in the second for shortness of life and comparative narrowness of range. The quality and opportuneness of poetry are in each case undeniable. Since the deaths of Herrick and Vaughan, England had not seen any one who had the finer lyrical gifts of the poet as Blake had them. Since the death of Dunbar, Scot-land had not seen such strength and intensity of poetic genius (joined in this case to a gift of melody which Dunbar never had) as were shown by Burns. There was scarcely more than a twelvemonth between their births ; for Blake was born in 1757 (the day appears not to be known), and Burns in January 1759. But Blake long outlived Burns, and did not die till 1828, while

Burns was no more in July 1796. Neither the long life nor the short one provided any events which demand chronicling here. Both poets were rather fortunate in their wives, though Blake clave to Catherine Boucher more constantly than Burns to his Jean. Neither was well provided with this world's goods ; Burns wearing out his short life in difficulties as farmer and as excise-man, while all the piety of biographers has left it something of a mystery how Blake got through his long life with no better resources than a few very poorly paid private commissions for his works of design, the sale of his hand-made books of poetry and prophecy, and such occasional employment in engraving as his unconventional style and his still more unconventional habits and temper allowed him to accept or to keep. In some respects the two were different enough according to commonplace standards, less so perhaps according to others. The forty years of Burns, and the more than seventy of Blake, were equally passed in a rapture ; but morality has less quarrel with Blake, who was essentially a " God-intoxicated man ", and spent his life in one long dream of art and prophecy, than with Burns, who was generally in love, and not unfrequently in liquor. But we need no more either of antithesis or of comparison : the purely literary matter calls us.

It was in 1783 — a date which, in its close approximation to the first appearances of Crabbe and Cowper, makes the literary student think of another group of first appearances in the early " eighties " of the sixteenth century foreshadowing the outburst of Elizabethan literature — that Blake's first book appeared. His *Poetical Sketches*, now one of the rarest volumes of English poetry, was printed by subscription among a literary coterie who met at the house of Mr. and Mrs. Mathew ; but the whole edition was given to the author. He had avowedly taken little or no trouble to correct it, and the text is nearly as corrupt as that of the *Supplices ;* nor does it seem that he took any trouble to make it " go off," nor that it did go off in any appreciable manner. Yet if many ears had then been open to true poetical music, some of them could not have mistaken sounds the like of which had not, as has been said, been heard since the deaths of Herrick and Vaughan. The merit of the contents is unequal to a degree not to be accounted for by the mere neglect to prepare carefully for press, and the influence of *Ossian* is, as throughout Blake's work, much more prominent for evil than for good. But the chaotic play of *Edward the Third* is not mere Elizabethan imitation; and at least half a dozen of the songs and lyrical pieces are of the most exquisite quality — snatches of Shakespeare or Fletcher as Shakespeare or Fletcher might have written them in Blake's time. The finest of all no doubt is the magnificent "Mad Song." But others — "How sweet I roamed from Field to Field" (the most eighteenth century in manner, but showing how even that manner could be strengthened and sweetened); "My Silks and Fine Array," beautiful, but more like an Elizabethan imitation than most; "Memory Hither Come," a piece of ineffable melody — these are things which at once showed Blake to be free of the very first company of poets, to be a poet who for real essence of poetry excelled everything the century had yet seen, and everything, with the solitary exception of the *Lyrical Ballads* at its extreme end, that it was to see.

Unfortunately it was not by any means as a poet that Blake regarded himself. He knew that he was an artist, and he thought that he was a prophet; and for the rest of his life, deviating only now and then into engraving as a mere breadwinner, he devoted himself to the joint cultivation of these two gifts, inventing for the purpose a method or vehicle of publication excellently suited to his genius, but in other respects hardly convenient. This method was to execute text and illustrations at once on copper-plates, which were then treated in slightly different fashions. Impressions worked off from these by hand-press were coloured by hand, Blake and his wife executing the entire process. In this fashion were produced the lovely little gems of literature and design called *Songs of Innocence* (1789) and *Songs of Experience* (1794); in this way for the most part, but with some modifica-tions, the vast and formidable mass of the so-called "Prophetic"

Books. With the artistic qualities of Blake we are not here concerned, but it is permissible to remark that they resemble his
literary qualities with a closeness which at once explains and is
explained by their strangely combined method of production.
That Blake was not entirely sane has never been doubted except
by a few fanatics of mysticism, who seem to think that the denial
of complete sanity implies a complete denial of genius. And
though he was never, in the common phrase, " incapable of man-
aging " such very modest affairs as were his, the defect appears
most in the obstinate fashion in which he refused to perfect and
co-ordinate his work. He could, when he chose and would give
himself the trouble, draw quite exquisitely ; and he always drew
with marvellous vigour and imagination. But he would often
permit himself faults of drawing quite inexplicable and not very
tolerable. So, too, though he had the finest gift of literary expression, he chose often to babble and still oftener to rant at large.
Even the *Songs of Innocence and Experience* — despite their double
charm to the eye and the ear, and the presence of such things as
the famous " Tiger," as the two " Introductions " (two of Blake's
best things), and as " The Little Girl Lost " — show a certain
poetical declension from the highest heights of the *Poetical
Sketches*. The poet is no longer a poet pure and simple ; he has
got purposes and messages, and these partly strangle and partly
render turbid the clear and spontaneous jets of poetry which
refresh us in the " Mad Song " and the " Memory." And after
the *Songs* Blake did not care to put forth anything bearing the
ordinary form of poetry. We possess indeed other poetical work
of his, recovered in scraps and fragments from MSS., and some of
it is beautiful. But it is as a rule more chaotic than the *Sketches*
themselves ; it is sometimes defaced (being indeed mere private
jottings never intended for print) by personality and coarseness ; and it is constantly puddled with the jargon of Blake's
mystical philosophy, which, borrowing some of its method from
Swedenborg and much of its imagery and nomenclature from
Ossian, spreads itself unhampered by any form whatever over the

Prophetic Books. The literary merit of these in parts is often very high, and their theosophy (for that is the best single word for it) is not seldom majestic. But despite the attempts of some disciples to evolve a regular system from them, students of philosophy as well as of literature are never likely to be at much odds as to their real character. " Ravings " they are not, and they are very often the reverse of " nonsense." But they are the work of a man who in the first place was very slightly acquainted with the literature and antecedents of his subject, who in the second was distinctly *non compos* on the critical, though admirably gifted on the creative side of his brain, and who in the third had the ill luck to fall under the fullest sway of the Ossianic influence. To any one who loves and admires Blake — and the present writer deliberately ranks him as the greatest and most delectable poet of the eighteenth century proper in England, reserving Burns as specially Scotch — it must always be tempting to say more of him than can be allowed on such a scale as the present; but the scale must be observed.

There is all the more reason for the observance that Blake exercised on the literary *history* of his time no influence, and occupied in it no position. He always had a few faithful friends and patrons who kept him from starvation by their commissions, admired him, believed in him, and did him such good turns as his intensely independent and rather irritable disposition would allow. But the public had little opportunity of seeing his pictures, and less of reading his books; and though the admiration of Lamb led to some appreciation from Southey and others, he was practically an unread man. This cannot be said of Robert Burns, who, born as was said a year or two after Blake, made his first literary venture three years after him, in 1786. Most people know that the publication, now famous and costly, called " the Kilmarnock Edition," was originally issued in the main hope of paying the poet's passage to Jamaica after an unfortunate youth of struggle, and latterly of dissipation. Nay, even after the appearance of the *Poems* and their welcome he still proposed to go abroad. He was

summoned back to Edinburgh to reprint them, to make a considerable profit by them, and to be lionised without stint by the society
of the Scottish capital. He then settled down, marrying Jean
Armour, at Ellisland in Dumfriesshire, on a small farm and a post
in the Excise, which, when his farming failed and he moved to
Dumfries itself, became his only regular means of support. He
might have increased this considerably by literature ; but as it was
he actually gave away, or disposed of for trifling equivalents, most
of the exquisite songs which he wrote in his later years. These
years were unhappy. He hailed the French Revolution with a
perfectly innocent, because obviously ignorant, Jacobinism which,
putting all other considerations aside, was clearly improper in a
salaried official of the Crown, and thereby got into disgrace with
the authorities, and also with society in and about Dumfries. His
habits of living, though their recklessness has been vastly exaggerated, were not careful, and helped to injure both his reputation
and his health. Before long he broke down completely, and died
on the first of July 1796, his poetical powers being to the very last
in fullest perfection.

Burns' work, which even in bulk — its least remarkable characteristic — is very considerable when his short life and his unfavourable education and circumstances are reckoned, falls at
once into three sharply contrasted sections. There are his poems
in Scots ; there are the verses that, in obedience partly to the
incompetent criticism of his time, partly to a very natural mistake
of ambition and ignorance, he tried to write in conventional
literary English ; and there is his prose, taking the form of more
or less studied letters. The second class of the poems is almost
worthless, and fortunately it is not bulky. The letters are of
unequal value, and have been variously estimated. They show
indeed that, like almost all poets, he might, if choice and fate
had united, have become a very considerable prose-writer, and
they have immense autobiographic value. But they are sometimes, and perhaps often, written as much in falsetto as the division
of verse just ruled out ; their artificiality does not take very good

models; and their literary attraction is altogether second-rate.
How far different the value of the Scots poems is, four generations
have on the whole securely agreed. The moral discomfort of
Principal Shairp, the academic distaste of Mr. Matthew Arnold
for a world of "Scotch wit, Scotch religion, and Scotch drink,"
and the purely indolent and ignorant reluctance of others to
grapple with Scottish dialect, need not trouble the catholic critic
much. The two first may be of some use as cautions and drags;
the third may be thrown aside at once. Scots, though a dialect,
is not a patois; it has a great and continuous literature; it combines in an extraordinary degree the consonant virtues of English
and the vowel range of the Latin tongues. It is true that Burns'
range of subject, as distinct from that of sound, was not extremely
wide. He could give a voice to passion — passion of war, passion of
conviviality, passion above all of love — as none but the very greatest
poets ever have given or will give it; he had also an extraordinary
command of *genre*-painting of all kinds, ranging from the merely
descriptive and observant to the most intensely satirical. Perhaps
he could only do these two things — could not be (as he certainly
has not been) philosophical, deeply meditative, elaborately in
command of the great possibilities of nature, political, moral,
argumentative. But what an "only" have we here! It amounts
to this, that Burns could "only" seize, could "only" convey the
charms of poetical expression to, the more primitive thought and
feeling of the natural man, and that he could do this supremely.
His ideas are — to use the rough old Lockian division — ideas of
sensation, not of reflection; and when he goes beyond them he is
sensible, healthy, respectable, but not deep or high. In his own
range there are few depths or heights to which he has not soared
or plunged.

That he owed a good deal to his own Scottish predecessors,
especially to Ferguson, is not now denied; and his methods of
composing his songs are very different from those which a lesser
man, using more academic forms, could venture upon without
the certainty of the charge of plagiarism. We shall never under-

stand Burns aright if we do not grasp the fact that he was a "folk-poet," into whom the soul of a poet of all time and all space had entered. In all times and countries where folk-poetry has a genuine existence, its forms and expressions are much less the property of the individual than of the race. The business of collecting ballads is one of the most difficult and doubtful, not to say dangerous, open to the amateur. But it is certain that any collector who was not a mere simpleton would at once reject as spurious a version which he heard in identically the same terms from two different subjects. He would know that they must have got it from a printed or at least written source. Now Burns is, if not our only example, our only example of the very first quality, of the poet who takes existing work and hands it on shaped to his own fashion. Not that he was not perfectly competent to do without any existing canvas; while, when he had it, he treated it without the very slightest punctilio. Of some of the songs which he reshaped into masterpieces for Johnson and Thomson he took no more than the air and measure; of others only the refrain or the first few lines; of others again stanzas or parts of stanzas. But everywhere he has stamped the version with something of his own — something thenceforward inseparable from it, and yet characteristic of him. In the expression of the triumph and despair of love, not sicklied over with any thought as in most modern poets, only Catullus and Sappho can touch Burns. " Green grow the Rashes O," "Yestreen I had a Pint of Wine," the farewell to Clarinda, and the famous deathbed verses to Jessie Lewars, make any advance on them impossible in point of spontaneous and unreflecting emotion; while a thousand others (the number is hardly rhetorical) come but little behind. " Willie brew'd a Peck o' Maut " in the same way rides sovereign at the head of a troop of Bacchanalian verses; and the touches of rhetoric and convention in "Scots wha hae " cannot spoil, can hardly even injure it. To some it really seems that the much praised lines " To Mary in Heaven " and others where the mood is less boisterous, show Burns at less advantage, not because the kind is inferior, but because he was less at home in it; but it is almost impossible to praise too highly the equally famous "Mouse," and some other things. It was in this tremendous force of natural passion and affection, and in his simple observation of common things, that Burns' great lesson for his age and country lay. None even of the reformers had dared to be passionate as yet. In Cowper indeed there was no passion except of religious despair, in Crabbe none except that of a grim contemplation of the miseries and disappointments of life, while although there was plenty of passion in Blake it had all conveyed itself into the channel of mystical dreaming. It is a little pathetic, and more than a little curious, to compare "The Star that shines on Anna's Breast," the one approach to passionate expression of Cowper's one decided love, with any one of a hundred outbursts of Burns, sometimes to the very same name.

The other division of the Poems, at the head of which stand *The Jolly Beggars, Tam o' Shanter*, and *The Holy Fair*, exhibit an equal power of vivid feeling and expression with a greater creative and observant faculty, and were almost equally important as a corrective and alterative to their generation. The age was not ill either at drama, at manners-painting, or at satire; but the special kind of dramatic, pictorial, and satiric presentation which Burns manifested was quite unfamiliar to it and in direct contradiction to its habits and crotchets. It had had a tendency to look only at upper and middle-class life, to be conventional in its very indecorum, to be ironic, indirect, parabolical. It admired the Dutch painters, it had dabbled in the occult, it was Voltairian enough; but it had never dared to outvie Teniers and Steen as in *The Jolly Beggars*, to blend naturalism and *diablerie* with the overwhelming *verve* of *Tam o' Shanter*, to change the jejune freethinking of two generations into an outspoken and particular attack on personal hypocrisy in religion as in *Holy Willie's Prayer* and *The Holy Fair*. Even to Scotsmen, we may suspect (or rather we pretty well know, from the way in which Robertson and Blair, Hume and Mackenzie, write), this burst of genial racy humour from

c

the *terræ filius* of Kilmarnock must have been somewhat startling ; and it speaks volumes for the amiable author of the *Man of Feeling* that, in the very periodical where he was wont to air his mild Addisonian hobbies, he should have warmly commended the Ayrshire ploughman.

In a period where we have so many great or almost great names to notice, it cannot be necessary to give the weakest writers of its weakest part more than that summary mention which is at once necessary and sufficient to complete the picture of the literary movement of the time. And this is more especially the case with reference to the minor verse of the end of the eighteenth century. The earliest work of the really great men who re-created English poetry, though in some cases chronologically *in*, is not in the least *of* it. For the rest, it would be almost enough to say that William Hayley, the preface to whose *Triumphs of Temper* is dated January 1781, and therefore synchronised very closely with the literary appearance of Cowper, Crabbe, and Blake, was one of the most conspicuous, and remains one of the most characteristic of them. Hayley's personal relations with the first and last of these poets — relations which have kept and will keep his name in some measure alive long after the natural death of his verse — were in both cases conditioned by circumstances in a rather trying way, but were not otherwise than creditable to him. His verse itself is impossible and intolerable to any but the student of literary history, who knows that all things are possible, and finds the realisation of all in its measure interesting. The heights, or at least the average levels, of Hayley may be fairly taken from the following quotation : —

> Her lips involuntary catch the chime
> And half articulate the soothing rhyme ;
> Till weary thought no longer watch can keep,
> But sinks reluctant in the folds of sleep —

of which it can only be said that any schoolboy could write it ; his not infrequent depths from the couplet : —

> Her airy guard prepares the softest down
> From Peace's wing to line the nuptial crown.

where the image of a guardian angel holding Peace with the
firmness of an Irish housewife, and plucking her steadily in order
to line a nuptial crown (which must have been a sort of sun-
bonnet) with the down thereof, will probably be admitted to be
not easily surpassable. Of Hayley's companions in song, I have
been dispensed by my predecessor from troubling myself with
Erasmus Darwin, who was perhaps intellectually the ablest of
them, though the extreme absurdity of the scheme of his *Botanic
Garden* brought him, as the representative of the whole school,
under the lash of the *Anti-Jacobin* in never-dying lines.   Darwin's
friend and townswoman, Anna Seward ; Mrs. Barbauld, the
author of the noble lines, " Life, we've been long together " — the
nobility of which is rather in its sentiment than in its expression —
. and of much tame and unimportant stuff; Merry, who called
himself Della Crusca and gathered round him the school of
gosling imitators that drew on itself the lash of Gifford ; the
Laureate Pye ; and others who, less fortunate than the victims of
Canning and Frere, have suffered a second death in the forgetting
of the very satires in which they met their deserts, can be barely
named now.   Two, however, may claim, if no great performance, a
remarkable influence on great performers.   Dr. Sayers, a member
of the interesting Norwich school, directly affected Southey, and
not Southey only, by his unrhymed verse ; while the sonnets of
William Lisle Bowles, now only to be read with a mild esteem by
the friendliest critic most conscious of the historic allowance,
roused Coleridge to the wildest enthusiasm and did much to
form his poetic taste.   To Bowles, and perhaps to one or two
others, we may find occasion to return hereafter.

The satires, however, which have been more than once
referred to in the preceding paragraph, form a most important
feature, and a perhaps almost more important symptom, of the
literary state of the time.   They show, indeed, that its weakness
did not escape the notice of contemporaries; but they also show
that the very contemporaries who noticed it had nothing better to
give in the way of poetry proper than that which they satirised.

In fact, one of the chief of these satirists, Wolcot, has left a considerable mass of not definitely satirical work which is little if at all better than the productions of the authors he lampooned.

This very remarkable body of satirical verse, which extends from the *Rolliad* and the early satires of Peter Pindar at the extreme beginning of our present time to the *Pursuits of Literature* and the *Anti-Jacobin* towards its close, was partly literary and partly political, diverging indeed into other subjects, but keeping chiefly to these two and intermixing them rather inextricably. The *Pursuits of Literature*, though mainly devoted to the subject of its title, is also to a great extent political; the *Rolliad* and the *Probationary Odes*, intensely political, were also to no small extent literary. The chief examples were among the most popular literary productions of the time; and though few of them except the selected *Poetry of the Anti-Jacobin* are now read, almost all the major productions deserve reading. The great defect of contemporary satire — that it becomes by mere lapse of time unintelligible — is obviated to no small extent here by the crotchet (rather fortunate, though sometimes a little tedious) which these writers, almost without exception, had for elaborate annotation. Of the chief of them, already indicated more than once by reference or allusion, some account may be given.

The Rolliad is the name generally given for shortness to a collection of political satires originating in the great Westminster election of 1784, when Fox was the Whig candidate. It derived its name from a Devonshire squire, Mr. Rolle, who was a great supporter of Pitt; and, with the *Political Eclogues*, the mock *Probationary Odes* for the laureateship (vacant by Whitehead's death), and the *Political Miscellanies*, which closed the series, was directed against the young Prime Minister and his adherents by a knot of members of Brooks' Club, who are identified rather by tradition and assertion than by positive evidence. Sheridan, Tierney, Burgoyne, Lord John Townshend, Burke's brother Richard, and other public men probably or certainly contributed, as did Ellis — afterwards to figure so conspicuously in the same way on

the other side. But the chief writers were a certain Dr. Lawrence, a great friend of Burke, who was in a way the editor ;
Tickel, a descendant of Addison's friend and a connection of the
Sheridans ; and another Irishman named Fitzpatrick. The various
"skits" of which the book or series is composed show considerable
literary skill, and there is a non-political and extraneous interest
in the fact that it contains some *rondeaux* believed to be the only,
or almost the only, examples of that form written in England
between Cotton in the seventeenth century and the revival of it
not very many years ago. The fun is often very good fun, and
there is a lightness and brightness about the verse and phrasing
which had been little seen in English since Prior. But the tone
is purely personal ; there are no principles at stake, and the book,
besides being pretty coarse in tone, is a sort of object lesson in
the merely intriguing style of politics which had become characteristic of England under the great seventy years' reign of the
Whigs.

Coarseness and personality, however, are in the *Rolliad* refined
and high-minded in comparison with the work of "Peter Pindar,"
which has the redeeming merit of being even funnier, with the
defect of being much more voluminous and unequal. John
Wolcot was a Devonshire man, born in May 1738 at Kingsbridge,
or rather its suburb Dodbrooke, in Devonshire. He was educated
as a physician, and after practising some time at home was taken
by Sir William Trelawney to Jamaica. Here he took orders and
received a benefice ; but when he returned to England after Trelawney's death he practically unfrocked himself and resumed the
cure of bodies. Although he had dabbled both in letters and in
art, it was not till 1782 that he made any name ; and he did it
then by the rather unexpected way of writing poetical satires
in the form of letters to the members of the infant Royal
Academy. From this he glided into satire of the political kind,
which, however, though he was a strong Whig and something
more, did not so much devote itself to the attack or support of
either of the great parties as to personal lampoons on the king,

his family, and his friends. Neither Charles the Second at the hands of Marvell, nor George the Fourth at the hands of Moore, received anything like the steady fire of lampoon which Wolcot for years poured upon the most harmless and respectable of English monarchs. George the Third had indeed no vices, — unless a certain parsimony may be dignified by that name, — but he had many foibles of the kind that is more useful to the satirist than even vice. Wolcot's extreme coarseness, his triviality of subject, and a vulgarity of thought which is quite a different thing from either, are undeniable. But *The Lousiad* (a perfect triumph of cleverness expended on what the Greeks called rhyparography), the famous pieces on George and the Apple Dumplings and on the King's visit to Whitbread's Brewery, with scores of other things of the same kind (the best of all, perhaps, being the record of the Devonshire Progress), exhibit incredible felicity and fertility in the lower kinds of satire. This satire Wolcot could apply with remarkable width of range. His artistic satires (and it must be admitted that he had not bad taste here) have been noticed. He riddled the new devotion to physical science in the unlucky person of Sir Joseph Banks ; the chief of his literary lampoons, a thing which is quite a masterpiece in its way, is his "Bozzy and Piozzi," wherein Boswell and Mrs. Thrale are made to string in amœbean fashion the most absurd or the most laughable of their respective reminiscences of Johnson into verses which, for lightness and liveliness of burlesque representation, have hardly a superior. Until the severe legislation which followed the Jacobin terror in France cowed him, and to some extent even subsequently, Wolcot maintained a sort of Ishmaelite attitude, by turns attacking and defending himself against men of eminence in literature and politics, after a fashion the savagery whereof was excused sometimes by its courage and nearly always by an exuberant good-humour which both here and elsewhere accompanies very distinct ill-nature. His literary life in London covered about a quarter of a century, after which, losing his sight, he retired once more to the West, though he is said to have died at

Somers Town in 1819. The best edition of his works is in five
good-sized volumes, but it is known not to be complete.

Both the *Rolliad* men and Wolcot had been on the Whig,
Wolcot almost on the Republican side ; and for some years they
had met with no sufficient adversaries, though Gifford soon engaged
" Peter " on fairly equal terms. The great revulsion of feeling,
however, which the acts of the French Revolution induced among
Englishmen generally drew on a signal rally on the Tory part.
The *Anti-Jacobin* newspaper, with Gifford as its editor, and
Canning, Ellis (now a convert), and Frere as its chief contributors,
not merely had at its back the national sentiment and the official
power, but far outstripped in literary vigour and brilliancy the
achievements of the other side. The famous collection above
referred to, *The Poetry of the Anti-Jacobin*, which has been again
and again reprinted, shows no signs of losing its attraction, — a
thing almost unparalleled in the case of satirical work nearly a
century old. Its very familiarity makes it unnecessary to dwell
much on it, but it is safe to say that nothing of the kind more
brilliant has ever been written, or is very likely ever to be written,
than the parodies of Southey's Sapphics and " Henry Martin "
sonnet, the litany of the Jacobins, French and English, the
" skits " on Payne Knight and Darwin, *The Rovers*, — mocking
the new German sentimentalism and mediævalism, — and the
stately satire of " The New Morality," — where, almost alone, the
writers become serious, and reach a height not attained since
Dryden.

Gifford and Mathias differ from the others just mentioned in
being less directly political in writing and inspiration, though
Gifford at least was a strong politician. He was, like Wolcot, a
Devonshire man, born at Ashburton in 1757, and, as his numerous
enemies and victims took care often to remind him, of extremely
humble birth and early breeding, having been a shoemaker's
apprentice. Attracting attention as a clever boy, he was sent to
Exeter College and soon attained to influential patronage. To do
him justice, however, he made his reputation by the work of his

own hand, — his satires of *The Baviad*, 1794, and *The Mæviad* next year, attacking and pretty nearly extinguishing Merry and his Della Cruscans, a set of minor bards and mutual admirers who had infested the magazines and the libraries for some years.[1] The *Anti-Jacobin* and the editing of divers English classics put Gifford still higher ; and when the *Quarterly Review* was established in opposition to the *Edinburgh*, his appointment (1809) to the editorship, which he held almost till his death (he gave it up in 1824 and died in 1826), completed his literary position. Gifford is little read nowadays, and a name which was not a very popular one even on his own side during his lifetime has, since the triumph of the politics and of some of the literary styles which he opposed, become almost a byword for savage and unfair criticism. The penalty of unfairness is usually and rightly paid in kind, and Gifford has paid it very amply. The struggles of his youth and lifelong ill-health no doubt aggravated a disposition at no time very sweet ; and the feuds of the day, both literary and political, were apt to be waged, even by men far superior to Gifford in early and natural advantages, with the extremest asperity and without too much scruple. But Gifford is perhaps our capital example in English of a cast of mind which is popularly identified with that of the critic, though in truth nothing is more fatal to the attainment of the highest critical competence. It was apparently impossible for him (as it has been, and, it would seem, is for others, to regard the author whom he was criticising, the editor who had preceded him in his labours, or the adversary with whom he was carrying on a polemic, as anything but a being partly idiotic and partly villainous, who must be soundly scolded, first for having

---

[1] Although *The Baviad* and *The Mæviad* are well worth reading, it may be questioned whether they are as amusing as their chief quarry, *The British Album*, "containing the poems of Della Crusca, Anna Matilda, Benedict, Cesario, The Bard, etc.," the two little volumes of which attained their third edition in 1790. "Della Crusca," or Robert Merry (1755–98), was a gentleman by birth, and of means, with a Harrow and Oxford training, and some service in the army. Strange to say, there is testimony of good wits that he was by no means a fool ; yet such drivelling rubbish as he and his coadjutors wrote even the present day has hardly seen.

done what he did, and secondly to prevent him from doing it again. So ingrained was this habit in Gifford that he could refrain from indulging it, neither in editing the essays of his most distinguished contributors, nor in commenting on the work of these contributors, outside the periodicals which he directed. Yet he was a really useful influence in more ways than one. The service that he did in forcibly suppressing the Della Cruscan nuisance is even yet admitted, and there has been plentiful occasion, not always taken, for similar literary *dragonnades* since. And his work as an editor of English classics was, blemishes of manner and temper excepted, in the main very good work.

Thomas James Mathias, the author of *The Pursuits of Literature,* was a much nearer approach to the pedant pure and simple. For he did not, like Gifford, redeem his rather indiscriminate attacks on contemporaries by a sincere and intelligent devotion to older work ; and he was, much more than Gifford, ostentatious of such learning as he possessed. Accordingly the immense popularity of his only book of moment is a most remarkable sign of the times. De Quincey, who had seen its rise and its fall, declares that for a certain time, and not a very short one, at the end of the last century and the beginning of this, *The Pursuits of Literature* was the most popular book of its own day, and as popular as any which had appeared since ; and that there is not very much hyperbole in this is proved by its numerous editions, and by the constant references to it in the books of the time. Colman, who was one of Mathias' victims, declared that the verse was a "peg to hang the notes on"; and the habit above referred to certainly justified the gibe to no small extent. If the book is rather hard reading nowadays (and it is certainly rather difficult to recognise in it even the "demon of originality" which De Quincey himself grants rather grudgingly as an offset to its defects of taste and scholarship), it is perhaps chiefly obscured by the extreme desultoriness of the author's attacks and the absence of any consistent and persistent target. Much that Mathias reprehends in Godwin and Priestley, in Colman and Wolcot, and a whole crowd of lesser men, is justifiably censured ; much that he lays down is sound and good enough. But the whole — which, after the wont of the time, consists of several pieces jointed on to each other and all flooded with notes — suffers from the twin vices of negation and divagation. Indeed, its chief value is that, both by its composition and its reception, it shows the general sense that literature was not in a healthy state, and that some renaissance, some reaction, was necessary.

The prominence of the French Revolution, which has already appeared more than once in the above account of late eighteenth century poetry, is still more strongly reflected in the prose writing of the period. Indeed, many of its principal writers devoted their chief attention either to describing, to attacking, or to defending the events and principles of this portentous phenomenon. The chief of them were John Moore, Arthur Young, Helen Maria Williams, Thomas Paine, William Godwin, Richard Price, Mary Wollstonecraft, and Thomas Holcroft. Of these Price, a veteran who had nearly reached his sixtieth year when our period commences, chiefly belongs to literature as an antagonist of Burke, as does Priestley, whose writing was very extensive, but who was as much more a " natural philosopher " than a man of letters as Price was much less a man of letters than a moralist and a statistician. Both, moreover, have been mentioned in the preceding volume, and it is not necessary to say much about them, or about John Horne Tooke (1736–1812), philologist and firebrand.

Of the others something may, and in some cases not a little must, appear. Dr. John Moore, sometimes called " Zeluco " Moore (from his most popular book), and father of the general who fell at Corunna, was born at Stirling in the winter of 1729–30. Studying medicine at Glasgow, he was apprenticed (as Smollett had been earlier) to Dr. John Gordon, and entered the army as surgeon's mate for the Laufeldt campaign. He then lived two years in Paris, perfecting himself in medicine, after which he established himself in Glasgow. After many years' practice there, he accompanied the young Duke of Hamilton on various travels through Europe, and in 1778 settled in London. This was his headquarters for the rest of his life, till his death at Richmond on 21st January 1803. The chief interruption to his residence there was his memorable journey with Lord Lauderdale to Paris in the latter half of 1792, which resulted in one of the most vivid and trustworthy accounts by an eyewitness of the opening scenes of the Terror. This *Journal during a Residence in France* was published during the next two years. But Moore had earlier than this, though not very early in his own life, become an author. His *View of Society and Manners in France, Switzerland, and Germany*, the result of his journeyings with the Duke, appeared in 1779, with a continuation relating to Italy two years later; and in 1786 he published his one famous novel *Zeluco*. After the *Journal* he returned to novel writing in *Edward* (1796) and *Mordaunt* (1800) — books by no means contemptible, but suffering from the want of a central interest and of a more universal grasp of character and manners. He contributed a Life of Smollett and an Essay on Romance to an edition of his friend's works in 1797. One or two medical books also stand to his credit, while he had rather unadvisedly added to his admirable *Journal* a *View of the Causes of the French Revolution* which is not worthy of it. His complete works fill seven volumes.

Of these, the earlier travels are readable enough, and sometimes very noteworthy in matter. It is almost enough to say that they contain some of the latest accounts by an Englishman of France while it was still merry, and of Venice while it was still independent; an early picture of Alpine travel; very interesting personal sketches of Voltaire and Frederick the Great; and one memorable passage (remembered and borrowed by Scott in *Redgauntlet*) telling how at Florence the shadow of Prince Charlie, passing the Duke of Hamilton in the public walks, fixed his eyes earnestly on the Duke, as though saying, "Our ancestors were better acquainted." *Zeluco* and the *Journal* alone deserve much attention from any one but a professed student of literature. The value of the latter has been admitted by all competent authorities, and it is enhanced by the fact that Moore was a strong Whig, and was even accused by some zealots of favouring Jacobinism. His picture, therefore, of the way in which political revolution glides into ethical anarchy is certainly unbiassed the other way. Of *Zeluco* everybody, without perhaps a very clear knowledge of its authorship, knows one passage — the extremely humorous letter containing the John Bull contempt of the sailor Dawson for the foolish nation which clothes its troops in "white, which is absurd, and blue, which is only fit for the artillery and the blue horse." But few know much more, though there is close by a much more elaborate and equally good piece of Smollettian fun in the quarrel of Buchanan and Targe, the Scotch Whig and Jacobite, over the reputation of Queen Mary. The book, however, besides the unlucky drawback that almost all its interest lies in the latter part, has for hero a sort of lifeless monster of wickedness, who is quite as uninteresting as a faultless one, and shows little veracity of character except in the minor personages and episodes. In these, and indeed throughout Moore's work, there is a curious mixture of convention with extreme shrewdness, of somewhat commonplace expression with a remarkably pregnant and humorous conception. But he lacks concentration and finish, and is therefore never likely to be much read again as a whole.

There may appear to be some slight inconsistency is giving a paragraph, if only a short one, to Arthur Young where distinct mention has been refused to Price and Priestley. But Olivier de Serres has secured a place in all histories of French literature as a representative of agricultural writing, and Young is our English Serres. Moreover, his *Survey of France* has permanent attraction for its picture of the state of that country just before, and in the earliest days of, the Revolution. And though his writing is extremely incorrect and unequal, though its literary effect is much injured by the insertion of statistical details which sometimes turn it for pages together into a mere set of tables, he has constant racy phrases, some of which have passed into the most honourable state of all — that of unidentified quotation — while more

deserve it. He was born in 1741, the son of a Suffolk clergyman, was connected by marriage with the Burneys, and very
early developed the passion for agricultural theory and practice
which marked his whole life, even when in his later years (he
lived till 1820) he fell under the influence of religious crotchets.
His French travels were published in 1792–94, and form by far his
most attractive book, though his surveys of England and Ireland
contain much that is good. Young was a keen, though not a
very consistent or clear-sighted politician, especially on the side of
political economy. But, like other men of his time, he soon fell
away from his first love for the French Revolution. In the
literary, historical, and antiquarian associations of the places he
visited, he seems to have felt no interest whatever.

Helen Maria Williams, with Young and Moore, is our chief
English witness for the state of France and Paris just before and
during the early years of the Revolution. She was one of
Johnson's girl pets in his latest years, but Boswell is certainly
justified in suggesting that if the sage had lived a little longer he
would certainly not have repeated his elegant compliment: "If
I am so ill when you are near, what should I be when you are
away?" She outlived this phase also of her life, and did not
die till 1828, being then sixty-five. Even in the early days she
had been a Girondist, not a Jacobin ; but she happened to live in
Paris during the outbreak of the Revolution, wrote *Letters from
France*, which had a great popularity, and was hand in glove with
most of the English and Irish revolutionary leaders. Wolfe
Tone in his diary speaks of her as "Miss Jane Bull completely,"
but neither prudery nor patriotism would have struck persons less
prejudiced than the leader of the United Irishmen as the leading
points of Helen Maria. Her poems, published in 1786, during
her pre-revolutionary days, are dedicated to Queen Charlotte, and
nearly half the first of the two pretty little volumes (which have a
horrific frontispiece of the Princes in the Tower, by Maria
Cosway) is occupied by a stately list of subscribers, with the
Prince of Wales at their head. They have little merit, but are

not uninteresting for their "signs of the times": sonnets, a tale called *Edwin and Eltruda*, an address to Sensibility, and so forth. But the longest, *Peru*, is in the full eighteenth century couplet with no sign of innovation. The *Letters from France*, which extend to eight volumes, possess, besides the interest of their subject, the advantage of a more than fair proficiency on the author's part in the formal but not ungraceful prose of her time, neither unduly Johnsonian nor in any way slipshod. But it may perhaps be conceded that, but for the interest of the subject, they would not be of much importance.

The most distinguished members of the Jacobin school, from the literary point of view, were Thomas Paine and William Godwin. Paine was only a literary man by accident. He was born at Thetford on 29th January 1737, in the rank of small trades- man, and subsequently became a custom-house officer. But he lost his place for debt and dubious conduct in 1774, and found a more congenial home in America, where he defended the rebellion of the Colonies in a pamphlet entitled *Common Sense*. His new compatriots rewarded him pretty handsomely, and after about a dozen years he returned to Europe, visiting England, which, however, he left again very shortly (it is said owing to the persuasion of Blake), just in time to escape arrest. He had already made friends in France, and his publication of *The Rights of Man* (1791–92), in answer to Burke's attack on the Revolution, made him enormously popular in that country. He was made a French citizen, and elected by the Pas de Calais to the Convention. His part here was not discreditable. He opposed the King's execution, and, being expelled the Convention and imprisoned by the Jacobins, wrote his other notorious work, *The Age of Reason* (1794–95), in which he maintained the Deist position against both Atheism and Christianity. He recovered his liberty and his seat, and was rather a favourite with Napoleon. In 1802 he went back to America, and died there (a confirmed drunkard it is said and denied) seven years later. A few years later still, Cobbett, in one of his sillier moods, brought

Paine's bones back to England, which did not in the least want them.

The coarse and violent expression, as well as the unpopular matter, of Paine's works may have led to his being rather unfairly treated in the hot fights of the Revolutionary period ; but the attempts which have recently been made to whitewash him are a mere mistake of reaction, or paradox, or pure stupidity. The charges which used to be brought against his moral character matter little ; for neither side in these days had, or in any days has, a monopoly of loose or of holy living. But two facts will always remain : first, that Paine attacked subjects which all require calm, and some of them reverent, treatment, in a tone of the coarsest violence ; and, secondly, that he engaged in questions of the widest reach, and requiring endless thought and reading, with the scanty equipments and the superabundant confidence of a self-educated man. No better instance of this latter characteristic could be produced or required than a sentence in the preface to the second part of the *Age of Reason*. Here Paine (who admitted that he had written the first part hastily, in expectation of imprisonment, without a library, and without so much as a copy of the Scriptures he was attacking at hand, and who further confessed that he knew neither Hebrew nor Greek nor even Latin) observes : " I have produced a work that no Bible-believer, though writing at his ease and with a library of Church books about him, can refute." In this charming self-satisfaction, which only natural temper assisted by sufficient ignorance can attain in perfection, Paine strongly resembles his disciple Cobbett. But the two were also alike in the effect which this undoubting dogmatism, joined to a very clear, simple, and forcible style, less correct in Paine's case than in Cobbett's, produced upon readers even more ignorant than themselves, and greatly their inferiors in mental strength and literary skill. Paine, indeed, was as much superior to Cobbett in logical faculty as he was his inferior in range of attainments and charm of style ; while his ignorance and his arbitrary assumption and exclusion of premises passed unnoticed by the classes whom he more particularly addressed. He was thus among the lower and lower middle classes by far the most formidable propagator of anarchist ideas in religion and politics that England produced ; and his influence lasted till far into the present century, being, it is said, only superseded by new forms of a similar spirit. But he never could have had much on persons of education, unless they were prepared to sympathise with him, or were of singularly weak mind.

William Godwin, on the other hand, affected the "educated persons," and those of more or less intellectual power, even more forcibly than Paine affected the vulgar. This influence of his, indeed, is a thing almost unique, and it has perhaps never yet been succinctly examined and appraised. Born at Wisbech in 1756, the son of a dissenting minister, he himself was thoroughly educated for the Presbyterian ministry, and for some five years discharged its functions. Then in 1783 (again the critical period) he became unorthodox in theology, and took to literature, addicting himself to Whig politics. He also did a certain amount of tutoring. It was not, however, till nearly ten years after he had first taken to writing that he made his mark, and attained the influence above referred to by a series of works rather remarkably different in character. 1793 saw the famous *Inquiry concerning Political Justice*, which for a time carried away many of the best and brightest of the youth of England. Next year came the equally famous and more long-lived novel of *Caleb Williams*, and an extensive criticism (now much forgotten, but at the time of almost equal importance with these), published in the *Morning Chronicle*, of the charge of Lord Chief-Justice Eyre in the trial of Horne Tooke, Holcroft, and others for high treason. Godwin himself ran some risk of prosecution ; and that he was left un-molested shows that the Pitt government did not strain its powers, as is sometimes alleged. In 1797 he published *The Enquirer*, a collection of essays on many different subjects ; and in 1799 his second remarkable novel (it should be said that in his early years of struggle he had written others which are quite forgotten)

St. Leon. The closing years of the period also saw first his connection and then his marriage with Mary Wollstonecraft, who will be noticed immediately after him.

It is rather curious that Godwin, who was but forty-four at the beginning of the nineteenth century, and continued to be a diligent writer as well as a publisher and bookseller till his death in 1836, his last years being made comfortable by a place under the Reform Ministry, never did anything really good after the eighteenth century had closed. His tragedy *Antonio* only deserves remembrance because of Lamb's exquisite account of its damnation. His *Life of Chaucer* (1801) was one of the earliest examples of that style of padding and guesswork in literary biography with which literature has been flooded since. His later novels — *Fleetwood, Mandeville, Cloudesley,* etc. — are far inferior to *Caleb Williams* (1794) and *St. Leon* (1799). His *Treatise of Population* (1820), in answer to Malthus, was belated and ineffective ; and his *History of the Commonwealth,* in four volumes, though a very respectable compilation, is nothing more. Godwin's character was peculiar, and cannot be said to be pleasing. Though regarded (or at least described) by his enemies as an apostle of license, he seems to have been a rather cold-blooded person, whose one passion for Mary Wollstonecraft was at least as much an affair of the head as of the heart. He was decidedly vain, and as decidedly priggish ; but the worst thing about him was his tendency to " sponge " — a tendency which he indulged not merely on his generous son-in-law Shelley, but on almost everybody with whom he came in contact. It is, however, fair to admit that this tendency (which was probably a legacy of the patronage system) was very wide-spread at the time ; that the mighty genius of Coleridge succumbed to it to a worse extent even than Godwin did ; and that Southey himself, who for general uprightness and independence has no superior in literary history, was content for years to live upon the liberality not merely of an uncle, but of a school comrade, in a way which in our own days would probably make men of not half his moral worth seriously uncomfortable.

D

Estimates of the strictly formal excellence of Godwin's writing have differed rather remarkably. To take two only, his most recent biographer, Mr. Kegan Paul, is never weary of praising the "beauty" of Godwin's style; while Scott, a very competent and certainly not a very savage critic, speaks of the style of the Chaucer as "uncommonly depraved, exhibiting the opposite defects of meanness and of bombast." This last is too severe; but I am unable often to see the great beauty, the charm, and so forth, which Godwin's admirers have found in his writings. He shows perhaps at his best in this respect in *St. Leon*, where there are some passages of a rather artificial, but solemn and grandiose beauty; and he can seldom be refused the praise of a capable and easily wielded fashion of writing, equally adapted to exposition, description, and argument. But that Godwin's taste and style were by no means impeccable is proved by his elaborate essay on the subject in the *Enquirer*, where he endeavours to show that the progress of English prose-writing had been one of unbroken improvement since the time of Queen Elizabeth, and pours contempt on passages of Shakespeare and others where more catholic appreciation could not fail to see the beauty. In practice his special characteristic, which Scott (or Jeffrey, for the criticism appeared in the *Edinburgh*) selected for special reprobation in the context of the passage quoted above, was the accumulation of short sentences, very much in the manner of which, in the two generations since his death, Macaulay and the late Mr. J. R. Green have been the chief exponents. Hazlitt probably learnt this from Godwin; and I think there is no doubt that Macaulay learnt it from Hazlitt.

It may, however, be freely admitted that whatever Godwin had to say was at least likely not to be prejudicially affected by the manner in which he said it. And he had, as we have seen, a great deal to say in a great many kinds. The "New Philosophy," as it was called, of the *Political Justice* was to a great extent softened, if not positively retracted, in subsequent editions and publications; but its quality as first set forth accounts both for the conquest

which it, temporarily at least, obtained over such minds as those
of Wordsworth and Coleridge, and for the horror with which it was
regarded elsewhere. Godwin's system was not too consistent, and
many of its parts were borrowed more or less directly from others :
from Locke, from Hume, from the French materialists, from
Jonathan Edwards, and, by way of reaction as well as imitation,
from Rousseau. But Godwin's distinctive claim, if not exactly
glory, is that he was the first systematic Anarchist. His cardinal
principle was that government in itself, and with all its consequences of law, restriction, punishment, etc., is bad, and to be got
rid of. He combined this (logically enough) with perfectibilism
— supposing the individual to be infinitely susceptible of " melior-
ation " by the right use of reason — and (rather illogically) with
necessarianism. In carrying out his views he not only did not
hesitate at condemning religion, marriage, and all other restrictions
of the kind, but indulged in many curious crotchets as to the
uselessness, if not mischievousness, of gratitude and other sentiments generally considered virtuous. The indefinite development
of the individual by reason and liberty, and the general welfare of
the community at large, were the only standards that he admitted.
And it should be said, to his credit, that he condemned the use of
violence and physical force *against* government quite as strongly
as their use *by* government. The establishment of absolute liberty,
in the confidence that it will lead to absolute happiness, was, at
first at any rate, the main idea of the *Political Justice*, and it is
easy to understand what wild work it must have made with heads
already heated by the thunder-weather of change that was pervading Europe.

Godwin has been frequently charged with alarm at the
anarchist phantom he had raised. It is certain not merely that
he altered and softened the *Political Justice* not a little, but that
in his next work of the same kind, *The Enquirer*, he took both
a very different line of investigation and a different tone of
handling. In the preface he represents it as a sort of inductive
complement to the high *a priori* scheme of his former work ; but

this is not a sufficient account of the matter. It is true that his paradoxical rebellion against conventions appears here and there ; and his literary criticism, which was never strong, may be typified by his contrast of the " hide-bound sportiveness " of Fielding with the " flowing and graceful hilarity " of Sterne. Indeed, this sentence takes Godwin's measure pretty finally, and shows that he was of his age, not for all time. But, on the other hand, it is fair to say that the essays on " The Study of the Classics " and the " Choice of Reading," dealing with subjects on which, both then and since, oceans of cant and nonsense have been poured forth, are nearly as sound as they can be.

In his purely imaginative work he presents a contrast not much less strange. We may confine attention here to the two capital examples of it. *Caleb Williams* alone has survived as a book of popular reading, and it is no small tribute to its power that, a full century after its publication, it is still kept on sale in sixpenny editions. Yet on no novel perhaps is it so difficult to adjust critical judgment, either by the historical or the personal methods. Both its general theme — the discovery of a crime committed by a man of high reputation and unusual moral worth, and the persecution of the discoverer by the criminal — and its details, are thoroughly leavened and coloured by Godwin's political and social views at the time ; and either this or some other defect has made it readable with great difficulty at all times by some persons, among whom I am bound to enrol myself. Yet the ingenuity of its construction, in spite of the most glaring impossibilities, the striking situations it contains, and no doubt other merits, have always secured readers for it. *St. Leon*, a romance of the *elixir vitæ*, has no corresponding central interest, and, save in the amiable but very conventional figure of the heroine Marguerite, who is said to have been studied from Mary Wollstonecraft, no interest of character ; while its defects of local colour and historical truth are glaring. But Godwin, who was in so many ways a mirror of the new thought of the time, had caught by anticipation something of its nascent spirit of romance. He is altogether a rather puzzling person; and perhaps the truest explanation of the puzzle, as well as certainly the most comfortable to the critic, is that his genius and literary temperament were emphatically crude and undeveloped, that he was a prophet rather than anything else, and that he had the incoherencies and the inconsistencies almost inseparable from prophecy.

Even if fate and metaphysical aid had not conjoined Godwin and Mary Wollstonecraft in the closest bond possible between man and woman, it would have been proper to mention their names together as authors. For as Godwin's "New Philosophy" was the boldest attempt made by any man of the time in print to overthrow received conventions of the relations of man to man, and incidentally of man to woman, so was his wife's *Vindication of the Rights of Woman* a complement of it in relation to the status of the other sex as such. She was rather hardly treated in her own time; Horace Walpole calling her, it is said (I have not verified the quotation), a "hyena in petticoats": it would be at least as just to call Lord Orford a baboon in breeches. And though of late years she has been made something of a heroine, it is to be feared that admiration has been directed rather to her crotchets than to her character. This last appears to have been as lovable as her hap was ill. The daughter of an Irishman of means, who squandered them and became a burden on his children; the sister of an attorney who was selfishly indifferent to his sisters — she had to fend for herself almost entirely. At one time she and her sisters kept school; then she was, thanks to the recommendation of Mr. Prior, a master at Eton, introduced as governess to the family of Lord Kingsborough; then, after doing hack-work for Johnson, the chief Liberal publisher of the period, she went to Paris, and unluckily fell in with a handsome scoundrel, Gilbert Imlay, an American soldier. She lived with him, he deserted her, and she nearly committed the suicide which was actually the fate of her unfortunate daughter by him, Fanny Imlay or Godwin. Only at the last had she a glimpse of happiness. Godwin, who had some weaknesses, but who was not a scoundrel, met her, and fell in love with her, and as both had independently demonstrated that marriage was a failure, they naturally married ; but she died a week after giving birth to a daughter — the future Mrs. Shelley.   The *Vindication of the Rights of Woman*, on which Mary Wollstonecraft's fame as an author almost wholly rests, is in some ways a book nearly as faulty as it can be.   It is not well written ; it is full of prejudices quite as wrong-headed as those it combats ; it shows very little knowledge either of human nature or of good society ; and its " niceness," to use the word in what was then its proper sense, often goes near to the nasty.   But its protest on the one hand against the " proper " sentimentality of such English guides of female youth as Drs. Fordyce and Gregory, on the other against the " improper " sentimentality of Rousseau, is genuine and generous.   Many of its positions and contentions may be accepted unhesitatingly to-day by those who are by no means enamoured of advanced womanhood ; and Mary, as contrasted with most of her rights-of-women followers, is curiously free from bumptiousness and the general qualities of the virago.   She had but ill luck in life, and perhaps showed no very good judgment in letters, but she had neither bad brains nor bad blood; and the references to her, long after her death, by such men as Southey, show the charm which she exercised.

With Godwin also is very commonly connected Thomas Holcroft (or, as Lamb always preferred to spell the name, "*Ould*croft "), a curiosity of literature and a rather typical figure of the time.   Holcroft was born in London in December 1745, quite in the lowest ranks, and himself rose from being stable-boy at Newmarket, through the generally democratic trade of shoemaking, to quasi-literary positions as schoolmaster and clerk, and then to the dignity of actor.   He was about thirty-five when he first began regular authorship ; and during the rest of his life he wrote four novels, some score and a half of plays, and divers other works, none of which is so good as his Autobiography, published after his death by Hazlitt, and said to be in part that writer's work.   It would have been fortunate for Holcroft if he had confined himself to literature ; for some of his plays, notably *The Road to Ruin*, brought him in positively large sums of money, and his novels were fairly popular. But he was a violent democrat, — some indeed attributed to him the origination of most of the startling things in Godwin's *Political Justice,* — and in 1794 he was tried, though with no result, for high treason, with Horne Tooke and others. This brought him into the society of the young Jacobin school, — Coleridge, and the rest, — but was disastrous to the success of his plays ; and when he went abroad in 1799 he entered on an extraordinary business of buying old masters (which were rubbish) and sending them to England, where they generally sold for nothing. He returned, however, and died on 23rd March 1809.

Holcroft's theatre will best receive such notice as it requires in connection with the other drama of the century. Of his novels, *Alwyn*, the first, had to do with his experiences as an actor, and *Hugh Trevor* is also supposed to have been more or less autobiographical. Holcroft's chief novel, however, is *Anna St. Ives*, a book in no less than seven volumes, though not very large ones, which was published in 1792, and which exhibits no small affinities to Godwin's *Caleb Williams*, and indeed to the *Political Justice* itself. And Godwin, who was not above acknowledging mental obligations, if he was rather ill at discharging pecuniary ones, admits the influence which Holcroft had upon him. *Anna St. Ives*, which, like so many of the other novels of its day, is in letters, is worth reading by those who can spare the time. But it cannot compare, for mere amusement, with the very remarkable *Memoir* above referred to. Only about a fourth of this is said to be in Holcroft's own words ; but Hazlitt has made excellent matter of the rest, and it includes a good deal of diary and other authentic work. In his own part Holcroft shows himself a master of the vernacular, as well as (what he undoubtedly was) a man of singular shrewdness and strength of mental temper.

The Novel school of the period (to which Holcroft introduces us) is full and decidedly interesting, though it contains at the best one masterpiece, *Vathek*, and a large number of more or less meritorious attempts in false styles. The kind was very largely written — much more so than is generally thought. Thus Godwin, in his early struggling days, and long before the complete success of *Caleb Williams*, wrote, as has been mentioned, for trifling sums of money (five and ten guineas), two or three novels which even the zeal of his enthusiastic biographer does not seem to have been able to recover. Nor did the circulating library, even then a flourishing institution, lack hands more or less eminent to work for it, or customers to take off its products. The Minerva Press, much cited but little read, had its origin in this our time ; and this time is entitled to the sole and single credit of starting and carrying far a bastard growth of fiction, the "tale of terror," which continued to be cultivated in its simplest form for at least half a century, and which can hardly be said to be quite obsolete yet. But as usual we must proceed by special names, and there is certainly no lack of them. "Zeluco" Moore has been dealt with already; Day, the eccentric author of *Sanford and Merton*, belongs mainly to an earlier period, and died, still a young man, in the year of the French Revolution ; but, besides Holcroft, Beckford, Bage, Cumberland, Mrs. Radcliffe, and Monk Lewis, with Mrs. Inchbald, are distinctly "illustrations" of the time, and must have more or less separate mention.

William Beckford is one of the problems of English literature. He was one of the richest men in England, and his long life — 1760 to 1844 — was occupied for the most part not merely with the collection, but with the reading of books. That he could write as well as read he showed as a mere boy by his satirical *Memoirs of Painters*, and by the great-in-little novel of *Vathek* (1783), respecting the composition of which in French or English divers fables are told. Then he published nothing for forty years, till in 1834 and 1835 he issued his *Travels in Italy, Spain, and Portugal*, recollections of his earliest youth. These travels have extraordinary merits of their kind ; but *Vathek* is a kind almost to itself. The history of the Caliph, in so far as it is a satire on unlimited power, is an eighteenth century commonplace; while many traits in it are obviously imitated from Voltaire. But the figure of Nouronihar, which Byron perhaps would have equalled if he could, stands alone in literature as a fantastic projection of the potentiality of evil magnificence in feminine character; and the closing scenes in the domain of Eblis have the grandeur of Blake combined with that finish which Blake's temperament, joined to his ignorance of literature and his lack of scholarship, made it impossible for him to give. The book is quite unique. It could hardly, in some of its weaker parts especially, have been written at any other time; and yet its greater characteristics have nothing to do with that time. In the florid kind of supernatural story it has no equal. Only Dante, Beckford, and Scott in *Wandering Willie's Tale* have given us Hells that are worthy of the idea of Hell.

Except that both were very much of their time, it would be impossible to imagine a more complete contrast than that which exists between Beckford and Bage. The former was, as has been said, one of the richest men in England, the creator of two "Paradises" at Fonthill and Cintra, the absolute arbiter of his time and his pleasures, a Member of Parliament while he chose to be so, a student, fierce and recluse, the husband of a daughter of the Gordons, and the father of a mother of the Hamiltons, the collector, disperser, bequeather of libraries almost unequalled in magnificence and choice. Robert Bage, who was born in 1728 and died in 1801, was in some ways a typical middle-class Englishman. He was a papermaker, and the son of a paper-maker; he was never exactly affluent nor exactly needy; he was apparently a Quaker by education and a freethinker by choice; and between 1781 and 1796, obliged by this reason or that to stain the paper which he made, he produced six novels: *Mount Henneth, Barham Downs, The Fair Syrian, James Wallace, Man as he is*, and *Hermsprong*. The first, second, and fourth of these were admitted by Scott to the "Ballantyne Novels," the others, though *Hermsprong* is admittedly Bage's best work, were not.

It is impossible to say that there is genius in Bage ; yet he is a very remarkable writer, and there is noticeable in him that singular *fin de siècle* tendency which has reasserted itself a century later. An imitator of Fielding and Smollett in general plan, — of the latter specially in the dangerous scheme of narrative by letter, — Bage added to their methods the purpose of advocating a looser scheme of morals and a more anarchical system of government. In other words, Bage, though a man well advanced in years at the date of the Revolution, exhibits for us distinctly the spirit which brought the Revolution about. He is a companion of Godwin and of Mary Wollstonecraft ; and though it must be admitted that, as in other cases, the presence of "impropriety" in him by no means implies the absence of dulness, he is full of a queer sort of undeveloped and irregular cleverness.

The most famous, though not the only novel of Richard Cumberland, *Henry*, shows the same tendency to break loose from British decorum, even such decorum as had really been in the main observed by the much-abused pens of Fielding, Smollett, and Sterne himself ; but it has little purpose and indeed little vigour of any kind. Cumberland clung as close as he could to the method of Fielding, including the preliminary dissertation or meditation, but he would be a very strange reader who should mistake the two.

The school of Bage and Cumberland, the former of whom bears some little resemblance to his countrywoman George Eliot, was, with or without Bage's purpose, continued more or less steadily ; indeed, it may be said to be little more than a variant, with local colour, of the ordinary school of novel-writing. But it was not this school which was to give tone to the period. The "tale of terror" had been started by Horace Walpole in the *Castle of Otranto*, and had, as we have seen, received a new and brilliant illustration in the hands of Beckford. But the genius of the author of *Vathek* could not be followed ; the talent of the author of the *Castle of Otranto* was more easily imitated. How far the practice of the Germans (who had themselves imitated Walpole, and whose work began in the two last decades of the century to have a great reflex influence upon England) was responsible for the style of story which, after Mrs. Radcliffe and Monk Lewis had set the fashion, dominated the circulating libraries for years, is a question not easy and perhaps not necessary to answer positively. I believe myself that no foreign influence ever causes a change in national taste ; it merely coincides therewith. But the fact of the set in the tide is unmistakable and undeniable. For some years the two authors just mentioned rode paramount in the affections of English novel readers ; before long Miss Austen devoted her early and delightful effort, *Northanger Abbey*, to satirising the taste for them, and quoted or invented a well-known list of blood-curdling titles ;[1] the morbid talent of Maturin gave a fresh impulse to it, even after the healthier genius of Scott had already revolutionised the general scheme of novel-writing ; and yet later still an industrious literary hack, Leitch Ritchie, was able to issue, and it may be presumed to find readers for, a variety of romance the titles of which might strike a hasty practitioner of the kind of censure usual in biblical criticism as a designed parody of Miss Austen's own catalogue. The style, indeed, in the wide sense has never lost favour. But in the special Radcliffian form it reigned for some thirty years, and was widely popular for nearly fifty.

Anne Radcliffe, whose maiden name was Ward, was born on 9th July 1764 and died on 7th February 1822. One of her novels, *Gaston de Blondeville*, was published posthumously ; but otherwise her whole literary production took place between the years 1789 and 1797. The first of these years saw *The Castles of Athlin and Dunbayne*, a very immature work ; the last *The Italian*, which is perhaps the best. Between them appeared *A Sicilian Romance* (1790), *The Romance of the Forest* (1791), and the far-

---

[1] I used to think these titles sprouts of the author's brain ; but a correspondent assured me that one or two at least are certainly genuine. Possibly, therefore, all are.

famed *Mysteries of Udolpho* in 1795. Matthew Gregory Lewis, who, like Beckford, was a West-Indian landowner and member for Hindon, and was well-to-do if not extremely wealthy, was nine years younger than Mrs. Radcliffe, and did not produce his famous *Monk* till the same year which saw *Udolpho*. He published a good deal of other work in prose, verse, and drama ; the most noteworthy of the second class being *Tales of Terror*, to which Scott contributed, and the most noteworthy of the third *The Castle Spectre*. Lewis, who, despite some foibles, was decidedly popular in the literary and fashionable society of his time, died in 1818 at the age of forty-five on his way home from the West Indies. Although he would have us understand that *The Monk* was written some time before its actual publication, Lewis' position as a direct imitator of Mrs. Radcliffe is unmistakable ; and although he added to the characteristics of her novels a certain appeal to "Lubricity" from which she was completely free, the general scheme of the two writers, as well as that of all their school, varies hardly at all. The supernatural in Mrs. Radcliffe's case is mainly, if not wholly, what has been called "the explained supernatural," — that is to say, the apparently ghostly, and certainly ghastly, effects are usually if not always traced to natural causes, while in most if not all of her followers the demand for more highly spiced fare in the reader, and perhaps a defect of ingenuity in the writer, leaves the devils and witches as they were. In all, without exception, castles with secret passages, trap-doors, forests, banditti, abductions, sliding panels, and other apparatus and paraphernalia of the kind play the main part. The actual literary value is, on the whole, low ; though Mrs. Radcliffe is not without glimmerings, and it is exceedingly curious to note that, just before the historical novel was once for all started by Scott, there is in all these writers an absolute and utter want of comprehension of historical propriety, of local and temporal colour, and of all the marks which were so soon to distinguish fiction. Yet at the very same time the yearning after the historical is shown in the most unmistakable fashion

from Godwin down to the Misses Lee, Harriet and Sophia (the
latter of whom in 1783 produced, in *The Recess*, a preposterous
Elizabethan story, which would have liked to be a historical
novel), and other known and unknown writers.

Another lady deserves somewhat longer notice. Hannah
More, once a substantially famous person in literature, is now
chiefly remembered by her association with great men of letters,
such as Johnson in her youth, Macaulay and De Quincey in her
old age. She was born as early as 1745 near Bristol, and all
her life was a Somerset worthy. She began — a curious beginning for so serious a lady, but with reforming intentions — to write
for the stage, published *The Search after Happiness* when she
was seventeen, and had two rather dreary tragedies, *Percy* and
the *Fatal Secret,* acted, Garrick being a family friend of hers.
Becoming, as her day said, "pious," she wrote "Sacred Dramas,"
and at Cowslip Green, Barley Wood, and Clifton produced "Moral
Essays," the once famous novel of *Cœlebs in Search of a Wife*,
and many tracts, the best known of which is *The Shepherd of
Salisbury Plain.* She died at a great age on 7th September 1833.
Hannah More is not to be spoken of with contempt, except
by ignorance or incompetence. She had real abilities, and
was a woman of the world. But she was very unfortunately
parted in respect of time, coming just before the days when it
became possible for a lady to be decent in literature without being
dull.

If a book and not a chapter were allowed about this curious,
and on the whole rather neglected and undervalued, Fifth Act of
the eighteenth century, many of its minor literary phenomena
would have to be noticed : such as the last state of periodicals
before the uprising of the *Edinburgh Review,* and the local literary
coteries, the most notable of which was that of Norwich, with the
Aldersons, Sayers the poet, who taught Southey and others to try
blank verse in other measures than the decasyllabic, William
Taylor, the apostle of German literature in England, and others.
But, as it is, we must concentrate our attention on its main lines.

In these lines the poetical pioneers, the political and other satirists, the revolutionary propagandists, and the novelists of terror, are the four classes of writers that distinguish the period 1780 to 1800 ; and perhaps they distinguish it sufficiently, at least for those with whom historical genesis and connection atone to some extent for want of the first order of intrinsic interest. In less characteristic classes and in isolated literary personalities the time was not extremely rich, though it was not quite barren. We can here only notice cursorily the theological controversialists who, like Paley, Horsley, and Watson, waged war against the fresh outburst of aggressive Deism coinciding with the French Re- volution : the scholars, such as, in their different ways, Dr. Parr, the Whig " moon " of Dr. Johnson ; Porson, the famous Cambridge Grecian, drinker, and democrat ; Taylor the Platonist, a strange person who translated most of the works of Plato and was said to have carried his discipleship to the extent of a positive Pagan- ism ; Gilbert Wakefield, a miscellaneous writer who wrote rapidly and with little judgment, but with some scholarship and even some touches of genius, on a great variety of subjects ; Jacob Bryant, mythologist, theologian, and historical critic, a man of vast learning but rather weak critical power ; and many others. Of some of these we may indeed have more to say later, as also of the much-abused Malthus, whose famous book, in part one of the consequences of Godwin, appeared in 1798 ; while as for drama, we shall return to that too. Sheridan survived through the whole of the time and a good deal beyond it ; but his best work was done, and the chief dramatists of the actual day were Colman, Holcroft, Cumberland, and the farce-writer O'Keefe, a man of humour and a lively fancy.

One, however, of these minor writers has too much of what has been called " the interest of origins " not to have a paragraph to himself. William Gilpin, who prided himself on his connection with Bernard Gilpin, the so-called " Apostle of the North " in the sixteenth century, was born at Carlisle. But he is best known in connection with the New Forest, where, after taking his degree at Oxford, receiving orders, and keeping a school for some time, he was appointed to the living of Boldre. This he held till his death in 1814. Gilpin was not a secularly-minded parson by any means ; but his literary fame is derived from the series of Picturesque Tours (*The Highlands*, 1778 ; *The Wye and South Wales*, 1782 ; *The Lakes*, 1789 ; *Forest Scenery*, 1791 ; and *The West of England and the Isle of Wight*, 1798) which he published in the last quarter of the century. They were extremely popular, they set a fashion which may be said never to have died out since, and they attained the seal of parody in the famous *Dr. Syntax* of William Combe (1741–1823), an Eton and Oxford man who spent a fortune and then wrote an enormous amount of the most widely various work in verse and prose, of which little but *Syntax* itself (1812 *sqq.*) is remembered. Gilpin himself is interesting as an important member of " the naturals," as they have been oddly and equivocally called. His style is much more florid and less just than Gilbert White's, and his observation correspondingly less true. But he had a keen sense of natural beauty and did much to instil it into others.

In all the work of the time, however, great and small, from the half-unconscious inspiration of Burns and Blake to the common journey-work of book-making, we shall find the same character — incessantly recurring, and unmistakable afterwards if not always recognisable at the time — of transition, of decay and seed-time mingled with and crossing each other. There are no distinct spontaneous literary schools : the forms which literature takes are either occasional and dependent upon outward events, such as the wide and varied attack and defence consequent upon the French Revolution, or else fantastic, trivial, reflex. Sometimes the absence of any distinct and creative impulse reveals itself in work really good and useful, such as the editing of old writers, of which the labours of Malone are the chief example and the forgeries of Ireland the corresponding corruption ; or the return to their study æsthetically, in which Headley, a now forgotten critic, did good work. Sometimes it resulted in such things as the literary reputation (which was an actual thing after a kind) of persons like Sir James Bland Burges, Under-Secretary of State, poetaster, connoisseur, and general fribble. Yet all the while, in schools and universities, in London garrets and country villages, there was growing up, and sometimes showing itself pretty unmistakably, the generation which was to substitute for this trying and trifling the greatest work in verse, and not the least in prose, that had been done for two hundred years. The *Lyrical Ballads* of 1798, the clarion-call of the new poetry, so clearly sounded, so inattentively heard, might have told all, and did tell some, what this generation was about to do.

CHAPTER II

THE NEW POETRY

THE opening years of the eighth decade of the eighteenth century saw, in unusually close conjunction, the births of the men who were to be the chief exponents, and in their turn the chief determining forces, of the new movement. The three greatest were born, Wordsworth in 1770, Scott in 1771, and Coleridge in 1772; Southey, who partly through accident was to form a trinity with Wordsworth and Coleridge, and who was perhaps the most typical instance of a certain new kind of man of letters, followed in 1774; while Lamb and Hazlitt, the chief romantic pioneers in criticism, Jeffrey and Sydney Smith, the chief classical reactionaries therein, were all born within the decade. But the influence of Scott was for various reasons delayed a little; and critics naturally come after creators. So that the time-honoured eminence of the "Lake Poets"—Wordsworth, Coleridge, and Southey—need not be disturbed.

The day of the birth of William Wordsworth was the 7th of April, the place Cockermouth. His father was an attorney, and, as Lord Lonsdale's agent, a man of some means and position; but on his death in 1783 the eccentric and unamiable character of the then Lord Lonsdale, by delaying the settlement of accounts, put the family in considerable difficulties. Wordsworth, however, was thoroughly educated at Hawkshead Grammar School and St. John's College, Cambridge, where he took his B.A. degree in 1791. He travelled in France, and for a time, like many young men, was a fervent Republican; but, like all the nobler of those who had "hailed the dawn of the French Revolution," he lived to curse its noon. He published early, his first volume of poems bearing the date 1793; but, though that attention to nature which was always his chief note appeared here, the work is not by any means of an epoch-making character. He was averse from every profession; but the fates were kind to him, and a legacy of £900 from his friend Raisley Calvert made a man of such simple tastes as his independent, for a time at least. On the strength of it he settled first at Racedown in Dorset, and then at Alfoxden in Somerset, in the companionship of his sister Dorothy; and at the second of the two places in the neighbourhood of Coleridge. Massive and original as Wordsworth's own genius was, it is almost impossible to exaggerate the effect, both in stimulus and guidance, of the influence of these two; for Dorothy Wordsworth was a woman of a million, and Coleridge, marvellous as were his own powers, was almost more marvellous in the unique Socratic character of his effect on those who possessed anything to work upon. The two poets produced in 1798 the *Lyrical Ballads*, among the contents of which it is sufficient to mention *Tintern Abbey* and *The Ancient Mariner;* and they subsequently travelled together in Germany. Then Wordsworth returned to his native lakes and never left them for long, abiding first at or near Grasmere, and from 1813 at his well-known home of Rydal Mount. When Lord Lonsdale died in 1802, his successor promptly and liberally settled the Wordsworth claims. The poet soon married his cousin Mary Hutchinson; and Lord Lonsdale, not satisfied with atoning for his predecessor's injustice, procured him, in the year of his migration to Rydal, the office of Distributor of Stamps for Westmoreland — an office which was almost a sinecure, and was, for a man of Wordsworth's tastes, more than amply paid. It is curious, and a capital instance to prove that the malignity of fortune has itself been maligned, that the one English poet who was constitutionally incapable of writing for bread never was under any necessity to do so. For full sixty years Wordsworth wandered much, read little, meditated without stint, and wrote, though never hurriedly, yet almost incessantly. The dates of his chief publications may be best given in a note.[1] For some years his poems were greeted by the general public and by a few of its critical guides with storms of obloquy and ridicule; but Words-worth, though never indifferent to criticism, was severely disdainful of it, and held on his way. From the first the brightest spirits of England had been his passionate though by no means always un-discriminating admirers; and about the end of the first quarter of the century the public began to come round. Oxford, always first to recognise, if not always first to produce, the greatest achiev-ments of English literature, gave him its D.C.L. in 1839. He received a pension of £300 a year in 1842 from Sir Robert Peel, who, unlike most English Prime Ministers, cared for men of letters; the laureateship fell to him in right of right on Southey's death in 1843, and he died on the 23rd of April 1850, having come to fourscore years almost without labour, and without many heavy sorrows.

Of his character not much need be said. Like that of Milton, whom he in many ways resembled (they had even both, as Hartley Coleridge has pointed out, brothers named Christopher), it was not wholly amiable, and the defects in it were no doubt aggravated by his early condition (for it must be remembered that till he was two and thirty his prospects were of the most disquieting char-acter), by the unjust opposition which the rise of his reputation met with, and by his solitary life in contact only with worshipping friends and connections. One of these very worshippers con-fesses that he was " inhumanly arrogant "; and he was also, what all arrogant men are not, rude. He was entirely self-centred, and his own circle of interests and tastes was not wide. It is said that he would cut books with a buttery knife, and after that it is

---

[1] *Lyrical Ballads*, 1798, and with additions 1800; *Poems*, 1807 (in these four volumes even adorers have allowed all his greatest work to be included); *The Excursion*, 1814; *The White Doe of Rylston*, 1815; *Sonnets on the River Duddon*, and others, 1819-20. In 1836 he brought out a collected edition of his poems in six volumes. *The Prelude* was posthumous.

probably unnecessary to say any more, for the fact " surprises by itself " an indictment of almost infinite counts.

But his genius is not so easily despatched. I have said that it is now as a whole universally recognised, and I cannot but think that Mr. Matthew Arnold was wrong when he gave a contrary opinion some fifteen years ago. He must have been biassed by his own remembrance of earlier years, when Wordsworth was still a bone of contention. I should say that never since I myself was an undergraduate, that is to say, for the last thirty years, has there been any dispute among Englishmen whose opinion was worth taking, and who cared for poetry at all, on the general merits of Wordsworth. But this agreement is compatible with a vast amount of disagreement in detail ; and Mr. Arnold's own estimate, as where he compares Wordsworth with Molière (who was not a poet at all, though he sometimes wrote very tolerable verse), weighs him with poets of the second class like Gray and Manzoni, and finally admits him for his dealings with " life," introduces fresh puzzlements into the valuation. There is only one principle on which that valuation can properly proceed, and this is the question, " Is the poet rich in essentially poetical moments of the highest power and kind ? " And by poetical moments I mean those instances of expression which, no matter what their subject, their intention, or their context may be, cause instantaneously in the fit reader a poetical impression of the intensest and most moving quality.

Let us consider the matter from this point of view.[1]

The chief poetical influences under which Wordsworth began

[1] It must be remembered that Wordsworth was a prose writer of considerable excellence and of no small volume. Many people no doubt were surprised when Dr. Grosart, by collecting his pamphlets, his essays, his notes, and his letters, managed to fill three large octavo volumes. But his poetry so far outweighs his prose (though, like most poets, he could write admirably in his pedestrian style when he chose) that his utterances in " the other harmony " need not be specially considered. The two most considerable examples of this prose are the pamphlet on *The Convention of Cintra* and the five and twenty years later *Guide to the Lakes*. But minor essays, letters of a more or less formal character, and prefaces and notes to the poems, make up a goodly total; and always display a genius germane to that of the poems.

to write appear to have been those of Burns and Milton; both were upon him to the last, and both did him harm as well as good. It was probably in direct imitation of Burns, as well as in direct opposition to the prevailing habits of the eighteenth century, that he conceived the theory of poetic diction which he defended in prose and exemplified in verse. The chief point of this theory was the use of the simplest and most familiar language, and the double fallacy is sufficiently obvious. Wordsworth forgot that the reason why the poetic diction of the three preceding generations had become loathsome was precisely this, that it had become familiar; while the familiar Scots of Burns was in itself unfamiliar to the English ear. On the other hand, he borrowed from Milton, and used more and more as he grew older, a distinctly stiff and unvernacular form of poetic diction itself. Few except extreme and hopeless Wordsworthians now deny that the result of his attempts at simple language was and is far more ludicrous than touching. The wonderful *Affliction of Margaret* does not draw its power from the neglect of poetic diction, but from the intensity of emotion which would carry off almost any diction, simple or affected; while on the other hand such pieces as " We are Seven," as the " Anecdote for Fathers," and as " Alice Fell," not to mention " Betty Foy " and others, which specially infuriated Wordsworth's own contemporaries, certainly gain nothing from their namby-pamby dialect, and sometimes go near to losing the beauty that really is in them by dint of it. Moreover, the Miltonic blank verse and sonnets — at their best of a stately magnificence surpassed by no poet — have a tendency to become heavy and even dull when the poetic fire fails to fuse and shine through them. In fact it may be said of Wordsworth, as of most poets with theories, that his theories helped him very little, and sometimes hindered him a great deal.

His real poetical merits are threefold, and lie first in the inexplicable, the ultimate, felicity of phrase which all great poets must have, and which only great poets have; secondly, in his matchless power of delineating natural objects; and lastly, more properly,

and with most special rarity of all, in the half-pantheistic mysticism which always lies behind this observation, and which every
now and then breaks through it, puts it, as mere observation, aside,
and blazes in unmasked fire of rapture. The summits of Wordsworth's poetry, the " Lines Written at Tintern Abbey " and the
" Ode on Intimations of Immortality," — poems of such astonishing magnificence that it is only more astonishing that any one
should have read them and failed to see what a poet had come
before the world, — are the greatest of many of these revelations
or inspirations. It is indeed necessary to read Wordsworth
straight through — a proceeding which requires that the reader
shall be in good literary training, but is then feasible, profitable,
and even pleasant enough — to discern the enormous height at
which the great Ode stands above its author's other work. The
Tintern Abbey lines certainly approach it nearest : many smaller
things — " The Affliction of Margaret," " The Daffodils," and
others — group well under its shadow, and innumerable passages
and even single lines, such as that which all good critics have noted
as lightening the darkness of the *Prelude* —

> Voyaging through strange seas of thought, alone —

must of course be added to the poet's credit. But the Ode remains
not merely the greatest, but the one really, dazzlingly, supremely
great thing he ever did. Its theory has been scorned or impugned
by some ; parts of it have even been called nonsense by critics of
weight. But, sound or unsound, sense or nonsense, it is poetry,
and magnificent poetry, from the first line to the last — poetry than
which there is none better in any language, poetry such as there is
not perhaps more than a small volume-full in all languages. The
second class of merit, that of vivid observation, abounds where-
ever the poems are opened. But the examples of the first are
chiefly found in the lyrics " My Heart Leaps up," " The Sparrow's
Nest " ; the famous daffodil poem which Jeffrey thought " stuff,"
which some say Dorothy wrote chiefly, and which is almost
perfect of its kind ; the splendid opening of the " Lines to Hart-

ley Coleridge," which connect themselves with the " Immortality
Ode"; the exquisite group of the "Cuckoo," the best patches
of the Burns poems, and the three "Yarrows"; the "Peel
Castle" stanzas; and, to cut a tedious catalogue short, the
hideously named but in parts perfectly beautiful " Effusion on the
Death of James Hogg," the last really masterly thing that the poet
did. In some of these we may care little for the poem as a whole,
nothing for the moral the poet wishes to draw. But the poetic
moments seize us, the poetic flash dazzles our eyes, and the
whole divine despair or not more divine rapture which poetry
causes comes upon us.

One division of Wordsworth's work is so remarkable that it
must have such special and separate mention as it is here possible
to give it; and that is his exercises in the sonnet, wherein to some
tastes he stands only below Shakespeare and on a level with
Milton. The sonnet, after being long out of favour, paying for its
popularity between Wyatt and Milton by neglect, had, principally
it would seem on the very inadequate example of Bowles (see
infra), become a very favourite form with the new Romantics.
But none of them wrote it with the steady persistence, and none
except Keats with the occasional felicity, of Wordsworth. Its
thoughtfulness suited his bent, and its limits frustrated his
prolixity, though, it must be owned, he somewhat evaded this
benign influence by writing in series. And the sonnets on "The
Venetian Republic," on the " Subjugation of Switzerland," that
beginning "The world is too much with us," that in November
1806, the first " Personal Talk," the magnificent " Westminster
Bridge," and the opening at least of that on Scott's departure
from Abbotsford, are not merely among the glories of Wordsworth,
they are among the glories of English poetry.

Unfortunately these moments of perfection are, in the poet's
whole work, and especially in that part of it which was composed
in the later half of his long life, by no means very frequent.
Wordsworth was absolutely destitute of humour, from which it
necessarily followed that his self-criticism was either non-existent

or constantly at fault. His verse was so little facile, it paid so little regard to any of the common allurements of narrative-interest or varied subject, it was so necessary for it to reach the full white heat, the absolute instant of poetic projection, that when it was not very good it was apt to be scarcely tolerable. It is nearly impossible to be duller than Wordsworth at his dullest, and unluckily it is as impossible to find a poet of anything like his powers who has given himself the license to be dull so often and at such length. The famous " Would he had blotted a thousand " applies to him with as much justice as it was unjust in its original application ; and it is sometimes for pages together a positive struggle to remember that one is reading one of the greatest of English poets, and a poet whose influence in making other poets has been second hardly to that of Spenser, of Keats, or of the friend who follows him in our survey.

Samuel Taylor Coleridge was born in Devonshire, at Ottery St. Mary, of which place his father was vicar, on the 21st October 1772. The family was merely respectable before his day, but since it has been of very unusual distinction, intellectual and other. He went to Christ's Hospital when he was not quite ten years old, and in 1791 was admitted to an exhibition at Jesus College, Cambridge, with his thoughts already directed to poetry by the sonnets of Bowles above mentioned, and with a reputation, exaggerated perhaps, but certainly not invented, in Lamb's famous " Elia " paper on his old school. Indeed, high as is Coleridge's literary position on the strength of his writing alone, his talk and its influence on hearers have been unanimously set higher still. He did very well at first, gaining the Browne Medal for Greek Verse and distinguishing himself for the Craven Scholarship ; but he speedily fell in love, in debt, it is suspected in drink, and it is known into various political and theological heresies. He left Cambridge and enlisted at Reading in the 15th Light Dragoons. He obtained his discharge, however, in three or four months, and no notice except a formal admonition appears to have been taken of his resuming his position at Cambridge. Indeed he was shortly after elected to a Foundation Scholarship. But in the summer of 1794 he visited Oxford, and after he had fallen in with Southey, whose views were already Jacobinical, the pair engaged themselves to Pantisocracy[1] and the Miss Frickers. This curious and often told story cannot be even summarised here. Its immediate result was that Coleridge left the University without taking a degree, and, though not at once, married Sarah Fricker on October 1795. Thenceforward he lived on literature and his friends, especially the latter. He tried Unitarian preaching and newspaper work, of which at one time or another he did a good deal. The curious ins and outs of Coleridge's strange though hardly eventful life have, after being long most imperfectly known, been set forth in fullest measure by Mr. Dykes Campbell. It must suffice here to say that, after much wandering, being unable or unwilling to keep house with his own family, he found asylums, first with some kind folk named Morgan, and then in the house of Mr. Gillman at Hampstead, where for years he held forth to rising men of letters, and where he died on the 25th June 1834. His too notorious craving for opium had never been conquered, though it had latterly been kept in some check.

Despite this unfortunate failing and his general inability to carry out any schemes of work on the great scale, Coleridge's literary production was very considerable, and, except the verse, it has never been completely collected or systematically edited. He began verse-writing very early, and early found a vent for it in the *Morning Chronicle*, then a Radical organ. He wrote *The Fall of Robespierre* in conjunction with Southey in 1794, and published it. Some prose pamphlets followed, and then Cottle, the Bristol providence of this group of men of letters, offered thirty guineas for a volume of poems, which duly appeared in 1796. Meanwhile Coleridge had started a singular newspaper called *The Watchman*, which saw ten numbers, appearing every

---

[1] This word, as well as "Aspheterism," which has had a less general currency, was a characteristic coinage of Coleridge's to designate a kind of Communism, partly based on the speculations of Godwin, and intended to be carried into practice in America.

eighth day. *The Lyrical Ballads* followed in 1798, and meanwhile Coleridge had written the play of *Osorio* (to appear long afterwards as *Remorse*), had begun *Christabel*, and had contributed some of his best poems to the *Morning Post*. His German visit (see *ante*) produced among other things the translation of *Wallenstein*, a translation far above the original. Some poetry and much newspaper work filled the next ten years, with endless schemes; but in 1807 Coleridge began to lecture at the Royal Institution — a course somewhat irregularly delivered, and almost entirely unreported. 1809 saw his second independent periodical venture, *The Friend*, the subsequent reprint of which as a book is completely rewritten. In 1811–12 he delivered his second course of lectures, this time on his own account. It was followed by two others, and in 1813 *Remorse* was produced at Drury Lane, had a fair success, and brought the author some money. *Christabel*, with *Kubla Khan*, appeared in 1816, and the *Biographia Literaria* next year; *Zapolya* and the rewritten *Friend* the year after, when also Coleridge gave a new course of lectures, and yet another, the last. *Aids to Reflection*, in 1825, was the latest important work he issued himself, though in 1828 he superintended a collection of his poems. Such of the rest of his work as is in existence in a collected form has been printed or reprinted since.

A more full account of the appearance of Coleridge's work than is desirable or indeed possible in most cases here has been given, because it is important to convey some idea of the astonishingly piecemeal fashion in which it reached the world. To those who have studied the author's life of opium-eating; of constant wandering from place to place; of impecuniousness so utter that, after all the painstaking of the modern biographer, and after full allowance for the ravens who seem always to have been ready to feed him, it is a mystery how he escaped the workhouse; of endless schemes and endless non-performance — it is only a wonder that anything of Coleridge's ever reached the public except in newspaper columns. As it was, while his most ambitiously planned books were never written at all, most of those which did reach the press were years in getting through it ; and Southey, on one occasion, after waiting fifteen months for the conclusion of a contribution of Coleridge's to *Omniana*, had to cancel the sheet in despair. The collection, after many years, by Mr. Ernest Coleridge of his grandfather's letters has by no means completely removed the mystery which hangs over Coleridge's life and character. We see a little more, but we do not see the whole ; and we are still unable to understand what strange impediments there were to the junction of the two ends of power and performance. A rigid judge might almost say, that if friends had not been so kind, fate had been kinder, and that instead of helping they hindered, just as a child who is never allowed to tumble will never learn to walk.

The enormous tolerance of friends, however, which alone enabled him to produce anything, was justified by the astonishing genius to which its possessor gave so unfair a chance. As a thinker, although the evidence is too imperfect to justify very dogmatic conclusions, the opinion of the best authorities, from which there is little reason for differing, is that Coleridge was much more stimulating than intrinsically valuable. His *Aids to Reflection*, his most systematic work, is disappointing ; and, with *The Friend* and the rest, is principally valuable as exhibiting and inculcating an attitude of mind in which the use of logic is not, as in most eighteenth century philosophers, destructive, but is made to consist with a wide license for the employment of imagination and faith. He borrowed a great deal from the Germans, and he at least sometimes forgot that he had borrowed a great deal from our own older writers.

So, too, precise examination of his numerous but fragmentary remains as a literary critic makes it necessary to take a great deal for granted. Here, also, he Germanised much ; and it is not certain, even with the aid of his fragments, that he was the equal either of Lamb or of Hazlitt in insight. Perhaps his highest claim is that, in the criticism of philosophy, of religion, and of literature alike he expressed, and was even a little ahead of, the nobler bent and sympathy of his contemporaries. We are still content to assign to Coleridge, perhaps without any very certain title-deeds, the invention of that more catholic way of looking at English literature which can relish the Middle Ages without doing injustice to contemporaries, and can be enthusiastic for the seventeenth century without contemning the eighteenth.[1] To him more than to any single man is also assigned (and perhaps rightly, though some of his remarks on the Church, even after his rally to orthodoxy, are odd) the great ecclesiastical revival of the Oxford movement; and it is certain that he had not a little to do with the abrupt discarding of the whole tradition of Locke, Berkeley and Hartley only excepted. Difficult as it may be to give distinct chapter and verse for these assignments from the formless welter of his prose works, no good judge has ever doubted their validity, with the above and other exceptions and guards. It may be very difficult to present Coleridge's assets in prose in a liquid form ; but few doubt their value.

It is very different with his poetry. Here, too, the disastrous, the almost ruinous results of his weaknesses appear. When one begins to sift and riddle the not small mass of his verse, it shrinks almost appallingly in bulk. *Wallenstein*, though better than the original, is after all only a translation. *Remorse* (either under that name or as *Osorio*) and *Zapolya* are not very much better than the contemporary or slightly later work of Talfourd and Milman. *The Fall of Robespierre* is as absurd and not so amusing as Southey's unassisted *Wat Tyler*. Of the miscellaneous verse with which, after these huge deductions, we are left, much is verse-impromptu, often learned and often witty, for Coleridge was (in early days at any rate) abundantly provided with both wit and humour, but quite occasional. Much more consists of mere Juvenilia. Even of the productions of his best times (the last lustrum of the eighteenth century and a lucid interval about 1816)

---

[1] Yet this praise can only be assigned to Coleridge with large allowance. He was always unjust to his own *immediate* predecessors, Johnson, Gibbon, etc.; and he was not too sensible of the real merits of Pope or even of Dryden. In this respect Leigh Hunt, an immeasurably weaker thinker, had a much more catholic taste. And it is not certain that, as a mere prose writer, Coleridge was a very good prose writer.

much is not very good. *Religious Musings*, though it has had its admirers, is terribly poor stuff. *The Monody on the Death of Chatterton* might have been written by fifty people during the century before it. *The Destiny of Nations* is a feeble rant; but the *Ode on the Departing Year*, though still unequal, still conventional, strikes a very different note. *The Three Graves*, though injured by the namby-pambiness which was still thought incumbent in ballads, again shows no vulgar touch. And then, omitting for the moment *Kubla Khan*, which Coleridge said he wrote in 1797, but of which no mortal ever heard till 1816, we come to *The Rime of the Ancient Mariner* and the birth of the new poetry in England. Here the stutters and flashes of Blake became coherent speech and steady blaze ; here poetry, which for a century and a half had been curbing her voice to a genteel whisper or raising it only to a forensic declamation, which had at best allowed a few woodnotes to escape here and there as if by mistake, spoke out loud and clear.

If this statement seems exaggerated (and it is certain that at the time of the appearance of the *Ancient Mariner* not even Wordsworth, not even Southey quite relished it, while there has always been a sect of dissidents against it), two others will perhaps seem more extravagant still. The second is that, with the exception of this poem, of *Kubla Khan*, of *Christabel*, and of *Love*, all of them according to Coleridge written within a few months of each other in 1797–98, he never did anything of the first class in poetry. The third is that these four — though *Christabel* itself does not exceed some fifteen hundred lines and is decidedly unequal, though the *Ancient Mariner* is just over six hundred and the other two are quite short — are sufficient between them to rank their author among the very greatest of English poets. It is not possible to make any compromise on this point ; for upon it turns an entire theory and system of poetical criticism. Those who demand from poetry a " criticism of life," those who will have it that " all depends on the subject," those who want " moral " or " construction " or a dozen other things, — all good

in their way, most of them compatible with poetry and even helpful to it, but none of them essential thereto, — can of course never
accept this estimate.   Mrs. Barbauld said that *The Ancient
Mariner* was "improbable"; and to this charge it must plead
guilty at once.   *Kubla Khan*, which I should rank as almost the
best of the four, is very brief, and is nothing but a dream, and a
fragment of a dream.   *Love* is very short too, and is flawed by
some of the aforesaid namby-pambiness, from which none of the
Lake school escaped when they tried passion.   *Christabel*, the
most ambitious if also the most unequal, does really underlie the
criticism that, professing itself to be a narrative and holding out
the promise of something like a connected story, it tells none, and
does not even offer very distinct hints or suggestions or what its
story, if it had ever been told, might have been.   A thousand
faults are in it; a good part of the thousand in all four.

But there is also there something which would atone for faults
ten thousand times ten thousand; there is what one hears at most
three or four times in English, at most ten or twelve times in all
literature — the first note, with its endless echo-promise, of a new
poetry.   The wonderful cadence-changes of *Kubla Khan*, its
phrases, culminating in the famous distich so well descriptive of
Coleridge himself —

> For he on honey dew hath fed,
>   And drunk the milk of Paradise,

the splendid crash of the

> Ancestral voices prophesying war,

are all part of this note and cry.   You will find them nowhere
from Chaucer to Cowper — not even in the poets where you will
find greater things as you may please to call them.   Then in the
Mariner comes the gorgeous metre, — freed at once and for the
first time from the "butter-woman's rank to market" which had
distinguished all imitations of the ballad hitherto, — the more gorgeous imagery and pageantry here, the simple directness there, the

tameless range of imagination and fancy, the fierce rush of rhythm : —

> The fair breeze blew, the white foam flew,
>   The furrow followed free :
> We were the first that ever burst
>   Into that silent sea.

And thereafter the spectre of Life-in-Death, the water-snakes, the rising of the dead men, the snapping of the spell. There had been nothing like all this before ; and in all the hundred years, for all the great poetry we have seen, we have seen nothing so *new* as it. *Love* gave the magnificent opening stanza, the motto and defence at once of the largest, the most genuine, the most delightful part of poetry. And *Christabel*, independently of its purple patches, such as the famous descant on the quarrels of friends, and the portents that mark the passage of Geraldine, gave what was far more important — a new metre, destined to have no less great and much more copious influence than the Spenserian stanza itself. It might of course be easy to pick out anticipations in part of this combination of iambic dimeter, trochaic, and ana-pæstic ; but it never had taken thorough form before. And how it seized on the imagination of those who heard it is best shown by the well-known anecdote of Scott, who, merely hearing a little of it recited, at once developed it and established it in *The Lay of the Last Minstrel*. In verse at least, if not in prose, there is no greater *master* than Coleridge.

Robert Southey, the third of this curiously dissimilar trio whom partly chance and partly choice have bound together for all time, was born at Bristol on 12th August 1774. His father was only a linen-draper, and a very unprosperous one ; but the Southeys were a respectable family, entitled to arms, and possessed of con-siderable landed property in Somerset, some of which was left away from the poet by unfriendly uncles to strangers, while more escaped him by a flaw in the entail. His mother's family, the Hills, were in much better circumstances than his father, and like the other two Lake Poets he was singularly lucky in finding helpers. First his mother's brother the Rev. Herbert Hill, chaplain to the English factory at Lisbon, sent him to Westminster, where he did very well and made invaluable friends, but lost the regular advancement to Christ Church owing to the wrath of the head-master Dr. Vincent at an article which Southey had contributed to a school magazine, the *Flagellant*. He was in fact expelled ; but the gravest consequences of expulsion from a public school of the first rank did not fall upon him, and he matriculated without objection at Balliol in 1793. His college, however, which was then distinguished for loose living and intellectual dulness, was not congenial to him ; and developing extreme opinions in politics and religion, he decided that he could not take orders, and left without even taking a degree. His disgrace with his own friends was completed by his engaging in the Pantisocratic scheme, and by his attachment to Edith Fricker, a penniless girl (though not at all a " milliner at Bath ") whose sisters became Mrs. Coleridge and Mrs. Lovell. And when the ever-charitable Hill invited him to Portugal he married Miss Fricker the very day before he started. After a residence at Lisbon, in which he laid the foundation of his unrivalled acquaintance with Peninsular history and literature, he returned and lived with his wife at various places, nominally studying for the law, which he liked not better but worse than the Church. After divers vicissitudes, including a fresh visit (this time not as a bachelor) to Portugal, and an experience of official work as secretary to Corry the Irish Chancellor of the Exchequer, he at last, at the age of thirty, established himself at Greta Hall, close to Keswick, where Coleridge had already taken up his abode. This, as well as much else in his career, was made possible by the rare generosity of his friend of school-days and all days, Charles Wynn, brother of the then Sir Watkin, and later a pretty well known politician, who on coming of age gave him an annuity of £160 a year. This in 1807 he relinquished on receiving a government pension of practically the same amount. The Laureateship in 1813 brought him less than another hundred ; but many years afterwards

Sir Robert Peel, in 1835, after offering a baronetcy, put his declining years out of anxiety by conferring a further pension of £300 a year on him. These declining years were in part unhappy. As early as 1816 his eldest son Herbert, a boy of great promise, died; the shock was repeated some years later by the death of his youngest and prettiest daughter Isabel; while in the same year as that in which his pension was increased his wife became insane, and died two years later. A second marriage in 1839 to the poetess Caroline Bowles brought him some comfort; but his own brain became more and more affected, and for a considerable time before his death on 21st March 1843 he had been mentally incapable.

Many morals have been drawn from this melancholy end as to the wisdom of too prolonged literary labour, which in Southey's case had certainly been prodigious, and had been carried so far that he actually read while he was taking constitutional walks. It is fair to say, however, that, just as in the case of Scott the terrible shock of the downfall of his fortunes has to be considered, so in that of Southey the successive trials to which he, a man of exceptionally strong domestic affections, was exposed, must be taken into account. At the same time it must be admitted that Southey's production was enormous. His complete works never have been, and are never likely to be collected; and, from the scattered and irregular form in which they appeared, it is difficult if not impossible to make even a guess at the total. The list of books and articles (the latter for the most part written for the *Quarterly Review*, and of very great length) at the end of his son's *Life* fills nearly six closely printed pages. Two of these entries — the *Histories of Brazil* and of the *Peninsular War* — alone represent six large volumes. The Poems by themselves occupy a royal octavo in double columns of small print running to eight hundred pages; the correspondence, very closely printed in the six volumes of the *Life*, and the four more of *Letters* edited by the Rev. J. W. Warter, some five thousand pages in all; while a good deal of his early periodical work has never been identified,

F

and there are large stores of additional letters — some printed, more in MS. Nor was Southey by any means a careless or an easy writer. He always founded his work on immense reading, some of the results of which, showing the laborious fashion in which he performed it, were published after his death in his *Commonplace Book*. He did not write very rapidly; and he corrected, both in MS. and in proof, with the utmost sedulity. Of the nearly 14,000 books which he possessed at his death, it is safe to say that all had been methodically read, and most read many times; while his almost mediæval diligence did not hesitate at working through a set of folios to obtain the information or the corrections necessary for a single article.

It is here impossible to mention more than the chief items of this portentous list. They are in verse — *Poems*, by R. Southey and R. Lovell, 1794; *Joan of Arc*, 1795; *Minor Poems*, 1797–99; *Thalaba*, 1801; *Metrical Tales* and *Madoc*, 1805; *The Curse of Kehama*, 1810; *Roderick*, 1814; with a few later volumes, the chief being the unlucky *Vision of Judgment*, 1821, in hexameters. A complete edition of the Poems, except one or two posthumously printed, was published by himself in ten volumes in 1837, and collected into one ten years later with the additions. This also includes *Wat Tyler*, a rhapsody of the poet's youth, which was (piratically and to his infinite annoyance) published in 1817.

In prose Southey's most important works are the *History of Brazil*, 1810–19 (this, large as it is, is only a kind of offshoot of the projected *History of Portugal*, which in a way occupied his whole life, and never got published at all); the *History of the Peninsular War*, 1822–32; the *Letters from England by Don Manuel Espriella*, 1812; the *Life of Nelson* (usually thought his masterpiece), 1813; the *Life of Wesley*, 1820; *The Book of the Church*, 1824; *Colloquies on Society* (well known, if not in itself, for Macaulay's review of it), 1829; *Naval History*, 1833–40; and the great humorous miscellany of *The Doctor* (seven volumes), 1834–47; to which must be added editions, often containing some of his best work, of Chatterton, Amadis of Gaul, Palmerin of England, Kirke White, Bunyan, and Cowper, with divers *Specimens* of the British Poets, the charming prose and verse *Chronicle of the Cid*, the miscellany of *Omniana*, half-way between table- and commonplace-book, the *Commonplace Book* itself, and not a little else, besides letters and articles innumerable.

Certain things about Southey are uncontested and uncontestable. The uprightness and beauty of his character, his wonderful helpfulness to others, and the uncomplaining way in which he bore what was almost poverty, — for, high as was his reputation, his receipts were never a tithe of the rewards not merely of Scott or Byron or Tom Moore, but of much lesser men — are not more generally acknowledged than the singular and pervading excellence of his English prose style, the robustness of his literary genius, and his unique devotion to literature. But when we leave these accepted things he becomes more difficult if not less interesting. He himself had not the slightest doubt that he was a great poet, and would be recognised as such by posterity, though with a proud humility he reconciled himself to temporary lack of vogue. This might be set down to an egotistic delusion. But such an easy explanation is negatived by even a slight comparison of the opinions of his greatest contemporaries. It is somewhat staggering to find that Scott, the greatest Tory man of letters who had strong political sympathies, and Fox, the greatest Whig politician who had keen literary tastes, enjoyed his long poems enthusiastically. But it may be said that the eighteenth century leaven which was so strong in each, and which is also noticeable in Southey, conciliated them. What then are we to say of Macaulay, a much younger man, a violent political opponent of Southey, and a by no means indiscriminate lover of verse, who, admitting that he doubted whether Southey's long poems would be read after half a century, had no doubt that if read they would be admired? And what are we to say of the avowals of admiration wrung as it were from Byron, who succeeded in working himself up, from personal, political, and literary motives combined, into a frantic hatred of Southey, lampooned him in print, sent him a challenge (which luckily was not delivered) in private, and was what the late Mr. Mark Pattison would have called "his Satan"?

The half century of Macaulay's prophecy has come, and that prophecy has been fulfilled as to the rarity of Southey's readers as a poet. Has the other part come true too? I should hesitate to say that it has. Esteem not merely for the man but for the writer can never fail Southey whenever he is read by competent persons : admiration may be less prompt to come at call. Two among his smaller pieces — the beautiful "Holly Tree," and the much later but exquisite stanzas "My days among the dead are past" — can never be in any danger ; the grasp of the grotesque-terrific, which the poet shows in the "Old Woman of Berkley" and a great many other places, anticipates the *Ingoldsby Legends* with equal ease but with a finer literary gift ; some other things are really admirable and not a little pleasing. But the longer poems, if they are ever to live, are still dry bones. *Thalaba*, one of the best, is spoilt by the dogged craze against rhyme, which is more, not less, needed in irregular than in regular verse. *Joan of Arc, Madoc, Roderick*, have not escaped that curse of blank verse which only Milton, and he not always, has conquered in really long poems. *Kehama*, the only great poem in which the poet no longer disdains the almost indispensable aid to poetry in our modern and loosely quantified tongue, is much better than any of the others. The Curse itself is about as good as it can be, and many other passages are not far below it ; but to the general taste the piece suffers from the remote character of the subject, which is not generally and humanly interesting, and from the mass of tedious detail.

To get out of the difficulty thus presented by indulging in contemptuous ignoring of Southey's merits has been attempted many times since Emerson foolishly asked "Who is Southey?" in his jottings of his conversation with Landor, Southey's most dissimilar but constant friend and panegyrist. It is extremely easy to say who Southey is. He is the possessor of perhaps the purest and most perfect English prose style, of a kind at once simple and scholarly, to be found in the language. He has written (in the *Life of Nelson*) perhaps the best short biography in that language, and other things not far behind this. No Englishman has ever excelled him in range of reading or in intelligent comprehension and memory of what he read. Unlike many bookworms, he had an exceedingly lively and active humour. He has scarcely an equal, and certainly no superior, in the rare and difficult art of discerning and ranging the material parts of an historical account : the pedant may glean, but the true historian will rarely reap after him. And in poetry his gifts, if they are never of the very highest, are so various and often so high that it is absolutely absurd to pooh-pooh him as a poet. The man who could write the verses " In my Library " and the best parts of *Thalaba* and *Kehama* certainly had it in his power to write other things as good, probably to write other things better. Had it been in his nature to take no thought not merely for the morrow but even for the day, like Coleridge, or in his fate to be provided for without any trouble on his own part, and to take the provision with self-centred indifference, like Wordsworth, his actual production might have been different and better. But his strenuous and generous nature could not be idle ; and idleness of some sort is, it may be very seriously laid down, absolutely necessary to the poet who is to be supreme.

The poet who, though, according to the canons of poetical criticism most in favour during this century, he ranks lower than either Wordsworth or Coleridge, did far more to popularise the general theory of Romantic poetry than either, was a slightly older man than two of the trio just noticed ; but he did not begin his poetical career (save by one volume of translation) till some years after all of them had published. Walter Scott was born in Edinburgh on the 15th of August 1771. His father, of the same name as himself, was a Writer to the Signet ; his mother was Anne Rutherford, and the future poet and novelist had much excellent Border blood in him, besides that of his direct ancestors the Scotts of Harden. He was a very sickly child ; and though he grew out of this he was permanently lame. His early childhood was principally spent on the Border itself, with a considerable interval at Bath; and he was duly sent to the High School and University of Edinburgh, where, like a good many other future men of letters, he was not extremely remarkable for what is called scholarship. He was early imprisoned in his father's office, where the state of relations between father and son is supposed to be pretty accurately represented by the story of those between Alan Fairford and his father in *Redgauntlet;* and, like Alan, he was called to the bar. But even in the inferior branch of the profession he enjoyed tolerable liberty of wandering about and sporting, besides sometimes making expeditions on business into the Highlands and other out-of-the-way parts of the country.

He thus acquired great knowledge of his fatherland; while (for he was, if not exactly a scholar, the most omnivorous of readers) he was also acquiring great knowledge of books. And it ought not to be omitted that Edinburgh, in addition to the literary and professional society which made it then and afterwards so famous, was still to no small extent the headquarters of the Scotch nobility, and that Scott, long before his books made him famous, was familiar with society of every rank. His first love affair did not run smooth, and he seems never to have entirely forgotten the object of it, who is identified (on somewhat more solid grounds than in the case of other novelists) with more than one of his heroines. But he consoled himself to a certain extent with a young lady half French, half English, Miss Charlotte Carpenter or Charpentier, whom he met at Gilsland and married at Carlisle on Christmas Eve 1797. Scott was an active member of the yeomanry as well as a barrister, an enthusiastic student of German as well as a sportsman; and the book of translations (from Bürger) above referred to appeared in 1796. But he did nothing important till after the beginning of the present century, when the starting of the *Edinburgh Review* and some other things brought him forward; though he showed what he could do by contributing two ballads, "Glenfinlas" and "The Eve of St. John," to a collection of terror-pieces started by Monk Lewis, and added Goethe's

Götz von Berlichingen to his translations. He had become in 1799 independent, though not rich, by being appointed Sheriff of Selkirkshire.

His beginnings as an author proper were connected, as was all his subsequent career, partly for good but more for ill, with a school friendship he had early formed for two brothers named Ballantyne at Kelso. He induced James, the elder, to start a printing business at Edinburgh, and unfortunately he entered into a secret partnership with this firm, which never did him much good, which caused him infinite trouble, and which finally ruined him. But into this complicated and still much debated business it is impossible to enter here. James Ballantyne printed the *Border Minstrelsy*, which appeared in 1802, — a book ranking with Percy's *Reliques* in its influence on the form and matter of subsequent poetry, — and then Scott at last undertook original work of magnitude. His task was *The Lay of the Last Minstrel*, published in 1805. It may almost be said that from that day to his death he was the foremost — he was certainly, with the exception of Byron, the most popular — man of letters in Great Britain. His next poems — *Marmion* (1808) and *The Lady of the Lake* (1810) — brought him fame and money such as no English poet had gained before ; and though Byron's following — for following it was — for the time eclipsed his master, the latter's *Rokeby*, *The Lord of the Isles*, and others, would have been triumphs for any one else.

How, when the taste for his verse seemed to cool, he struck out a new line in prose and achieved yet more fame and yet more money than the verse had ever given him, will concern us in the next chapter. But as it would be cumbrous to make yet a third division of his work, the part of his prose which is not fiction may be included here, as well as the rest of his life. He had written much criticism for the *Edinburgh*, until he was partly disgusted by an uncivil review of *Marmion*, partly (and more) by the tone of increasing Whiggery and non-intervention which Jeffrey was imposing on the paper ; and when the *Quarterly* was founded in opposition he transferred his services to that. He edited a splendid and admirably done issue of Dryden (1808) and another not quite so thoroughly executed of Swift (1814), and his secret connection with the Ballantynes induced him to do much other editing and miscellaneous work. In the sad last years of his life he laboured with desperation at a great *Life of Napoleon*, which was a success pecuniarily but not in many other ways, produced the exquisite *Tales of a Grandfather* on Scottish history, and did much else. He even wrote plays, which have very little merit, and, except abstract philosophy, there is hardly a division of literature that he did not touch ; for he composed a sermon or two of merit, and his political pamphlets, the *Letters of Malachi Malagrowther*, opposing what he thought an interference with Scottish privileges in currency matters, are among the best of their kind.

His life was for many years a very happy one ; for his marriage, if not passionately, was fairly successful, he was extremely fond of his children, and while his poems and novels began before he had fully reached middle life to make him a rich man, his Sheriffship, and a Clerkship of Session which was afterwards added (though he had to wait some time for its emoluments), had already made him secure of bread and expectant of affluence. From a modest cottage at Lasswade he expanded himself to a rented country house at Ashestiel on the Tweed, having besides a comfortable town mansion in Edinburgh ; and when he was turned out of Ashestiel he bought land and began to build at Abbotsford on the same river. The estate was an ill-chosen and unprofitable one. The house grew with the owner's fortunes, which, founded in part as they were on the hardest and most honest work that author ever gave, were in part also founded on the quicksand of his treacherous connection with men, reckless, ill-judging, and, though perhaps not in intention dishonest, perpetually trading on their secret partner's industry and fame. In the great commercial crash of 1825, Constable, the publisher of most of the novels, was involved ; he dragged the Ballantynes down with him ; and the whole of Scott's fortune, except his appointments and the little

settled on his wife and children, was liable for the Ballantynes'
debts.   But he was not satisfied with ruin.   He must needs set to
work at the hopeless task of paying debts which he had never,
except technically, incurred, and he actually in the remaining years
of his life cleared off the greater part of them.   It was at the cost
of his life itself.   His wife died, his children were scattered ; but
he worked on till the thankless, hopeless toil broke down his
strength, and after a fruitless visit to Italy, he returned, to die at
Abbotsford on 21st September 1832.

Scott's poetry has gone through various stages of estimate, and
it can hardly be said even now, a hundred years after the
publication of his first verses, to have attained the position, practically accepted by all but paradoxers, which in that time a poet
usually gains, unless, as the poets of the seventeenth century did
in the eighteenth, he falls, owing to some freak of popular taste,
out of really critical consideration altogether.   The immense
popularity which it at first obtained has been noted, as well as the
fact that it was only ousted from that popularity by, so to speak,
a variety of itself.   But the rise of Byron in the long run did it
far less harm than the long-delayed vogue of Wordsworth and
Coleridge and the success even of the later schools, of which
Tennyson was at once the pioneer and the commander-in-chief.
At an uncertain time in the century, but comparatively early, it
became fashionable to take Scott's verse as clever and spirited
improvisation, to dwell on its over-fluency and facility, its lack of
passages in the grand style (whatever the grand style may be), to
indicate its frequent blemishes in strictly correct form and phrase.
And it can hardly be said that there has been much reaction from
this tone among professed and competent critics.

To a certain extent, indeed, this undervaluation is justified,
and Scott himself, who was more free from literary vanity than
any man of letters of whom we have record, pleaded guilty again
and again.   Dropping as he did almost by accident on a style
which had absolutely no forerunners in elaborate formal literature,
a style almost absolutely destitute of any restrictions or limits, in

which the length of lines and stanzas, the position of rhymes, the change from narrative to dialogue, and so forth, depended wholly and solely on the caprice of the author, it would have been extremely strange if a man whose education had been a little lacking in scholastic strictness, and who began to write at a time when the first object of almost every writer was to burst old bonds, had not been somewhat lawless, even somewhat slipshod. *Christabel* itself, the first in time, and, though not published till long afterwards, the model of his *Lay*, has but a few score verses that can pretend to the grand style (whatever that may be). Nor yet again can it be denied that, acute as was the sense which bade Scott stop, he wrote as it was a little too much in this style, while he tried others for which he had far less aptitude.

Yet it seems to me impossible, on any just theory of poetry or of literature, to rank him low as a poet. He can afford to take his trial under more than one statute. To those who say that all depends on the subject, or that the handling and arrangement of the subject are, if not everything, yet something to be ranked far above mere detached beauties, he can produce not merely the first long narrative poems in English, which for more than a century had honestly enthralled and fixed popular taste, but some of the very few long narrative poems which deserve to do so. Wordsworth, in a characteristic note on the *White Doe of Rylstone*, contrasts, with oblique depreciation of Scott, that poem and its famous predecessors in the style across the border ; but he omits to notice one point of difference — that in Scott the *story* interests, and in himself it does not. For the belated " classical " criticism of the *Edinburgh Review*, which thought the story of the *Last Minstrel* childish, and that of *Marmion* not much better, it may have been at least consistent to undervalue these poems. But the assumptions of that criticism no longer pass muster. On the other hand, to those who pin their poetical faith on "patches," the great mass of Scott's poetical work presents examples of certainly no common beauty. The set pieces of the larger poems, the Melrose description in *The Lay*, the battle in *Marmion*, the Fiery Cross in the *Lady of the Lake*, are indeed inferior in this respect to the mere snatches which the author scattered about his novels, some of which, especially the famous "Proud Maisie," have a beauty not inferior to that of the best things of his greatest contemporaries. And in swinging and dashing lyric, again, Scott can hold his own with the best, if indeed "the best" can hold *their* own in this particular division with "Lochinvar" and "Bonnie Dundee," with Elspeth's ballad in the *Antiquary*, and the White Lady's comfortable words to poor Father Philip.

The most really damaging things to be said against Scott as a poet are two. First, that his genius did not incline him either to the expression of the highest passion or to that of the deepest meditation, in which directions the utterances of the very greatest poetry are wont to lie. In the second place, that the extreme fertility and fluency which cannot be said to have improved even his prose work are, from the nature of the case, far more evident, and far more damagingly evident, in his verse. He is a poet of description, of action, of narration, rather than of intense feeling or thought. Yet in his own special divisions of the simpler lyric and of lyrical narrative he sometimes attains the exquisite, and rarely sinks below a quality which is fitted to give the poetical delight to a very large number of by no means contemptible persons. It appears to me at least, that on no sound theory of poetical criticism can Scott be ranked as a poet below Byron, who was his imitator in narrative and his inferior in lyric. But it may be admitted that this was not the opinion of most contemporaries of the two, and that, much as the poetry of Byron has sunk in critical estimation during the last half century, and slight as are the signs of its recovery, those who do not think very highly of the poetry of the pupil do not, as a rule, show much greater enthusiasm for that of the master.

Byron, it is true, was only half a pupil of Scott's, and (oddly enough for the poet, who, with Scott, was recognised as leader by the Romantic schools of all Europe) had more than a hankering after the classical ideals in literature. Yet how much of this was due to wilful "pose" and a desire not to follow the prevailing school of the day is a question difficult to answer — as indeed are many connected with Byron, whose utterances, even in private letters, are very seldom to be taken with absolute confidence in their sincerity. The poet's character did no discredit to the doctrines of heredity. His family was one of considerable distinction and great age; but his father, Captain John Byron, who never came to the title, was a *roué* of the worst character, and the cousin whom the poet succeeded had earned the name of the Wicked Lord. His mother, Catherine Gordon of Gight, was of an excellent Scotch stock, and an heiress; though her rascally husband made away with her money. But she had a most violent temper, and seems to have had absolutely no claims except those of birth to the title of lady. Byron was born in Holles Street, Cavendish Square, on 22nd January 1788; and his early youth, which was spent with his mother at Aberdeen, was one of not much indulgence or happiness. But he came to the title, and to an extremely impoverished succession, at ten years old, and three years later was sent to Harrow. Here he made many friends, distinguishing himself by obtruding mentions and memories of his rank in a way not common with the English aristocracy, and hence, in 1805, he proceeded to Trinity College, Cambridge. He spent about the usual time there, but took no degree, and while he was still an undergraduate printed his *Hours of Idleness*, first called *Juvenila*. It appeared publicly in March 1807, and a year later was the subject of a criticism, rather excessive than unjust, in the *Edinburgh Review*. Byron, who had plenty of pluck, and who all his life long inclined in his heart to the Popian school, spent a considerable time upon a verse-answer, *English Bards and Scotch Reviewers*, in which he ran amuck generally, but displayed ability which it was hopeless to seek in his first production. Then he went abroad, and the excitement of his sojourn in the countries round the Mediter-

ranean for the next two years not only aroused, but finally determined and almost fully developed, his genius.

On his return home he took his seat and went into society
with the success likely to attend an extremely handsome young
man of twenty-three, with a vague reputation both for ability and
naughtiness, a fairly old title, and something of an estate. But
his position as a "lion" was not thoroughly asserted till the
publication, in February 1812, of *Childe Harold*, which with
some difficulty he had been induced by his friend Dallas, his
publisher Murray, and the critic Gifford to put before some frigid
and trivial *Hints from Horace*. Over *Childe Harold* the English
public went simply mad, buying seven editions in five weeks; and
during the next three years Byron produced, in rapid succession,
The Giaour, *The Bride of Abydos*, *The Corsair*, *Lara*, *The Siege
of Corinth*, and *Hebrew Melodies*. He could hardly write fast
enough for the public to buy. Then the day after New Year's
Day 1814, he married Miss Milbanke, a great heiress, a future
baroness in her own right, and handsome after a fashion, but of a
cold, prim, and reserved disposition, as well as of a very unforgiv-
ing temper. It probably did not surprise any one who knew the
pair when, a year later, they separated for ever.

The scandals and discussions connected with this event are
fortunately foreign to our subject here. The only important result
of the matter for literature is that Byron (upon whom public
opinion in one of its sudden fits of virtuous versatility threw even
more of the blame than was probably just) left the country and
journeyed leisurely, in the company of Mr. and Mrs. Shelley for
the most part, to Venice. He never returned alive to England;
and Venice, Ravenna, Pisa, and Genoa were successively his headquarters till 1823. Then the Greek Insurrection attracted him,
he raised what money he could, set out for Greece, showed in the
distracted counsels of the insurgents much more practical and
untheatrical heroism than he had hitherto been credited with, and
died of fever at Missolonghi on the 19th of April 1824. His
body was brought home to England and buried in the parish

church of Hucknall Torkard, near Newstead Abbey, his Notting-hamshire seat, which, however, he had sold some time before. The best of Byron's poems by far date from this latter period of his life : the later cantos of *Childe Harold*, the beautiful short poems of *The Dream* and *Darkness*, many pieces in dramatic form (the chief of which are *Manfred, Cain, Marino Faliero*, and *Sardanapalus*), *Mazeppa*, a piece more in his earlier style but greatly superior to his earlier work, a short burlesque poem *Beppo*, and an immense and at his death unfinished narrative satire entitled *Don Juan*.

Although opinions about Byron differ very much, there is one point about him which does not admit of difference of opinion. No English poet, perhaps no English writer except Scott (or rather "The Author of Waverley "), has ever equalled him in popularity at home ; and no English writer, with Richardson and Scott again as seconds, and those not very close ones, has equalled him in contemporary popularity abroad. The vogue of Byron in England, though overpowering for the moment, was even at its height resisted by some good judges and more strait-laced moralists ; and it ebbed, if not as rapidly as it flowed, with a much more enduring movement. But abroad he simply took possession of the Continent of Europe and kept it. He was one of the dominant influences and determining causes of the French Romantic movement ; in Germany, though the failure of literary talent and activity of the first order in that country early in this century made his school less important, he had great power over Heine, its one towering genius ; and he was almost the sole master of young Russia, young Italy, young Spain, in poetry. Nor, though his active and direct influence has of course been exhausted by time, can his reputation on the Continent be said to have ever waned.

These various facts, besides being certain in themselves, are also very valuable as guiding the inquirer in regions which are more of opinion. The rapidity of Byron's success everywhere, the extent of it abroad (where few English writers before him had

had any at all), and the decline at home, are all easily connected
with certain peculiarities of his work. That work is almost as
fluent and facile as Scott's, to which, as has been said, it owes
immense debts of scheme and manner ; and it is quite as faulty.
Indeed Scott, with all his indifference to a strictly academic
correctness, never permitted himself the bad rhymes, the bad
grammar, the slipshod phrase in which Byron unblushingly in-
dulges. But Byron is much more monotonous than Scott, and
it was this very monotony, assisted by an appearance of intensity,
which for the time gave him power. The appeal of Byron consists
very mainly, though no doubt not wholly, in two things : the lavish
use of the foreign and then unfamiliar scenery, vocabulary, and
manners of the Levant, and the installation, as principal character,
of a personage who was speedily recognised as a sort of fancy
portrait, a sketch in cap and yataghan, of Byron himself as he
would like to be thought. This Byronic hero has an ostentatious
indifference to moral laws, for the most part a mysterious past
which inspires him with deep melancholy, great personal beauty,
strength, and bravery, and he is an all-conquering lover. He is
not quite so original as he seemed, for he is in effect very little
more than the older Romantic villain-hero of Mrs. Radcliffe, the
Germans, and Monk Lewis, costumed much more effectively,
placed in scheme and companionship more picturesquely, and
managed with infinitely greater genius. But it is a common experience in literary history that a type more or less familiar
already, and presented with striking additions, is likely to be
more popular than something absolutely new. And accordingly
Byron's bastard and second-hand Romanticism, though it owed
a great deal to the terrorists and a great deal more to Scott, for
the moment altogether eclipsed the pure and original Romanticism
of his elders Coleridge and Wordsworth, of his juniors Shelley
and Keats.

But although the more extreme admirers of Byron would no
doubt dissent strongly from even this judgment, it would probably
be subscribed, with some reservations and guards, by not a few

good critics from whom I am compelled to part company as to other parts of Byron's poetical claim. It is on the question how much of true poetry lies behind and independent of the scenery and properties of Byronism, that the great debate arises. Was the author of the poems from *Childe Harold* to *Don Juan* really gifted with the poetical " sincerity and strength " which have been awarded him by a critic of leanings so little Byronic in the ordinary sense of Matthew Arnold? Is he a poetic star of the first magnitude, a poetic force of the first power, at all? There may seem to be rashness, there may even seem to be puerile insolence and absurdity, in denying or even doubting this in the face of such a European concert as has been described and admitted above. Yet the critical conscience admits of no transaction ; and after all, as it was doubted by a great thinker whether nations might not go mad like individuals, I do not know why it should be regarded as impossible that continents should go mad like nations.

At any rate the qualities of Byron are very much of a piece, and, even by the contention of his warmest reasonable admirers, not much varied or very subtle, not necessitating much analysis or disquisition. They can be fairly pronounced upon in a judgment of few words. Byron, then, seems to me a poet distinctly of the second class, and not even of the best kind of second, inasmuch as his greatness is chiefly derived from a sort of parody, a sort of imitation, of the qualities of the first. His verse is to the greatest poetry what melodrama is to tragedy, what plaster is to marble, what pinchbeck is to gold. He is not indeed an impostor ; for his sense of the beauty of nature and of the unsatisfactoriness of life is real, and his power of conveying this sense to others is real also. He has great, though uncertain, and never very *fine*, command of poetic sound, and a considerable though less command of poetic vision. But in all this there is a singular touch of illusion, of what his contemporaries had learnt from Scott to call gramarye. The often cited parallel of the false and true Florimels in Spenser applies here also. The really great poets do not injure each other in the very least by comparison, different as

they are.   Milton does not "kill" Wordsworth ; Spenser does not
injure Shelley ; there is no danger in reading Keats immediately
after Coleridge.   But read Byron in close juxtaposition with any
of these, or with not a few others, and the effect, to any good
poetic taste, must surely be disastrous ; to my own, whether good
or bad, it is perfectly fatal.   The light is not that which never was
on land or sea; it is that which is habitually just in front of the
stage : the roses are rouged, the cries of passion even sometimes
(not always) ring false.   I have read Byron again and again ; I
have sometimes, by reading Byron only and putting a strong con-
straint upon myself, got nearly into the mood to enjoy him.   But
let eye or ear once catch sight or sound of real poetry, and the
enchantment vanishes.

   Attention has already been called to the fact that Byron,
though generally ranking with the poets who have been placed
before him in this chapter as a leader in the nineteenth century
renaissance of poetry, was a direct scholar of Scott, and in point
of age represented, if not a new generation, a second division of
the old.   This was still more the case in point of age, and almost
infinitely more so in point of quality, as regards Shelley and Keats.
There was nothing really new in Byron ; there was only a great
personal force directing itself, half involuntarily and more than
half because of personal lack of initiative, into contemporary ways.
The other two poets just mentioned were really new powers.
They took some colour from their elders ; but they added more
than they took, and they would unquestionably have been great
figures at any time of English literature and history.   Scott had
little or no influence on them, and Wordsworth not much ; but
they were rather close to Coleridge, and they owed something to
a poet of much less genius than his or than their own — Leigh
Hunt.

   Percy Bysshe Shelley, the elder of the two, was Byron's junior
by four years, and was born at Field Place in Sussex in August
1792.   He was the heir of a very respectable and ancient
though not very distinguished family of the squirearchy ; and he

G

had every advantage of education, being sent to Eton in 1804, and to University College, Oxford, six years later. The unconquerable unconventionality of his character and his literary tastes had shown themselves while he was still a schoolboy, and in the last year of his Etonian and the first of his Oxonian residence he published two of the most absurd novels of the most absurd novel kind that ever appeared, *Zastrozzi* and *St. Irvyne*, imitations of Monk Lewis. He also in the same year collaborated in two volumes of verse, *The Wandering Jew* (partly represented by *Queen Mab*), and "*Poems* by Victor and Cazire" (which has vindicated the existence of reviewers by surviving only in its reviews, all copies having mysteriously perished). His stay at Oxford was not long; for having, in conjunction with a clever but rather worthless friend, Thomas Jefferson Hogg (afterwards his biographer), issued a pamphlet on "The Necessity of Atheism" and sent it to the heads of colleges, he was, by a much greater necessity, expelled from University on 25th March 1811. Later in the same year he married Harriet Westbrook, a pretty and lively girl of sixteen, who had been a school-fellow of his sister's, but came from the lower middle class. His apologists have said that Harriet threw herself at his head, and that Shelley explained to her that she or he might depart when either pleased. The responsibility and the validity of this defence may be left to these advocates.

For nearly three years Shelley and his wife led an exceedingly wandering life in Ireland, Wales, Devonshire, Berkshire, the Lake District, and elsewhere, Shelley attempting all sorts of eccentric propagandism in politics and religion, and completing the crude but absolutely original *Queen Mab*. Before the third anniversary of his wedding-day came round he had parted with Harriet, against whose character his apologists, as above, have attempted to bring charges. The fact is that he had fallen in love with Mary Godwin, daughter of the author of *Political Justice* (whose writings had always had a great influence on Shelley, and who spunged on him pitilessly) and of Mary Wollstonecraft. The pair fled to

monosyllabic noun at the end of the line, and a strong cæsura about two-thirds through that line. All the rest is Shelley, and wonderful.

It may be questioned whether, fine as *The Revolt of Islam* is, the Spenserian stanza was quite so well suited as the " Pindaric " or as blank verse, or as lyrical measures, to Shelley's genius. It is certainly far excelled both in the lyrics and in the blank verse of *Prometheus Unbound*, the first poem which distinctly showed that one of the greatest lyric poets of the world had been born to England. *The Cenci* relies more on subject, and, abandoning the lyric appeal, abandons what Shelley is strongest in ; but *Hellas* restores this. Of his comic efforts, the chief of which are *Swellfoot the Tyrant* and *Peter Bell the Third*, it is perhaps enough to say that his humour, though it existed, was fitful, and that he was too much of a partisan to keep sufficiently above his theme. The poems midway between, large and small — *Prince Athanase, The Witch of Atlas* (an exquisite and glorious fantasy piece), *Rosalind and Helen, Adonian Epipsychidion*, and the *Triumph of Life* — would alone have made his fame. But it is in Shelley's smallest poems that his greatest virtue lies. Not even in the seventeenth century had any writer given so much that was so purely exquisite. " To Constantia Singing," the "Ozymandias " sonnet, the "Lines written among the Euganean Hills," the "Stanzas written in Dejection," the "Ode to the West Wind," the hackneyed "Cloud," and "Skylark," "Arethusa," the "World's Wanderers," "Music, when soft voices die," "The flower that smiles to-day," "Rarely, rarely, comest thou," the "Lament," "One word is too often profaned," the "Indian Air," the second "Lament," "O world ! O life ! O time !" (the most perfect thing of its kind perhaps, in the strict sense of perfection, that all poetry contains), the "Invitation," and the "Recollection," — this long list, which might have been made longer, contains things absolutely consummate, absolutely unsurpassed, only rivalled by a few other things as perfect as themselves.

Shelley has been foolishly praised, and it is very likely that the praise given here may seem to some foolish. It is as hard for praise to keep the law of the head as for blame to keep the law of the heart. He has been mischievously and tastelessly excused for errors both in and out of his writings which need only a kindly silence. In irritation at the "chatter" over him some have even tried to make out that his prose — very fine prose indeed, and preserved to us in some welcome letters and miscellaneous treatises, but capable of being dispensed with — is more worthy of attention than his verse, which has no parallel and few peers. But that one thing will remain true in the general estimate of competent posterity I have no doubt. There are two English poets, and two only, in whom the purely poetical attraction, exclusive of and sufficient without all others, is supreme, and these two are Spenser and Shelley.

The life of John Keats was even shorter and even less marked by striking events than that of Shelley, and he belonged in point of extraction and education to a somewhat lower class of society than any of the poets hitherto mentioned in this chapter. He was the son of a livery stable keeper who was fairly well off, and he went to no school but a private one, where, however, he received tolerable instruction and had good comrades. Born in 1795, he was apprenticed to a surgeon at the age of fifteen, and even did some work in his profession, till in 1817 his overmastering passion for literature had its way. He became intimate with the so-called "Cockney school," or rather with its leaders Leigh Hunt and Hazlitt — an intimacy, as far as the former was concerned, not likely to chasten his own taste, but chiefly unfortunate because it led, in the rancorous state of criticism then existing, to his own efforts being branded with the same epithet. His first book was published in the year above mentioned: it did not contain all the verse he had written up to that time, or the best of it, but it confirmed him in his vocation. He broke away from surgery, and, having some little means, travelled to the Isle of Wight, Devonshire, and other parts of England, besides becoming more and more familiar with men of letters. It was in the Isle of Wight chiefly that he wrote *Endymion*, which appeared in 1818. This was savagely and stupidly attacked in *Blackwood* and the *Quarterly;* the former article being by some attributed, without a tittle of evidence, to Lockhart. But the supposed effect of these attacks on Keats' health was widely exaggerated by some contemporaries, especially by Byron. The fact was that he had almost from his childhood shown symptoms of lung disease, which developed itself very rapidly. The sense of his almost certain fate combined with the ordinary effects of passion to throw a somewhat hectic air over his correspondence with Miss Fanny Brawne. His letters to her contain nothing discreditable to him, but ought never to have been published. He was, however, to bring out his third and greatest book of verse in 1820; and then he sailed for Italy, to die on the 23rd of February 1821. He spoke of his name as "writ in water." Posterity has agreed with him that it is—but in the Water of Life.

Nothing is more interesting, even in the endless and delightful task of literary comparison, than to contrast the work of Shelley and Keats, so alike and yet so different. A little longer space of work, much greater advantages of means and education, and a happier though less blameless experience of passion, enabled Shelley to produce a much larger body of work than Keats has to his name, even when this is swollen by what Mr. Palgrave has justly stigmatised as "the incomplete and inferior work" withheld by Keats himself, but made public by the cruel kindness of admirers. And this difference in bulk probably coincides with a difference in the volume of genius of the two writers. Further, while it is not at all improbable that if Shelley had lived he would have gone on writing better and better, the same probability is, I think, to be more sparingly predicated of Keats.

On the other hand, by a not uncommon connection or consequence, Keats has proved much more of a "germinal" poet than Shelley. Although the latter was, I think, by far the greater, his poetry had little that was national and very little that was imitable about it. He has had a vast influence; but it has been in the main the influence, the inspiration of his unsurpassed exciting power. No one has borrowed or carried further any specially Shelleian turns of phrase, rhythm, or thought. Those who have attempted to copy and urge further the Shelleian attitude towards politics, philosophy, ethics, and the like, have made it generally ludicrous and sometimes disgusting. He is, in his own famous words, "something remote and afar." His poetry is almost poetry in its elements, uncoloured by race, language, time, circumstance, or creed. He is not even so much a poet as Poetry accidentally impersonated and incarnate.

With Keats it is very different. He had scarcely reached maturity of any kind when he died, and he laboured under the very serious disadvantages, first of an insufficient acquaintance with the great masters, and secondly of coming early under the influence of a rather small master, yet a master, Leigh Hunt, who taught him the fluent, gushing, slipshod style that brought not merely upon him, but upon his mighty successor Tennyson, the harsh but not in this respect wholly unjust lash of conservative and academic criticism. But he, as no one of his own contemporaries did, felt, expressed, and handed on the exact change wrought in English poetry by the great Romantic movement. Coleridge, Wordsworth, Scott, and even Southey to some extent, were the authors of this; but, being the authors, they were necessarily not the results of it. Byron was fundamentally out of sympathy with it, though by accidents of time and chance he had to enlist; Shelley, an angel, and an effectual angel, of poetry, was hardly a man, and still less an Englishman. But Keats felt it all, expressed what of it he had time and strength to express, and left the rest to his successors, helped, guided, furthered by his own example. Keats, in short, is the father, directly or at short stages of descent, of every English poet

born within the present century who has not been a mere
"sport" or exception. He begat Tennyson, and Tennyson
begat all the rest.

The evidences of this are to be seen in almost his earliest
poems — not necessarily in those contained in his earliest volume.
Of course they are not everywhere. There were sure to be,
and there were, mere echoes of eighteenth century verse and
mere imitations of earlier writers. But these may be simply
neglected. It is in such pieces as "Calidore" that the new note
is heard; and though something in this note may be due to Hunt
(who had caught the original of it from Wither and Browne),
Keats changed, enriched, and refashioned the thing to such an
extent that it became his own. It is less apparent (though
perhaps not less really present) in his sonnets, despite the magnificence of the famous one on Chapman's *Homer*, than in the
couplet poems, which are written in an extremely fluent and
peculiar verse, very much "enjambed" or overlapped, and with
a frequent indulgence in double rhymes. Hunt had to a certain extent started this, but he had not succeeded in giving
it anything like the distinct character which it took in Keats'
hands.

Endymion was written in this measure, with rare breaks; and
there is little doubt that the lusciousness of the rhythm, combined
as it was with a certain lusciousness both of subject and (again
in unlucky imitation of Hunt) of handling, had a bad effect on
some readers, as also that the attacks on it were to a certain
extent, though not a very large one, prompted by genuine disgust
at the mawkishness, as its author called it, of the tone. Keats, who
was always an admirable critic of his own work, judged it correctly
enough later, except that he was too harsh to it. But it is a
delightful poem to this day, and I do think that it is quite just to
call it, as it has been called, "not Greek, but Elizabethan-Ro-
mantic." It seems to me quite different from Marlowe or the
author of *Britain's Ida*, and really Greek, but Greek mediæval,
Greek of the late romance type, refreshed with a wonderful new

blood of English romanticism. And this once more was to be the note of all the best poetry of the century, the pouring of this new English blood through the veins of old subjects — classical, mediæval, foreign, modern. We were to conquer the whole world of poetical matter with our English armies, and Keats was the first leader who started the adventure.

The exquisite poetry of his later work showed this general tendency in all its latest pieces, — clearly in the larger poems, the fine but perhaps somewhat overpraised *Hyperion*, the admirable *Lamia*, the exquisite *Eve of St. Agnes*, but still more in the smaller, and most of all in those twin peaks of all his poetry, the " Ode on a Grecian Urn " and " La Belle Dame sans Merci." He need indeed have written nothing but these two to show himself not merely an exquisite poet but a captain and leader of English poetry for many a year, almost for many a generation to come. Wordsworth may have given him a little, a very quiet hint for the first, the more Classical masterpiece ; Coleridge something a little louder for the second, the Romantic. But in neither case did the summons amount to anything like a cue or a call-bell ; it was at best seed that, if it had not fallen on fresh and fruitful soil, could have come to nothing.

As it is, and if we wish to see what it came to, we must simply look at the whole later poetry of the nineteenth century in England. The operations of the spirit are not to be limited, and it is of course quite possible that if Keats had not been, something or somebody would have done his work instead of him. But as it is, it is to Keats that we must trace Tennyson, Rossetti, Mr. Swinburne, Mr. Morris ; to Keats that even not a little of Browning has to be affiliated ; to Keats, directly or indirectly, that the greater part of the poetry of nearly three generations owes royalty and allegiance.

Of him, as of Shelley, some foolish and hurtful things have been said. In life he was no effeminate " æsthetic " or " decadent," divided between sensual gratification and unmanly *Katzenjammer*, between paganism and puerility, but an honest, manly Englishman, whose strength only yielded to unconquerable disease, whose impulses were always healthy and generous. Despite his origin, — and, it must be added, some of his friendships,— there was not a touch of vulgarity about him ; and if his comic vein was not very full-pulsed, he had a merry laugh in him. There is no "poisonous honey stolen" from anywhere or extracted by himself from anything in Keats ; his sensuousness is nothing more than is, in the circumstances, "necessary and voluptuous and right." But these moral excellences, while they may add to the satisfaction with which one contemplates him, hardly enhance — though his morbid admirers seem to think that the absence of them would enhance — the greatness and the value of his poetical position, both in the elaboration of a new poetic style and language, and still more in the indication of a new road whereby the great poetic exploration could be carried on.

Round or under these great Seven — for that Byron was great in a way need not be denied ; Southey, the weakest of all as a poet, had a very strong influence, and was one of the very greatest of English men of letters — must be mentioned a not inconsiderable number of men who in any other age would have been reckoned great. The eldest of these, both in years and in reputation, holds his position, and perhaps always held it, rather by courtesy than by strict right. Samuel Rogers[1] was born in London on 30th July 1763, and was the son of a dissenting banker, from whom he derived Whig principles and a comfortable fortune. It is said that he once, as a very young man, went to call on Dr. Johnson, but was afraid to knock ; but though shyness accompanied him through life, the amiability which it is sometimes supposed to betoken did not. He published a volume of poems in 1786, and his famous *Pleasures of Memory*, the piece that

---

[1] Curiously enough, there was another and slightly older Samuel Rogers, a clergyman, who published verse in 1782, just before his namesake, and who dealt with Hope—

> Hope springs eternal in the *aspiring* breast.

His verse, of which specimens are given in Southey's *Modern English Poets*, is purely eighteenth century. He died in 1790.

made his reputation, in 1792. Twenty years afterwards *Columbus* followed, and yet two years later, in 1814, *Jacqueline;* while in 1822 *Italy*, on which, with the *Pleasures of Memory*, such fame as he has rests, was published, to be reissued some years afterwards in a magnificent illustrated edition, and to have a chance (in a classical French jest) *se sauver de planche en planche*. He did not die till 1855, in his ninety-third year : the last, as he had been the first, of his group.

Rogers had the good luck to publish his best piece at a time when the general and popular level of English poetry was at the lowest point it has reached since the sixteenth century, and to be for many years afterwards a rich and rather hospitable man, the acquaintance if not exactly the friend of most men of letters, of considerable influence in political and general society, and master of an excessively sharp tongue. A useful friend and a dangerous enemy, it was simpler to court or to let him alone than to attack him, and his fame was derived from pieces too different from any work of the actual generation to give them much umbrage. It may be questioned whether Rogers ever wrote a single line of poetry. But he wrote some polished and pleasant verse, which was vigorous by the side of Hayley and " correct " by the side of Keats. In literature he has very little interest ; in literary history he has some.

Felix opportunitate in the same way, but a far greater poet, was Thomas Campbell, who, like Rogers, was a Whig, like him belonged rather to the classical than to the romantic school in style if not in choice of subject, and like him had the good luck to obtain, by a poem with a title very similar to that of Rogers' masterpiece, a high reputation at a time when there was very little poetry put before the public. Campbell was not nearly so old a man as Rogers, and was even the junior of the Lake poets and Scott, having been born at Glasgow on the 27th July 1777. His father was a real Campbell, and as a merchant had at one time been of some fortune ; but the American War had impoverished him, and the poet was born to comparative indigence. He did, however, well at the college of his native city, and on leaving it took a tutorship in Mull. His *Pleasures of Hope* was published in 1799 and was extremely popular, nor after it had its author much difficulty in following literature. He was never exactly rich, but pensions, legacies, editorships, high prices for his not extensive poetical work, and higher for certain exercises in prose bookmaking which are now almost forgotten, maintained him very comfortably. Indeed, of the many recorded ingratitudes of authors to publishers, Campbell's celebrated health to Napoleon because "he shot a bookseller" is one of the most ungrateful. In the last year of the eighteenth century he went to Germany, and was present at (or in the close neighbourhood of) the battle of Hohenlinden. This he afterwards celebrated in really immortal verse, which, with "Ye Mariners of England" and the "Battle of the Baltic," represents his greatest achievement. In 1809 he published *Gertrude of Wyoming*, a short-long poem of respectable *technique* and graceful sentiment. In 1824 appeared a volume of poems, of which the chief, *Theodric* (not as it is constantly misspelled *Theodoric*), is bad ; and in 1842 another, of which the chief, *The Pilgrim of Glencoe*, is worse. He died in 1844 at Boulogne, after a life which, if not entirely happy (for he had ill-health, not improved by incautious habits, some domestic misfortunes, and a rather sour disposition), had been full of honours of all kinds, both in his own country, of where he was Lord Rector of Glasgow University, and out of it.

If Campbell had written nothing but his longer poems, the comparison above made with Rogers would be wholly, instead of partly, justified. Although both still retain a sort of conventional respect, it is impossible to call either the *Pleasures of Hope* or *Gertrude of Wyoming* very good poetry, while enough has been said of their successors. Nor can very high praise be given to most of the minor pieces. But the three splendid war-songs above named — the equals, if not the superiors, of anything of the kind in English, and therefore in any language — set him in a position from which he is never likely to be ousted. In a handful of others — " Lochiel," the exquisite lines on " A Deserted Garden in Argyleshire," with, for some flashes at least, the rather over-famed " Exile of Erin," " Lord Ullin's Daughter," and a few more — he also displays very high, though rather unequal and by no means unalloyed, poetical faculty ; and " The Last Man," which, by the way, is the latest of his good things, is not the least. But his best work will go into a very small compass : a single octavo sheet would very nearly hold it, and it was almost all written before he was thirty. He is thus an instance of a kind of poet, not by any means rare in literature, but also not very common, who appears to have a faculty distinct in class but not great in volume, who can do certain things better than almost anybody else, but cannot do them very often, and is not quite to be trusted to do them with complete sureness of touch. For it is to be noted that even in Campbell's greatest things there are distinct blemishes, and that these blemishes are greatest in that which in its best parts reaches the highest level — " The Battle of the Baltic." Many third and some tenth rate poets would never have left in their work such things as " The might of England flushed *To anticipate the scene*," which is half fustian and half nonsense : no very great poet could possibly have been guilty of it. Yet for all this Campbell holds, as has been said, the place of best singer of war in a race and language which are those of the best singers and not the worst fighters in the history of the world — in the race of Nelson and the language of Shakespeare. Not easily shall a man win higher praise than this.

In politics, as well as in a certain general kind of literary attitude and school, another Thomas, Moore, classes himself both historically and naturally with Rogers and Campbell ; but he was a very much better poet than Rogers, and, though he never reached quite the same height as Campbell at his narrow and exceptional best, a far more voluminous verse writer and a much freer writer of good verse of many different kinds. He was born in Dublin on 28th May 1779 ; his father being a grocer, his mother somewhat higher in social rank. He was well educated, and was sent to Trinity College, Dublin, where he had but surmounted political difficulties ; for his time as an undergraduate coincided with " Ninety-eight," and though it does not seem that he had meddled with anything distinctly treasonable, he had " Nationalist " friends and leanings. Partly to sever inconvenient associations, partly in quest of fortune, he was sent to London in that year, and entered at the Temple. In a manner not very clearly explained, but connected no doubt with his leaning to the Whig party, which was then much in need of literary help, he became a protégé of Lord Moira's, by whom he was introduced to the Prince of Wales. The Prince accepted the dedication of some translations of Anacreon, etc., which Moore had brought over with him, and which were published in 1800 ; while two years later the *Poems of Thomas Little,* a punning pseudonym, appeared, and at once charmed the public by their sugared versification and shocked it by their looseness of tone — a looseness which is not to be judged from the comparatively decorous appearance they make in modern editions. But there was never much harm in them. Next year, in 1803, Moore received a valuable appointment at Bermuda, which, though he actually went out to take possession of it and travelled some time in North America, he was allowed to transfer to a deputy. He came back to England, published another volume of poems, and fought a rather famously futile duel with Jeffrey about a criticism on it in the *Edinburgh Review.* He began the *Irish Melodies* in 1807, married four years later, and from that time fixed his headquarters mostly in the country : first near Ashbourne in Derbyshire, then near Devizes in Wiltshire, to be near his patrons Lord Moira and Lord Lansdowne. But he was constantly in London on visits, and much in the society of men of letters, not merely of his own party. In particular he became, on the whole, Byron's most intimate friend, and preserved towards that very difficult person an attitude (tinged neither with the servility nor with the exaggerated independence of the *parvenu*) which did him a great deal of credit. He was rather a strong partisan, and, having a brilliant vein of poetical satire, he wrote in 1813 *The Twopenny Post Bag* — the best satiric verse of the poetical kind since the *Anti-Jacobin*, and the best on the Whig side since the *Rolliad*.

Nor did he fail to take advantage of the popular appetite for long poems which Scott and Byron had created; his *Lalla Rookh*, published in 1817, being very popular and very profitable. It was succeeded by another and his best satirical work, *The Fudge Family*, a charming thing.

Up to this time he had been an exceedingly fortunate man; and his good luck, aided it must be said by his good conduct, — for Moore, with all his apparent weaknesses, was thoroughly sound at the core, — enabled him to surmount a very serious reverse of fortune. His Bermuda deputy was guilty of malversation so considerable that Moore could not meet the debt, and he had to go abroad. But Lord Lansdowne discharged his obligations; and Moore paid Lord Lansdowne. He returned to England in 1823, and was a busy writer for all but the last years of the thirty that remained to him; but the best of his work was done, with one exception. Byron left him his *Memoirs*, which would of course have been enormously profitable. But Lady Byron and others of the poet's connections were so horrified at the idea of the book appearing that, by an arrangement which has been variously judged, but which can hardly be regarded as other than disinterested on Moore's part, the MS. was destroyed, and instead of it Moore brought out in 1830 his well-known *Life of Byron*. This, some not incompetent judges have regarded as ranking next to Lockhart's *Scott* and Boswell's *Johnson*, and though its main attraction may be derived from Byron's very remarkable letters, still shows on the part of the biographer very unusual dexterity, good feeling, and taste. The lives of *Sheridan* and *Lord Edward Fitzgerald* had, and deserved to have, less success; while a *History of Ireland* was, and was bound to be, an almost complete failure. For, though a very good prose writer, Moore had little of the erudition required, no grasp or faculty of political argument, and was at this time of his life, if not earlier, something of a trimmer, certain to satisfy neither the "ascendency" nor the "nationalist" parties. His prose romance of *The Epicurean* is much better, and a really remarkable, piece of work; and though the *Loves of the Angels*, his last long poem, is not very good, he did not lose his command either of sentimental or of facetious lyric till quite his last days. These were clouded; for, like his contemporaries Scott and Southey, he suffered from brain disease for some time before his death, on 25th February 1852.

During his lifetime, especially during the first half or two-thirds of his literary career, Moore had a great popularity, and won no small esteem even among critics; such discredit as attached to him being chiefly of the moral kind, and that entertained only by very strait-laced persons. But as the more high-flown and impassioned muses of Wordsworth, of Shelley, and of Keats gained the public ear in the third and later decades of the century, a fashion set in of regarding him as a mere melodious trifler; and this has accentuated itself during the last twenty years or so, though quite recently some efforts have been made in protest. This estimate is demonstrably unjust. It is true that of the strange and high notes of poetry he has very few, of the very strangest and highest none at all. But his long poems, *Lalla Rookh* especially, though somewhat over-burdened with the then fashionable deck cargo of erudite or would-be erudite notes, possess merit which none but a very prejudiced critic can, or at least ought to, overlook. And in other respects he is very nearly, if not quite, at the top of at least two trees, which, if not quite cedars of Lebanon, are not mere grass of Parnassus. Moore was a born as well as a trained musician. But whereas most musicians have since the seventeenth century been exceedingly ill at verbal numbers, he had a quite extraordinary knack of composing what are rather disrespectfully called "words." Among his innumerable songs there are not one or two dozens or scores, but almost hundreds of quite charmingly melodious things, admirably adjusted to their music, and delightful by themselves without any kind of instrument, and as said not sung. And, what is more, among these there is a very respectable number to which it would be absolutely absurd to give the name of trifle. " I saw from the beach " is not a trifle, nor " When in death I shall calm recline," nor " Oft in the stilly night," nor " Tell me, kind sage, I pray thee," nor many others. They have become so hackneyed to us in various ways, and some of them happen to be pitched in a key of diction which, though not better or worse than others, is so out of fashion, that it seems as if some very respectable judges could not " focus " Moore at all. To those who can he will seem, not of course the equal, or anything like the equal, of Burns or Shelley, of Blake or Keats, but in his own way, — and that a way legitimate and not low, — one of the first lyrical writers in English. And they will admit a considerable addition to his claims in his delightful satirical verse, mainly but not in the least offensively political, in which kind he is as easily first as in the sentimental song to music.

Something not dissimilar to the position which Moore occupies on the more classical wing of the poets of the period is occupied on the other by Leigh Hunt. Hunt (Henry James Leigh, who called himself and is generally known by the third only of his Christian names) was born in London on the 19th October 1784, was educated at Christ's Hospital, began writing very early, held for a short time a clerkship in a public office, and then joined his brother in conducting the *Examiner* newspaper. Fined and imprisoned for a personal libel on the Prince Regent (1812), Hunt became the fashion with the Opposition ; and the *Story of Rimini*, which he published when he came out of gaol, and which was written in it, had a good deal of influence. He spent some years in Italy, to which place he had gone with his family in 1822 to edit *The Liberal* and to keep house with Byron — a very disastrous experiment, the results of which he recorded in an offensive book on his return. Hunt lived to 18th August 1859, and was rescued from the chronic state of impecuniosity in which, despite constant literary work, he had long lived, by a Crown pension and some other assistance in his latest days. Personally, Leigh Hunt was an agreeable and amiable being enough, with certain foibles which were rather unfairly magnified in the famous caricature of him as Harold Skimpole by his friend Dickens, but which were accompanied by some faults of taste of which Mr. Skimpole is not accused.

In letters he was a very considerable person ; though the best and far the largest part of his work is in prose, and will be noticed hereafter. His verse is not great in bulk, and is perhaps more original and stimulating than positively good. His wide and ardent study of the older English poets and of those of Italy had enabled him to hit on a novel style of phrase and rhythm, which has been partly referred to above in the notice of Keats ; his narrative faculty was strong, and some of his smaller pieces, from his sonnets downwards, are delightful things. " Abou ben Adhem " unites (a rare thing for its author) amiability with dignity, stateliness with ease ; the " Nile " sonnet is splendid ; " Jenny kissed me," charming, if not faultless ; " The Man and the Fish," far above vulgarity. The lack of delicate taste which characterised his manners also marred his verse, which is not unfrequently slipshod, or gushing, or trivially fluent, and perhaps never relatively so good as the best of his prose. But he owed little to any but the old masters, and many contemporaries owed not a little to him.

A quaint and interesting if not supremely important figure among the poets of this period, and, if his poetry and prose be taken together, a very considerable man of letters,— perhaps the most considerable man of letters in English who was almost totally uneducated, — was James Hogg, who was born in Ettrick Forest in the year 1772. He was taken from school to mind sheep so early that much later he had to teach himself even reading and writing afresh ; and, though he must have had the song-gift early, it was not till he was nearly thirty that he published anything. He was discovered by Scott, to whom he and his mother supplied a good deal of matter for the *Border Minstrelsy*, and he published again in 1803. The rest of his life was divided between writing — with fair success, though with some ill-luck from bankrupt publishers — and sheep-farming, on which he constantly lost, though latterly he sat rent free under the Duke of Buccleuch. He died on 21st November 1835.

Even during his life Hogg underwent a curious process of mythopœia at the hands of Wilson and the other wits of *Blackwood's Magazine*, who made him — partly with his own consent, partly not — into the famous "Ettrick Shepherd" of the *Noctes Ambrosianæ*. "The Shepherd" has Hogg's exterior features and a good many of his foibles, but is endowed with considerably more than his genius. Even in his published and acknowledged works, which are numerous, it is not always quite easy to be sure of his authorship ; for he constantly solicited, frequently received, and sometimes took without asking, assistance from Lockhart and others. But enough remains that is different from the work of any of his known or possible coadjutors to enable us to distinguish his idiosyncrasy pretty well. In verse he was a very fluent and an exceedingly unequal writer, who in his long poems chiefly, and not too happily, followed Scott, but who in the fairy poem of "Kilmeny" displayed an extraordinary command of a rare form of poetry, and who has written some dozens of the best songs in the language. The best, but only a few of the best, of these are "Donald Macdonald," "Donald M'Gillavry," "The Village of Balmanhapple," and the "Boy's Song." In prose he chiefly attempted novels, which have no construction at all, and few merits of dialogue or style, but contain some powerful passages ; while one of them, *The Confessions of a Justified Sinner*, if it is entirely his, which is very doubtful, is by far the greatest thing he wrote, being a story of *diablerie* very well designed, wonderfully fresh and enthralling in detail, and kept up with hardly a slip to the end. His other chief prose works are entitled *The Brownie of Bodsbeck, The Three Perils of Man, The Three Perils of Woman,* and *Altrive Tales*, while he also wrote some important, and in parts very offensive, but also in parts amusing, *Recollections of Sir Walter Scott*. His verse volumes, no one of which is

good throughout, though hardly one is without good things, were
*The Mountain Bard, The Queen's Wake, Mador of the Moor, The
Pilgrims of the Sun, Jacobite Relics* (some of the best forged by
himself), *Queen Hynde*, and *The Border Garland*.

A greater writer, if his work be taken as a whole, than any
who has been mentioned since Keats, was Walter Savage Landor,
much of whose composition was in prose, but who was so alike
in prose and verse that the whole had better be noticed together
here. Landor (who was of a family of some standing in Warwickshire, and was heir to considerable property, much of which he
wasted later by selling his inheritance and buying a large but
unprofitable estate in Wales) was born at Ipsley Court, in 1775.
He went to school at Rugby, and thence to Trinity College,
Oxford, at both of which places he gained considerable scholarship but was frequently in trouble owing to the intractable and
headstrong temper which distinguished him through life. He was
indeed rusticated from his college, and subsequently, owing to his
extravagant political views, was refused a commission in the Warwickshire Militia. He began to write early, but the poem of
Gebir, which contains in germ or miniature nearly all his characteristics of style, passed almost unnoticed by the public, though it
was appreciated by good wits like Southey and De Quincey.
After various private adventures he came into his property and
volunteered in the service of Spain, where he failed, as usual, from
impracticableness. In 1811, recklessly as always, he married
a very young girl of whom he knew next to nothing, and the
marriage proved anything but a happy one. The rest of his long
life was divided into three residences : first with his family at
Florence ; then, when he had quarrelled with his wife, at Bath ; and
lastly (when he had been obliged to quit Bath and England
owing to an outrageous lampoon on one lady, which he had
written, as he conceived, in chivalrous defence of another) at
Florence again. Here he died in September 1864, aged very
nearly ninety.

Landor's poetical productions, which are numerous, are

spread over the greater part of his life ; his prose, by which he is chiefly known, dates in the main from the last forty years of it, the best being written between 1820 and 1840. The greater part of this prose takes the form of " Imaginary Conversations " — sometimes published under separate general headings, sometimes under the common title — between characters of all ages, from the classical times to Landor's. Their bulk is very great ; their perfection of style at the best extraordinary, and on the whole remarkably uniform ; their value, when considerations of matter are added to that of form, exceedingly unequal. For in them Landor not only allowed the fullest play to the ungovernable temper and the childish crotchets already mentioned, but availed himself of his opportunities (for, though he endeavoured to maintain a pretence of dramatic treatment, his work is nearly as personal as that of Byron) to deliver his sentiments on a vast number of subjects, sometimes without too much knowledge, and constantly with a plentiful lack of judgment. In politics, in satiric treatment, and especially in satiric treatment of politics, he is very nearly value-less. But his intense familiarity with and appreciation of clas-sical subjects gave to almost all his dealings with them a value which, for parallel reasons, is also possessed by those touching Italy. And throughout this enormous collection of work (which in the compactest edition fills five large octavo volumes in small print), whensoever the author forgets his crotchets and his rages, when he touches on the great and human things, his utterance reaches the very highest water-mark of English literature that is not absolutely the work of supreme genius.

For supreme genius Landor had not. His brain was not a great brain, and he did not possess the exquisite alertness to his own weaknesses, or the stubborn knack of confinement to things suitable to him, which some natures much smaller than the great ones have enjoyed. But he had the faculty of elaborate style — of style elaborated by a careful education after the best models and vivified by a certain natural gift — as no one since the seven-teenth century had had it, and as no one except Mr. Ruskin and

the late Mr. Pater has had since. Also, he was as much wider
in his range and more fertile in his production than Mr. Pater
as he was more solidly grounded on the best models than Mr.
Ruskin. Where Landor is quite unique is in the apparent
indifference with which he was able to direct this gift of his into
the channels of prose and poetry — a point on which he parts
company from both the writers to whom he has been compared,
and in which his only analogue, so far as I am able to judge, is
Victor Hugo. The style of no Englishman is so alike in the two
harmonies as is that of Landor. And it is perhaps not surprising
that, this being the case, he shows at his best in prose when he
tries long pieces, in verse when he tries short ones. Some of
Landor's prose performances in *Pericles and Aspasia*, in the
Pentameron (where Boccaccio and Petrarch are the chief interlocutors), and in not a few of the separate conversations, are altogether unparalleled in any other language, and not easy to parallel
in English. They are never entirely or perfectly natural; there is
always a slight " smell of the lamp," but of a lamp perfumed and
undying. The charm is so powerful, the grace so stately, that it
is impossible for any one to miss it who has the faculty of recognising charm and grace at all. In particular, Landor is remarkable —
and, excellent as are many of the prose writers whom we have
had since, he is perhaps the most remarkable — for the weight, the
beauty, and the absolute finish of his phrase. Sometimes these
splendid phrases do not mean very much ; occasionally they mean
nothing or nonsense. But their value as phrase survives, and the
judge in such things is often inclined and entitled to say that
there is none like them.

This will prepare the reader who has some familiarity with
literature for what is to be said about Landor's verse. It always
has a certain quality of exquisiteness, but this quality is and could
not but be unequally displayed in the short poems and the long.
The latter can hardly attain, with entirely competent and impartial judges, more than a success of esteem. *Gebir* is couched in
a Miltonic form of verse (very slightly shot and varied by Romantic

admixture) which, as is natural to a young adventurer, caricatures the harder and more ossified style of the master. Sometimes it is great ; more usually it intends greatness. The "Dialogues in Verse" (very honestly named, for they are in fact rather dialogues in verse than poems), though executed by the hand of a master both of verse and dialogue, differ in form rather than in fact from the Conversations in prose. The *Hellenics* are mainly dialogues in verse with a Greek subject. All have a quality of nobility which may be sought in vain in almost any other poet ; but all have a certain stiffness and frigidity, some a certain empti- ness. They are never plaster, as some modern antiques have been ; but they never make the marble of which they are com- posed wholly flesh. Landor was but a half-Pygmalion.

The vast collection of his miscellaneous poems contains many more fortunate attempts, some of which have, by common consent of the fittest, attained a repute which they are never likely to lose. " Rose Aylmer " and " Dirce," trifles in length as both of them are, are very jewels of poetic quality. And among the hundreds and almost thousands of pieces which Landor produced there are some which come not far short of these, and very many which attain a height magnificent as compared with the ordinary work of others. But the hackneyed comparison of amber does something gall this remarkable poet and writer. Everything, great and small, is enshrined in an imperishable coating of beautiful style ; but the small things are somewhat out of pro- portion to the great, and, what is more, the amber itself always has a certain air of being deliberately and elaborately produced— not of growing naturally. Landor — much more than Dryden, of whom he used the phrase, but in the same class as Dryden — is one of those who " wrestle with and conquer time." He has conquered, but it is rather as a giant of celestial nurture than as an unquestioned god.

Even after enumerating these two sets of names — the first all of the greatest, and the greatest of the second, Landor, equalling the least of the first — we have not exhausted the poetical riches of this remarkable period. It is indeed almost dangerous to embark on the third class of poets ; yet its members here would in some cases have been highly respectable earlier, and even at this time deserve notice either for influence, or for intensity of poetic vein, or sometimes for the mere fact of having been once famous and having secured a " place in the story." The story of literature has no popular ingratitude ; and, except in the case of distinct impostors, it turns out with reluctance those who have once been admitted to it. Sometimes even impostors deserve a renewal of the brand, if not a freshening up of the honourable inscription.

The first of this third class in date, and perhaps the first in influence, though far indeed from being the first in merit, was William Lisle Bowles, already once or twice referred to. He was born on 24th September 1762 ; so that, but for the character and influence of his verse, he belongs to the last chapter rather than to this. Educated at Winchester, and at Trinity College, Oxford, he took orders, and spent nearly the last half century of his very long life (he did not die till 1850) in Wiltshire, as Prebendary of Salisbury and Rector of Bremhill. It was in the year of the French Revolution that he published his *Fourteen Sonnets* [afterwards enlarged in number], *written chiefly on Picturesque Spots during a Journey*. These fell early into Coleridge's hands ; he copied and recopied them for his friends when he was a blue-coat boy, and in so far as poetical rivers have any single source, the first tricklings of the stream which welled into fulness with the Lyrical Ballads, and some few years later swept all before it, may be assigned to this very feeble fount. For in truth it is exceedingly feeble. In the fifth edition (1796), which lies before me exquisitely printed, with a pretty aquatint frontispiece by Alken, and a dedication of the previous year to Dean Ogle of Winchester, the Sonnets have increased to twenty-seven, and are supplemented by fifteen " miscellaneous pieces." One of these latter is itself a sonnet " written at Southampton," and in all respects similar to the rest. The others — " On Leaving Winchester," " On the

Death of Mr. Headley" the critic, a man of worth,[1] "To Mr. Burke on his Reflections," and so forth — are of little note. The same may be said of Bowles' later poetical productions, which were numerous ; but his edition of Pope, finished in 1807, brought about a hot controversy not yet forgotten (nor, to tell the truth, quite settled) on the question Whether Pope was a poet? That Bowles can have had scant sympathy with Pope is evident from the very first glance at the famous sonnets themselves. Besides their form, which, as has been said, was of itself something of a reactionary challenge, they bear strong traces of Gray, and still stronger traces of the picturesque mania which was at the same time working so strongly in the books of Gilpin and others. But their real note is the note which, ringing in Coleridge's ear, echoed in all the poetry of the generation, the note of unison between the aspect of nature and the thought and emotion of man. In the sonnets "At Tynemouth," "At Bamborough Castle," and indeed in all, more or less, there is first the attempt to paint directly what the eye sees, not the generalised and academic view of the type-scene by a type-poet which had been the fashion for so long ; and secondly, the attempt to connect this vision with personal experience, passion, or meditation. Bowles does not do this very well, but he tries to do it ; and the others, seeing him try, went and did it.

His extreme importance as an at least admitted "origin" has

[1] Henry Headley, who, like Bowles and Landor, was a member of Trinity College, Oxford, and who died young, after publishing a few original poems of no great value, deserves more credit for his *Select Beauties of Ancient English Poetry*, published in two volumes, with an exquisite title-page vignette, by Cadell in 1787, than has sometimes been allowed him by the not numerous critics who have noticed him recently, or by those who immediately followed him. His knowledge was soon outgrown, and therefore looked down upon ; and his taste was a very little indiscriminate. But it was something to put before an age which was just awakening to the appetite for such things two volumes full of selections from the too little read poets of the seventeenth, with a few of the sixteenth century. Moreover, Headley's biographical information shows very praiseworthy industry, and his critical remarks a great deal of taste at once nice and fairly catholic. A man who in his day could, while selecting and putting forth Drayton and Carew, Daniel and King, speak enthusiastically of Dryden and even of Goldsmith, must have had the root of the matter in him as few critics have had.

procured him notice somewhat beyond his real deserts ; over others we must pass more rapidly.   Robert Bloomfield, born in 1760, was one of those unfortunate "prodigy" poets whom mistaken kindness encourages.   He was the son of a tailor, went early to agricultural labour, and then became a shoemaker.   His *Farmer's Boy*, an estimable but much over-praised piece, was published in 1800, and he did other things later.   He died mad, or nearly so, in 1823 — a melancholy history repeated pretty closely a generation later by John Clare.   Clare, however, was a better poet than Bloomfield, and some of the "Poems written in an Asylum"[1] have more than merely touching merit.   James Montgomery,[1] born at Irvine on 4th November 1771, was the son of a Moravian minister, and intended for his father's calling.   He, however, preferred literature and journalism, establishing himself chiefly at Sheffield, where he died as late as 1854 (30th April).   He had, as editor of the *Sheffield Iris*, some troubles with the law, and in 1835 was rewarded with a pension.   Montgomery was a rather copious and fairly pleasing minor bard, no bad hand at hymns and short occasional pieces, and the author of longer things called *The Wanderer of Switzerland, The West Indies, The World before the Flood*, and *The Pelican Island*.   Bernard Barton, an amiable Quaker poet, will probably always be remembered as the friend and correspondent of Charles Lamb ; perhaps also as the father-in-law of Edward FitzGerald.   His verse commended itself both to Southey (who had a kindly but rather disastrous weakness for minor bards) and to Byron, but has little value.   Barton died in 1849.

The same pair of enemies joined in praising Henry Kirke White, who was born in 1785 and died when barely twenty-one. Here indeed Southey's unsurpassed biographical skill enforced the poetaster's merit in a charming *Memoir*, which assisted White's

---

[1] Not to be confounded with *Robert*, or "Satan" Montgomery, his junior by many years, and a much worse poet, the victim of Macaulay's famous classical example of what is called in English "slating," and in French *éreintement*.   There is really nothing to be said about this person that Macaulay has not said ; though perhaps one or two of the things he has said are a little strained.

rather pathetic story. He was the son of a butcher, a diligent but reluctant lawyer's clerk, an enthusiastic student, a creditable undergraduate at St. John's, Cambridge, and a victim of consumption. All this made his verse for a time popular. But he really deserved the name just affixed to him : he was a poetaster, and nothing more. The "genius" attributed to him in Byron's well-known and noble though rather rhetorical lines may be discovered on an average in about half a dozen poets during any two or three years of any tolerable poetic period. His best things are imitations of Cowper in his sacred mood, such as the familiar "Star of Bethlehem," and even these are generally spoilt by some feebleness or false note. At his worst he is not far from Della Crusca.[1]

In the same year with Kirke White was born a much better poet, and a much robuster person in all ways, mental and physical. Allan Cunningham was a Dumfriesshire man born in the lowest rank, and apprenticed to a stone-mason, whence in after years he rose to be Chantrey's foreman. Cunningham began — following a taste very rife at the time — with imitated, or to speak plainly, forged ballads ; but the merit of them deserved on true grounds the recognition it obtained on false, and he became a not inconsiderable man of letters of all work. His best known prose work is the "Lives of the Painters." In verse he is ranked, as a song writer in Scots, by some next to Burns, and by few lower than Hogg. Some of his pieces, such as "Fair shines the sun in France," have the real, the inexplicable, the irresistible song-gift. Cunningham, who was the friend of many good men and was liked by all of them, died on 29th October 1842. His elder by eleven years, Robert Tannahill, who was born in 1774 and died (probably by suicide) in 1810, deserves a few lines in this tale of Scots singers. Tannahill, like Cunningham in humble circumstances originally, never became more than a weaver. His verse has not

---

[1] Some fifteen years ago, in a little book on Dryden, I called Kirke White a "miserable poetaster," and was rebuked for it by those who perhaps knew Byron's lines and nothing more. Quite recently Mr. Gosse was rebuked more loudly for a less severe denunciation. I determined that I would read Kirke White again ; and the above judgment is the mildest I can possibly pronounce after the reading. A good young man with a pathetic career ; but a poetaster merely.

the *gusto* of Allan or of Hogg, but is sweet and tender enough. William Motherwell too, as much younger than Allan as Tannahill was older (he was born in 1797 and died young in 1835), deserves mention, and may best receive it here.   He was a Conservative journalist, an antiquary of some mark, and a useful editor of Minstrelsy.   Of his original work, "Jeanie Morrison" is the best known ; and those who have read, especially if they have read it in youth, "The Sword Chant of Thorstein Raudi," will not dismiss it as Wardour Street; while he did some other delightful things. Earlier (1812) the heroicomic *Anster Fair* of William Tennant (1784–1848) received very high and deserved no low praise ; while William Thom, a weaver like Tannahill, who was a year younger than Motherwell and lived till 1848, wrote many simple ballads in the vernacular, of which the most touching are perhaps "The Song of the Forsaken" and "The Mitherless Bairn."

To return to England, Bryan Waller Procter, who claimed kindred with the poet from whom he took his second name, was born in 1790, went to Harrow, and, becoming a lawyer, was made a Commissioner of Lunacy.   He did not die till 1874 ; and he, and still more his wife, were the last sources of direct informa- tion about the great race of the first third of the century.   He was, under the pseudonym of " Barry Cornwall," a fluent verse writer of the so-called cockney school, and had not a little reputa- tion, especially for songs about the sea and things in general.   They still, occasionally from critics who are not generally under the bond- age of traditional opinion, receive high praise, which the present writer is totally unable to echo.   A loyal junior friend to Lamb, a wise and kindly senior to Beddoes, liked and respected by many or by all, Procter, as a man, must always deserve respect.   If

> The sea, the sea, the open sea,
> The blue, the fresh, the ever free,

and things like it are poetry, I admit myself, with a sad humility, to be wholly destitute of poetical appreciation.

The Church of England contributed two admirable verse

writers of this period in Henry Cary and Reginald Heber. Cary, who was born in 1772 and was a Christ Church man, was long an assistant librarian in the British Museum. His famous translation of the *Divina Commedia*, published in 1814, is not only one of the best verse translations in English, but, after the lapse of eighty years, during which the study of Dante has been constantly increasing in England, in which poetic ideas have changed not a little, and in which numerous other translations have appeared, still attracts admiration from all competent scholars for its combination of fidelity and vigour. Heber, born in 1783 and educated at Brasenose, gained the Newdigate with *Palestine*, a piece which ranks with *Timbuctoo* and a few others among unforgotten prize poems. He took orders, succeeding to the family living of Hodnet, and for some years bid fair to be one of the most shining lights of the English Church, combining admirable parochial work with good literature, and with much distinction as a preacher. Unfortunately he thought it his duty to take the Bishopric of Calcutta when it was offered him ; and, arriving there in 1824, worked incessantly for nearly two years and then died. His *Journal in India* is very pleasant reading, and some of his hymns rank with the best in English.

Ebenezer Elliott, the " Corn-Law Rhymer," was born in Yorkshire on 7th March 1781. His father was a clerk in an iron-foundry. He himself was early sent to foundry work, and he afterwards became a master-founder at Sheffield. From different points of view it may be thought a palliation — and the reverse — of the extreme virulence with which Elliott took the side of workmen against landowners and men of property, that he attained to affluence himself as an employer, and was never in the least incommoded by the " condition-of-England " question. He early displayed a considerable affection for literature, and was one, and about the last, of the prodigies whom Southey, in his inexhaustible kindness for struggling men of letters, accepted. Many years later the Laureate wrote good-naturedly to Wynn : "I mean to read the Corn-Law Rhymer a lecture, not without some hope, that as I taught him the art of poetry I may teach him something better." The "something better" was not in Elliott's way ; for he is a violent and crude thinker, with more smoke than fire in his violence, though not without generosity of feeling now and then, and with a keen admiration of the scenery — still beautiful in parts, and then exquisite — which surrounded the smoky Hades of Sheffield. He himself acknowledges the influence of Crabbe and disclaims that of Wordsworth, from which the cunning may anticipate the fact that he is deeply indebted to both. His earliest publication or at least composition, " The Vernal Walk," is said to date from the very year of the *Lyrical Ballads*, and of course owes no royalty to Wordsworth, but is in blank verse, a sort of compound of Thomson and Crabbe. " Love " (in Crabbian couplets slightly tinged with overlapping) and " The Village Patriarch " (still smacking of Crabbe in form, though irregularly arranged in rhymed decasyllables) are his chief other long poems. He tried dramas, but he is best known by his " Corn-Law Rhymes " and " Corn-Law Hymns," and deserves to be best known by a few lyrics of real beauty, and many descriptions. How a man who could write " The Wonders of the Lane " and " The Dying Boy to the Sloe Blossom " could stoop to malignant drivel about " palaced worms," " this syllabub-throated logician," and so forth, is strange enough to understand, especially as he had no excuse of personal suffering. Even in longer poems the mystery is renewed in " They Met Again " and " Withered Wild Flowers " compared with such things as " The Ranter," though the last exhibits the author at both his best and worst. However, Elliott is entitled to the charity he did not show ; and the author of such clumsy Billingsgate as " Arthur Bread-Tax Winner," " Faminton," and so forth, may be forgiven for the flashes of poetry which he exhibits. Even in his political poems they do not always desert him, and his somewhat famous Chartist (or ante-Chartist) " Battle-Song " is as right-noted as it is wrong-headed.

Sir Aubrey de Vere (1788–1846), a poet and the father of a poet still alive, was a friend and follower of Wordsworth, and the author of sonnets good in the Wordsworthian kind. But he cannot be spared much room here ; nor can much even be given to the mild shade of a poetess far more famous in her day than he. " Time that breaks all things," according to the dictum of a great poet still living, does not happily break all in literature ; but it is to be feared that he has reduced to fragments the once not inconsiderable fame of Felicia Hemans. She was born (her maiden name was Felicia Dorothea Browne) at Liverpool on 25th September 1794, and when she was only eighteen she married a Captain Hemans. It was not a fortunate union, and by far the greater part of Mrs. Hemans' married life was spent, owing to no known fault of hers, apart from her husband. She did not live to old age, dying on 26th April 1835. But she wrote a good deal of verse meanwhile — plays, poems, " songs of the affections," and what not. Her blameless character (she wrote chiefly to support her children) and a certain ingenuous tenderness in her verse, saved its extreme feebleness from severe condemnation in an age which was still avid of verse rather than discriminating in it ; and children still learn " The boy stood on the burning deck," and other things. It is impossible, on any really critical scheme, to allow her genius ; but she need not be spoken of with any elaborate disrespect, while it must be admitted that her latest work is her best — always a notable sign. " Despondency and Aspiration," dating from her death-year, soars close to real sublimity ; and of her smaller pieces " England's Dead " is no vulgar thing.

Between the death of Byron and the distinct appearance of Tennyson and the Brownings there was a kind of interregnum or twilight of poetry, of which one of its strangest if not least illumi- native stars or meteors, Beddoes, has given a graphic but uncom- plimentary picture in a letter : " owls' light " he calls it, with adjuncts. Wordsworth, Coleridge, and Southey ; Scott, Campbell, and Moore, were all living, but the poetic production of all had on the whole ceased. Shelley and Keats would have been in time the natural, and in genius the more than sufficient sun and

moon of the time; but they had died before Byron. So the
firmament was occupied by rather wandering stars : some of them
elders already noticed, others born in the ten or twelve years
between Keats (1795) and the eldest of the Tennysons (1807).
The chief of these were the pair of half-serious, half-humorous
singers, Hood and Praed. Next in public estimation come
Talfourd, Hartley Coleridge, Macaulay, Sir Henry Taylor, the
Irish poet Mangan, R. H. Horne, and the first Lord Lytton;
while a third class — of critics' rather than readers' favourites —
varying in merit, but, at the best of the best of them, ranking
higher than any of the above, may be made up of George
Darley, C. J. Wells, the Dorsetshire poet Barnes, Beddoes,
Charles Whitehead, R. S. Hawker, and Thomas Wade. To the
second class must be added " L. E. L.," the poetess who filled
the interval between Mrs. Hemans and Mrs. Browning.

Wells, Whitehead, and Wade may be dismissed without disrespect as, if not critical mares'-nests, at any rate critical hobbies.
Persons of more or less distinction (and of less or more crotchet)
have at different times paid very high compliments to the *Joseph
and his Brethren* (1823, revised later) of Charles Jeremiah Wells
(1800–1879), a friend of Keats, and a person who seems to have
lived much as he pleased; to the *Solitary* of Charles Whitehead
(1804–1862), a Bohemian ne'er-do-weel, who also showed talent
as a novelist and miscellanist; and to the *Mundi et Cordis
Carmina* (1835) of Thomas Wade (1805–1875), a playwright and
journalist. Of the three, Wade appears to me to have had the
greatest poetical talent. But I do not think that any one who on
the one hand uses epithets in poetical criticism with caution, and
on the other has read a great deal of minor poetry as it appears,
could put any one of them very high. All were born late
enough to breathe the atmosphere of the new poetry young; all
had poetical velleities, and a certain amount, if not of originality,
of capacity to write poetry. But they were not poets; they were
only poetical curiosities.

Darley, Beddoes, and Horne belong in the main to the same

I

class, but rise high, in one case immeasurably, above them. George Darley (1795–1846) is perhaps our chief English example of " the poet who dies in youth while the man survives," and who becomes a critic. In him, however, the generation of the critic did not wait for the corruption of the poet. An Irishman, and of Trinity College, Dublin, he was one of the staff of the *London Magazine*, and wrote much verse bad and good, including the once famous " I've been Roaming," of which it is safe to say that not one in ten of those who have sung it could tell the author. His best work is contained in the charming pastoral drama of *Sylvia* (1827) and the poem entitled *Nepenthe* (1839). He was a good but rather a savage critic, and edited Beaumont and Fletcher. His work has never been collected, nor, it is believed, ever fully published ; and it has the marks of a talent that never did what was in it to do, and came at an unfortunate time. Some not bad judges in the forties ranked Darley with Tennyson in poetic possibilities, and thought the former the more promising of the two.

Except Donne, there is perhaps no English poet more difficult to write about, so as to preserve the due pitch of enthusiasm on the one hand and criticism on the other, than Thomas Lovell Beddoes, bore at Clifton on 20th July 1803. He was the son of a very famous physician, and of Anna Edgeworth, the youngest sister of the whole blood to the novelist. Beddoes, left fatherless at six years old, was educated at the Charterhouse and at Pembroke College, Oxford, and when he was barely of age went to Germany to study medicine, living thenceforth almost entirely on the Continent. Before this he had published two volumes, *The Improvisatore* and *The Bride's Tragedy ;* but his principal work is a wild Elizabethan play called *Death's Jest-Book* or *The Fool's Tragedy*, which he never absolutely finished. He died in 1848 at Basle by a complicated and ghastly kind of suicide. Three years later his Poems appeared, and they have been recently republished, with additions and a curious collection of letters.

Beddoes has sometimes been treated as a mainly bookish

poet deriving from the Elizabethans and Shelley. I cannot agree
with this. His very earliest work, written when he could not
know much either of Shelley or Keats, shows as they do
technique perhaps caught from Leigh Hunt. But this is quite
dropped later; and his Elizabethanism is not imitation but inspiration. In this inspiration he does not follow, but shares with,
his greater contemporaries. He is a younger and tragic counterpart to Charles Lamb in the intensity with which he has imbibed
the Elizabethan spirit, rather from the nightshade of Webster and
Tourneur than from the vine of Shakespeare. As wholes, his
works are naught, or naught but nightmares; though *Death's
Jest-Book*, despite its infinite disadvantages from constant rewrit-
ing and uncertainty of final form, has a strong grasp. But they
contain passages, especially lyrics, of the most exquisite fancy and
music, such as since the seventeenth century none but Blake and
Coleridge had given. Beddoes does not seem to have been at
all a pleasant person, and in his later days at any rate he would
appear to have been a good deal less than sane. But the author
of such things as the " Dirge for Wolfram " (" If thou wilt ease
thine heart ") in *Death's Jest-Book*, and the stanza beginning
" Dream-Pedlary," " If there were dreams to sell," with not a few
others of the same kind, attains to that small and disputed — but
not to those who have thought out the nature of poetry disputable
— class of poets who, including Sappho, Catullus, some mediæval
hymn-writers, and a few moderns, especially Coleridge, have, by
virtue of fragments only, attained a higher position than many
authors of large, substantive, and important poems. They
may be shockingly lacking in bulk, in organisation, in proper
choice of subject, in intelligent criticism of life ; but they are
like the summer lightning or the northern aurora, which, though
they shine only now and then, and only it may be for a few
moments, shine, when they do shine, with a beauty unapproachable by gas or candle, hardly approached by sun or moon, and
illuminate the whole of their world.

Although quotation is in the main impossible in this book,

Beddoes, despite the efforts of his friend Kelsall, of Mr. Swinburne, of Mr. Gosse (thanks to whom a quasi-complete edition has at last appeared), and others, is still so little known, that a short one may be allowed in his case. I have known a critic who said deliberately of the above-mentioned stanza in " Dream-Pedlary " —

> If there were dreams to sell,
>   What would you buy?
> Some cost a passing bell,
>   Some a light sigh
> That shakes from Life's fresh crown
> Only a roseleaf down.
> If there were dreams to sell —
> Merry and sad to tell —
> And the crier rung the bell,
>   What would you buy?

that these ten lines contain more pure poetry than the entire works of Byron. And the same touch will be found not merely in the " Wolfram Dirge " mentioned —

> If thou wilt ease thine heart
> Of Love and all its smart,
> Then sleep, dear, sleep.
>
> .   .   .   .
>
> But wilt thou *cure* thine heart
> Of Love and all its smart,
> Then die, dear, die —

but in several other dirges (for the dirge is the form natural to Beddoes), in the " Song from Torrismond," in " Love in Idleness," in the " Song on the Water " (which is pure early Tennyson), in the exquisite " Threnody," and in many other things. They have been called artificial : the epithet can be allowed in no other sense than in that in which it applies to all the best poetry. And they have the note, which only a few true but imperfect poets have, of anticipation. Shadows before, both of Tennyson and Browning, especially of the latter, appear in Beddoes. But after all his main note is his own : not theirs, not the Elizabethan, not Shelley's, not another's. And this is what makes a poet.

As Beddoes' forte lay in short and rather uncanny snatches,

so that of Richard Hengist Horne lay in sustained and dignified composition. He was not christened Hengist at all, but Henry. He had a curious life. In youth he knew Keats and Wells, having been, like them, at the private school of Mr. Clarke at Edmonton. He went to Sandhurst and was expelled for insubordination; joined the Mexican navy in the war of liberation; travelled widely; but seemed at about five and twenty to be settling down to literature and journalism in England. After writing various things, he produced in 1837 the fine but not quite "live" plays of *Cosmo de Medici* and *The Death of Marlowe*, and in 1843 the famous farthing epic, *Orion*, which was literally published at a farthing. This was the smallest part of a great literary baggage of very unequal value. In 1852 Horne, resuming the life of adventure, went to Australia, served in the gold police, and stayed at the Antipodes till 1869. Then he came home again and lived for fifteen years longer, still writing almost to his very death on 13th March 1884.

It is not true that *Orion* is Horne's only work of value; but it is so much better than anything else of his, and so characteristic of him, that by all but students the rest may be neglected. And it is an example of the melancholy but frequently exemplified truth, that few things are so dangerous, nay, so fatal to enduring literary fame, as the production of some very good work among a mass of, if not exactly rubbish, yet inferior stuff. I do not think it extravagant to say that if Horne had written nothing but *Orion* and had died comparatively young after writing it, he would have enjoyed very high rank among English poets. For, though doubtless a little weighted with "purpose," it is a very fine poem indeed, couched in a strain of stately and not second-hand blank verse, abounding in finished and effective passages, by no means destitute of force and meaning as a whole, and mixing some passion with more than some real satire. But the rather childish freak of its first publication probably did it no good, and it is quite certain that the author's long life and unflagging production did it much harm.

Of the other persons in the list above, Macaulay, Hartley Coleridge, and Lord Lytton are mainly something else than poets, and Talfourd, as a dramatist, will also be noticed elsewhere. Barnes and Hawker were both clergymen of the West of England : the former very highly ranked by some for his studies in Dorset dialect ; the latter the author of the famous "Song of the Western Men" (long thought a genuine antique), of the exquisite "Queen Gwennyvar's Round," of the fine "Silent Tower of Bottreaux," of some beautiful sonnets, and of the stately "Quest of the Sangreal." Whether James Clarence Mangan, whose most famous poem is "Dark Rosaleen," a musical and mystic celebration of the charms and wrongs of Erin, is a great poet to whom Saxon jealousy has refused greatness for political reasons, or a not ungifted but not consummately distinguished singer who added some study to the common Irish gift of fluent, melodious verse-making, is a question best solved by reading his work and judging for the reader's self. It is not by any sane account so important that to dismiss it thus is a serious *rifiuto*, and it is probably impossible for Irish enthusiasm and English judgment ever to agree on the subject. Of "L. E. L." Sir Henry Taylor, Hood, and Praed, some more substantive account must be given.

Although it is not easy, after two generations, to decide such a point accurately, it is probable that "L. E. L." was the most popular of all the writers of verse who made any mark between the death of Byron in 1824 and the time when Tennyson definitely asserted himself in 1842. She paid for this popularity (which was earned not merely by her verse, but by a pretty face, an odd social position, and a sad and apparently, though it seems not really, mysterious end) by a good deal of slightly unchivalrous satire at the time and a rather swift and complete oblivion afterwards. She was born (her full name being Letitia Elizabeth Landon) in London on 14th August 1802, and was fairly well connected and educated. William Jerdan, the editor of the *Literary Gazette* (a man whose name constantly occurs in the

literary history of this time, though he has left no special work
except an *Autobiography*), was a friend of her family, and she
began to write very early, producing novels and criticisms as well
as verse in newspapers, in the albums and *Souvenirs* which were
such a feature of the twenties and thirties, and in independent
volumes.   She was particularly active as a poet about 1824–35,
when appeared the works whose titles — *The Improvisatore, The
Troubadour, The Golden Violet*—suggested parodies to Thackeray.
Her best novel is held to be *Ethel Churchill*, published in 1837.
Next year she married Mr. Maclean, the Governor of Cape Coast
Castle ; and, going out with him to that not very salubrious clime,
died suddenly in about two months.   All sorts of ill-natured
suggestions were of course made ; but the late Colonel Ellis, the
historian of the colony, seems to have established beyond the
possibility of doubt that she accidentally poisoned herself with
prussic acid, which she used to take for spasms of the heart.

It is tolerably exact, and it is not harsh, to say that " L. E. L."
is a Mrs. Hemans with the influence of Byron added, not to the
extent of any "impropriety," but to the heightening of the
Romantic tone and of a native sentimentality.   Her verse is
generally musical and sweet : it is only sometimes silly.   But it
is too often characterised by what can but be called the " gush "
which seems to have affected all the poetesses of this period
except Sara Coleridge (1802–50) (who has some verses worthy
of even her name in *Phantasmion*, her only independent book),
and which appears in very large measure in the work of Mrs.
Browning.

Sir Henry Taylor's poetical repute illustrates the converse of
the proposition which is illustrated by that of Horne.   It is
probable that, if each is measured by his best things, *Orion* and
Philip Van Artevelde, Horne must be allowed to be a good deal
the better poet.   But a placid official life enabled Taylor both to
gain powerful friends and to devote himself to literature merely
when and how he pleased.   And so he has burdened his baggage
with no mere hack-work.   He was indeed a singularly lucky

person. The son of a man of fair family but reduced fortune who had taken to farming, Henry Taylor began in the navy. But he disliked the service very much, and either obtained or received his discharge after only nine months' sea life as a midshipman during the year 1814. Then he entered the public store-keeper's department, but was ousted by rearrangements after four years' service. These beginnings were not very promising; but his father allowed him to stay quietly at home till by pure luck he obtained a third post under Government in the Colonial Office. This he held for nearly fifty years, during which it gave him affluence and by degrees a very high position, and left him abundance of time for society and letters. He resigned it in 1872, and died on 27th March 1886. He wrote some prose of various kinds, and just before his death published a pleasant autobiography. But his literary fame rests on a handful of plays and poems, all of them, except *St. Clement's Eve*, which did not appear till 1862, produced at leisurely intervals between 1827 (*Isaac Comnenus*) and 1847 (*The Eve of the Conquest* and other poems). The intervening works were *Philip Van Artevelde* (his masterpiece, 1834), *Edwin the Fair* (1842), some minor poems, and the romantic comedy of *A Sicilian Summer* (first called *The Virgin Widow*), which was published with *St. Clement's Eve*. He had (as, it may be noted curiously, had so many of the men of the transition decade in which he was born) a singular though scanty vein of original lyric snatch, the best example of which is perhaps the song " Quoth tongue of neither maid nor wife " in *Van Artevelde ;* but his chief appeal lay in a very careful study of character and the presentation of it in verse less icy than Talfourd's and less rhetorical than Milman's. Yet he had, unlike either of these, very little direct eye to the stage, and therefore is classed here as a poet rather than as a dramatist. There is always a public for what is called " thoughtful " poetry, and Taylor's is more than merely thoughtful. But it may be suspected by observers that when Robert Browning came into fashion Henry Taylor went out. Citations of *Van Artevelde*, if not of the other pieces (none of which are contemptible, while the two last, inferior in weight to their predecessors, show advance in ease and grace), are very frequent between 1835 and 1865 : rare I think between 1865 and 1895.

And so we come at last to the twin poets, in the proper sense humorous, — that is to say, jesting with serious thoughts behind, — of the first division of this class. They were very close in many ways — indeed it is yet a moot point which of the two borrowed certain rhythms and turns of word and verse from the other, or whether both hit upon these independently. But their careers were curiously different ; and, except in comparative length of life (if that be an advantage), Praed was luckier than his comrade. Thomas Hood, who was slightly the elder, was born in 1798 or 1799 (for both dates are given) in the Poultry ; his father being a bookseller and publisher. This father died, not in good circum- stances, when the son was a boy, and Thomas, after receiving some though not much education, became first a merchant's clerk and then an engraver, but was lucky enough to enjoy between these uncongenial pursuits a long holiday, owing to ill-health, of some three years in Scotland. It was in 1820 or thereabouts that he fell into his proper vocation, and, as sub-editor of the *London Magazine*, found vent for his own talents and made acquaintance with most of its famous staff. He married, wrote some of his best serious poems and some good comic work, and found that while the former were neglected the latter was eagerly welcomed. It was settled that, in his own pathetic pun, he was to be " a lively Hood for a livelihood " thenceforward. It is difficult to say whether English literature lost or gained, except from one very practical point of view ; for Hood did manage to live after a fashion by his fun as he certainly could not have lived by his poetry. He had, however, a bare pittance, much bad health, and some ex- tremely bad luck, which for a time made him, through no fault of his own, an exile. His last five years were again spent in England, and in comparative, though very comparative, prosperity ; for he was editor first of the *New Monthly Magazine*, then of a magazine of his own, *Hood's Monthly*, and not long before his death he received from Sir Robert Peel a civil list pension of £100 a year. The death was due to consumption, inherited and long valiantly struggled with.

The still shorter life of Winthrop Mackworth Praed, on the other hand, was passed under sufficiently favourable stars. He was born in 1802, and his father, Serjeant Praed, possessed property, practice at the bar, and official position. Praed was sent to Eton, where he became a pillar of the famous school magazine *The Etonian*, and thence to Trinity College, Cambridge, where he did extremely well, made the acquaintance of Macaulay, and wrote in *Knight's Quarterly*. After a short interval of tutoring and reading for the bar he entered Parliament in 1830, and remained in it for the rest of his life, which closed on 15th July 1839. He had latterly been secretary to the Board of Control, and it was thought that, had he lived, he might have made a considerable political reputation both as speaker and administrator.

The almost unchequered sunshine of one of these careers and the little sun and much shadow of the other have left traces — natural though less than might be supposed — of difference between the produce of the two men; but perhaps the difference is less striking than the resemblance. That Hood — obliged to write for bread, and outliving Praed by something like a decade at the two ends — wrote a great deal more than Praed did is of little consequence, for the more leisurely writer is as unequal as the duty labourer. Hood had the deeper and stronger genius: of this there is no doubt, and the advantage more than made up for Praed's advantages in scholarship and in social standing and accomplishment. In this serious work of Hood's — *Lycus the Centaur, The Plea of the Midsummer Fairies, The Elm Tree, The Haunted House* — there is observable — to a degree never surpassed by any of the poets of this group except Beddoes, and more sustained and human, though less weird and sweet, than his — a strain of the true, the real, the ineffable tone of poetry proper. At this Praed never arrives: there are at most in him touches which may seem to a very charitable judgment to show that in other circumstances sorrow, passion, or the like might have roused him to display the hidden fire. On the other hand, neither Hood's breeding, nor, I think, his nature, allowed him to display the exquisite airiness, the delicate artificial bloom and perfection, of Praed's best *vers de société* — the *Season*, the *Letter of Advice*, and the rest. This last bloom has never been quite equalled — even Prior's touch is coarse to it, even that of the late Mr. Locker is laboured and deliberate. So too as there is nothing in Praed of the popular indignation — generous and fine but a little theatrical — which endears Hood to the general in *The Bridge of Sighs* and *The Song of the Shirt*, so there is nothing in Hood of the sound political sense, underlying apparent banter, of Praed's *Speaker Asleep* and other things.

But where the two poets come together, on a ground which they have almost to themselves, is in a certain kind of humorous poetry ranging from the terrific-grotesque, as in Hood's *Miss Kilmansegg* and Praed's *Red Fisherman*, to the simple, humorously tender study of characters, as in a hundred things of Hood's and in not a few of Praed's with *The Vicar* at their head. The resemblance here is less in special points than in a certain general view of life, conditioned in each case by the poet's breeding, temperament, and circumstance, but alike in essence and quality : in a certain variety of the essentially English fashion of taking life with a mixture of jest and earnest, of humour and sentiment. Hood, partly influenced by the need of caring for the public, partly by his pupilship to Lamb, perhaps went to further extremes both in mere fun and in mere sentiment than Praed did, but the central substance is the same in both.

Yet one gift which Hood has and Praed has not remains to be noticed — the gift of exquisite song writing. Compared with the admired inanities of Barry Cornwall, his praised contemporary, Hood's " Fair Ines," his " Time of Roses," his exquisite " Last Stanzas," and not a few other things, are as gold to gilt copper. Praed has nothing to show against these ; but he, like Hood, was no inconsiderable prose writer, while the latter, thanks to his apprenticeship to the burin, had an extraordinary faculty of illus-trating his own work with cuts, contrary to all the canons, but inimitably grotesque.

It is probable that even in this long survey of the great poetical production of the first third of this century some gaps may be detected by specialists. But it seemed to me impossible to give more than the barest mention here to the " single speech " accident of Charles Wolfe, the author of the " Burial of Sir John Moore," which everybody knows, and of absolutely nothing else that is worth a single person's knowing; to the gigantic and impossible labours of Edwin Atherstone; to the industrious translation of Rose and Sotheby; to the decent worth of Caroline Bowles, and the Hood-and-water of Laman Blanchard. And there are others perhaps who cannot be even mentioned; for there must be an end.

CHAPTER III

THE NEW FICTION

ALTHOUGH, as was shown in the first chapter, the amount of novel writing in the last decades of the eighteenth century was very considerable, and the talent displayed by at least some of the practitioners of the form distinctly great, it can hardly have been possible for any careful observer of it, either during the last ten years of the old age or the first fifteen of the new, to be satisfied with it on the whole, or to think that it had reached a settled or even a promising condition. Miss Burney (now Madame d'Arblay), whose brilliant début with *Evelina* was made just before the date at which this book begins, had just after that date produced *Cecilia*, in which partial and contemporary judges professed to see no falling off. But though she was still living and writing, — though she lived and wrote till the present century was nearly half over, — *Camilla* (1796) was acknowledged as a doubtful success, and *The Wanderer* (1814) as a disastrous failure; nor after this did she attempt the style again.

The unpopularity of Jacobinism and the growing distaste for the philosophy of the eighteenth century prevented much attempt being made to follow up the half political, half philosophical novel of Godwin, Holcroft, and Bage. No such causes, however, were in operation as concerning the "Tale of Terror," the second founder of which, Monk Lewis, was indeed no inconsiderable figure during the earlier part of the great age of 1810–30, while Charles Robert Maturin improved considerably upon Lewis himself. Maturin was born in Ireland (where he principally lived) in 1782, and died there in 1824. He took orders, but was too eccentric for success in his profession, and his whole heart was set on literature and the drama. Befriended by Scott and Byron, though very severely criticised by Coleridge, he succeeded in getting his tragedy of *Bertram* acted at Drury Lane with success; but his later theatrical ventures (*Manuel, Fredolpho*) were less fortunate. He also published sermons; but he lives in literature only by his novels, and not very securely by these. He produced three of them — *The Fatal Vengeance : or, The Family of Montorio, The Wild Irish Boy*, and the *Milesian Chief* — under a pseudonym before he was thirty; while after the success of *Bertram* he avowed *Women* (1818), *Melmoth the Wanderer* (1820), and *The Albigenses* (1824), the last in a sort of cross style between his earlier patterns and Scott. But his fame had best be allowed to rest wholly on *Melmoth*, a remarkable book dealing with the supposed selling of a soul to the devil in return for prolonged life; the bargain, however, being terminable if the seller can induce some one else to take it off his hands. Although far too long, marvellously involved with tales within tales, and disfigured in parts by the rant and the gush of its class, *Melmoth* is really a powerful book, which gave something more than a passing shudder to its own generation (it specially influenced Balzac), and which has not lost its force even now. But the usual novel of this kind, which was written in vast numbers, was simply beneath contempt.

The exquisite artist who, as mentioned formerly, had taken these tales of terror as part subject of her youthful satire, had begun to write some years before the close of the eighteenth century. But Miss Austen's books were long withheld from the press, and she was considerably preceded in publication by Maria Edgeworth. These last are the only novels of the first decade of the nineteenth century which have held any ground, though they were but few among the crowds not merely of tales of terror but of fashionable novels, " Minerva Press " inanities,

attempts in the bastard and unsuccessful kind of historical romance
which preceded Scott's, and others.   Miss Edgeworth, who was
born in 1767, the daughter of an eccentric busybody of good
family and property in Ireland, and who lived till 1848, had a
great fame in her own day, deserved it, never entirely lost it,
and has lately had it revived ; while Scott declared (but in such
matters Scott was a little apt to let his good-nature and his freedom from personal vanity get the better of strict critical truth)
that her Irish novels had supplied the suggestion of his Scotch
ones.   Her chief works in this kind were *Castle Rackrent* (1801),
a book with little interest of the strictly "novel" kind, but
a wonderful picture of the varieties of recklessness and misconduct which in the course of a generation or two ruined or crippled
most of the landlords of Ireland ; *Belinda* (1803), her most
ambitious and elaborate if not her most successful effort, which
includes a very vivid and pregnant sketch of the feminine dissipation of the end of the last century ; *Tales of Fashionable Life*,
including the admirable *Absentee;* and *Ormond*, the most vivid of
her Irish stories next to *Castle Rackrent.*   She continued to write
novels as late as 1834 (*Helen*), while some very charming letters
of hers, though privately printed a good many years ago, were
not published till 1894.   Miss Edgeworth's father, Richard, was
himself something of a man of letters, and belonged to the class
of Englishmen who, without imbibing French freethinking, had
eagerly embraced the "utility" doctrines, the political economy,
and some of the educational and social crazes of the French
philosophes; and he did his daughter no good by thrusting into
her earlier work a strain of his own crotchet and purpose.   Indirectly, however, this brought about in *The Parent's Assistant,* in
other books for children, and in the *Moral Tales,* some of her most
delightful work.   In the novels (which besides these mentioned
include *Leonora, Harrington, Ennui,* and *Patronage,* the longest of
all) Miss Edgeworth occupies a kind of middle position between
the eighteenth century novelists, of whom Miss Burney is the last,
and those of the nineteenth, of whom Miss Austen is the first.

This is not merely, though no doubt it is partly, due to the fact that the society which she saw (and she mixed in a great deal, from the highest downwards) was itself in a kind of transition state : it was at least as much owing to a certain want of distinct modernness and distinct universality in her own character, thought, and style. Miss Edgeworth, though possessed of delightful talents falling little short of genius, and of much humour (which last is shown in the charming *Essay on Irish Bulls*, as well as in her novels and her letters), missed, as a rule, the last and greatest touches ; and, except some of her Irish characters, who are rather types than individuals, she has not created many live persons, while sometimes she wanders very far from life. Her touch, in short, though extremely pleasant, was rather uncertain. She can tell a story to perfection, but does not often invent it perfectly ; and by herself she can hardly be said to have originated anything, though of course, if we could accept the above quoted statement of Scott's, she indirectly originated a very great deal.

Very different is the position occupied by Jane Austen, who was born at Steventon in Hampshire on 16th December 1775, being the daughter of the rector of that place, lived a quiet life chiefly at various places in her native county, frequented good society in the rank of not the richest country squires, to which her own family belonged, and died at Winchester unmarried on 24th July 1817. Of her six completed novels, *Sense and Sensibility*, *Pride and Prejudice*, *Mansfield Park*, and *Emma* were published during the last seven years of her life, while *Northanger Abbey* and *Persuasion* appeared, for the first time with an author's name, the year after her death. They had no enormous or sudden popularity, but the best judges, from Scott downwards, at once recognised their extraordinary merit ; and it is not too much to say that by the best judges, with rare exceptions, that merit has been acknowledged with ever increasing fulness at once of enthusiasm and discrimination to the present day. With Scott, Miss Austen is the parent of nineteenth century fiction ; or, to speak with greater exactness, she is the mother of the nineteenth century novel, just as he is the father of the nineteenth century romance.

One indeed of the most wonderful things about her is her earliness. Even the dates of publication of her first books precede those of any novelist of the same rank and the same modernity; but these dates are misleading. *Northanger Abbey* was written more than twenty years before it appeared, and the bulk of *Pride and Prejudice* (which some hold to be the best and most characteristic of all) is known to have been as old at least as *Northanger Abbey*. That is to say, almost at the very time of the appearance of *Camilla* (to which, by the way, Miss Austen was an original subscriber), a book not strikingly more nineteenth century in tone than the novels of Richardson, though a little more so in manners, a girl even younger than Miss Burney herself had been when she wrote *Evelina* was drawing other girls, who, putting aside the most trivial details of dress, speech, and so forth, might be living girls to-day.

The charm and the genius of Miss Austen are not universally admitted; the touch of old fashion in external detail apparently discontenting some readers, the delicate and ever-present irony either escaping or being distasteful to others, while the extreme quietness of the action and the entire absence of excitement probably revolt a third class. But the decriers do not usually attempt formal criticism. However, they sometimes do, and such an attempt once came under the notice of the present historian. It was urged that to extol Miss Austen's method is a masculine delusion, that method being nothing but the throwing into literature of the habit of minute and semi-satiric observation natural to womankind. It did not apparently occur to this critic that he (or she) was in the first place paying Miss Austen an extraordinarily high compliment — a compliment almost greater than the most enthusiastic "Janites" have ventured — inasmuch as no higher literary triumph can be even conceived than thus to focus, formulate, and crystallise the special talent and gift of an entire sex into a literary method. Nor did it

K

probably occur to him that he was laying himself open to the damaging, or rather ruinous retort, " Then how is it that, of all the women who have preceded and followed Miss Austen as novelists, no other has displayed this specially and universally feminine gift?"

It is no doubt true that there is something feminine about the method, which, with the addition of a certain *nescio quid*, giving it its modern difference, may be said to combine the peculiarities of Fielding and of Richardson, though it works on a much smaller scale than either. It has the intense and pervading, though not the exuberant and full-blooded, *livingness* of Fielding, and it also has something not unlike a feminine counterpart and complement of his pervading irony; while it is not unlike Richardson in building up the characters and the stories partly by an infinity of tiny strokes of detail, often communicated in conversation, partly by the use of an exceedingly nice and delicate analysis of motive and temperament. It is in the former respect that Miss Austen stands apart from most, if not from all, women who have written novels. Irony is by no means a frequent feminine gift; and as women do not often possess it in any great degree, so they do not as a rule enjoy it. Miss Austen is only inferior among English writers to Swift, to Fielding, and to Thackeray — even if it be not improper to use the term inferiority at all for what is after all not much more than difference — in the use of this potent but most double-edged weapon. Her irony indeed is so subtle that it requires a certain dose of subtlety to appreciate it, and it is not uncommon to find those who consider such personages as Mr. Collins in *Pride and Prejudice* to be merely farcical, instead of, as they are in fact, preachers of the highest and most Shakespearian comedy. But there would be no room here to examine Miss Austen's perfections in detail; the important thing for the purposes of this history is to observe again that she " set the clock," so to speak, of pure novel writing to the time which was to be nineteenth century time to this present hour. She discarded violent and romantic adventure. She did not rely in the very least degree on describing popular or passing fashions, amusements, politics ; but confined herself to the most strictly ordinary life. Yet she managed in some fashion so to extract the characteristics of that life which are perennial and human, that there never can be any doubt to fit readers in any age finding themselves at home with her, just as they find themselves at home with all the greatest writers of bygone ages. And lastly, by some analogous process she hit upon a style which, though again true to the ordinary speech of her own day, and therefore now reviled as "stilted" and formal by those who have not the gift of literary detachment, again possesses the universal quality, and, save in the merest externals, is neither ancient nor modern.

For the moment, however, Miss Austen's example had not so much little influence as none at all. A more powerful and popular force, coming immediately afterwards and coinciding with the bent of general taste, threw for the time the whole current of English novel writing into quite a different channel ; and it was not till the first rush of this current had expended itself, after an interval of thirty or forty years, that the novel, as distinguished from the romance and from nondescript styles partaking now of the romance itself, now of something like the eighteenth century story, engaged the popular ear. This new development was the historical novel proper ; and the hand that started it at last was that of Scott. At last — for both men and women had been trying to write historical novels for about two thousand years, and for some twenty or thirty the attempts had come tolerably thick and fast. But before Scott no one, ancient or modern, Englishman or foreigner, had really succeeded. In the first place, until the eighteenth century was pretty far advanced, the conception and the knowledge of history as distinguished from the mere writing and reading of chronicles had been in a very rudimentary condition. Exceedingly few historians and no readers of history, as a class and as a rule, had practised or acquired the art of looking at bygone ages with any attempt to realise and revive the ideas of those ages themselves, or even, while looking at them with the eyes of the present, to keep in mind that these were quite different eyes from those of contemporaries. In the same way no attempt at getting "local colour," at appropriateness of dialect, and so forth, had been made. These negligences in the hands of genius had been as unimportant as the negligences of genius always are. If Shakespeare's "godlike Romans" are not entirely free from anachronism, nobody of sense would exchange them for anything else than themselves; and though Dante practically repeated in the *Commedia* the curious confusion which in less gifted *trouvères* and romances mixed up Alexander with Charlemagne and blended Greek and Gothic notions in one inextricable tangle, this also was supremely unimportant, if not even in a manner interesting. But when, at the end of the eighteenth century, writers, of secondary powers at best, engaging in a new and unengineered way, endeavoured to write historical novels, they all, from Godwin and Mrs. Radcliffe to Miss Reeves and the Misses Lee, made the merest gallimaufries of inaccurate history, questionable fiction, manners heedlessly jumbled, and above all dialogue destitute of the slightest semblance of verisimilitude, and drawn chiefly from that of the decadent tragic and comic drama of the time.

It is not possible — it never is in such cases — to give a very exact account of the causes which led Walter Scott, when the public seemed to be a little tiring of the verse-romances which have been discussed in the last chapter, to take to romances in prose. The example of Miss Edgeworth, if a true cause at all, could affect only his selection of Scotch manners to illustrate his histories, not his adoption of the historical style itself. But he did adopt it; and, fishing out from an old desk the beginnings of a story which he had left unfinished, or rather had scarce commenced, years earlier, he fashioned it into *Waverley*. This appearing in the year 1814 at a serious crisis in his own affairs, opened at once a new career of fame and fortune to him, and a previously unknown field of exploit and popularity to the English novel.

The extraordinary greatness of Scott — who in everything but pure style, and the expression of the highest raptures of love, thought, and nature, ranks with the greatest writers of the world — is not better indicated by any single fact than by the fact that it is impossible to describe his novels in any simple formula. He practically created the historical novel; and, what is more, he elaborated it to such an extent that no really important additions to his scheme have been made since. But not all his novels are historical. The two which immediately succeeded *Waverley*, and which perhaps the best judges consider his best, — *Guy Mannering* and *The Antiquary*, — have only the faintest touch of history about them, and might have none at all without affecting their excellence; while one of the most powerful of his later books, *St. Ronan's Well*, is almost absolutely virgin of fact. So also, though his incomparable delineation of national manners, speech, and character, of the *cosas de Escócia* generally, is one of the principal sources of his interest, *Ivanhoe*, which has perhaps been the most popular of all his books, *Kenilworth*, which is not far below it in popularity or in merit, and one or two others, have nothing at all of Scotland in them; and the altogether admirable romance of *Quentin Durward*, one of his four or five masterpieces, so little that what there is plays the smallest part in the success. So yet again, historical novelist as Scott is, and admirably as he has utilised and revivified history, he is by no means an extremely accurate historical scholar, and is wont not merely to play tricks with history to suit his story, — that is probably always allowable, — but to commit anachronisms which are quite unnecessary and even a little teasing.

There is no doubt that the single gift underlying all these and other things — the gift which enabled Scott not merely, as has been said, to create the historical novel, but to give the novel generally an entirely new start and direction, to establish its popularity, to clear its reputation from the smirch of frivolity on the one side and immorality on the other, to put it in the position occupied at other times or in other countries by the drama and the sermon, and to make it a rival of the very newspaper which was being refashioned at the same moment, while providing opportunities for the production of literature proper not inferior to those of any literary kind except poetry — that this was a gift of higher scope, if of vaguer definition, than any of those referred to. It was that gift which no one except Shakespeare has ever possessed in larger measure, though others have possessed it in greater partial intensity and perfection — the gift of communicating life to the persons, the story, the dialogue. To some extent Scott had this treasure in an earthen vessel. He could not, like Thackeray, like Fielding, like Miss Austen even, make everybody that he touched alive : his heroes very generally are examples to the contrary. And as a rule, when he did perform this function of the wizard, — a name given to him by a more than popular appropriateness, — he usually did it, not by the accumulation of a vast number of small strokes, but by throwing on the canvas, or rather panel, large outlines, free sweeps of line, and breadths of colour, instinct with vivacity and movement. Yet he managed wholly to avoid that fault of some creative imaginations which consists in personifying and individualising their figures by some easily recognisable label of mannerism. Even his most mannered characters, his humourists in the seventeenth century sense, of whom Dugald Dalgetty is the prince and chief — the true commander of the whole *stift* of this *Dunkelspiel* — stand poles asunder from those inventions of Dickens and of some others who are ticketed for us by a gesture or a phrase repeated *ad nauseam*. And this gift probably is most closely connected with another : the extraordinary variety of Scott's scene, character, and — so far as the term is applicable to his very effective but rather loose fashion of story-telling — plot. It is a common and a just complaint of novelists, especially when they are fertile rather than barren, that with them scene, plot, and character all run into a kind of mould, that their stories with a little trouble can be thrown into a sort of common form, that their persons simply "change from the blue bed to the brown," and that the blue and brown beds themselves are seen, under their diverse colours, to have a singular and not very welcome uniformity of pattern and furniture. Even Scott does not escape this almost invariable law of the brain-artist: it is one of the sole Shakespearian characteristics that Shakespeare does escape it entirely and altogether. A certain form of huddled and not altogether probable catastrophe, a knack of introducing in the earlier part of the story, as if big with fate, personages who afterwards play but a subordinate part, and one or two other things, might be urged against Sir Walter. But, on the whole, no artist is less chargeable with stereotype than he. His characters are hardly ever doubles; their relationships (certain general connections excepted, which are practically the scaffolding of the romance in itself) do not repeat themselves; the backgrounds, however much or however little strict local colour they may have, are always sufficiently differentiated. They have the variety, as they have the truth, of nature.

No detailed account can here be attempted of the marvellous rapidity and popularity of the series of novels from the appearance of *Waverley* till just before the author's death eighteen years later. The anecdotage of the matter is enormous. The books were from the first anonymous, and for some time the secret of their authorship was carefully and on the whole successfully preserved. Even several years after the beginning, so acute a judge as Hazlitt, though he did not entertain, thought it necessary seriously to discuss, the suggestion that Godwin wrote them, — a suggestion which, absurd as, with our illegitimate advantage of distance and perspective, we see it to be, was less nonsensical than it seems to those who forget that at the date of the appearance of *Waverley* there was no novelist who could have been selected with more plausibility. After a time this and that were put together, and a critic of the name of Adolphus constructed an argument of much ingenuity and shrewdness to show that the author of *Marmion* and the *Lady of the Lake* must be the author of *Waverley*. But the secret was never regularly divulged till Sir Walter's misfortunes, referred to in the section on his poetry, made further concealment not so much useless as impossible in the first place, and positively detrimental in the second. The series was dauntlessly continued, despite the drag of the *Napoleon*, the necessity of attempting other work that would bring in money, and above all the strain on the faculties both of imagination and labour which domestic as well as pecuniary misfortunes imposed. Nor did Scott, it may be fearlessly asserted, though it is not perhaps the general opinion, ever publish any "dotages," with the possible exception of *Castle Dangerous*, which was not only finished but begun when the fatal disease of the brain which killed him had got the upper hand. The introduction to the *Chronicles of the Canongate*, written in 1827, is one of the most exquisite and masterly things that he ever did, though, from its not actually forming part of one of the novels, it is comparatively little known. The *Fair Maid of Perth*, a year later, has been one of the most popular of all abroad, and not the least so at home ; and there are critics who rank *Anne of Geierstein*, in 1829, very high indeed. Few defenders are found for *Count Robert of Paris*, which was in fact written in the valley of the shadow ; and it may be admitted that in his earlier days Scott would certainly have been able to give it a fuller development and a livelier turn. Yet the opening scene, though a little too long, the escape from the vaults of the Blachernal, and not a few other things, would be recognised as marvellous if they could be put before a competent but unbiassed taste, which knew nothing of Sir Walter's other work, but was able to compare it not merely with the work of his predecessors but with that of his imitators, numerous and enterprising as they were, at the time that *Count Robert* appeared.

In such a comparison Scott at his worst excels all others at their best. It is not merely that in this detail and in that he has the mastery, but that he has succeeded in making novel writing in general turn over a completely new leaf, enter upon a distinctly

different competition. With the masterpieces of the eighteenth
century novel he does not enter into comparison at all: he is
working on a different scene, addressing a different audience,
using different tools, colours, methods. Every successful novelist
up to his time had, whatever his ostensible "*temp.* of tale,"
quietly assumed the thoughts, the speech, the manners, even to a
great extent the dress and details of his own day. And in this
assumption all but the greatest had inevitably estranged from them
the ears and eyes of days that were not their own, which days, no
doubt, were in turn themselves rapidly hastening to change, but
never to revert to the original surroundings. Scott had done in
prose fiction what the poets and the dramatists had sometimes
done, what very rare philosophers had sometimes done likewise.
Ostensibly going to the past, and to some extent really borrowing its
circumstances, he had in reality gone straight to man as man; he
had varied the particular trapping only to exhibit the universal
substance. The Baron of Bradwardine, Dandie Dinmont, Edie
Ochiltree, Mause Headrigg, Bailie Jarvie, and the long list of
originals down to Oliver Proudfute and even later, their less
eccentric companions from Fergus MacIvor to Queen Margaret,
may derive part of their appeal from dialect and colouring, from
picturesque "business" and properties. But the chief of that
appeal lies in the fact that they are all men and women of the
world, of life, of time in general; that even when their garments,
even when their words are a little out of fashion, there is real
flesh and blood beneath the garments, real thought and feeling
behind the words. It may be urged by the Devil's Advocate, and
is not wholly susceptible of denial by his opponent, that, after the
first four or five books, the enormous gains open to Scott first
tempted, and the heroic efforts afterwards demanded of him later
compelled, the author to put not quite enough of himself and his
knowledge into his work, to "pad" if not exactly to "scamp" a
little. Yet it is the fact that some of his very best work was not
only very rapidly written, but written under such circumstances
of bodily suffering and mental worry as would have made any work

at all impossible to most men. And, on the whole, it is perhaps as idle to speculate whether this work might have been better, as it is ungenerous to grumble that it ought to have been. For after all it is such a body of literature as, for complete liberation from any debts to models, fertility and abundance of invention, nobility of sentiment, variety and keenness of delight, nowhere else exists as the work of a single author in prose.

It was certain that an example so fascinating in itself, and of such extraordinary profit in fame and fortune to the author, would be followed. It was said with sufficient accuracy that Scott's novels, at the best of his career, brought him in about £15,000 a year, a sum previously undreamt of by authors; while their reputation overshadowed not only all others in England, but all others throughout Europe. And it is rather surprising, and shows how entirely Scott had the priority in this field, that it was not for six or seven years at least that any noteworthy attempts in his manner appeared, while it can scarcely be said that in England anything of very great value was published in it before his death. In the last ten years of his life, however, imitations, chiefly of his historical style, did appear in great numbers ; and he has left in his diary an extremely interesting, a very good-natured, but a very shrewd and just criticism upon them in general, and upon two in particular — the *Brambletye House* of Horace Smith, one of the authors of the delightful parodies called *Rejected Addresses*, and the first book, *Sir John Chiverton*, of an author who was to continue writing for some half century, and at times to attain very great popularity. This was Harrison Ainsworth, and G. P. R. James also began to publish pretty early in the third decade of the century. James' *Richelieu*, his first work of mark, appeared in 1825, the same year as *Sir John Chiverton ;* but he was rather the older man of the two, having been born in 1801, while Ainsworth's birth year was 1805. The latter, too, long outlived James, who died in 1860, while holding the post of English Consul in Venice, while Ainsworth survived till 1882. Both were exceedingly prolific, James writing history and other work as well as the novels —

Darnley, *Mary of Burgundy*, *Henry Masterton*, *John Marston Hall*, and dozens of others — which made his fame; while Ainsworth (*Jack Sheppard*, *The Tower of London*, *Crichton*, *Rookwood*, *Old St. Paul's*, etc.) was a novelist only. Both, especially between 1830 and 1850, achieved considerable popularity with the general public; and they kept it much longer (if indeed they have yet lost it) with schoolboys. But while the attempt of both to imitate Scott was palpable always, the success of neither could be ranked very high by severe criticism. James wrote better than Ainsworth : his historical knowledge was of a much wider and more accurate kind, and he was not unimbued with the spirit of romance. But the sameness of his situations (it became a stock joke to speak of the " two horsemen " who so often appeared in his opening scenes), the exceedingly conventional character of his handling, and the theatrical feebleness of his dialogue, were always reprehended and open to reprehension. Harrison Ainsworth, on the other hand, had a real knack of arresting and keeping the interest of those readers who read for mere excitement : he was decidedly skilful at gleaning from memoirs and other documents scraps of decoration suitable for his purpose, he could in his better days string incidents together with a very decided knack, and, till latterly, his books rarely languished. But his writing was very poor in strictly literary merit, his style was at best bustling prose melodrama, and his characters were scarcely ever alive.

The chief follower of Sir Walter Scott in " Scotch " novels — for Miss Ferrier, the Scottish counterpart of Miss Edgeworth and Miss Austen, was, though his friend, hardly his follower, and *Marriage* was mainly written before *Waverley* — was John Galt, who also has some claim to priority. He was born (2nd May 1779) at Irvine in Ayrshire, the scene of his best work, but passed most of his youth at Greenock. His father was a retired West India captain ; and Galt's biographers do not make it very clear whence he obtained the capital for the various travels and enterprises which occupied his not exactly eventful, but busy and varied life. He had entered the Custom-house; but went to London in 1804, and tried literature in many forms, and for the most part with very little success. While travelling in the Levant he met Byron, of whom long afterwards he published a rather absurd life; and after his return home his *Ayrshire Legatees* found welcome and popularity in *Blackwood*. This was in 1821, and after five years' busy writing Galt went to Canada in charge of a great scheme of colonisation and commerce called the Canada Company. This, after fair prospects, broke down completely. He came back again, wrote hard, and schemed incessantly. But fortune was not kind to him; and he died, in a way a broken man, at Greenock on 11th April 1839.

Galt, though with some of the national characteristics which have not always made Scotchmen popular, appears to have been a person of worth and amiability. He got on well with Byron, a very uncommon thing; and from Carlyle, whom he met when they were both on the staff of *Fraser*, he receives unwontedly amiable notice. His literary production was vast and totally uncritical; his poems, dramas, etc., being admittedly worthless, his miscellaneous writing mostly book-making, while his historical novels are given up by all but devotees. He had, however, a special walk — the delineation of the small humours and ways of his native town and county — in which, if not exactly supreme, he has seldom been equalled. The *Ayrshire Legatees* is in main scheme a pretty direct and not very brilliant following of *Humphrey Clinker;* but the letters of the worthy family who visit London are read in a home circle which shows Galt's peculiar talent. It is shown better still in his next published work, *The Annals of the Parish*, which is said to have been written long before, and in the pre-Waverley days to have been rejected by the publishers because "*Scotch* novels could not pay." It is not exactly a novel, being literally what its title holds out — the annals of a Western Parish by its minister, the Rev. Mr. Balwhidder, a Presbyterian Parson Adams of a less robust type, whose description of himself and parishioners is always good, and at times charming. *Sir Andrew Wylie* (a fantastic book of much good fun and much good feeling), *The Entail*, and *The Provost* (the last two sometimes ranked next to the *Annals*), followed rapidly, and are all good in a way which has been oddly revived of late years by some of our most popular novelists. A better writer than Galt, though a less fertile, was Dr. Moir ("Delta"), another *Blackwood* man, whose chief single performance is *Mansie Wauch*, but who wrote both prose and verse, both tales and essays, with considerable accomplishment of style, and with a very agreeable mixture of serious and comic power.

Meanwhile, the historical novel did not by any means absorb the attention of the crowds of aspirants who hurried to try their fortune in the wake of Scott. Lady Morgan (or rather Miss Sydney Owenson) did, in *The Wild Irish Girl* (1806) and other things, some "rattling Hibernian stories" quite early ; John Banim (1798–1842) coincided with the two Englishmen and exceeded them in *goût du terroir;* and the *Fairy Legends* (1826) of Crofton Croker (1798–1854) are at their best simply exquisite. But the older styles continued after a fashion, or underwent slight changes, before the novel of purely ordinary life, on a plan midway between Scott and Miss Austen, triumphed in the middle of the century. One of the most popular of novelists in the reigns of George IV. and William IV. was Theodore Hook (1788–1841), a man of respectable connections and excellent education, who, having made himself a favourite with the Regent and many persons of quality as a diner-out and improvisatore, received a valuable appointment at the Mauritius, laid himself open by carelessness to a prosecution for malversation, and, returning to England, never entirely escaped from the effects of this, though he was extremely successful both as a novelist, and as a newspaper writer and editor, in the *John Bull* chiefly. Some of Hook's political squibs and light verses still retain attraction ; and the tradition of his extraordinary faculties in improvising both words, music, and dramatic arrangement remains. But his novels (*Sayings and Doings, Gilbert Gurney, Gurney Married, Maxwell*, etc.) have become very dead-alive. They have little plot; a sort of rattling adventure in a modernised following of Smollett, which is their chief source of interest; manners true enough to their own day to be out-of-date now, but not handled with sufficient art ever to regain the attraction of revived antiquity; and a very careless and undistinguished style.

The first series of Hook's *Sayings and Doings* appeared in 1824, the year before that of the novels of James and Ainsworth above noticed. Three years later, and five before Scott's death, appeared *Falkland*, the first (anonymous) novel of a writer far surpassing any of the hour in talent, and credited by some with positive genius. Edward George Earle Lytton Bulwer, afterwards Sir Edward Lytton-Bulwer, and later still Lord Lytton (born in 1800), was the youngest son of General Bulwer of Wood Dalling and Haydon in Norfolk, while he on his mother's side represented an ancient Hertfordshire family seated at Knebworth. He was a Cambridge man: he obtained the Chancellor's prize for English verse in 1825, and his first books were in poetical form. He became a Member of Parliament, being returned in the Whig interest for St. Ives before the Reform Bill passed, and in the first Reform Parliament for Lincoln, and he held this seat for a decade, receiving his baronetcy in 1835. For another decade he was out of the House of Commons, though he succeeded to the Knebworth estate in 1844. He was returned for Hertfordshire in 1852, and, joining Lord Derby's reconstituted party, ranked for the rest of his life as a Conservative of a somewhat Liberal kind. In the second Derby administration he was Colonial Secretary, but took no part in that of 1867, and died just before the return of the Tories to power in 1873.

This sufficiently brilliant political career was complicated by literary production and success in a manner not equalled by any Englishman of his time, and only approached by Macaulay and by Mr. Disraeli. *Falkland* was succeeded by *Pelham*, which was published with his name, and which was the first, perhaps the most successful, and by far the most brilliant, of the novels in

which authors have endeavoured to secure the rank of man of the
world even more than that of man of letters, taking the method
chiefly of fashionable, and therefore somewhat ephemeral, epigram.
Nor did Bulwer (as he was known in the heyday of his popularity)
ever cease novel writing for the forty-five years which were left to
him, while the styles of his production varied with fashion in a
manner impossible to a man of less consummate versatility and
talent, though perhaps equally impossible to one of a very decided
turn of genius. The fashionable novel, the crime novel, the romance
of mystery, the romance of classical times, the historical novel, by
turns occupied him ; and it is more easy to discover faults in *Paul
Clifford, Eugene Aram, The Pilgrims of the Rhine, The Last
Days of Pompeii, Ernest Maltravers, Zanoni, Rienzi, The Last of
the Barons*, and *Harold*, than to refuse admiration to their extraordinary qualities. Then their author, recognising the public
taste, as he always did, or perhaps exemplifying it with an almost
unexampled quickness, turned to the domestic kind, which was at
last, more than thirty years after Miss Austen's death, forcing its
way, and wrote *The Caxtons, My Novel*, and *What will he do with
it ?* — books which to some have seemed his greatest triumphs. The
veering of that taste back again to tales of terror was acknowledged
by *A Strange Story*, which, in 1861, created an excitement rarely,
if ever, caused by the work of a man who had been writing for
more than a generation ; while *The Haunted and the Haunters*, a
brief ghost-story contributed to *Blackwood's Magazine*, has always
seemed to the present writer the most perfect thing that he ever
did, and one of the most perfect things of its kind ever done.
In the very last years of his life, the wonderful *girouette* of his
imagination felt other popular gales, and produced — partly as
novels of actual society, partly as Janus-faced satires of what was
and what might be — *The Coming Race, Kenelm Chillingly*, and
the posthumous *Parisians*.

But this list of novels, which does not include by name much
more than two-thirds of his actual production, by no means
exhausts Lord Lytton's literary work. For some years, chiefly

before he had passed middle life, he was an active dramatist, and at least three of his plays— *The Lady of Lyons*, *Richelieu*, and *Money*— had a success (not merely passing, and in the first case at least permanent) which few if any other plays of the century have had. He was always returning to verse, though never with real poetical success; the exceptions which may be urged most forcibly being his translations from Schiller, a congenial original. He was at one time editor of the *New Monthly Magazine*. He translated freely, he wrote much criticism, —which is often in isolated passages, if not so often in general drift and grasp, extremely good, —and he was a constant essayist in very various kinds. It is probable that if his entire works were ever collected, which is not likely, few, if any, authors of the nineteenth century, though it be one of unbridled writing and printing, could equal him in volume; while it is certain that very few indeed could produce more numerous testimonials of the kind given by the immediate, and not merely immediate, success of separate works.

Yet it has been sometimes complained, sometimes boasted, that " with the critics Bulwer is dead "; and it is not very certain that with the faithful herd of uncritical readers the first Lord Lytton keeps any great place. Even many years ago he had ceased to be, if he ever was, a general favourite with those who specially loved literature; and it is rather doubtful whether he will ever regain even a considerable vogue of esteem. Perhaps this may be unjust, for he certainly possessed ability in bulk, and perhaps here and there in detail, far surpassing that of all but the very greatest of his contemporaries. Even the things which were most urged against him by contemporary satirists, and which it is to be feared are remembered at second-hand when the first-hand knowledge of his work has declined, need not be fatal. A man may write such things as " There is an eloquence in Memory because it is the nurse of Hope " without its being necessary to cast up his capital letters against him in perpetuity, or to inquire without ceasing whether eloquence is an inseparable property of nurses. But he had two great faults — want of concentration and want of reality; and the very keenness, the very delicacy of his appreciation of the shiftings of popular taste may seem without unfairness to argue a certain shallowness of individual soil, a literary compost wherein things spring up rapidly because they have no depth of earth, but also because they have no depth of earth, rapidly vanish and wither away. The novel and the magazine have beyond all doubt given us much admirable work which without them we should not have had; they have almost as certainly, and in no case much more certainly than in Bulwer's, over-forced and over-coaxed into hasty and ephemeral production talents which, with a little more hardening and under less exacting circumstances, might have become undoubted genius. Sentimental grandiloquence is not by itself fatal: the fashion which tempts to it, which turns on it, may return to it again; and it is never impossible to make allowance for its excesses, especially when, as in the case under discussion, it is accompanied by a rare and true satiric grasp of life. In these early externals of his, Bulwer was only the most illustrious of the innumerable victims of Byron. But his failure to make his figures thoroughly alive is more serious; and this must be put down partly to incapacity to take pains.

It was nearly ten years after the first success of Bulwer, and more than half as much after the death of Scott, that a novelist greater than any the century had seen, except Scott himself and Miss Austen, appeared. Charles Dickens and Lord Lytton became rather intimate friends; but their origins and early experiences were curiously different. Dickens' father had been in a government office; but after the Peace he took to the press, and his son (born in 1812), after some uncomfortable early experiences which have left their mark on *David Copperfield*, fled to the same refuge of the destitute in our times. He was a precocious, but not an extraordinary precocious writer; for he was four and twenty when the *Sketches by Boz* were printed in a volume after appearing in the *Morning Chronicle*. But the *Sketches*

L

by Boz, though containing some very sprightly things, are but as farthing candles to sunlight when compared with the wonderful and wholly novel humour of *The Pickwick Papers*, which (Dickens having been first (1836) employed to write them as mere letter-press to the sporting sketches of the caricaturist Seymour) appeared as a book in 1838. From that time their author had a success which in money came second to that of Scott, and which both pecuniarily and otherwise enabled him to write pretty much as he pleased. So to the last the style of his novels never bore much reference to any public taste or demand ; and he developed himself more strictly according to his own bent than almost any writer of English who was not born to fortune. During the last twenty years of his life, which ended suddenly on 9th June 1870, he was a newspaper editor — first of *Household Words*, then of *All the Year Round;* but these very periodicals were of his own making and design. He made two journeys to America : one very early in 1842, with a literary result (*American Notes*) of very sharp criticism of its people ; the other late in 1867, when he made large sums by reading from his works — a style of entertainment which, again, was almost of his own invention, and which gave employment to a very strong dramatic and histrionic faculty that found little other vent. But his life was extremely uneventful, being for its last two and thirty years simply one long spell of hard though lavishly rewarded literary labour.

The brilliancy and the originality of the product of this can never be denied. True to his general character of independence, Dickens owes hardly anything to any predecessor except Smollett, to whom his debts are rather large, and perhaps to Theodore Hook, to whom, although the fact has not been generally recognised, they exist. He had had no regular education, had read as a boy little but the old novelists, and never became as a man one of either wide learning or much strictly literary taste. His temperament indeed was of that insubordinate middle-class variety which rather resents the supremacy of any classics ; and he carried the same feeling into art, into politics, and into the discussion of the vague problems of social existence which have so much occupied the last three-quarters of the century. Had this icono-clastic but ignorant zeal of his (which showed itself in his second novel, *Nicholas Nickleby*, and was apparent in his last completed one, *Our Mutual Friend*) been united with less original genius, the result must have been infinitely tedious, and could not have been in any way profitable. For Dickens' knowledge, as has been said, was very limited; his logical faculties were not strong; and while constantly attempting to satirise the upper classes, he knew extremely little about them, and has never drawn a single "aristocrat," high government official, or "big-wig" gener-ally, who presents the remotest resemblance to a living being. But he knew the lower and lower middle classes of his own day with wonderful accuracy; he could inform this knowledge of his with that indefinable comprehension of man as man which has been so often noted; and over and above this he possessed an imagination, now humorous, now terrible, now simply grotesque, of a range and volume rarely equalled, and of a quality which stands entirely by itself, or is approached at a distance, and with a difference, only by that of his great French contemporary Balzac. This imagination, essentially plastic, so far outran the strictly critical knowledge of mankind as mankind just mentioned that it has invested Dickens' books and characters with a peculiarity found nowhere else, or only in the instance just excepted. They are never quite real : we never experience or meet anything or anybody quite like them in the actual world. And yet in their own world they hold their position and play their parts quite perfectly and completely : they obey their own laws, they are consistent with their own surroundings. Occasionally the work is marred by too many and too glaring tricks of mannerism : this was especially the case with the productions of the period between 1855 and 1865. The pathos of Dickens was always regarded as slightly conventional and unreal by critical judges. But his humour, though never again attaining the same marvellous flow of unforced merriment which the *Pickwick Papers* had shown, was almost unfailing; and, thanks to the gift of projecting imaginative character, above noticed, it was never exactly the same.

These and other gifts were shown in a long line of novels covering just thirty years, from *Boz* to *Our Mutual Friend;* for the last few years of his life, disturbed by his American tour, by increasing ill-health, and other things, produced nothing but the beginnings of an unfinished novel, *Edwin Drood.* He attempted little besides novels, and what he did attempt outside of them was not very fortunate, except the delightful *Uncommercial Traveller,* wherein in his later days he achieved a sort of mellowed version of the *Boz* sketches, subdued more to the actual, but not in the least tamed or weakened. Although a keen lover of the theatre and an amateur actor of remarkable merit, he had the sense and self-denial never to attempt plays except in an indirect fashion and in one or two instances, nor ever in his own name solely. His *Child's History of England* (1854) is probably the worst book ever written by a man of genius, except Shelley's novels, and has not, like them, the excuse of extreme youth. His *Pictures from Italy* (1845), despite vivid passages, are quite unworthy of him; and even the *American Notes* could be dispensed with without a sigh, seeing that we have *Martin Chuzzlewit.* But his novels, despite their many faults, could not be dispensed with, — no one who understands literary value would give up even the worst of them, — while his earlier " Christmas Books " (during the fancy for these things in the forties) and his later contributions to the Christmas numbers of his periodicals contain some of his best fantastic and pathetic work. *Pickwick* was immediately followed by *Oliver Twist,* — a very popular book, and in parts a very powerful one, but containing in germ most of the faults which afterwards developed themselves, and, with the exception of the " Artful Dodger," not bringing out any of his great character-creations. *Nicholas Nickleby* (1838) is a story designed to fix a stigma on cheap private schools, and marred by some satire as cheap as the schools themselves on the fashionable and aristo-

cratic society of which to his dying day Dickens never knew
anything ; but it is of great interest as a story, and full of admirable
humoristic sketches, which almost if not quite excused not merely
the defect of knowledge just referred to, but the author's unfortunate proneness to attempt irony, of which he had no command,
and argument, of which he had if possible less. His next two
stories, *The Old Curiosity Shop* and *Barnaby Rudge,* were enshrined (1840–41) in an odd framework of fantastic presentation,
under the general title of *Master Humphrey's Clock,* — a form
afterwards discarded with some advantage, but also with some loss.
The Old Curiosity Shop, strongly commended to its own public
and seriously hampered since by some rather maudlin pathos,
improved even upon *Nicholas Nickleby* in the humoristic vein ;
and while Dick Swiveller, Codlin and Short, Mr. Chuckster, and
others remain as some of the best of Dickens' peculiar characters of the lighter sort, the dwarf Quilp is perhaps his only
thoroughly successful excursion into the grimmer and more horrible
kind of humour. *Barnaby Rudge* is in part a historical novel,
and the description of the riots of Eighty is of extraordinary
power ; but the real appeal of the book lies in the characters of
the Varden family, with the handmaid Miss Miggs and the ferocious apprentice Tappertit. Sir John Chester, a sort of study
from Chesterfield, is one of the most disastrous of this author's
failures ; but Dennis the Hangman may have a place by Quilp.
Then (1843) came *Martin Chuzzlewit,* which, as observed, embodied his American experiences in a manner which may or may
not have been fair, but which was exquisitely funny. It also
added the immortal figure of Mrs. Gamp (not unattended by any
means) to the glorious list of his comic creations. It was in
Dombey and Son (1846–48) that the Dickens of the decadence first
appeared ; the maudlin strain of *The Old Curiosity Shop* being
repeated in Paul Dombey, while a new and very inauspicious
element appeared in certain mechanical tricks of phrase, and in a
totally unreal style of character exemplified in the Bagstocks, the
Carkers, and so forth. Yet Captain Cuttle, his friend Bunsby,

Miss Nipper, and the inestimable Toots put in ample bail for this also. And it was followed (1849–50) by *David Copperfield*, one of the capital books of English fiction. This was to some extent obviously autobiographic; but, setting some questions of taste aside, not unduly so. Even the hero is too real to be frigid; and of the two heroines, Dora, if an idiot, is saved by pathos different from that of Paul and Nell, while the insipidity of Agnes does not greatly spoil the story, and the commonplace theatricality of the Steerforth and Little Em'ly episode can be neglected. On the other hand, Miss Trotwood, David Copperfield's schools and schoolfellows, Uriah Heap (not wholly good as he is), and above all the priceless Mr. Micawber, would suffice to keep twenty books alive.

But this book, though by no means Dickens' Corunna or even his Malplaquet, was certainly the climax of his career, and no impartial and competent critic could ever give him the same praise again. In two long stories, *Bleak House* and *Little Dorrit*, and in a shorter one, *Hard Times*, which appeared between 1852 and 1857, the mania of " purpose " and the blemish of mechanical mannerism appeared to a far worse degree than previously, though in the first named at any rate there were numerous consolations of the old kind. The *Tale of Two Cities* (1859) has been more differently judged than any other of his works; some extolling it as a great romance, if not quite a great historical novel, while others see in it little more than mixed mannerism and melodrama. Something of the same difference prevails about *Great Expectations* (1860–61), the parties as a rule changing sides, and those who dislike the *Tale of Two Cities* rejoicing in *Great Expectations*, Dickens' closest attempt at real modern life (with a fantastic admixture of course), and in its heroine, Estella, his almost sole creation of a live girl. *Our Mutual Friend* (1864–65), though not a return to the great days, brought these parties somewhat together again, thanks to the Doll's Dressmaker and Rogue Riderhood. And then, for it is impossible to found any sound critical judgment on the fragment of *Edwin Drood*, the building of the most extraordinary monument of the fantastic in literature ceased abruptly.

That exactly the same fate befell the great successor, rival, and foil of Dickens in novel writing during the middle of the century was due to no metaphysical aid but to the simple and prosaic fact that at the time publication in parts, independently or in perodicals, was the usual method. Although the life of William Makepeace Thackeray was as little eventful as Dickens' own, their origin and circumstances were as different as their work. Dickens, as has been said, was born in distinctly the lower section of the middle class, and had, if any education, a very irregular one. Thackeray, who was born at Calcutta in 1811, belonged to a good family, regularly connected with English public schools and universities, inherited a small but comfortable fortune, and was himself educated at the Charterhouse and at Trinity College, Cambridge, though he took no degree. Unsuccessful as an artist (it is one of the chief pieces of literary anecdote of our times that he offered himself fruitlessly to Dickens as an illustrator), and having by imprudence or accident lost his private means, he began to write, especially in the then new and audacious *Fraser's Magazine*. For this, for other periodicals, and for *Punch* later, he performed a vast amount of miscellaneous work, part only of which, even with the considerable addition made some ten years ago, has ever been enshrined in his collected works. It is all very remarkable, and can easily be seen now to be quite different from any other work of the time (the later thirties) ; but it is very unequal and distinctly uncertain in touch. These qualities or defects also appear in his first publications in volume — the *Paris* (1840) and *Irish* (1843) *Sketch Books*, and the novels of *Catherine* and *Barry Lyndon*. The *Punch* work (which included the famous *Book of Snobs* and the admirable attempts in misspelling on the model of Swift and Smollett known as the *Memoirs of Mr. Yellowplush*, with much else) marked a distinct advance in firmness of handling and raciness of humour ; while the author, who, though now a very poor man, had access to the best society, was constantly adding to his stock of observation as well as to his literary practice. It was not, however, till 1846, when he began *Vanity Fair*, that any very large number of persons began to understand what a star had risen in English letters; nor can even *Vanity Fair* be said to have had any enormous popularity, though its author's powers were shown in a different way during its publication in parts by the appearance of a third sketch book, the *Journey from Cornhill to Grand Cairo*, more perfect than either of its forerunners, and by divers extremely brilliant Christmas books. *Vanity Fair* was succeeded in 1849 (for Thackeray, a man fond of society and a little indolent, was fortunately never a very rapid writer) by *Pendennis*, which holds as autobiography, though not perhaps in creative excellence, the same place among his works as *Copperfield* does among those of Dickens. Several slighter things accompanied or followed this, Thackeray showing himself at once an admirable lecturer, and an admirable though not always quite judicial critic, in a series of discourses afterwards published as a volume on *The English Humourists of the Eighteenth Century*. But it was not till 1852 that the marvellous historical novel of *Esmond* — the greatest book in its own special kind ever written — appeared, and showed at once the fashion in which the author had assimilated the Queen Anne period and his grasp of character and story. He returned to modern times in *The Newcomes* (1853-55), which some put at the head of his work as a contemporary painter of manners. After this he had seven years of life which were well filled. He followed up *Esmond* with *The Virginians* (1857-58), a novel of the third quarter of the eighteenth century, which has not been generally rated high, but which contains some of his very best things ; he went to America and lectured on *The Four Georges* (lectures again brilliant in their kind) ; he became (1860) editor of the *Cornhill Magazine* and wrote in it two stories, *Lovel the Widower* and *Philip;* while he struck out a new line in a certain series of contributions called *The Roundabout Papers*, some of which were among his very last, and nearly all of them among his most characteristic and perfect work. He had begun yet another novel, *Denis Duval*, which was to deal with the last quarter of the century he knew so well; but he died suddenly two days before Christmas 1863, leaving it a mere fragment. He had unsuccessfully attempted play writing in *The Wolves and the Lamb*, an earlier and dramatic version of *Lovel the Widower*. And during almost his whole literary career he had been a sparing but an exquisite writer of a peculiar kind of verse, half serious half comic, which is scarcely inferior in excellence to his best prose. " The Ballad of Bouillabaisse " and " The Age of Wisdom," to take only two examples, are unmatched in their presentation of pathos that always keeps clear of the maudlin, and is wide-eyed if not dry-eyed in view of all sides of life; while such things as " Lyra Hibernica " and " The Ballads of Policeman X " have never been surpassed as verse examples of pure, broad, roaring farce that still retains a certain reserve and well-bred scholarship of tone.

But his verse, however charming and unique, could never have given him the exalted and massive pedestal which his prose writings, and especially his novels, provide. Even without the novels, as without the verse, he would still occupy a high place among English writers for the sake of his singular and delightful style, and for the attitude both to life and to letters, corresponding with that style, which his essays and miscellanies exhibit. This style is not by any means free from minor blemishes, though it discarded many of these as time went on. But it has an extraordinary vivacity; a manner entirely its own, which yet seldom or never approaches mannerism; a quality of humour for which no word would be so fit as the old-fashioned " archness," if that had not been so hopelessly degraded before even the present century opened; at need, an unsurpassed pathos which never by any chance or exception succumbs to the demon of the gushing or maudlin; a flexibility and facility of adaptation to almost all (not quite all) subjects which is hard to parallel.

And this style reflects with more than common exactness, even in these minor works, the attitude above spoken of, which is not less unique and not less inestimable than the style itself. Towards some of the "great subjects" Thackeray indeed adopts not quite a Shakespearian silence, but a slightly uneasy respect. Never irreligious as he was, there was something in him of his own beloved eighteenth century's dislike and discomfort in face of religious dogma and religious enthusiasm; he had no metaphysical head; his politics (he once stood for Parliament) were a little childish. It was his, in short, not so much to argue as to observe, to feel, to laugh with no unkindness but with infinite comprehension, to enjoy, to suffer. Of all the innumerable cants that ever were canted, the cant about Thackeray's "cynicism" was the silliest and the most erroneous. He knew the weakness of man, and laughed at it as the wise knows and laughs, "knowing also," as the poet says, "that he himself must die." But he did not even despise this weakness, much less is he harsh to it. On the contrary, he is milder not only than Swift, but even than Addison or Miss Austen, and he is never wroth with human nature save when it is not only weak but base.

All these good gifts and others, such as incomparable power of presenting scene and personage to the necessary extent and with telling detail, appear in his novels, with the addition of a greater gift than any of them — the gift most indispensable of all others to the novelist — the gift of creating and immortalising character. Of mere story, of mere plot, Thackeray was not a great master; and he has made himself appear a less great master than he was by his fancy for interlarding his narratives with long addresses to the reader, and by his other fancy for extending them over very great spaces of time. The unities are no doubt in fiction, if not in drama, something of a caricature; but it is seldom possible to neglect them to the extent of years and decades without paying the penalty; and Thackeray is not of those who have evaded payment. But in the creation of living character he stands simply alone among novelists: above even Fielding, though his characters may have something less of massiveness; much above Scott, whose consummate successes are accompanied by not a few failures;

and out of sight of almost every one else except Miss Austen, whose world is different, and, as a world, somewhat less of flesh and blood. In *Vanity Fair* he is still in this respect not quite at his acme ; and the magnificent character of Becky Sharp (the attempt to rival whom by her almost exact contemporary, Valerie Marneffe, is a singular critical error), supported as it is by the lesser successes of Jos and Rawdon, of George Osborne and Lord Steyne, does not find itself, save now and then, especially in the crowning scene of the scandal in Curzon Street, completely parted or completely put in scene. And so at the other end of the list, from *The Virginians*, fine as much of that is, onwards, it is permissible, without unreason or want of generosity, to discern a slight, a very slight, flagging, not in the quality or kind of the power, but in the vigour and freshness with which it is applied. But in *Pendennis*, in *Esmond*, and in *The Newcomes*, it appears as it does nowhere else in English, or in any literature. It is not so much the holding up of the mirror to life as the presentation of life itself. Although the figures, the scheme of thought and sentiment and sense, differ from what we find in Shakespeare by the whole difference between poetry and prose, there is, on the lower level, a positive gain in vividness by the absence of the restraints and conventions of the drama and the measured line. Every act, every scene, every person in these three books is real with a reality which has been idealised just up to and not beyond the necessities of literature. It does not matter what the acts, the scenes, the personages may be. Whether we are at the height of romantic passion with Esmond's devotion to Beatrix, and his transactions with the duke and the prince over diamonds and title deeds ; whether the note is that of the simplest human pathos, as in Colonel Newcome's death-bed ; whether we are indulged with society at Baymouth and Oxbridge ; whether we take part in Marlborough's campaigns or assist at the Back Kitchen — we are in the House of Life, a mansion not too frequently opened to us by the writers of prose fiction. It was impossible that Thackeray should live long or write very many novels when he had once found his way. The lesson of the greatest imagination of his great contemporary and master settles that. Not the "Peau de Chagrin" itself could have enabled any man to produce a long succession of novels such as *Vanity Fair* and *Esmond*.

During the time before the century reached its middle, in which Bulwer and Dickens were the most popular of novelists, while Thackeray was slowly making his way to the place that was properly his, the demand for novels, thoroughly implanted in the public by the success of Scott, was constantly met by work of all sorts, very little of which survives except in country circulating libraries and on the shelves of houses the ownership of which has not changed hands for some considerable time. Very little of it, indeed, much deserved to survive. Lockhart, an exceedingly judicious critic, thought it necessary not long after the appearance of *Vanity Fair* to apologise for the apparent extravagance of the praise which he had given to his friend Theodore Hook by observing that, except Dickens, there was no novelist of the first class between the death of Scott and the rise of Thackeray himself. But about the time of that rise, and for a good many years after it, what may be called the third generation of the novelists of the century began to make its appearance, and, as has been partly observed above, to devote itself to a somewhat different description of work, which will be noticed in a future chapter.

The historical novel, though some of its very best representatives were still to make their appearance, ceased to occupy the first place in popular esteem ; and the later varieties of the novel of more or less humorous adventure, whether in the rather commonplace form of Hook or in the highly individual and eccentric form of Dickens, also ceased to be much cultivated, save by Dickens himself and his direct imitators. The vogue set in for a novel of more or less ordinary life of the upper middle class, and this vogue lasted during the whole of the third quarter, if not of the second half, of the century, though about 1870 the historical novel revived, and, after some years of uncertain popular taste, seems in the last decade to have acquired almost as great popularity (with its companion study of purely fantastic adventure) as ever. Yet we must, before passing to other departments, and interrupting the account of fiction, notice not a few other writers of the time previous to 1850.

The descent, in purely literary merit, from Dickens and Thackeray, and perhaps from Bulwer, to some of those who must now be mentioned, is great. Yet the chief naval and the chief military novelist of England need surely not appear by allowance; and if affection and frequent reading count for any-thing, it is not certain that some technically much greater names might not shine with lesser lustre than those of Marryat and Lever. Frederick Marryat, the elder of the pair, was born in 1792, early enough to see a good deal of service in the later years of the Great War, partly under the brilliant if eccentric leadership of Lord Cochrane. His promotion was fairly rapid : he became a commander in 1815, and afterwards distinguished himself as a post captain in the Burmese War, being made a C.B. in 1825. But the increasing dearth of active service was not suitable to a character like that of Marryat, who, moreover, was not likely to be popular with " My Lords "; and his discovery of a faculty for writing opened up to him, both as novelist and magazine editor, a very busy and profitable literary career, which lasted from 1830 to 1848, when he died. Marryat's works, which are very numerous (the best being perhaps *Peter Simple, Mr. Midshipman Easy*, and *Jacob Faithful*, though there is hardly one that has not special adherents), resemble Smollett's more than those of any other writer, not merely in their sea-scenes, but in general scheme and character. Some of Smollett's faults, too, which are not necessarily connected with the sea — a certain ferocity, an over-fondness for practical jokes, and the like — appear in Marryat, who is, moreover, a rather careless and incorrect writer, and liable to fits both of extravagance and of dulness. But the spirit and humour of the best of his books throughout, and the best parts of the others, are unmistakable and unsurpassed. Nor should it be forgotten that he had a rough but racy gift of verse, the best, though by no means the only good example of which is the piece beginning, "The Captain stood on the carronade."

The range of Charles Lever, who was born in 1806, was as much wider than Marryat's as his life was longer and his experience (though in a purely literary view oddly similar) more varied. He was educated at Trinity College, Dublin, and after some sojourn both on the Continent and in America became (1837) physician to the British Embassy at Brussels. At this time the Continent was crowded with veterans, English and other, of the Great War ; while Lever's Irish youth had filled him with stories of the last generation of madcap Irish squires and squireens. He combined the two in a series of novels of wonderful *verve* and spirit, first of a military character, the chief of which were *Harry Lorrequer, Charles O'Malley* (his masterpiece), and *Tom Burke of Ours*. He had, after no long tenure of the Brussels appointment, become (1842) editor of the *Dublin University Magazine,* where for many years his books appeared. After a time, when his stores of military anecdote were falling low and the public taste had changed, he substituted novels partly of Irish partly of Continental bearing (*Roland Cashel, The Knight of Gwynne,* and many others) ; while in the early days of Dickens' *All the Year Round* he adventured a singular piece entitled *A Day's Ride, a Life's Romance,* which the public did not relish, but which was much to the taste of some good judges. He had by this time gone to Florence, became Vice-Consul at Spezzia in 1852, whence, in 1867, he was transferred as British Consul to Trieste, and died there in 1872.

For some years before his death he had been industrious in a third and again different kind of novel, not merely more thoughtful and less "rollicking," but adjusted much more closely to actual life and character. Indeed Lever at different times of his life manifested almost all the gifts which the novelist requires, though unfortunately he never quite managed to exhibit them all together. His earlier works, amusing as they are and full of dash and a certain kind of life, sin not only by superficiality but by a reckless disregard of the simplest requirements of story-telling, of the most rudimentary attention to chronology, probability, and general keeping. His later, vastly amended in this respect, and exhibiting, moreover, a deeper comprehension of human character as distinguished from mere outward "humours," almost necessarily present the blunted and blurred strokes which come from the loss of youth and the frequent repetition of literary production. Indeed Lever, with Bulwer, was the first to exemplify the evil effects of the great demand for novels, and the facilities for producing them given by the spread of periodicals.

To descend to the third, or even the lower second class in fiction is almost more dangerous here than a similar laxity in any other department; and we can no more admit Lord John Russell because he wrote a story called *The Nun of Arrouca*, than we can exhume any equally forgotten production of writers less known in non-literary respects. It can hardly, however, be improper to mention in connection with Marryat, the greatest of them all, some other members of the interesting school of naval writers who not unnaturally arose after the peace had turned large numbers of officers adrift, and the rise of the demand for essays, novels, and miscellaneous articles had offered temptation to writing. The chief of these were, in order of rising excellence, Captains Glascock, Chamier, and Basil Hall, and Michael Scott, a civilian, but by far the greatest writer of the four. Glascock, an officer of distinction, was the author of the *Naval Sketch Book*, a curious olla-podrida of "galley" stories, criticisms on naval books, and miscellanies, which appeared in 1826. It is not very well written, and in parts very dull, but provides some genuine things. Chamier, who was born in 1796 and did not die till 1870, was a post captain and a direct imitator of Marryat, as also was Captain Howard, Marryat's sub-editor for a time on the *Metropolitan*, and the part author with him of some books which have caused trouble to bibliographers. Chamier's books — *Ben Brace, The Arethusa, Tom Bowling*, etc. — are better than Howard's *Rattlin the Reefer* (commonly ascribed to Marryat), *Jack Ashton*, and others, but neither can be called a master.

Captain Basil Hall, who was born of a good Scotch family at Edinburgh in 1788 and died at Haslar Hospital in 1844, was a better writer than either of these three; but he dealt in travels, not novels, and appears here as a sort of honorary member of the class. His *Travels in America* was one of the books which, in the second quarter of the century, rightly or wrongly, excited American wrath against Englishmen; but his last book, *Fragments of Voyages and Travels*, was his most popular and perhaps his best. Captain Basil Hall was a very amiable person, and though perhaps a little flimsy as a writer, is yet certainly not to be spoken of with harshness.

A very much stronger talent than any of these was Michael Scott, who was born in Glasgow in 1789 and died in 1835, having passed the end of his boyhood and the beginning of his manhood in Jamaica. He employed his experiences in composing for *Blackwood's Magazine*, and afterwards reducing to book shape, the admirable miscellanies in fiction entitled *Tom Cringle's Log* and *The Cruise of the Midge*, which contain some of the best fighting, fun, tropical scenery, and description generally, to be found outside the greatest masters. Very little is known of Scott, and he wrote nothing else.

One unique figure remains to be noticed among novelists of the first half of the century, though as a matter of fact his last novel was not published till within twenty years of its close. Benjamin Disraeli, Earl of Beaconsfield, belongs, as a special person, to another story than this. But this would be very incomplete without him and his novels. They were naturally written for the most part before, in 1852, he was called to the leadership of the House of Commons, but in two vacations of office later he added to them *Lothair* (1870) and *Endymion* (1881). It is, however, in his earlier work that his chief virtue is to be found. It is especially in its first division, — the stories of *Vivian Grey, The Young Duke, Contarini Fleming, Alroy, Venetia*, and *Henrietta Temple*, — published between 1827 and 1837. They are more like Bulwer's than like anybody else's work, but *Vivian Grey* appeared

in the same year with *Falkland* and before *Pelham*. Later novels
— *Coningsby* (1844), *Sybil* (1845), and *Tancred* (1847) — are more
directly political; while certain smaller and chiefly early tales —
Ixion, The Infernal Marriage, Popanilla, etc. — are pure fantasy
pieces with a satirical intent, and the first of them is, with perhaps
Bedford's *Vathek* as a companion, the most brilliant thing of its
kind in English. In these more particularly, but in all more or
less, a strong Voltairian influence is perceptible; but on the
whole the set of books may be said to be like nothing else. They
have grave faults, being sometimes tawdry in phrase and imagery,
sometimes too personal, frequently a little unreal, and scarcely
ever finally and completely adjusted to the language in which and
the people of whom they are written. Yet the attraction of them is
singular; and good judges, differing very widely in political and
literary tastes, have found themselves at one as to the strange
way in which the reader comes back to them as he advances in
life, and as to the marvellous cleverness which they display. Let
it be added that *Henrietta Temple*, a mere and sheer love story
written in a dangerous style of sentimentalism, is one of the most
effective things of its kind in English, and holds its ground despite
all drawbacks of fashion in speech and manners, which never tell
more heavily than in the case of a book of the kind; while in
Venetia the story of Byron is handled with remarkable closeness,
and yet in good taste.

Two other novelists belonging to the first half of the century,
and standing even further out of the general current than did
Disraeli, both of them also possessing greater purely literary genius
than his, must also be mentioned here. Thomas Love Peacock,
the elder of them, born a long way within the eighteenth century
(in 1785), passed a studious though irregularly educated youth
and an idle early manhood, but at a little more than thirty (1817)
produced, after some verse, the curious little satirical romance of
Headlong Hall. This he followed up with others — *Melincourt,
Nightmare Abbey, Maid Marian, The Misfortunes of Elphin*, and
Crotchet Castle — at no great intervals until 1830, after which,

M

having in the meantime been appointed to a valuable and important office under the East India Company, he published no other book for thirty years. Then in 1860 he put forth *Gryll Grange*, and some five years later died, a very old man, in 1866. Peacock at all times was a writer of verse, and the songs which diversify his novels are among their most delightful features; but his more ambitious poetical efforts, which date from his earlier years, *The Genius of the Thames* and *Rhododaphne*, are not of much mark. The novels themselves, however, have a singular relish, and are written in a style always piquant and attractive and latterly quite admirable. They may all be described as belonging to the fantastic-satirical order of which the French tale-tellers (instigated, however, by an Englishman, Anthony Hamilton) had set the example during the previous century. Social, political, economic, and other fads and crazes are all touched in them; but this satire is combined with a strictly realistic presentation of character, and, except in the romances of *Maid Marian* and *Elphin*, with actual modern manners. Peacock's satire is always very sharp, and in his earlier books a little rough as well; but as he went on he acquired urbanity without losing point, and became one of the most consummate practitioners of Lucianic humour adjusted to the English scheme and taste. More than thirty years after date *Gryll Grange* is not obsolete even as a picture of manners; while *Crotchet Castle*, obsolete in a few externals, is as fresh as ever in substance, owing to its close grasp of essential humanity. In verse Peacock was the last, and one of the best, of the masters of the English drinking-song; and some of his examples are unmatched for their mixture of joviality, taste, sense, and wit.

George Borrow, who was eighteen years Peacock's junior, and outlived him by fifteen, was a curious counterpart-analogue to him. Like Peacock, he was irregularly educated, and yet a wide and deep student; but, unlike Peacock, he devoted himself not so much to the ancient as to the more out-of-the-way modern tongues, and became a proficient not merely in Welsh, the Scandinavian tongues, Russian, Spanish, and other literary languages, but in Romany or Gipsy, having associated much with the "folk of Egypt" during his youth. After some very imperfectly known youthful experiences, which formed at least the basis of his later novels, *Lavengro* (1851) and *The Romany Rye* (1857), he received an appointment as colporteur to the Bible Society, first in Russia, then in Spain; and his adventures in the latter country formed the basis of a study called *The Gipsies of Spain* (1840), which has much, and a volume of travel and autobiography, *The Bible in Spain* (1843), which has unique, interest. Returning home, he married a wife with some money, and spent the remainder of a long life in his native county of Norfolk, producing, besides the books just named, *Wild Wales* (1862), and dying in 1881. There is, in fact, not very much difference between Borrow's novels and his travel-books. The former had at least some autobiographic foundation, and the latter invest actual occurrences with the most singular flavour of romance. For his mere style Borrow was a little indebted to Cobbett, though he coloured Cobbett's somewhat drab canvas with the most brilliant fantastic hues. But his attitude, his main literary quality, is quite unique. It might be called, without too much affectation, an adjustment of the picaresque novel to dreamland, retaining frequent touches of solid and everyday fact. Peacock's style has found a good many, though no very successful, imitators; Borrow's is quite inimitable.

Harriet Martineau, one of the numerous writers, of both sexes, whom the polygraphic habits of this century make it hard to "class," was born at Norwich in 1802, and belonged to one of the families that made up the remarkable literary society which distinguished that city at the end of the last century and the beginning of this. She began as a religious writer according to the Unitarian persuasion; she ended as a tolerably active opponent of religion. But she found her chief vocation (before, as she did in her middle and later days, becoming a regular journalist) in writing stories on political economy, a proceeding doubtless determined by the previous exercises in didactic story-telling of Miss Edge-worth and Mrs. Marcet. These *Illustrations of Political Economg* (1832) exactly hit the taste of their time and were very popular. Her less adulterated children's books (of which the best perhaps is *Feats on the Fiord*) and her novel *Deerbrook* (1839), owing much to Miss Edgeworth in conception, display a good faculty of narrative, and she did a great deal of miscellaneous work. As she became less religious she became more superstitious, and indulged in curious crazes. She lived latterly at the Lakes, and died on 27th June 1876. Harriet Martineau was the object of rather absurd obloquy from Conservative critics as an advanced woman in her day, and of still more absurd eulogy by Liberal sympathisers both in that day and since. Personally she seems to have been amiable and estimable enough. Intellectually she had no genius; but she had a good deal of the versatile talent and craftsmanship for which the literary conditions of this century have produced unusual stimulus and a fair reward.

There was something (though not so much as has been repre-sented) of the masculine element about Miss Martineau; a con-temporary Miss M. was delightfully feminine. Mary Russell Mit-ford, born at Alresford, the town of Wither, on 16th December 1786, was the daughter of a doctor and a rascal, who, when she was a child, had the incredible meanness to squander twenty thou-sand pounds which she won in a lottery, and later the constant courage to live on her earnings. She published poems as early as 1810; then wrote plays which were acted with some success; and later, gravitating to the *London Magazine*, wrote for it essays only second to those of Elia — the delightful papers collectively called *Our Village*, and not completed till long after the death of the *London* in 1832. The scenery of these is derived from the banks of the Loddon, for the neighbourhood of Reading was in various places her home, and she died at Swallowfield on 10th January 1855. Latterly she had a civil-list pension; but, on the whole, she supported herself and her parents by writing. Not much, if anything, of her work is likely to survive except *Our*

Village ; but this is charming, and seems, from the published *Life* of her and the numerous references in contemporary biography, to express very happily the character and genius of its author — curiously sunny, healthy, and cheerful, not in the least namby-pamby, and coinciding with a faculty of artistic presentation of observed results, not very imaginative but wonderfully pleasing.

To these authors and books, others of more or less " single-speech " fame might be added : the vivid and accurate Persian tale of *Hajji Baba* by James Morier, the *Anastatius* of Thomas Hope, excellently written and once very much admired, the fashionable *Granby* and *Tremaine* of Lister, the famous *Frankenstein* of Mrs. Shelley, are examples.   But even these, and much more other things not so good as they, compose in regard to the scheme of such a book as this the *numerus,* the crowd, which, out of no disrespect, but for obvious and imperative reasons, must be not so much neglected as omitted.   All classes of literature contribute to this, but, with the exception of mere compilations and books in science or art which are outgrown, none so much as prose fiction.   The safest of life (except poetry) of all literary kinds when it is first rate, it is the most certain of death when it is not ; and it pays for the popularity which it often receives to-day by the oblivion of an unending morrow.

CHAPTER IV

THE DEVELOPMENT OF PERIODICALS

PERHAPS there is no single feature of the English literary history of the nineteenth century, not even the enormous popularisation and multiplication of the novel, which is so distinctive and characteristic as the development in it of periodical literature. For this did not, as the extension of novel writing did, concern a single department only. The periodical — it may almost for short-ness' sake be said the newspaper — not only became infinitely multiplied, but it gradually absorbed almost every department, or a share of almost every department, into itself. Very large numbers of the best as well as of the worst novels themselves have originally appeared in periodicals; not a very small pro-portion of the most noteworthy nineteenth century poetry has had the same origin; it may almost be said that all the best work in essay, whether critical, meditative, or miscellaneous, has thus been ushered into the world. Even the severer and more academic divisions of history, philosophy, theology, and their sisters, have condescended to avail themselves of this means of obtaining a public audience; and though there is still a certain conventional decency in apologising for reprints from periodicals, it is quite certain that, had such reprints not taken place, more than half the most valuable books of the age in some departments, and a considerable minority of the most valuable in others, would never have appeared as books at all.

The first division of our time, the last twenty years of the eighteenth century, though it witnessed a very great development of the mere newspaper, with which we have little to do, did not see very much of this actual " development of periodical literature" which concerns us. These twenty years saw the last attempts in the line of the Addisonian essay; they saw the beginnings of some modern newspapers which exist at the present day; they beheld in the *Anti-Jacobin* perhaps the most brilliant specimen of political persiflage in newspaper form that had or has ever been seen. But they did not see — though they saw some fumbling attempts at it — anything like those strangely different but mutually complementary examples of periodical criticism which were given just after the opening of the new age by *The Edinburgh Review* (1802) and Cobbett's *Weekly Register;* and they saw nothing at all like the magazine, or combination of critical and creative matter, in which *Blackwood* was, some years later, to lead the way. At the close of the eighteenth century such magazines were in an exceedingly rudimentary state, and criticism was mainly still in the hands of the old *Monthly* and *Critical Reviews*, the respective methods of which had drawn from Johnson the odd remark that the *Critical* men, being clever, said little about their books, which the *Monthly* men, being " duller fellows," were glad to read and analyse. These Reviews and their various contemporaries had indeed from time to time enjoyed the services of men of the greatest talent, such as Smollett earlier and Southey just at the last. But, as a rule, they were in the hands of mere hacks; they paid so wretchedly that no one, unless forced by want or bitten by an amateurish desire to see himself in print, would contribute to them; they were by no means beyond suspicion of political and commercial favouritism; and their critiques were very commonly either mere summaries or scrappy " puffs" and " slatings," seldom possessing much grace of style, and scarcely ever adjusted to any scheme of artistic criticism.

This is a history of literature, not of the newspaper press, and it is necessary to proceed rather by giving account of the authors who were introduced to the public by — or who, being otherwise known, availed themselves of — this new development of periodicals. It may be sufficient to say here that the landmarks of the period, in point of the birth of papers, are, besides the two above mentioned, the starting of the *Quarterly Review* as a Tory opponent to the more and more Whiggish *Edinburgh* in 1809, of the *Examiner* as a Radical weekly in 1808, of *Blackwood's Magazine* as a Tory monthly in 1817, of the *London Magazine* about the same time, and of *Fraser* in 1830.

It was a matter of course that in the direction or on the staff of these new periodicals some of the veterans of the older system, or of the men who had at any rate already some experience in journalism, should be enlisted. Gifford, the first editor of the *Quarterly*, was in all respects a writer of the old rather than of the new age. Southey had at one time wholly, and for years partly, supported himself by writing for periodicals ; Coleridge was at different times not merely a contributor to these, but an actual daily journalist ; and so with others. But, as always happens when a really new development of literature takes place, new regiments raised themselves to carry out the new tactics, as it were, spontaneously. Many of the great names and the small mentioned in the last three chapters — perhaps indeed most of them — took the periodical shilling at one time or other in their lives. But those whom I shall now proceed to mention — William Cobbett, Francis Jeffrey, Sydney Smith, John Wilson, Charles Lamb, Leigh Hunt as a prose writer, William Hazlitt, Thomas De Quincey, John Gibson Lockhart, and some others — were, if not exactly journalists (an incorrect, but the only single designation), at any rare such frequent contributors to periodical literature of one kind or another that in some cases nothing, in most comparatively little, would be left of their work if contributions to newspapers, reviews, and magazines were to be excluded from it.

William Cobbett, not the greatest, but the most singular and original of the group, with the exception of Lamb, and as superior to Lamb in fertility and massive vigour as he was inferior to him in exquisite delicacy and finish, was the son of a very small farmer little above the labouring rank, and was born near Farnham in 1762. He was first a ploughboy, next an attorney's clerk, and then he enlisted in the 24th regiment. He served very creditably for seven or eight years, became serjeant-major, improved himself very much in education, and obtained his discharge. But, by one of the extraordinary freaks which mark his whole career, he first took it into his head to charge the officers of his regiment with malversation, and then ran away from his own charge with his newly married wife, first to France and then to America. Here he stayed till the end of the century, and here he began his news-paper experiments, keeping up in *Peter Porcupine's Journal* a vio-lent crusade against French Jacobins and American Democrats. He returned to England in June 1800, and was encouraged by the Government to set up what soon became his famous *Weekly Register* —a paper which, after being (as Cobbett's politics had been up to this time) strongly Tory, lapsed by rapid degrees into a strange kind of fantastic Radicalism shot with Tory gleams. This remained Cobbett's creed till his death. The paper was very profitable, and for some time Cobbett was able to lead something like a country gentleman's life at Botley in Hampshire. But he met with two years' imprisonment for a violent article on flogging in the army, he subsequently got into money difficulties, and in 1817 he made a second voyage to America, which was in fact a flight both from his creditors and from the risk of another Government prosecution under the Six Acts. Through all his troubles the *Register*, except for a month or two, had continued to appear ; and so it did to the last. Its proprietor, editor, and in the main author, stood for Parliament several times, and, after a trial for sedition in 1831, was at last returned for Oldham in 1832. He was not much of a success there, and died on 18th June 1835 near Guildford ; for he always clung to the marches of Surrey and Hampshire.

Some such details of Cobbett's life are necessary even in the most confined space, because they are intimately connected with his singular character and his remarkable works. These latter are enormous in bulk and of the most widely diversified character. *Peter Porcupine* fills twelve not small volumes ; the mere selections from the *Register*, which are all that has been republished of it, six very bulky ones ; with a wilderness of separate works besides— *Rural Rides*, a *History of the Reformation*, books on husbandry, gardening, and rural economy generally, some on the currency, an *English Grammar*, and dozens of others. Of these the *Rural Rides* is the most interesting in matter and the most picturesque in style, while it affords a fair panorama of its author's rugged but wonderfully varied and picturesque mind and character ; the *History of the Reformation* is the most wrong-headed and unfair ; the currency writings the most singular example of the delusion that strong prejudices and a good deal of mother-wit will enable a man to write, without any knowledge, about the most abstruse and complicated subjects ; the agricultural books and the *English Grammar* the best instances of genial humours, shrewdness, and (when crotchets do not come in too much) sound sense. But hardly anything that Cobbett writes is contemptible in form, however weak he may often be in argument, knowledge, and taste. He was the last, and he was not far below the greatest, of the line of vernacular English writers of whom Latimer in the sixteenth, Bunyan in the seventeenth, and Defoe in the eighteenth, are the other emerging personalities. To a great extent Cobbett's style was based on Swift ; but the character of his education, which was not in the very least degree academic, and still more the idiosyncrasy of his genius, imposed on it almost from the first, but with ever-increasing clearness, a manner quite different from Swift's, and, though often imitated since, never reproduced. The "Letter to Jack Harrow," the "Letter to the People of Botley," the "Letters to Old George Rose," and that to "Alexander Baring, Loan Monger," to take examples almost at random from the *Register*, are quite unlike anything before them or anything after them. The best-known parody of Cobbett, that in *Rejected Addresses*, gives rather a poor idea of his style ; exhibiting no doubt his intense egotism, his habit of half trivial divagation, and his use of strong language, but quite failing to give the immense force, the vivid clearness, and the sterling though not precisely scholarly English which characterise his good work. The best imitation to be found is in some of the anonymous pamphlets in which, in his later days, government writers replied to his powerful and mischievous political diatribes, and which in some cases, if internal evidence may be trusted, must have been by no mean hands.

Irrational as Cobbett's views were, — he would have adjusted the entire concerns of the nation with a view to the sole benefit of the agricultural interest, would have done away with the standing army, wiped out the national debt, and effected a few other trifling changes with a perfectly light heart, while in minor matters his crotchets were not only wild but simply irreconcilable with each other, — his intense if narrow earnestness, his undoubting belief in himself, and a certain geniality which could co-exist with very rough language towards his opponents, would give his books a certain attraction even if their mere style were less remarkable than it is. But it is in itself, if the most plebeian, not the least virile, nor even the least finished on its own scheme of the great styles in English. For the irony of Swift, of which, except in its very roughest and most rudimentary forms, Cobbett had no command or indeed conception, it substitutes a slogging directness nowhere else to be found equalled for combination of strength and, in the pugilistic sense, " science " ; while its powers of description, within certain limits, are amazing. Although Cobbett's newspaper was itself as much of an Ishmaelite and an outsider as its director, it is almost impossible to exaggerate the effect which it had in developing newspapers generally, by the popularity which it acquired, and the example of hammer-and-tongs treatment of political and economic subjects which it set. The faint academic far-off-ness of the eighteenth century handling, which is visible even in the much-praised *Letters of Junius*, which is visible in the very ferocity of Smollett's *Adventures of an Atom*, which put up with " Debates of the Senate of Lilliput " and so forth, has been blown away to limbo, and the newspaper (at first at some risk) takes men and measures, politics and policies, directly and in their own names, to be its province and its prey.

It is a far cry from Cobbett to the founders of the *Edinburgh Review*, who, very nearly at the same time as that at which he launched his *Register*, did for the higher and more literary kind of periodical what he was doing for the lower and vernacular kind.   I say the founders, because there is a still not quite settled dispute whether Francis Jeffrey or Sydney Smith was the actual founder of the famous "Blue and Yellow."   This dispute is not uninteresting ; because the one was as typically Scotch, with some remarkable differences from other Scotchmen, as the other was essentially English, with some points not commonly found in men of English blood.   Jeffrey, the younger of the two by a couple of years, was still a member of the remarkable band who, as has been noticed so often already, were all born in the early seventies of the eighteenth century ; and his own birthday was 23rd October 1773.   He was an Edinburgh man ; and his father, who was of a respectable though not distinguished family, held office in the Court of Session and was a strong Tory.   Jeffrey does not seem to have objected to his father's profession, though he early revolted from his politics ; and, after due study at the High School of his birthplace, and the Universities of Glasgow, Edinburgh, and Oxford (at which latter, however, he only remained a year, deriving very little benefit or pleasure from his sojourn at Queen's College), he was called to the Scottish bar.   He practised at first with very little success, and in 1798 had serious thoughts of taking up literary life in London.   But he could obtain no footing, and, returning to Edinburgh and marrying a cousin, he fell into the company of Sydney Smith, who was there with a pupil.   It seems to be admitted that the idea of a new *Review* — to be entirely free from the control or influence of publishers, to adopt an independent line of criticism (independent, but somewhat mistaken ; for the motto *Judex damnatur cum nocens absolvitur* gives a very one-sided view of the critic's office), and to be written for fair remuneration by persons of more or less distinct position, and at any rate of education — originated with Sydney Smith. He is also sometimes spoken of as the first " editor," which would appear to be a mistake. At first (the original issue was in October 1802) the review appears to have been a kind of republic ; the contributors being, besides Jeffrey and Sydney, a certain Francis Horner (who died too soon to demonstrate the complete falsity of the golden opinions entertained of him by his friends), Brougham, and some Professors of Edinburgh University. But no such plan has ever succeeded, though it has been more than once tried, and very soon accident or design showed that Jeffrey was the right man to take the command of the ship. The *Review* was not ostensibly a political one at first, and for some years Tories, the greatest of whom was Scott, wrote in it. But the majority of the contributors were Whigs, and the whole cast of the periodical became more and more of that complexion, till at last, private matters helping public, a formidable secession took place, and the *Quarterly* was founded.

From time to time students of literature turn to the early numbers of these famous periodicals, of the *Edinburgh* especially, with the result, usually of a certain, sometimes of a considerable, disappointment. With the exception of a few things already known from their inclusion in their authors' collected works, the material as a whole is apt to seem anything but extraordinarily good ; and some wonder is often expressed at the effect which it originally had. This arises from insufficient attention to a few obvious, but for that very reason easily neglected, truths. The inquirers as a rule have in their minds much more what has followed than what has gone before ; and they contrast the early numbers of the *Edinburgh*, not with its jejune forerunners, but with such matured instances as Macaulay's later essays ; the early numbers of the *Quarterly*, not with the early numbers of the *Edinburgh*, but with their own successors. Again it is apt to be forgotten that the characteristics of joint-stock periodical-writing make as much for general inequality as for occasional goodness. That which is written by many hands will seldom be as bad, but can never be as good, as that which is written by one ; that which takes its texts and starting-points from suggested matters of the moment will generally escape the occasional dulness, but can rarely attain the occasional excellence, of the meditated and original sprout of an individual brain.

The *Edinburgh* in its early years was undoubtedly surpassed by itself later and by its rivals ; but it was a far greater advance upon anything that had gone before it. It had the refreshing audacity, the fly-at-all character of youth and of intellectual opposition to established ideas ; it was, if even from the first not free from partisanship, at any rate not chargeable with the dull venal unfairness of the mere bookseller's hack who attacks Mr. Bungay's books because he is employed by Mr. Bacon, or *vice versa*. And it had a very remarkable staff, comprising the learning and trained intelligence of men like Leslie and Playfair, the unrivalled wit of Sydney Smith, the restless energy and occasional genius of Brougham, the solid profundity of Horner, the wide reading and always generous temper of Scott, and other good qualities of others, besides the talents of its editor Jeffrey himself.

Of these talents there is no doubt, though they were initially somewhat limited and not seldom misdirected afterwards. Jeffrey's entire energies were absorbed by the *Review* between its foundation and his resignation of the editorship after nearly thirty years' tenure, soon after which, his party at last coming into power, he was rewarded first by the Lord Advocateship and then by a seat on the Bench. He made a very fair judge, and held the post almost till his death in 1850. But his life, for the purposes of literature, is practically comprised between 1802 and 1829, during which he was far more than titulary the guiding spirit of the *Review*. Recently, or at any rate until quite recently (for there has been some reaction in the very latest days), the conception of an editor has been of one who writes not very much, and, though choosing his contributors with the best care he can give, does not

interfere very much with them when they are chosen. This was
very far from being the Jeffreyan ideal. He wrote a great deal,
—often in the earlier years as many as half a dozen articles in a
number,—and he "doctored" his contributors' articles (except in
the case of persons like Sydney Smith, who were of too unconquerable idiosyncrasy and too valuable) with the utmost freedom. At
the present day, however, his management of the *Review* is less
interesting than his own work, which he himself in his later years
collected and selected in an ample definitive edition. It is
exceedingly interesting, and for a good many years past it has
been distinctly undervalued ; the common, though very uncritical,
mistake having been made of asking, not whether Jeffrey made a
good fight for his own conclusions from his own premises, but
whether he approved or disapproved authors whom we now consider great. From this latter point of view he has no doubt small
chance. He began by snubbing Byron, and did not change his
tone till politics and circumstances combined made the change
obligatory; he pooh-poohed and belittled his own contributor
and personal friend Scott ; he pursued Wordsworth with equal
relentlessness and ill-success. And these three great examples
might be reinforced with whole regiments of smaller ones. A
more serious fault perhaps was the tone which he, more than any
one else, impressed on the *Review*, and which its very motto
expressed, as though an author necessarily came before the critic
with a rope about his neck, and was only entitled to be exempted
from being strung up *speciali gratia*. This notion, as presumptuous
as it is foolish, is not extinct yet, and has done a great deal of
harm to criticism, both by prejudicing those who are not critical
against critics, and by perverting and twisting the critic's own
notion of his province and duty.

Nevertheless, Jeffrey had great merits. His literary standpoint was a little unfortunate. Up to a certain extent he had
thoroughly sympathised with the Romantic movement, and he
never was an advocate for the Augustan period in English.
But either some curiosity of idiosyncrasy, or the fact that Scott

and the Lake Poets were all in different ways pillars of Toryism, set him against his own Romantic contemporaries in a very strange fashion. Still, in some ways he was a very great critic. His faculty of summarising a period of literature has rarely been equalled, and perhaps never surpassed; he had, when prejudice of some sort did not blind him, an extraordinary faculty of picking out the best passages in a book; and, above all, he arranged his critical judgments on something like a regular and co-ordinated system. Even his prejudices and injustices were systematic: they were linked to each other by arguments which might sometimes be questionable, but which were always arguments. And though, even when, as in the cases of Keats and Shelley, his extra-literary bias was not present to induce him wrong, he showed a deplorable insensibility to the finer strokes of poetry, he was in general, and taking literature all round, as considerable a critic as we have had in English.

Sydney Smith was a curious contrast to Jeffrey in almost every respect except in politics, and even there the resemblance was rather fortuitous than essential. The second son of a man of eccentric character and some means, he was born in 1771, was sent to Winchester, and proceeded thence to New College, Oxford, where he became Fellow and resided for a considerable time; but unusually little is recorded either of his school or of his college days. He took orders and was appointed to a curacy on Salisbury Plain, where the squire of the parish took a fancy to him and made him tutor to his eldest son. Tutor and pupil went to Edinburgh, just then in great vogue as an educational centre, in 1798; and there Sydney, besides doing clerical duty, stumbled upon his vocation as reviewer. He abode in the Scottish capital for about five years, during which he married, and then removed to London, where he again did duty of various kinds, lectured on Moral Philosophy, and, when the Grenville administration came in, received a fairly valuable Yorkshire living, that of Foston. Here, after a time, he had, owing to new legislation about clerical absentees, to take up his residence, which

involved building a parsonage.   He had repaid his Whig patrons
by writing the exceedingly brilliant and passably scurrilous *Letters
of Peter Plymley on Catholic Emancipation*, and he reviewed steadily
for the *Edinburgh*, as indeed he did during almost the whole editorship of Jeffrey.   At last Lord Lyndhurst, a Tory, gave him a stall
at Bristol, and he was able to exchange Foston for Combe-Florey,
in the more genial latitude of Somerset.   The rest of his life was
fortunate in worldly ways ; for the Reform Ministry, though they
would not give him a bishopric, gave him a canonry at St. Paul's,
and divers legacies and successions made him relatively a rich
man.   He died five years before Jeffrey, in February 1845.

Besides the differences of their Scotch and English nationality
and education, the contrast between the two friends and founders
of the " Blue and Yellow " was curiously pervading.   Jeffrey, for all
his supposed critical savagery, was a sentimentalist, and had the
keenest love of literature as literature ; Sydney cared very little for
books as books, and had not a grain of sentiment in his composition.   Jeffrey had little wit and no humour ; Smith abounded in
both, and was one of the very wittiest of Englishmen.   Even in
his *Review* articles he constantly shocked his more solemn and
pedagogic editor by the stream of banter which he poured not
merely upon Tories and High Churchmen, but on Methodists and
Non-conformists ; his letters are full of the most untiring and
to this day the most sparkling pleasantry ; and his two chief works
outside his reviews, the earlier *Peter Plymley's Letters* and the later
Letters to Archdeacon Singleton (written when the author's early
Whiggism had crystallised into something different, and when he
was stoutly resisting the attempts of the reformed government to
meddle with cathedral establishments), rank among the capital
light pamphlets of the world, in company with those of Pascal and
Swift and Courier.   The too few remnants of his abundant conversation preserve faint sparks of the blaze of impromptu fun for
which in his day he was almost more famous than as a writer.
Sydney Smith had below the surface of wit a very solid substratum
of good sense and good feeling ; but his literary appeal consisted

N

almost wholly in his shrewd pleasantry, which, as it has been observed, might with even more appropriateness than Coleridge said it of Fuller, have been said to be "the stuff and substance of his intellectual nature." This wit was scarcely ever in writing — it seems to have been sometimes in conversation — forced or trivial; it was most ingeniously adjusted to the purpose of the moment, whether that purpose was a political argument, a light summary of a book of travels, or a mere gossiping letter to a friend; and it had a quality of its own which could only be displayed by extensive and elaborate citation. But if it be possible to put the finger on a single note, it is one distinguishing Sydney Smith widely from Fuller himself, bringing him a little nearer to Voltaire, and, save for the want of certain earnestness, nearer still to Swift — the perfect facility of his jokes, and the casual, easy man-of-the-worldliness with which he sets them before the reader and passes on. Amid the vigorous but slightly ponderous manners of the other early contributors to the *Review*, this must have been of inestimable value; but it is a higher credit to Sydney Smith that it does not lose its charm when collected together and set by itself, as the more extravagant and rollicking kinds of periodical humour are wont to do. It was probably his want of serious preoccupations of any kind (for his politics were merely an accident; he was, though a sincere Christian, no enthusiast in religion; and he had few special interests, though he had an honest general enjoyment of life) which enabled Sydney Smith so to perfect a quality, or set of qualities, which, as a rule, is more valuable as an occasional set-off than as the staple and solid of a man's literary fare and ware. If so, he points much the same general moral as Cobbett, though in a way as different as possible. But in any case he was a very delightful person, an ornament of English literature, such as few other literatures possess, in his invariable abstinence from unworthy means of raising a laugh, and, among the group of founders of the new periodical, the representative of one of its most important constituents — polished *persiflage*.

The other contributors of the first generation to the *Edinburgh Review* do not require much notice here; for Brougham was not really a man of letters, and belongs to political and social, not to literary history, while Mackintosh, though no one would contest his claims, will be better noticed under the head of philosophy. Nor do many of the first staff of the *Edinburgh's* great rival, the *Quarterly*, require notice; for Gifford, Canning, Ellis, Scott, Southey have all been noticed under other heads.

Two, however, not of the absolutely first rank, may be mentioned here more conveniently than anywhere else — Sir John Barrow and Isaac Disraeli. The former had a rather remarkable career; for he was born, in 1764, quite of the lower rank, and was successively a clerk in a workshop, a sailor, a teacher of mathematics, and secretary to Macartney on his famous embassy to China. After following the same patron to South Africa, Barrow, at the age of forty, became Secretary of the Admiralty, which post he held with one short break for more than forty years longer. He was made a baronet in 1835, and died in 1848. Barrow was a considerable writer on geography and naval history; and one of the pillars of the *Quarterly*. Isaac Disraeli, son of one Benjamin of that name and father of another, seems to have been as unlike his famous offspring as any father could be to any son. Born at Enfield in 1766, he showed absolutely no taste for business of any kind, and after some opposition was allowed to cultivate letters. His original work was worth little; indeed, one of the amiable sayings attributed to his friend Rogers was that Isaac Disraeli had "only half an intellect." He fell, however, pretty early (1791) into an odd but pleasant and profitable course of writing which amused himself during the remainder of a long life (he died blind in the same year with Barrow), and has amused a vast number of readers for more than a century. The *Curiosities of Literature*, the first part of which appeared at the date above mentioned, to be supplemented by others for more than forty years, were followed by the *Calamities of Authors* and the *Quarrels of Authors* (1812–14), a book on *Charles I.*,

and the *Amenities of Literature* (1840). Of these the *Curiosities*
is the type, and it is also the best of them. Isaac Disraeli was
not a good writer; and his original reflections may sometimes
make the reader doubt for a moment whether Rogers was not
more wrong in granting him half an intellect than in denying
him a whole one. But his anecdotage, though, as perhaps such
anecdotage is bound to be, not extremely accurate, is almost
inexhaustibly amusing, and indicates a real love as well as a wide
knowledge of letters.

The next periodicals, the founding of which enlisted or brought
out journalists or essay-writers of the true kind, were *Blackwood's
Magazine*, founded at Edinburgh in 1817, and the *London Magazine*,
of about the same date, the first with one of the longest as well as
the most brilliant careers to run that any periodical can boast of,
the latter as short-lived as it was brilliant. Indeed, the two had an
odd and — in the Shakespearian sense — metaphysical opposition.
Scotland and England, the country and the Cockney schools,
Toryism and Liberalism (though the *London* was by no means
so thorough-going on the Liberal side as *Blackwood* was on the
Tory, and some of its most distinguished contributors were either
Tory, as De Quincey, or neutral, as Lamb) fought out their
differences under the two flags. And by a climax of coincidence,
the fate of the *London* was practically decided by the duel which
killed John Scott, its editor, this duel being the direct result of an
editorial or contributorial quarrel between the two periodicals.

Both these magazines, besides being more frequent in appearance than the *Edinburgh* and the *Quarterly*, attempted, as their
very title of "magazine" expressed, a much wider and more
miscellaneous collection of subjects than the strict "review"
theory permitted. From the very first *Blackwood* gave a welcome
to fiction, to poetry, and to the widest possible construction of the
essay, while, in almost every respect, the *London* was equally
hospitable. Both had staffs of unusual strength, and of still more
unusual personality; and while the *London* could boast of Charles
Lamb, of Hazlitt, of De Quincey, of Hood, of Miss Mitford,

besides many lesser names, *Blackwood* was practically launched
by the triumvirate of Wilson, Lockhart, and the Ettrick Shepherd, with the speedy collaboration of Maginn.

The eldest of these, and if not the most vigorous, if very
nearly the least prolific, yet the most exquisite and singular in
literary genius, was Charles Lamb. He also was of the "Seventy
Club," as we may call it, which founded the literature of the
nineteenth century, and he was born in London on 18th February
1775. He was of rather lower birth than most of its other
members (if membership can be predicated of a purely imaginary
body), being the son of a lawyer's clerk and confidential servant;
but he was educated at Christ's Hospital, and, through the interest
of his father's employer, obtained, at the age of seventeen, a berth in
the East India House, which assured his modest fortunes through
life. But there was the curse of madness in his family, and
though he himself escaped with but one slight and passing attack
of actual lunacy, and at the cost of an eccentricity which only
imparted a rarer touch to his genius, his elder sister Mary was
subject to constant seizures, in one of which she stabbed her
mother to the heart. She was more gently dealt with than
perhaps would have been the case at present, and Lamb undertook the entire charge of her. She repaid him by unfailing care
and affection during her lucid intervals (which were long and
frequent), and by a sympathy with his own literary tastes, which
not seldom made her a valuable collaborator as well as sympathiser. But the shadow was on his whole life : it made it impossible for him to marry, as he evidently would have done if it
had not existed ; and it perhaps had something to do with a
venial but actual tendency on his part to take, rather fully, the
convivial license of the time. But Lamb had no other weakness,
and had not this in any ruinous degree. The quality of his
genius was unique. He had from the first been a diligent and
affectionate student of sixteenth and seventeenth century writers,
and some of his first literary efforts, after some early sonnets
(written with Coleridge and their friend Lloyd, and much fallen

foul of by the Tory wits of the *Anti-Jacobin*), were connected with these studies.   He and his sister wrote *Tales from Shakespeare*, which, almost alone of such things, are not unworthy of the original.   He executed an Elizabethan tragedy, *John Woodvil*, which is rather better than it has been generally said to be ; and he arranged a series (or rather two) of scenes from the Elizabethan drama itself, the short, interspersed, critical remarks of which, though occasionally a very little fanciful, contain the most exquisitely sympathetic criticism to be found anywhere in English literature.

It was not, however, till he had well reached middle age that the establishment of the *London*, the later publishers of which, Taylor and Hessey, were his friends, gave him that half accidental, and yet it would seem necessary, opening which has so often made the fame of men of genius, and which apparently they are by no means often able to make for themselves.   Lamb's poems have occasionally an exquisite pathos and more frequently a pleasant humour, but they would not by themselves justify a very high estimate of him ; and it is at least possible that, if we had nothing but the brief critical remarks on the dramatists above noticed, they would, independently of their extreme brevity, have failed to obtain for him the just reputation which they now hold, thanks partly to the fact that we have, as comments on them, the *Essays of Elia* and the delightful correspondence.   This latter, after being first published soon after Lamb's death in 1834 (nine years after he had been pensioned off from the India House), by Mr., afterwards Serjeant and Sir Thomas Talfourd, has been gradually augmented, till it has at last found an excellent and probably final editor in Canon Ainger.

It is in these two collections that Lamb presents himself in the character which alone can confer on any man the first rank in literature, the character of unicity — of being some one and giving something which no one before him has given or has been.   The *Essays of Elia* (a *nom de guerre* said to have been taken from an Italian comrade of the writer's elder brother John in the South

Sea House, and directed by Lamb himself to be pronounced
" Ell-ia") elude definition not merely as almost all works of genius
do, but by virtue of something essentially elvish and tricksy in their
own nature.   It is easy to detect in them — or rather the things
there are so obvious that there is no need of detection — an extraordinary familiarity with the great " quaint " writers of the seventeenth century — Burton, Fuller, Browne — which has supplied a
diction of unsurpassed brilliancy and charm ; a familiarity with
the eighteenth century essayists which has enabled the writer to
construct a form very different from theirs in appearance but
closely connected with it in reality; an unequalled command
over that kind of humour which unites the most fantastic merriment to the most exquisite pathos ; a perfect humanity ; a cast of
thought which, though completely conscious of itself, and not in
any grovelling sense humble (Lamb, forgiving and gentle as he
was, could turn sharply even upon Coleridge, even upon Southey,
when he thought liberties had been taken with him), was a thousand
miles removed from arrogance or bumptiousness ; an endlessly
various and attractive set of crotchets and whimsies, never divorced
from the power of seeing the ludicrous side of themselves ; a
fervent love for literature and a wonderful gift of expounding it ;
imagination in a high, and fancy almost in the highest degree.
But when all this has been duly set down, how much remains
both in the essays and in the letters, which in fact are chiefly
distinguished from one another by the fact that the essays are
letters somewhat less discursive and somewhat in fuller dress, the
letters essays in the rough.   For the style of Lamb is as indefinable
as it is inimitable, and his matter and method defy selection and
specification as much as the flutterings of a butterfly.   One thing
he has always, and that is charm ; as for the rest he is an epitome
of the lighter side of *belles lettres*, and not always of the lighter
side only.

No one who studies Lamb can fail to see the enormous
advantage which was given him by his possession of an official
employment which brought him a small but sufficient income

without very hard labour.   Such literary work as his could never be done (at any rate for a length of time) as "collar-work," and even if the best of it had by chance been so performed, it must necessarily have been mixed, as that of Leigh Hunt is, with a far larger quantity of mere work to order.   No such advantage was possessed by the third of the great trio of Cockney critics, or at least critics of the so-called Cockney school ; for William Hazlitt, as much the greatest of English critics in a certain way as Lamb is in another and Jeffrey in a third (though a lower than either), was a Cockney neither by extraction nor by birth, nor by early sojourn, nor even by continuous residence in later life.   His family was Irish, his father a Unitarian minister ; he was born at Maidstone in 1778.   When his father was officiating at Wem in Shropshire, in Hazlitt's twentieth year, Coleridge, who at times affected the same denomination, visited the place, and Hazlitt was most powerfully impressed by him.   He was, however, divided between art and literature as professions, and his first essays were in the former, which he practised for some time, visiting the Louvre during the peace, or rather armistice, of Amiens, to copy pictures for some English collectors, and to study them on his own account. Returning to London, he met Lamb and others of the literary set in the capital, and, after some newspaper work, married Miss Stoddart, a friend of Mary Lamb's, and a lady of some property. He and his wife lived for some years at her estate of Winterslow on Salisbury Plain (long afterwards still a favourite resort of Hazlitt's), and then he went in 1812 once more to London, where abundant work on periodicals of all kinds, on the Liberal side, from daily newspapers to the *Edinburgh Review*, soon fell into his hands.   But after a time he gave up most kinds of writing except literary, theatrical, and art criticism, the delivery of lectures on literature, and the composition of essays of a character less fanciful and less purely original than Lamb's, but almost as miscellaneous.

He lived till September 1830, the first of those early thirties. of the nineteenth century which were to be as generally fatal to his generation of great English men of letters as the seventies of the eighteenth had been prolific of them ; and his dying words, "Well, I have had a happy life," are noteworthy.   For certainly that life would hardly have seemed happy to many.   He quarrelled with his first wife, was divorced from her in Scotland, discreditably enough ; published to the world with astounding lack of reticence the details of a frantic passion for Sarah Walker, a lodging-house-keeper's daughter, who jilted him ; and after marrying a second time, was left by his second wife.   He had never been rich, and during the last years of his life was in positive difficulties, while for almost the whole period of his second sojourn in London he was the object of the most virulent abuse from the Tory organs, especially the *Quarterly* and *Blackwood* — abuse which, it must be confessed, he was both ready and able to repay in kind with handsome interest.   He appears to have played the part of firebrand and makebate in the John Scott duel already referred to.   Even with his friends he could not keep upon good terms, and the sincere gentleness of Lamb broke down at least once, as the easy good-nature of Leigh Hunt did many times, under the strain of his perverse and savage wrong-headedness.

But whether the critical and the unamiable temper are, as some would have it, essentially one, or whether their combination in the same person be mere coincidence, Hazlitt was beyond all question a great, a very great, critic — in not a few respects our very greatest.   All his work, or almost all that has much merit, is small in individual bulk, though the total is very respectable. His longest book, his *Life of Napoleon*, which was written late and as a counterblast to Scott's, from the singular standpoint of a Republican who was an admirer of Bonaparte, has next to no value ; and his earliest, a philosophical work in eighteenth century style on *The Principles of Human Action*, has not much.   But his essays and lectures, which, though probably not as yet by any means exhaustively collected or capable of being identified, fill nine or ten volumes, are of extraordinary goodness.   They may be divided roughly into three classes.   The first, dealing with art and

the drama, must take the lowest room, for theatrical criticism is of
necessity, except in so far as it touches on literature rather than
acting, of very ephemeral interest; and Hazlitt's education in art
and knowledge of it were not quite extensive enough, nor the
examples which in the first quarter of this century he had before
him in England important enough, to make his work of this kind
of the first importance.   The best of it is the *Conversations with
Northcote*, a painter of no very great merit, but a survivor of the
Reynolds studio; and these conversations very frequently and
very widely diverge from painting into literary and miscellaneous
matters.   The second class contains the miscellaneous essays
proper, and these have by some been put at the head of Hazlitt's
work.   But although some of them, indeed, nearly all, display a
spirit, a command of the subject, and a faculty of literary treatment which had never been given to the same subjects in the
same way before, although such things as the famous "Going to
a Fight," "Going a Journey," "The Indian Jugglers," "Merry
England," "Sundials," "On Taste," and not a few more would,
put together and freed from good but less good companions, make
a most memorable collection, still his real strength is not here.

Great as Hazlitt was as a miscellaneous and Montaignesque
essayist, he was greater as a literary critic.   Literature was, though
he coquetted with art, his first and most constant love; it was the
subject on which, as far as English literature is concerned (and he
knew little and is still less worth consulting about any other), he
had acquired the largest and soundest knowledge; and it is that
for which he had the most original and essential genius.   His
intense prejudices and his occasional inadequacy make themselves felt here as they do everywhere, and even here it is
necessary to give the caution that Hazlitt is never to be trusted
when he shows the least evidence of dislike for which he gives no
reason.   But to any one who has made a little progress in criticism
himself, to any one who has either read for himself or is capable
of reading for himself, of being guided by what is helpful and of
neglecting what is not, there is no greater critic than Hazlitt in any

language. He will sometimes miss — he is never perhaps so certain as his friends Lamb and Hunt were to find — exquisite individual points. Prejudice, accidental ignorance, or other causes may sometimes invalidate his account of authors or of subjects in general. But still the four great collections of his criticism, *The Characters of Shakespeare*, *The Elizabethan Dramatists*, *The English Poets*, and *The English Comic Writers*, with not a few scattered things in his other writings, make what is on the whole the best corpus of criticism by a single writer in English on English. He is the critics' critic as Spenser is the poets' poet ; that is to say, he has, errors excepted and deficiencies allowed, the greatest proportion of the strictly critical excellencies — of the qualities which make a critic — that any English writer of his craft has ever possessed.

Blackwood's Magazine, the headquarters, the citadel, the *place d'armes* of the opposition to the Cockney school and of criticism and journalism that were Tory first of all, enlisted a younger set of recruits than those hitherto mentioned, and the special style of writing which it introduced, though exceedingly clever and stimulating, lent itself rather less to dispassionate literary appreciation than even the avowedly partisan methods of the *Edinburgh*.   In its successful form (for it had a short and inglorious existence before it found out the way) it was launched by an audacious "skit" on the literati of Edinburgh written by John Wilson, John Gibson Lockhart, and James Hogg, while very soon after its establishment it was joined by a wild and witty Bohemian scholar from the south of Ireland, William Maginn, who, though before long he drifted away to other resorts, and ere many years established in *Fraser* a new abode of guerilla journalism, impressed on *Blackwood* itself, before he left it, several of its best-known features, and in particular is said to have practically started the famous *Noctes Ambrosianæ*. Of Hogg, enough has been said in a former chapter. For the critical purpose of " Maga," as *Blackwood's Magazine* loved to call itself, he was rather a butt, or, to speak less despiteously, a stimulant, than an originator ; and he had neither the education nor indeed the gifts of a critic. Of each of the others some

account must be given, and Maginn will introduce yet another
flight of brilliant journalists, some of whom, especially the greatest
of all, Carlyle, lived till far into the last quarter of the present
century.

Wilson, the eldest of those just mentioned, though a younger
man than any one as yet noticed in this chapter, and for many
years the guiding spirit (there never has been any "editor" of
Blackwood except the members of the firm who have published
it) of *Maga*, must at some time or other have taken to literature,
and would probably in any case have sooner or later written the
poems and stories which exist under his name, but do not in the
very least degree constitute its eminence. It was the chapter of
accidents that made him a journalist and a critic. He was born
in 1785, his father being a rich manufacturer of Paisley, was
educated at the universities of Glasgow and Oxford, came early
into a considerable fortune, married at twenty-six, and having
established himself at Elleray on Windermere, lived there the life
of a country gentleman, with more or less literary tastes. His
fortune being lost by bad luck and dishonest agency, he betook
himself to Edinburgh, and finding it impossible to get on with
Jeffrey (which was not surprising), threw himself heart and soul
into the opposition venture of *Blackwood*. He had, moreover,
the extraordinary good luck to obtain, certainly on no very solid
grounds (though he made at least as good a professor as another),
the valuable chair of Moral Philosophy in the University of Edinburgh, which of itself secured him from any fear of want or narrow
means. But no penniless barrister on his promotion could have
flung himself into militant journalism with more ardour than
did Wilson. He re-created, if he did not invent, the *Noctes
Ambrosianæ* — a series of convivial conversations on food, drink,
politics, literature, and things in general, with interlocutors at first
rather numerous, and not very distinct, but latterly narrowed down
to "Christopher North" (Wilson himself), the "Ettrick Shepherd" (Hogg), and a certain "Timothy Tickler," less distinctly
identified with Wilson's mother's brother, an Edinburgh lawyer of

the name of Sym. A few outsiders, sometimes real (as De Quincey), sometimes imaginary, were, till the last, added now and then. And besides these conversations, which are his great title to fame, he contributed, also under the *nom de guerre* of Christopher North, an immense number of articles, in part collected as *Christopher North in his Sporting Jacket,* substantive collections on Homer, on Spenser, and others, and almost innumerable single papers and essays on things in general. From the time when Lockhart (see below) went to London, no influence on *Blackwood* could match Wilson's for some ten or twelve years, or nearly till the end of the thirties. Latterly ill-health, the death of friends and of his wife, and other causes, lessened his energy, and for some years before his death in 1854 he wrote little. Two years before that time his increasing ailments caused him even to resign his professorship.

Wilson — whose stories are merely mediocre, and whose poems, *The Isle of Palms* (1812) and *The City of the Plague* (1816), merely show that he was an intelligent contemporary of Scott and Byron, and a neighbour of the Lake poets — developed in his miscellaneous journalism one of the most puissant and luxuriant literary faculties of the time ; and in particular was among the first in one, and perhaps the very first in another, kind of writing. The first and less valuable of the two was the subjection of most, if not all, of the topics of the newspaper to a boisterous but fresh and vigorous style of critical handling, which bears some remote resemblance to the styles of L'Estrange towards the end of the seventeenth century, and Bentley a little later, but is in all important points new. The second and higher was the attempt to substitute for the correct, balanced, exactly-proportioned, but even in the hands of Gibbon, even in those of Burke, somewhat colourless and jejune prose of the past age, a new style of writing, exuberant in diction, semi-poetical in rhythm, confounding, or at least alternating very sharply between, the styles of high-strung enthusiasm and extravagant burlesque, and setting at naught all precepts of the immediate elders. It

would be too much, no doubt, to attribute the invention of this
style to Wilson. It was "in the air"; it was the inevitable
complement of romantic diction in poetry; it had been anticipated to some extent by others, and it displayed itself in various
forms almost simultaneously in the hands of Landor, who kept
to a more classical form, and of De Quincey, who was modern.
But Wilson, unless in conversation with De Quincey, cannot be said
to have learnt it from any one else: he preceded most in the time,
and greatly exceeded all in the bulk and influence of his exercises,
owing to his position on the staff of a popular and widely-read
periodical.

The defect of both these qualities of Wilson's style (a defect
which extends largely to the matter of his writings in criticism
and in other departments) was a defect of sureness of taste; while
his criticism was more vigorous than safe. Except his Toryism
(which, however, was shot with odd flashes of democratic sentiment and a cross-vein of crotchety dislike not to England but
to London), he had not many pervading prejudices. But at the
same time he had not many clear principles: he was the slave
of whim and caprice in his individual opinions; and he never
seems to have been able to distinguish between a really fine
thing and a piece of fustian, between an urbane jest and a piece
of gross buffoonery, between eloquence and rant, between a
reasoned condemnation and a spiteful personal fling. Accordingly the ten reprinted volumes of his contributions to *Blackwood*
and the mass of his still uncollected articles contain the strangest
jumble of good and bad in matter and form that exists anywhere.
By turns trivial and magnificent, exquisite and disgusting, a
hierophant of literature and a mere railer at men of letters, a
prince of describers, jesters, enthusiasts, and the author of
tedious and commonplace newspaper "copy," Wilson is one of
the most unequal, one of the most puzzling, but also one of the
most stimulating and delightful, figures in English literature.
Perhaps slightly over-valued for a time, he has for many years
been distinctly neglected, if not depreciated and despised; and

the voluminousness of his work, coupled with the fact that it is difficult to select from it owing to the pervading inequality of its merits, may be thought likely to keep him in the general judgment at a lower plane than he deserves. But the influence which he exerted during many years both upon writers and readers by his work in *Blackwood* cannot be over-estimated. And it may be said without fear that no one with tolerably wide sympathies, who is able to appreciate good literature, will ever seriously undertake the reading of his various works without equal satisfaction and profit.

Wilson's principal coadjutor in the early days of *Blackwood*, and his friend of all days (though the mania for crying down not so much England as London made " Christopher North " indulge in some girds at his old comrade's editorship of the *Quarterly*), was a curious contrast to Wilson himself. This contrast may have been due partly, but by no means wholly, to the fact that there was ten years between them. John Gibson Lockhart was born at Cambusnethan, where his father was minister, on 14th July 1794. Like Wilson, he was educated at Glasgow and at Oxford, where he took a first-class at a very early age, and whence he went to Germany, a completion of "study-years" which the revolutionary wars had for a long time rendered difficult, if not dangerous. On returning home he was called to the Scottish Bar, where it would seem that he might have made some figure, but for his inability to speak in public. *Blackwood* gave him the very opening suited to his genius ; and for years he was one of its chief contributors, and perhaps the most dangerous wielder of the pretty sharp weapons in which its staff indulged. Shortly afterwards, in 1819, he published (perhaps with some slight assistance from Wilson) his first original book (he had translated Schlegel's *Lectures on History* earlier), *Peter's Letters to his Kinsfolk*. The title was a parody on Scott's account of his continental journey after Waterloo, the substance an exceedingly vivacious account of the things and men of Edinburgh at the time, something after the fashion of *Humphrey*

Clinker. Next year, on 29th April, Lockhart married Sophia, Scott's elder daughter; and the pair lived for some years to come either in Edinburgh or at the cottage of Chiefswood, near Abbotsford, Lockhart contributing freely to *Blackwood*, and writing his four novels and his *Spanish Ballads*. At the end of 1825 or the beginning of 1826, just at the time when his father-in-law's financial troubles set in, he received the appointment of editor of the *Quarterly Review* in succession, though not in immediate succession, to Gifford. He then removed to London, where he continued to direct the *Review*, to contribute for a time to *Fraser*, to be a very important figure in literary and political life, and after Scott's death to write an admirable *Life*. Domestic troubles came rather thickly on him after Scott's death, which indeed was preceded by that of Lockhart's own eldest son, the " Hugh Littlejohn " of the *Tales of a Grandfather*. Mrs. Lockhart herself died in 1837. In 1843 Lockhart received the auditorship of the duchy of Lancaster, a post of some value. Ten years later, in broken health, he resigned the editorship of the *Quarterly*, and died towards the end of the year.

Lockhart's works, at present uncollected, and perhaps in no small proportion irrecoverable, must have been of far greater bulk than those of any one yet mentioned in this chapter except Wilson, and not inconsiderably greater than his. They are also of a remarkable variety, and of an extraordinary level of excellence in their different kinds. Lockhart was not, like Wilson, an advocate or a practitioner of very ornate or revolutionary prose. On the contrary, he both practised, preached, and most formidably defended by bitter criticism of opposite styles, a manner in prose and verse which was almost classical, or which at least admitted no further Romantic innovation than that of the Lake poets and Scott. His authorship of the savage onslaught upon Keats in *Blackwood* is not proven ; but there is no doubt that he wrote the scarcely less ferocious, though much more discriminating and better-deserved, attack on Tennyson's early poems in the *Quarterly*. He was himself no mean writer of verse. His

Spanish Ballads (1823), in which he had both Southey and Scott as models before him, are of great excellence; and some of his occasional pieces display not merely much humour (which nobody ever denied him), but no mean share of the feeling which is certainly not often associated with his name. But verse was only an occasional pastime with him : his vocation was to write prose, and he wrote it with admirable skill and a seldom surpassed faculty of adaptation to the particular task. It is indeed probable — and it would be no discredit to him — that his reputation with readers as opposed to students will mainly depend, as it depends at present, upon his *Life of Scott*. Nor would even thus his plumes be borrowed over much. For though no doubt the letters and the diary of Sir Walter himself count for much in the interest of the book, though the beauty and nobility of Scott's character, his wonderful achievements, the pathetic revolution of his fortune, form a subject not easily matched, yet to be equal to such a subject is to be in another sense on an equality with it. Admiration for the book is not chequered or tempered, as it almost necessarily must be in the case of its only possible rival, Boswell's *Johnson*, with more or less contempt for the author ; still less is it (as some have contended that admiration for Boswell is) due to that contempt. The taste and spirit of Lockhart's book are not less admirable than the skill of its arrangement and the competency of its writing ; nor would it be easily possible to find a happier adjustment in this respect in the whole annals of biography.

But this great book ought not to obscure the other work which Lockhart has done. His biography of Burns is of remarkable merit ; it may be questioned whether to this day, though it may be deficient in a few modern discoveries of fact (and these have been mostly supplied in the edition by the late Mr. Scott Douglas), it is not the best book on the subject. The taste and judgment, the clear vision and sound sense, which distinguished Lockhart, are in few places more apparent than here. His abridgment of Scott's *Life of Napoleon* is no ordinary abridgment, and is a work of thorough craft, if not even of art. His novels, with one exception, have ceased to be much read ; and perhaps even that one can hardly be said to enjoy frequent perusal. *Valerius*, the first, is a classical novel, and suffers under the drawbacks which have generally attended its kind. *Reginald Dalton*, a novel in part of actual life at Oxford, and intended to be wholly of actual life, still shows something of the artificial handling, of the supposed necessity for adventure, which is observable in Hook and others of the time, and which has been sufficiently noticed in the last chapter. *Matthew Wald*, the last of the four, is both too gloomy and too extravagant : it deals with a mad hero. But *Adam Blair*, which was published in the same year (1821) with *Valerius,* is a wonderful little book. The story is not well told ; but the characters and the principal situation — a violent passion entertained by a pious widowed minister for his neighbour's wife — are handled with extraordinary power. *Peter's Letters*, which is half a book and half journalism, may be said to be, with rare exceptions (such as an obituary article on Hook, which was reprinted from the *Quarterly*), the only specimen of Lockhart's miscellaneous writing that is easily accessible or authentically known. He was still but in his apprenticeship here ; but his remarkable gifts are already apparent. These gifts included a faculty of sarcastic comment so formidable that it early earned him the title of "the Scorpion" ; a very wide and sound knowledge of literature, old and new, English and foreign ; some acquirements in art and in other matters ; an excellent style, and a solid if rather strait-laced theory of criticism. Except that he was, as almost everybody was then, too much given to violent personalities in his anonymous work, he was a very great journalist indeed, and he was also a very great man of letters.

Thomas de Quincey was not of the earliest *Blackwood* staff (in that respect Maginn should be mentioned before him), but he was the older as well as the more important man of the two, and there is the additional reason for postponing the founder of

Fraser, that this latter periodical introduced a fresh flight of birds of passage (as journalists both fortunate and unfortunate may peculiarly be called) to English literature. De Quincey was born in 1785 (the same year as his friend Wilson) at Manchester, where his father was a merchant of means. He was educated at the Grammar School of his native town, after some preliminary teaching at or near Bath, whither his mother had moved after his father's death. He did not like Manchester, and when he had nearly served his time for an exhibition to Brasenose College, Oxford, he ran away and hid himself. He went to Oxford after all, entering at Worcester, where he made a long though rather intermittent residence, but took no degree. In 1809 he took up his abode at Grasmere, married after a time, and lived there, at least as his headquarters, for more than twenty years. In 1830 he moved to Edinburgh, where, or in its neighbourhood, he resided for the rest of his long life, and where he died in December 1859. He has given various autobiographic handlings of this life — in the main it would seem quite trustworthy, but invested with an air of fantastic unreality by his manner of relation.

His life, however, and his personality, and even the whole of his voluminous published work, have in all probability taken colour in the general thought from his first literary work of any consequence, the wonderful *Confessions of an English Opium Eater*, which, with the *Essays of Elia*, were the chief flowers of the *London Magazine*, and appeared in that periodical during the year 1821. He had acquired this habit during his sojourn at Oxford, and it had grown upon him during his at first solitary residence at the Lakes to an enormous extent. Until he thus committed the results of his dreams, or of his fancy and literary genius working on his dreams, or of his fancy and genius by themselves, to print and paper, in his thirty-sixth year, he had been, though a great reader, hardly anything of a writer. But thenceforward, and especially after, in 1825, he had visited his Lake neighbour Wilson at Edinburgh, and had been by him introduced to *Blackwood*, he became a frequent contributor to different magazines, and continued to be so, writing far more even than he published, till his death. He wrote very few books, the chief being a very free translation of a German novel, forged as Scott's, and called *Walladmor;* a more original and stable, though not very brilliant, effort in fiction, entitled *Klosterheim;* and the *Logic of Political Economy*. Towards the end of his life he superintended an English collection — there had already been one in America — of his essays, and this has been supplemented more than once since.

It may, indeed, fairly be doubted whether so large a collection, of miscellaneous, heterogeneous, and, to tell the truth, very unequally interesting and meritorious matter, has ever been received with greater or more lasting popular favour, a fresh edition of the fourteen or sixteen volumes of the *Works* having been called for on an average every decade. There have been dissidents : and recently in particular something of a set has been made against De Quincey — a set to some extent helped by the gradual addition to the *Works* of a great deal of unimportant matter which he had not himself cared to reproduce. This, indeed, is perhaps the greatest danger to which the periodical writer is after his death exposed, and is even the most serious drawback to periodical writing. It is impossible that any man who lives by such writing can always be at his best in form, and he will sometimes be compelled to execute what Carlyle has called " honest journey-work in default of better," — work which, though perfectly honest and perfectly respectable, is mere journey-work, and has no claim to be disturbed from its rest when its journey is accomplished. Of this there was some even in De Quincey's own collection, and the proportion has been much increased since. Moreover, even at his very best, he was not a writer who could be trusted to keep himself at that best. His reading was enormous, — nearly as great perhaps as Southey's, though in still less popular directions, — and he would sometimes drag it in rather inappropriately. He had an unconquerable and sometimes very irritating habit of digression, of divagation, of aside. And, worst of all, his humour, which in its own peculiar vein of imaginative grotesque has seldom been surpassed, was liable constantly to degenerate into a kind of laboured trifling, inexpressibly exasperating to the nerves. He could be simply dull; and he can seldom be credited with the possession of what may be called literary tact.

Yet his merits were such as to give him no superior in his own manner among the essayists, and hardly any among the prose writers of the century. He, like Wilson, and probably before Wilson, deliberately aimed at a style of gorgeous elaboration, intended not exactly for constant use, but for use when required ; and he achieved it. Certain well-known passages, as well as others which have not become hackneyed, in the *Confessions of an Opium Eater*, in the *Autobiography*, in *The English Mail Coach*, in *Our Ladies of Sorrow*, and elsewhere, are unsurpassed in English or out of it for imaginative splendour of imagery, suitably reproduced in words. Nor was this De Quincey's only, though it was his most precious gift. He had a singular, though, as has been said, a very untrustworthy faculty of humour, both grim and quaint. He was possessed of extraordinary dialectic ingenuity, a little alloyed no doubt by a tendency to wire-drawn and over subtle minuteness such as besets the born logician who is not warned of his danger either by a strong vein of common sense or by constant sojourn in the world. He could expound and describe admirably ; he had a thorough grasp of the most complicated subjects when he did not allow will-o'-the-wisps to lure him into letting it go, and could narrate the most diverse kinds of action, such as the struggles of Bentley with Trinity College, the journey of the Tartars from the Ukraine to Siberia, and the fortunes of the Spanish Nun, Catalina, with singular adaptability. In his biographical articles on friends and contemporaries, which are rather numerous, he has been charged both with ill-nature and with inaccuracy. The first charge may be peremptorily dismissed, the second requires much argument and sifting in particular cases. To some who have given not a little attention to the matter it seems that De Quincey was never guilty of deliberate fabrication, and that he was not even careless in statement. But he was first of all a dreamer; and when it is true of a man that, in the words of the exquisite passage where Calderon has come at one with Shakespeare, his very dreams are a dream, it will often happen that his facts are not exactly a fact.

Nevertheless, De Quincey is a great writer and a great figure in literature, while it may plausibly be contended that journalism may make all the more boast of him in that it is probable that without it he would never have written at all. And he has one peculiarity not yet mentioned. Although his chief excellences may not be fully perceptible except to mature tastes, he is specially attractive to the young. Probably more boys have in the last forty years been brought to a love of literature proper by De Quincey than by any other writer whatever.

Of other contributors to these periodicals much might be said in larger space, as for instance of the poisoner-critic Thomas Griffiths Wainewright, the "Janus Weathercock" of the *London*, the original of certain well-known heroes of Bulwer and Dickens, and the object of a more than once recurrent and distinctly morbid attention from young men of letters since. Lamb, who was not given to think evil of his friends, was certainly unlucky in calling Wainewright "warm- as light-hearted"; for the man (who died a convict in Australia, though he cheated the gallows which was his due) was both an affected coxcomb and a callous scoundrel. But he was a very clever fellow, though indignant morality has sometimes endeavoured to deny this. That he anticipated by sixty years and more certain depravations in style and taste notorious in our own day is something: it is more that his achievement in gaudy writing and in the literary treatment of art was really considerable.

Wainewright, however, is only "curious" in more than one sense of that term: Leigh Hunt, who, though quite incapable of poisoning anybody, had certain points in common with Waine-wright on the latter's more excusable sides, and whose prose must

now be treated, is distinguished.   He reappears with even better
right here than some others of the more important constituents of
this chapter.   For all his best work in prose appeared in periodicals, though it is impossible to say that all his work that appeared in periodicals was his best work.   He was for fourteen
years editor of, and a large contributor to, the *Examiner*, which he
and his brother started in 1808.   After his liberation from prison
he not merely edited, but in the older fashion practically wrote the
Reflector (1810), the *Indicator* (1819–21), and the *Companion*
(1828).   His rather unlucky journey to Italy was undertaken to
edit the *Liberal*.   He was one of the rare and rash men of letters
who have tried to keep up a daily journal unassisted — a new *Tatler*,
which lasted for some eighteen months (1830–32) ; and a little
later (1834–35) he supported for full two years a similar but
weekly venture, in part original, in part compiled or borrowed,
called *Leigh Hunt's London Journal*.   These were not his only
ventures of the kind : he was an indefatigable contributor to
periodicals conducted by others; and most of his books now
known by independent titles are in fact collections of "articles"
— sometimes reprinted, sometimes published for the first time.

It was impossible that such a mass of matter should be all
good ; and it is equally impossible to deny that the combined
fact of so much production and of so little concentration argues
a certain idiosyncrasy of defect.   In fact the butterfly character
which every unprejudiced critic of Leigh Hunt has noticed, made
it impossible for him to plan or to execute any work on a great
scale.   He never could have troubled himself to complete missing
knowledge, to fill in gaps, to co-ordinate thinking, as the literary
historian, whose vocation in some respects he might seem to have
possessed eminently, must do — to weave fancy into the novelist's
solid texture, and not to leave it in thrums or in gossamer.   But
he was, though in both ways a most unequal, a delightful miscellanist and critic.   In both respects it is natural, and indeed
unavoidable, to compare him with Lamb and with Hazlitt, whom,
however, he really preceded, forming a link between them and the

eighteenth century essayists. His greater voluminousness, induced by necessity, puts him at a rather unfair disadvantage with the first; and we may perhaps never find in him those exquisite felicities which delight and justify the true "Agnist." Yet he has found some things that Lamb missed in Lamb's own subjects; and though his prejudices (of the middle-class Liberal and freethinking kind) were sometimes more damaging than any to which Lamb was exposed, he was free from the somewhat wilful eclecticism of that inimitable person. He could like nearly all things that were good — in which respect he stands above both his rivals in criticism. But he stands below them in his miscellaneous work; though here also, as in his poetry, he was a master, not a scholar. Lamb and Hazlitt improved upon him here, as Keats and Shelley improved upon him there. But what a position is it to be "improved upon" by Keats and Shelley in poetry, by Hazlitt and Lamb in prose !

Hartley Coleridge might with about equal propriety have been treated in the last chapter and in this; but the already formidable length of the catalogue of bards perhaps turns the scale in favour of placing him with other contributors to *Blackwood*, to which, thanks to his early friendship with Wilson, he enjoyed access, and in which he might have written much more than he did, and did actually write most of what he published himself, except the *Biographia Borealis*.

The life of Hartley was a strange and sad variant of his father's, though, if he lacked a good deal of S. T. C.'s genius, his character was entirely free from the baser stains which darkened that great man's weakness. Born (1796) at Clevedon, the first-fruits of the marriage of Coleridge and Sara, he was early celebrated by Wordsworth and by his father in immortal verse, and by Southey, his uncle, in charming prose, for his wonderful dreamy precocity; but he never was a great reader. Southey took care of him with the rest of the family when Coleridge disappeared into the vague; and Hartley, after schooling at Ambleside, was elected to a post-mastership at Merton College, Oxford. He missed the Newdi-

gate thrice, and only got a second in the schools, but was more
than consoled by a Fellowship at Oriel.   Unfortunately Oriel was
not only gaining great honour, but was very jealous of it ; and the
probationary Fellows were subjected to a most rigid system of
observation, which seems to have gone near to espionage.   If
ever there was a man born to be a Fellow under the old English
University scheme, that man was Hartley Coleridge ; and it is
extremely probable that if he had been let alone he would have
produced, in one form or another, a justification of that scheme,
worthy to rank with Burton's *Anatomy*.   But he was accused
of various shortcomings, of which intemperance seems to have
been the most serious, though it is doubtful whether it would
have sunk the beam if divers peccadilloes, political, social, and
miscellaneous, had not been thrown in.   Strong interest was made
in favour of mercy, but the College deprived him of his Fellowship, granting him, not too consistently, a *solatium* of £300.   This
was apparently in 1820.   Hartley lived for nearly thirty years
longer, but his career was closed.   He was, as his brother
Derwent admits, one of those whom the pressure of necessity
does not spur but numbs.   He wrote a little for *Blackwood;* he
took pupils unsuccessfully, and school-mastered with a little better
success ; and during a short time he lived with a Leeds publisher
who took a fancy to him and induced him to write his only large
book, the *Biographia Borealis*.   But for the most part he abode
at Grasmere, where his failing (it was not much more) of occasional intemperance was winked at by all, even by the austere
Wordsworth, where he wandered about, annotated a copy of
Anderson's *Poets* and some other books, and supported himself
(with the curious Coleridgean faculty of subsisting like the bird
of paradise, without either foot or foothold) till, at his mother's
death, an annuity made his prospects secure.   He died on 6th
January 1849, a little before Wordsworth, and shortly afterwards
his work was collected by his brother Derwent in seven small
volumes ; the *Poems* filling two, the *Essays and Fragments* two,
and the *Biographia Borealis* three.

This last (which appeared in its second form as *Lives of Northern Worthies*, with some extremely interesting notes by S. T. C.) is an excellent book of its kind, and shows that under more favourable circumstances Hartley might have been a great literary historian. But it is on the whole less characteristic than the volumes of *Poems* and *Essays*. In the former Hartley has no kind of *souffle* (or long-breathed inspiration), nor has he those exquisite lyrical touches of his father's which put Coleridge's scanty and unequal work on a level with that of the greatest names in English poetry. But he has a singular melancholy sweetness, and a meditative grace which finds its special home in the sonnet. In the " Posthumous Sonnets " especially, the sound — not an echo of, but a true response to, Elizabethan music — is unmistakable, and that to Shakespeare (" the soul of man is larger than the sky "), that on himself (" When I survey the course that I have run "), and not a few others, rank among the very best in English. Many of the miscellaneous poems contain beautiful things. But on the whole the greatest interest of Hartley Coleridge is that he is the first and one of the best examples of a kind of poet who is sometimes contemned, who has been very frequent in this century, but who is dear to the lover of poetry, and productive of delightful things. This kind of poet is wanting, it may be, in what is briefly, if not brutally, called originality. He might not sing much if others had not sung and were not singing around him ; he does not sing very much even as it is, and the notes of his song are not extraordinarily piercing or novel. But they are true, they are not copied, and the lover of poetry could not spare them.

It is improbable that Hartley Coleridge would ever have been a great poet : he might, if Fate or even if the Oriel dons had been a little kinder, have been a great critic. As it is, his essays, his introduction to Massinger and Ford, and his *Marginalia*, suffer on the one side from certain defects of reading ; for his access to books was latterly small, and even when it had been ample, as at Oxford, in London, or at Southey's house, he confesses that he had availed himself of it but little. Hence he is often wrong, and more often incomplete, from sheer lack of information. Secondly, much of his work is mere jotting, never in the very least degree intended for publication, and sometimes explicitly corrected or retracted by later jottings of the same kind. In such a case we can rather augur of the might-have-been than pronounce on the actual. But the two volumes are full of delicate critical views on literature ; and the longest series, " Ignoramus on the Fine Arts," shows how widely, with better luck and more opportunity, he might have extended his critical performances. In short, Hartley Coleridge, if a " sair sicht " to the moralist, is an interesting and far from a wholly painful one to the lover of literature, which he himself loved so much, and practised, with all his disadvantages, so successfully.

All the persons hitherto mentioned in this chapter appear by undoubted right in any history of English Literature : it may cause a little surprise to see that of Maginn figuring with them. Yet his abilities were scarcely inferior to those of any ; and he was kept back from sharing their fame only by infirmities of character and by his succumbing to that fatal Bohemianism which, constantly recurring among men of letters, exercised its attractions with special force in the early days of journalism in this century. William Maginn (1793), who was the son of a schoolmaster at Cork, took a brilliant degree at Trinity College, Dublin, and for some years followed his father's profession. The establishment, however, and the style of *Blackwood* were an irresistible attraction to him, and he drifted to Edinburgh, wrote a great deal in the earlier and more boisterous days of *Maga* under the pseudonym of Ensign O'Doherty, and has, as has been said, some claims to be considered the originator of the *Noctes*. Then, as he had gone from Ireland to Edinburgh, he went from Edinburgh to London, and took part in divers Tory periodicals, acting as Paris correspondent for some of them till, about 1830, he started, or helped in starting, a London *Blackwood* in *Fraser*. He had now every opportunity, and he gathered round him a staff almost more brilliant than that of the *Edinburgh*, of the *London*, of the *Quarterly*, or of *Black-*

wood itself. But he was equally reckless of his health and of his money. The acknowledged original of Thackeray's Captain Shandon, he was not seldom in jail; and at last, assisted by Sir Robert Peel almost too late, he died at Walton on Thames in August 1842, not yet fifty, but an utter wreck.

The collections of Maginn's work are anything but exhaustive, and the work itself suffers from all the drawbacks, probable if not inevitable, of work written in the intervals of carouse, at the last moment, for ephemeral purposes. Yet it is instinct with a perhaps brighter genius than the more accomplished productions of some much more famous men. The *Homeric Ballads*, though they have been praised by some, are nearly worthless; and the longer attempts in fiction are not happy. But Maginn's shorter stories in *Blackwood*, especially the inimitable " Story without a Tail," are charming; his more serious critical work, especially that on Shakespeare, displays a remarkable combination of wide reading, critical acumen, and sound sense; and his miscellanies in prose and verse, especially the latter, are characterised by a mixture of fantastic humour, adaptive wit, and rare but real pathos and melody, which is the best note of the specially Irish mode. It must be said, however, that Maginn is chiefly important to the literary historian as the captain of a band of distinguished persons, and as in a way the link between the journalism of the first and the journalism of the second third of the century. A famous plate by Maclise, entitled " The Fraserians," contains, seated round abundant bottles, with Maginn as president, portraits (in order by " the way of the sun," and omitting minor personages) of Irving, Gleig the Chaplain-General, Sir Egerton Brydges, Allan Cunningham, Carlyle, Count D'Orsay, Brewster, Theodore Hook, Lockhart, Crofton Croker of the Irish Fairy Tales, Jerdan, Dunlop of the " History of Fiction," Galt, Hogg, Coleridge, Harrison Ainsworth, Thackeray, Southey, and Barry Cornwall. It is improbable that all these contributed at one time, and tolerably certain that some of them were very sparing and infrequent contributors at any time, but the important point is the juxtaposition of the generation which was departing and the generation which was coming on—of Southey with Thackeray and of Coleridge with Carlyle. Yet it will be noticed (and the point is of some importance) that these new-comers are, at least the best of them, much less merely periodical writers than those who came immediately before them. In part no doubt this was accident; in part it was due to the greater prominence which novels and serial works of other kinds were beginning to assume; in part it may be to the fact that the great increase in the number of magazines and newspapers had lowered their individual dignity and perhaps their profitableness. But it is certain that of the list just mentioned, Thackeray and Carlyle, of the contemporary new generation of the *Edinburgh* Macaulay, of the nascent *Westminster* Mill, and others, were not, like Jeffrey, like Sydney Smith, like Wilson, and like De Quincey, content to write articles. They aspired to write, and they did write, books; and, that being so, they will all be treated in chapters other than the present, appropriated to the kinds in which their chief books were designed.

The name of John Sterling is that of a man who, with no great literary claims of his own, managed to connect it durably and in a double fashion with literature, first as the subject of an immortal biography by Carlyle, secondly as the name-giver of the famous Sterling Club, which about 1838, and hardly numbering more members than the century did years, included a surprising proportion of the most rising men of letters of the day, while all but a very few of its members were of literary mark. John Sterling himself was the son of a rather eccentric father, Edward Sterling, who, after trying soldiering with no great, and farming with decidedly ill, success, turned to journalism and succeeded brilliantly on the *Times*. His son was born in the Isle of Bute on 20th July 1806, was educated, first privately, then at Glasgow, and when about nineteen went to Trinity College, Cambridge, where he fell in with a famous and brilliant set. He migrated from Trinity College to Trinity Hall, took no degree, wrote a little for the then young *Athenæum*, was engaged in a romantic and in all ways rather unfortunate business of encouraging a rebellion in Spain, but married instead of taking active part in it, and went to the West Indies. When he came home he, it is said under Coleridgean influence, took orders, but soon developed heterodox views and gave up active duty. He lived, though under sentence of death by consumption, till 1843, spending much time abroad, but writing a little, chiefly for periodicals.

The chief characteristic of Sterling in life and thought appears to have been a vacillating impulsiveness, while in letters his production, small in bulk, is anything but strong in substance or form. But, like some other men who do not, in the common phrase, "do much," he seems to have been singularly effectual as a centre of literary friendship and following. The Sterling Club included not merely Tennyson, John Stuart Mill, Carlyle, Allan Cunningham, Lord Houghton, Sir Francis Palgrave, Bishop Thirlwall, who all receive separate notice elsewhere, but others who, being of less general fame, may best be noticed together here. There were the scholars Blakesley, Worsley, and Hepworth Thompson (afterwards Master of Trinity); H. N. Coleridge, the poet's nephew, son-in-law, and editor; Sir Francis Doyle, afterwards Professor of Poetry at Oxford, the author of some interesting reminiscences in prose, and in verse of some of the best songs and poems on military subjects to be found in the language, such as "The Loss of the Birkenhead," the "Private of the Buffs," and above all the noble and consummate "Red Thread of Honour"; Sir Edmund Head, Fellow of Merton and Governor-General of Canada, and a writer on art (not to be confounded with his namesake Sir Francis, the agreeable miscellanist, reviewer, and travel writer, who was also a baronet and also connected with Canada, where he was Governor of the Upper Province at the time of the Rebellion of 1835). There was Sir George Cornewall Lewis, a keen scholar and a fastidious writer, whose somewhat short life (1806–63) was chiefly occupied by politics; for he was a Poor-Law Commissioner, a Member of Parliament, and a holder of numerous offices up to those of Chancellor of the Exchequer and Secretary of State. Lewis, who edited the *Edinburgh* for a short time, wrote no very long work, but many on a great variety of subjects, the chief perhaps being *On the Influence of Authority in Matters of Opinion*, 1850 (a book interesting to contrast with one by a living statesman forty-five years later), the *Inquiry into the Credibility of the Ancient Roman History* (1855), and later treatises on *The Government of Dependencies* and the *Best Form of Government*. He was also an exact verbal scholar, was, despite the addiction to "dry" subjects which this list may seem to show, the author of not a few *jeux d'esprit*, and was famous for his conversational sayings, the most hackneyed of which is probably "Life would be tolerable if it were not for its amusements."

But even this did not exhaust the Sterling Club. There was another scholar, Malden, who should have been mentioned with the group above; the second Sir Frederick Pollock, who wrote too little but left an excellent translation of Dante, besides some reminiscences and other work; Philip Pusey, elder brother of the theologian, and a man of remarkable ability; James Spedding, who devoted almost the whole of his literary life to the study, championship, and editing of Bacon, but left other essays and reviews of great merit; Twisleton, who undertook with singular patience and shrewdness the solution of literary and historical problems like the Junius question and that of the African martyrs; and lastly George Stovin Venables, who for some five and thirty years was the main pillar in political writing of the *Saturday Review*, was a parliamentary lawyer of great diligence and success, and combined a singularly exact and wide knowledge of books and men in politics and literature with a keen judgment, an admirably forcible if somewhat mannered style, a disposition far more kindly than the world was apt to credit him with, and a famous power of conversation. All these men, almost without exception, were more or less contributors to periodicals; and it may certainly be said that, but for periodicals, it is rather unlikely that some of them would have contributed to literature at all.

Not as a member of the Sterling Club, but as the intimate

friend of all its greatest members, as a contributor, though a
rather unfrequent one, to papers, and as a writer of singular and
extraordinary quality but difficult to class under a more precise
head, may be noticed Edward FitzGerald, who, long a recluse,
unstintedly admired by his friends but quite unknown to the
public, became famous late in life by his translation of Omar
Khayyám, and familiar somewhat after his death through the
publication of his charming letters by Mr. Aldis Wright. He was
born on 31st March 1809, near Woodbridge in Suffolk, the neighbourhood which was his headquarters for almost his entire life,
till his death on a visit to a grandson of the poet Crabbe at
Merton in Norfolk, 14th June 1883. He went to school at Bury,
and thence to Cambridge, where he laid the foundation of his
acquaintance with the famous Trinity set of 1825–30. But on
taking his degree in the last named year and leaving college, he
took to no profession, but entered on the life of reading, thinking,
gardening, and boating, which he pursued for more than half a
century. Besides his Trinity contemporaries, from Tennyson and
Thackeray downwards, he had Carlyle for an intimate friend, and
he married the daughter of Bernard Barton, the poet-Quaker
and friend of Lamb. He published nothing till the second half of
the century had opened, when *Euphranor*, written long before at
Cambridge, or with reference to it, appeared. Then he learnt
Spanish, and first showed his extraordinary faculty of translation by
Englishing divers dramas of Calderon. Spanish gave way to Persian,
and after some exercises elsewhere the famous version, paraphrase,
or whatever it is to be called, of the Rubaiyat of Omar Khayyám
appeared in 1859, to be much altered in subsequent editions.

FitzGerald's works in the collected edition of 1889 fill three
pretty stout volumes, to which a considerable number of letters (he
was first of all and almost solely a letter-writer and translator)
have been added. In his prose (no disrespect being intended to
Euphranor, a dialogue Berkeleian in form and of great beauty,
and other things) he interests us doubly as a character and as a
critic, for the letters contain much criticism. Personally Fitz-

Gerald was a man of rather few and not obtrusive, but deep and warm sympathies, slow to make new friends but intensely tenacious of and affectionate towards the old, with a very strong distaste for crowds and general society, and undoubtedly somewhat of what the French call a *maniaque*, that is to say, a slightly hypochondriac crotcheteer. These characteristics, which make him interesting as a man, are still more interestingly reflected in his criticism, which is often one-sided and unjust, sometimes crotchety (as when he would not admit that even his beloved Alfred Tennyson had ever been at his best since the collection of 1842), but often also wonderfully delicate and true.

As a translator he stands almost alone, his peculiar virtue, noticeable alike in his versions from the Spanish and Greek, being so capitally and once for all illustrated in that of Omar Khayyám that in narrow space it is not necessary to go beyond this. From the purist and pedantic point of view FitzGerald, no doubt, is wildly unfaithful. He scarcely ever renders word for word, and will insert, omit, alter, with perfect freedom ; yet the total effect is reproduced as perhaps no other translator has ever reproduced it. Whether his version of the Rubaiyat, with its sensuous fatalism, its ridicule of asceticism and renunciation, and its bewildering kaleidoscope of mysticism that becomes materialist and materialism that becomes mystical, has not indirectly had influences, practical and literary, the results of which would have been more abhorrent to FitzGerald than to almost any one else, may be suggested. But the beauty of the poem as a poem is unmistakable and altogether astounding. The melancholy richness of the rolling quatrain with its unicorn rhymes, the quaint mixture of farce and solemnity, passion and playfulness, the abundance of the imagery, the power of the thought, the seduction of the rhetoric, make the poem actually, though not original or English, one of the greatest of English poems.

Of the periodical too, if not entirely, was Richard Harris Barham, "Thomas Ingoldsby," the author of the most popular book of light verse that ever issued from the press. His one

P

novel, *My Cousin Nicholas*, was written for *Blackwood;* the immortal *Ingoldsby Legends* appeared in *Bentley* and *Colburn*. Born at Canterbury in 1788, of a family possessed of landed property, though not of much, and educated at St. Paul's School and Brasenose College, Barham took orders, and, working with thorough conscience as a clergyman, despite his light literature, became a minor canon in St. Paul's Cathedral. He died in 1845. Hardly any book is more widely known than the collected *Ingoldsby Legends*, which originally appeared in the last eight years of their author's life. Very recently they have met with a little priggish depreciation, the natural and indeed inevitable result, first of a certain change in speech and manners, and then of their long and vast popularity. Nor would any one contend that they are exactly great literature. But for inexhaustible fun that never gets flat and scarcely ever simply uproarious, for a facility and felicity in rhyme and rhythm which is almost miraculous, and for a blending of the grotesque and the terrible which, if less *fine* than Praed's or Hood's, is only inferior to theirs — no one competent to judge and enjoy will ever go to Barham in vain.

The same difficulty which beset us at the end of the last chapter recurs here, the difficulty arising from the existence of large numbers of persons of the third or lower ranks whose inclusion may be desired or their exclusion resented. At the head, or near it, of this class stand such figures as that of Douglas Jerrold, a sort of very inferior Hook on the other side of politics, with a dash (also very inferior) of Hood, whose *Mrs. Caudle's Curtain Lectures* and similar things were very popular at and a little before the middle of the century, but whose permanent literary value is of the smallest, if indeed it can be said to exist. But of these — not a few of them more worthy if less prominent in their day than Jerrold — there could be no end ; and there would be little profit in trying to reach any. The successful " contributor," by the laws of the case, climbs on the shoulders of his less successful mates even more than elsewhere ; and the very impetus which lands him on the height rejects them into the depths.

CHAPTER V

AFTER the brilliant group of historians whose work illustrated the close of the period covered by the preceding volume, it was some time before a historical writer of the first rank again appeared in England ; and there were reasons for this. Not that, as in the case of purely creative literature, in prose as in verse, there is any natural or actual lull between different successive periods in this case ; on the contrary the writing of history is more likely to be stimulated by example, and requires rather the utmost talent than positive genius, except in those rare cases which, as in other departments, are not to be accounted for, either in their presence or in their absence, by observation or inference. But in the first place the greatest minds of the first generation of which we have to take account, who were born about the beginning of the third quarter of the eighteenth century, were, partly by time and partly by chance, directed for the most part either into poetry, or into politics, or into active life ; and the five and twenty years of the Revolutionary War in which they passed their manhood were more likely to provide materials for history, than history itself.

Yet history, after the example given by Hume, by Robertson, and above all by Gibbon, was not at all likely to cease, nor did some men of great talents in other ways fail to betake themselves to it. Godwin was a historian, and, considering his strong prejudices, the unkindness of fortune (for history demands leisure almost as much as poetry), and some defects of knowledge, not a contemptible historian in his way. Mackintosh, intended for a philosopher, was a historian. Southey was a very considerable historian, and master of one of the most admirable historical styles on record. But he was signally unfortunate in having that work of his which should have been most popular, the *History of the Peninsular War*, pitted against another by a younger man of professional competence, of actual experience, and of brilliant literary powers, Sir William Napier (1786–1860). The literary value of these two histories is more even than a generation which probably reads neither much and has almost forgotten Southey is apt to imagine ; and though there is no doubt that the Poet Laureate was strongly prejudiced on the Tory side, his competitor was even more partial and biassed against that side. But the difference between the two books is the difference between a task admirably performed, and performed to a certain extent *con amore*, by a skilled practitioner in task-work, and the special effort of one who was at once an enthusiast and an expert in his subject. It is customary to call Napier's *History of the Peninsular War* " the finest military history in the English language," and so, perhaps, it is. The famous description of the Battle of Albuera is only one of many showing eloquence without any mere fine writing, and with the knowledge of the soldier covering the artist's exaggeration.

Moore, Campbell, Scott himself, were all, as has been previously recorded in the notices of their proper work, historians by trade, though hardly, even to the extent to which Southey was, historians by craft. But an exception must be made for the exquisite *Tales of a Grandfather*, in which Sir Walter, without perhaps a very strict application of historical criticism, applied his creative powers, refreshed in their decay by combined affection for the subject and for the presumed auditor, to fashioning the traditional history of old Scotland into one of the most delightful narratives of any language or time. But Henry Hallam, a contemporary of these men (1778–1859), unlike them lives as a historian only, or as a historian and literary critic — occupations so frequently combined during the present century that perhaps an apology is due for the presentation of some writers under the general head of one class rather than under that of the other.   Hallam, the son of a Dean of Bristol, educated at Eton and Christ Church, an early *Edinburgh* reviewer, and an honoured pundit and champion of the Whig party, possessing also great literary tastes, much industry, and considerable faculty both of judging and writing, united almost all the qualifications for a high reputation; while his abstinence from public affairs, and from participation in the violent half-personal, half-political squabbles which were common among the literary men of his day, freed him from most of the disadvantages, while retaining for him all the advantages, of party connections.   Early, too, he obtained a post in the Civil Service (a Commissionership of Audit), which gave him a comfortable subsistence while leaving him plenty of leisure.   For thirty years, between 1818 and 1848, he produced a series of books on political and literary history which at once attained a very high reputation, and can hardly be said to have yet lost it.   These were a *View of the State of Europe during the Middle Ages*, published in the first, and supplemented by a volume of notes and corrections in the last, of the years just mentioned; a *Constitutional History of England* from Henry VII. to George II. (1827); and an *Introduction to the Literature of Europe in the Fifteenth, Sixteenth, and Seventeenth Centuries* (1837-39).

The value of Hallam as a political and as a literary historian is by no means the same.   In the former capacity he was perhaps too much influenced by that artificial and rather curious ideal of politics which distinguished the Whig party of the later eighteenth century, which was exaggerated, celebrated brilliantly, and perhaps buried by his pupil and younger contemporary, Macaulay, and which practically erects the result of a coincidence of accidents in English history into a permanent and rationally defensible form of government, comparable with and preferable to the earlier and unchanging forms of monarchy, aristocracy, and democracy with their sub-varieties.   A certain coldness and sluggishness of temperament and sympathy also marred this part of Hallam's work, though less mischievously than elsewhere. But to balance these drawbacks handsomely in his favour, he possessed an industry which, immense as have been the pains spent on his subjects since he wrote, leaves him in possession of a very fair part of the field as a still trustworthy authority; a mind, on the whole, judicial and fair; and an excellently clear and scholarly if not exactly brilliant or engaging style.

As a literary historian and critic Hallam deserves, except on the score of industry and width of reading, rather less praise; and his dicta, once quoted with veneration even by good authorities, and borrowed, with or without acknowledgment, by nearly all second-hand writers, are being more and more neglected by both. Nor is this unjust, for Hallam, though possessed, as has been said, of sound and wide scholarship, and of a taste fairly trustworthy in accepted and recognised matters, was too apt to be at a loss when confronted with an abnormal or eccentric literary personality, shared far too much the hide-bound narrowness of the rules which guided his friend Jeffrey, lacked the enthusiasm which not seldom melted Jeffrey's chains of ice, and was constantly apt to intrude into the court of literary judgments, methods, procedures, and codes of law which have no business there.

Many other estimable, and some excellent writers fill up the space of fifty years, which may be described best, both for remembrance and for accuracy, as the space between Gibbon and Carlyle. William Roscoe, who was born as far back as 1753 and did not die till 1831, was the son of a market-gardener near Liverpool, and had few advantages of education, but became an attorney, attached himself strenuously to literature, especially Italian literature, and in 1796 published his *Life of Lorenzo de Medici*, which, after finishing it, he followed up nine years later with the *Life of Leo the Tenth*. Both obtained not merely an English but a continental reputation, both became in a manner classics, and both retain value to this day, though the Italian Renaissance has been a specially favourite subject of modern

inquiry. Roscoe was a violent Whig, and not a very dispassionate student in some respects; but he wrote well, and he is an
early example of the diffusion of the historic spirit proper, in
which Gibbon had at once set the example and, with some lapses,
attained nearly to perfection.

William Mitford (1744–1827) was even an older man than
Roscoe, and belonged to a slightly less modern school of history-
writing. He was a man of means, a friend of Gibbon, his fellow-
officer in the militia, and like him a strong Tory, though unlike
him he could not keep his politics out of his history. Although
Mitford's hatred of democracy, whether well- or ill-founded, makes
him sometimes unfair, and though his *History of Greece* contains
some blunders, it is on the whole rather a pity that it should have
been superseded to the extent to which it actually has been by
those of Grote and Thirlwall. For it is not more prejudiced and
much better written than Grote's, while it has greater liveliness
and zest than the Bishop's. It occupied more than thirty years
in publication, the first volume appearing in 1784, the last in
1818.

While Roscoe and Mitford were thus dealing with foreign and
ancient subjects, English history became the theme of a somewhat younger pair of historians, one of whom, Sharon Turner,
was born in 1768 and died in 1847; while John Lingard, born
three years later, outlived Turner by four. Lingard was a Roman
Catholic priest, and after being educated at Douai, divided most
of his time between pastoral work and teaching at the newly
founded Roman Catholic school of Ushaw. He was the author
of what still retains the credit of being the best history of England on the great scale, in point of the union of accuracy, skilful
arrangement, fairness (despite his inevitable prepossessions), and
competent literary form, — no mean credit for a member of an
unpopular minority to have attained in a century of the most
active historical investigation. Turner was more of a specialist
and particularist, and his style is not very estimable. He wrote
many books on English history, those on the later periods being

of little value. But his *History of the Anglo-Saxons*, first issued in 1799, was based on thorough research, and may be said to have for the first time rescued the period of origins of English history from the discreditable condition of perfunctory, traditional, and second- or third-hand treatment in which most, if not all, previous historians of England had been content to leave it.

Sir Francis Palgrave, another historian to whom the student of early English history is deeply indebted, was born in London in 1788, his paternal name being Cohen. He took to the law, and early devoted himself both within and outside his profession to genealogical and antiquarian research. Before much attention had been paid in France itself to Old French, he published a collection of Anglo-Norman poems in 1818, and from these studies he passed to that of English history as such. He was knighted in 1832, and made Deputy-Keeper of the Records in 1838; his tenure of this post being only terminated by his death in 1861. Palgrave edited many State documents (writs, calendars, rolls, and so forth), and in his last years executed a *History of Normandy and England* of great value. His considerable literary power became more considerable still in two of his sons: the eldest, for some time past Professor of Poetry at Oxford, Mr. F. T. Palgrave, being still alive, and therefore merely to be mentioned; while the second, William Gifford, who was born in 1826 and died in 1888, Minister at Monte Video, was a man of the most brilliant talents and the most varied career. He was a soldier, a Jesuit, a traveller in the most forbidden parts of Arabia at the expense of a foreign country, and for nearly a quarter of a century a member of the consular and diplomatic service of his own. His *Narrative* of his Arabian journey, his *Dutch Guiana*, and some remarkable poems are only a few of his works, all of which have strong character.

Nearly contemporary with these was Dr. Thomas M'Crie (1772–1835), whose *Lives of Knox* (1812) and *Melville* (1819) entitle him to something like the title of Historian of Scotch Presbyterianism in its militant period. M'Crie, who was styled by Hallam (a person

not given to nicknames), "the Protestant Hildebrand," was a
worthy and learned man of untiring industry, and his subjects so
intimately concern not merely Scottish but British history for
nearly two centuries, that his handling of them could not but be
important. But he was desperately prejudiced, and his furious
attack on Sir Walter Scott's *Old Mortality*, by which he is
perhaps known to more persons than by his own far from uninteresting works, argues a crass deficiency in intellectual and
æsthetic comprehension.

The tenth decade of the eighteenth century was as much a
decade of historians as the eighth had been a decade of poets ;
and with Milman and Tytler born in 1791, Alison in 1792, Grote
in 1794, Arnold and Carlyle in 1795, Thirlwall in 1797, and
Macaulay in 1800, it may probably challenge comparison with
any period of equal length. The batch falls into three pretty
distinct classes, and the individual members of it are also pretty
widely separated in importance, so that it may be more convenient
to discuss them in the inverse order of their merit rather than in
the direct order of their births.

Patrick Fraser Tytler, son and grandson of historians (his
grandfather William being the first and not the worst champion
of Queen Mary against the somewhat Philistine estimates of
Hume and Robertson, and his father Alexander a Professor of
History, a Scotch Judge, and an excellent writer in various kinds
of *belles lettres*), was a man of the finest character, the friend of
most of the great men of letters at Edinburgh in the age of Scott
and Jeffrey, and the author of an excellent *History of Scotland*
from Alexander the Third to the Union of the Crowns. He was
born in 1791, was called to the Scotch Bar in 1813, and died
young for a historian (a class which has so much to do with Time
that he is apt to be merciful to it) in 1849. He was perhaps hardly
a man of genius, but he commanded universal respect. Sir Archibald Alison was the son of a clergyman of the same name, who, after
taking orders in England and holding some benefices there, became
known as the author of *Essays on the Principles of Taste*, which

possess a good deal of formal and some real merit.   Archibald the
younger was highly distinguished at the University of Edinburgh,
was called to the Scotch Bar, and distinguished himself there also,
being ultimately appointed Sheriff of Lanarkshire.   Like most of
the brighter wits among his immediate contemporaries in Scotland (we have the indisputable testimony of Jeffrey to the fact)
Alison was an out-and-out Tory, and a constant contributor to
Blackwood, while his literary activity took very numerous shapes.
At last he began, and in the twenty years from 1839 to 1859
carried through, a *History of Europe during the French Revolution*,
completed by one of *Europe from the Fall of the First to the
Accession of the Third Napoleon*.   He died in 1867.   It was
rather unfortunate for Alison that he did not undertake this great
work until the period of Liberal triumph which marked the
middle decades of the century had well set in.   It was still more
unlucky, and it could less be set down to the operations of unkind
chance, that in many of the qualifications of the writer in
general, and the historical writer in particular, he was deficient.
He had energy and industry ; he was much less inaccurate than
it was long the fashion to represent him ; a high sense of
patriotism and the political virtues generally, a very fair faculty
of judging evidence, and a thorough interest in his subject were
his.   But his book was most unfortunately diffuse, earning its
author the *sobriquet* of " Mr. Wordy," and it was conspicuously
lacking in grasp, both in the marshalling of events and in the
depicting of characters.   Critics, even when they sympathised,
have never liked it ; but contrary to the wont of very lengthy
histories, it found considerable favour with the public, who, as the
French gibe has it, were not " hampered by the style," and
who probably found in the popular explanation of a great series
of important and interesting affairs all that they cared for.   Nor
is it unlikely that this popularity rather exaggerated the ill-will of the
critics themselves.   Alison is not quotable ; he is, even after youth,
read with no small difficulty ; but it would be no bad thing if
other periods of history had been treated in his manner and spirit.

Henry Hart Milman belongs to very much the same class of historian as Hallam, but unlike Hallam he was a poet, and, though a Broad Churchman of the days before the nickname was given, more of an adherent to the imaginative and traditional side of things. His father was a King's Physician, and he was educated at Eton and Brasenose. He obtained the Newdigate, and after bringing out his best play *Fazio* (of which more will be said later), took orders and received the vicarage of St. Mary's, Reading. Some poems of merit in the second class, including some hymns very nearly in the first, followed, and in 1821 he became Professor of Poetry at Oxford, where six years later he was Bampton Lecturer. It was in 1829 that Milman, who had been a frequent contributor to the *Quarterly Review*, began the series of his works on ecclesiastical history with the *History of the Jews*, the weakest of them (for Milman was not a very great Hebraist, and while endeavouring to avoid rigid orthodoxy did not satisfy the demands of the newer heterodox criticism). The *History of Christianity to the Abolition of Paganism* was better (1840), and the *History of Latin Christianity* (1854) better still. This last indeed, based on an erudition which enabled Milman to re-edit Gibbon with advantage, is a great book, and will probably live. For Milman here really *knew;* he had (like most poets who write prose with fair practice) an excellent style ; and he was able — as many men who have had knowledge have not been able, and as many who have had style have not tried or have failed to do — to rise to the height of a really great argument, and treat it with the grasp and ease which are the soul of history. That he owed much to Gibbon himself is certain ; that he did not fail to use his pupilage to that greatest of historians so as to rank among the best of his followers is not less certain, and is high enough praise for any man. He received the Deanery of St. Paul's in 1849, and held it till his death in 1868, having worthily sustained the glory of this the most literary of all great preferments in the Church of England by tradition, and having earned among English ecclesiastical historians a place like that of Napier among their military comrades.

Hallam and Milman were both, as has been said, Oxford men, and the unmistakable impress of that University was on both, though less on Hallam than on Milman. It is all the more interesting that their chief historical contemporaries of the same class were, the one a Cambridge man, and one of the most distinguished, the other not a University man at all. Both Grote and Thirlwall, as it happens, were educated at the same public school, Charterhouse. George Grote, the elder of them, born in 1794, was the son of a banker, and himself carried on that business for many years of his life. He was an extreme Liberal, or as it then began to be called, Radical, and a chief of the Philosophical Radicals of his time — persons who followed Bentham and the elder Mill. He was elected member for the City in the first Reform Parliament and held the seat for nine years; though if he had not retired he would probably have been turned out. Leaving Parliament in 1841, he left business two years later, and gave himself up to his *History of Greece*, which was published in the ten years between 1846 and 1856. He died in 1871, and was buried in Westminster Abbey. So was, four years later, his school-fellow, fellow-historian of Greece, and junior by three years, Connop Thirlwall. Thirlwall was one of the rare examples of extraordinary infant precocity (he could read Latin at three and Greek at four) who have been great scholars and men of distinction in after life, and to a ripe age. He was of a Northumbrian family, but was born at Stepney. From Charterhouse he went rather early (in 1814) to Trinity College, Cambridge, where he had almost the most brilliant undergraduate career on record, and duly gained his fellowship. He entered Lincoln's Inn, was actually called to the Bar, but preferred the Church, and took orders in his thirtieth year. He had already shown a strong leaning to theology, and had translated Schleiermacher. He now returned to Cambridge, taking both tutorial work and cure of souls; but in 1834 his

Liberal views attracted the disfavour of Christopher Wordsworth, Master of Trinity, and Thirlwall, resigning his tutorship, was consoled by Brougham with a Yorkshire living. Nor was this long his only preferment, for the Whigs were not too well off for clergymen who united scholarship, character, and piety, and he was made Bishop of St. David's in 1840. He held the see for thirty-four years, working untiringly, earning justly (though his orthodoxy was of a somewhat Broad character, and he could reconcile his conscience to voting for the disestablishment of the Irish Church) the character of one of the most exemplary bishops of the century, and seldom dining without a cat on his shoulder.

Thirlwall wrote many Charges, some of them famous, some delightful letters, part of a translation of Niebuhr, and some essays, while Grote, besides his historical work, produced some political and other work before it, with a large but not very good book on Plato, and the beginning of another on Aristotle after it. But it is by their *Histories of Greece* that they must live in literature. These histories (of which Grote's was planned and begun as early as 1823, though not completed till long afterwards, while Thirlwall's began to appear in 1835, and was finished just after Grote's saw the light) were both written with a certain general similarity of point of view as antidotes to Mitford, and as putting the Liberal view of the ever memorable and ever typical history of the Greek states. But in other respects they diverge widely; and it has been a constant source of regret to scholars that the more popular, and as the French would say *tapageur*, of the two, to a considerable extent eclipsed the solid worth and the excellent form of Thirlwall. Grote's history displays immense painstaking and no inconsiderable scholarship, though it is very nearly as much a "party pamphlet" as Macaulay's own, the advocate's client being in this case not merely the Athenian democracy but even the Athenian demagogue. Yet it to a great extent redeems this by the vivid way in which it makes the subject alive, and turns Herodotus and Thucydides,

Demosthenes and Xenophon, from dead texts and school-books into theses of eager and stimulating interest. But it has absolutely no style; its scale is much too great; the endless discussions and arguments on quite minor points tend to throw the whole out of focus, and to disaccustom the student's eye and mind to impartial and judicial handling; and the reader constantly sighs for the placid Olympian grasp of Gibbon, nay, even for the confident dogmatism of Macaulay himself, instead of the perpetual singlestick of argument which clatters and flourishes away to the utter discomposure of the dignity of the Historic Muse.

It is possible, on the other hand, that Thirlwall may have sacrificed a little too much, considering his age and its demands, to mere dispassionate dignity. He is seldom picturesque, and indeed he never tries to be so. But to a scholarship naturally far superior to Grote's, he united a much fairer and more judicial mind, and the faculty of writing — instead of loose stuff not exactly ungrammatical nor always uncomely, but entirely devoid of any grace of style — an excellent kind of classical English, but slightly changed from the best eighteenth century models. And he had what Grote lacked, the gift of seeing that the historian need not — nay, that he ought not to — parade every detail of the arguments by which he has reached his conclusions; but should state those conclusions themselves, reserving himself for occasional emergencies in which process as well as result may be properly exhibited. It is fair to say, in putting this curious pair forward as examples respectively of the popular and scholarly methods of historical writing, that Grote's learning and industry were very much more than popular, while Thirlwall's sense and style might with advantage have put on, now and then, a little more pomp and circumstance. But still the contrast holds; and until fresh discoveries like that of the *Athenian Polity* accumulate to an extent which calls for and obtains a new real historian of Greece, it is Thirlwall and not Grote who deserves the first rank as such in English.

Intimately connected with all these historians in time and style, but having over them the temporary advantage of being famous in another way, and the, as some think, permanent disadvantage of falling prematurely out of public favour, was Thomas Arnold. He was born at Cowes, in the Isle of Wight, on 13th June 1795, and was educated at Winchester and at Corpus Christi College, Oxford. At the age of twenty he was elected a fellow of Oriel — a distinction which was, and remained for two decades, almost the highest in the University — and he gained both Chancellor's Essay prizes, for Latin and English. Oriel was not in his time, as it was very shortly afterwards, a centre of ecclesiastical orthodoxy; but rather the home of a curious transition blend of thought which in different persons took the high-and-dry or the Rationalist direction, and was only generally opposed to Evangelicalism. Arnold himself inclined to the Liberal side, and had also strong personal gifts for teaching. He took orders, but neither became a tutor nor took a living, and established himself at Laleham, on the Thames, to take private pupils. After ten years' practice here he was elected to the Headmastership of Rugby, a school then, after vicissitudes, holding little if anything more than a medium place among those English Grammar Schools which ranked below the great schools of Eton, Harrow, Westminster, Winchester, and Charterhouse. How he succeeded in placing it on something like an equality with these, and how on the other hand he became, as it were, the apostle of the infant Broad Church School which held aloof alike from Evangelicals and Tractarians, are points which do not directly concern us. His more than indirect influence on literature was great; for few schools have contributed to it, in the same time, a greater number of famous writers than Rugby did under his head-mastership. His direct connection with it was limited to a fair number of miscellaneous works, many sermons, an edition of Thucydides, and a *History of Rome* which did not proceed (owing to his death in 1842, just after he had been appointed Regius Professor of Modern History at Oxford) beyond the

Second Punic War. Arnold, once perhaps injudiciously ex-
tolled by adoring pupils, and the defender of a theory of
churchmanship which strains rather to the uttermost the principle of unorthodox economy, has rather sunk between the
undying disapproval of the orthodox and the fact that the unorthodox have long left his standpoint. But his style is undoubtedly
of its own kind scholarly and excellent ; the matter of his history
suffers from the common fault of taking Niebuhr at too high a
valuation.

Thomas Babington Macaulay (who may be conveniently discussed before Carlyle, though he was Carlyle's junior by five years,
inasmuch as, even putting relative critical estimate aside, he died
much earlier and represented on the whole an older style of
thought) was born at Rothley Temple in Leicestershire on 25th
October 1800. His father, Zachary Macaulay, though a very
active agitator against the Slave Trade, was a strong Tory ; and
the son's conversion to Whig opinions was effected at some not
clearly ascertained period after he had reached manhood. A
very precocious child, he was at first privately educated, but entered
Trinity College, Cambridge, at the age of eighteen. Here he
fell in with a set somewhat but not much less distinguished than
that of the famous time, about ten years later, of which Tennyson was the centre — a set the most brilliant member of which,
besides Macaulay, was the poet Praed. Praed had been accustomed to journalism before he left Eton, and had made acquaintance at Windsor with the bookseller Knight, for whose *Quarterly
Magazine* both he and Macaulay wrote some very good things.
Macaulay himself obtained the Chancellor's prize for English
poems on " Pompeii " and " Evening," in two successive years
1819 and 1820 ; and after a very distinguished undergraduate
career was elected fellow of his college. He went to the Bar,
and his father's fortune, which had been a good one, being lost,
his chances were for a time uncertain. In 1825, however, he won
the admiration of Jeffrey and a place on the *Edinburgh Review*
by his well-known, and slightly gaudy, but wonderfully fresh and

stimulating article on Milton ; and literature, which had always been his ideal employment, seemed already likely to yield him a fair subsistence — for review-writing was at that time much more highly paid than it is at present.   Moreover the Whigs, on the eve of their long postponed triumph, were looking out for young men of talent ; and Macaulay, being recruited by them, was put into Lord Lansdowne's pocket-borough of Calne.   In the Reform debates themselves he distinguished himself greatly, and after the Bill was carried, having been elected for Leeds, he was not long in receiving his reward.   It was munificent, for he, a man of little more than thirty, who had made no reputation at the Bar, though much elsewhere, was appointed Legal Member of Council in India with a salary very much of which could in those days be saved by a careful man, especially if, like Macaulay, he was un-married.   Accordingly when, after between four and five years' stay, Macaulay in 1838 returned home, he was in possession of means sufficient to enable him to devote himself without fear or hindrance to literary and political pursuits, while his fame had been raised higher during his absence by his contributions to the *Edinburgh Review*.   Indeed his Indian experiences furnished the information — erroneous in some cases and partisan in others, but brilliantly used — enabling him to write the famous essays on Clive and on Hastings, where his historical method is at almost its best.   He was elected member for Edinburgh, a very high compli-ment, in 1839 ; and next year became Secretary for War.   In 1842 and 1843 respectively he established his position in verse and prose by publishing the *Lays of Ancient Rome* and a collec-tion of his *Essays;* and in 1846 he was made Postmaster-General. But his support of the Maynooth Grant offended the Protestantism of his constituents, and he lost his seat, and for the time his polit-ical opportunities, in 1847.   The disaster was no disaster for liter-ature : he had long been employed on a *History of England from the Accession of James II.*, and being now able to devote his whole time to it, he published the first volumes in 1848 with astonishing success.

Q

He was re-elected for Edinburgh in 1852, published the third and fourth volumes of his History in 1855 with success greater in pecuniary ways and otherwise than even that of their fore-runners, was raised to the Upper House as Lord Macaulay of Rothley in 1857, and died two years later, on 28th December 1859, of heart disease. Some personal peculiarities of Macaulay's — his extraordinary reading and memory, his brilliant but rather tyrannical conversation, his undoubting self-confidence — were pretty well known in his lifetime, and did not always create a prejudice in his favour. But a great revolution in this respect was brought about by the *Life* of him, produced a good many years later by his nephew, Sir George Trevelyan — a Life, standing for the interest of its matter and the skill and taste of its manner, not too far below the masterpieces of Boswell and Lockhart.

The literary personality of Macaulay, though a great one in all respects, is neither complex nor unequally present, and it is there-fore desirable to discuss all its manifestations together. In the order of importance and of bulk his work may be divided into verse, prose-essays, and history, for his speeches less directly con-cern us, and are very little more than essays adroitly enough adjusted so as not to be tedious to the hearer. In all three capacities he was eminently popular; and in all three his popu-larity has brought with it a sort of reaction, partly justified, partly unjust. The worst brunt of this reaction has fallen upon his verse, the capital division of which, the *Lays of Ancient Rome*, was persistently decried by Mr. Matthew Arnold, the critic of most authority in the generation immediately succeeding Macaulay's. A poet of the very highest class Macaulay was not; his way of thought was too positive, too clear, too destitute either of mystery or of dream, to command or to impart the true poetical mirage, to "make the common as if it were not common." His best efforts of this kind are in small and not very generally known things, the "Jacobite's Epitaph," "The Last Buccaneer." But his ballads earlier and later, *Ivry, The Armada, Naseby*, and the Roman quartet, exhibit the result of a consummate literary faculty with a real native gift for rhythm and metre, applying the lessons of the great Romantic generation with extraordinary vigour and success, and not without considerable eloquence and refinement. It is a gross and vulgar critical error to deem Macaulay's poetical effects vulgar or gross. They are *popular;* they hit exactly that scheme of poetry which the general ear can appreciate and the general brain understand. They are coin for general circulation ; but they are not base coin. Hundreds and thousands of immature and 'prentice tastes have been educated to the enjoyment of better things by them ; thousands and tens of thousands of tastes, respectable at least, have found in them the kind of poetry which they can like, and beyond which they are not fitted to go. And it would be a very great pity if there were ever wanting critical appreciations which, while relishing things more exquisite and understanding things more esoteric, can still taste and savour the simple genuine fare of poetry which Macaulay offers. There are few wiser proverbs than that which cautions us against demanding " better bread than is made of wheat," and the poetical bread of the *Lays of Ancient Rome* is an honest household loaf that no healthy palate will reject.

In the second division, that of essay writing, Macaulay occupies a position both absolutely and relatively higher. That the best verse ranks above even the best prose is not easily disputable ; that prose which is among the very best of its own particular kind ranks above verse which though good is not the best, may be asserted without any fear. And in their own kind of essay, Macaulay's are quite supreme. Jeffrey, a master of writing and a still greater master of editing, with more than twenty years' practice in criticism, asked him " where he got that style ? " The question was not entirely unanswerable. Macaulay had taken not a little from Gibbon ; he had taken something from a then still living contributor of Jeffrey's own, Hazlitt. But his private and personal note was after all uppermost in the compound. It had appeared early (it can be seen in things of his written when he was an undergraduate). It owed much to the general atmosphere of the century, to the habit of drawing phrase, illustration, idea, not merely from the vernacular or from classical authorities, but from the great writers of earlier European literature. And it would probably have been impossible without the considerable body of forerunners which the *Edinburgh*, the *Quarterly*, and other things of which some notice has been given in a former chapter, had supplied. But still the individual character reigns supreme.

Macaulay's Essays are in something more than the ordinary loose acceptation of the term a household word; and it cannot be necessary to single out individual instances where almost all are famous, and where all deserve their fame. The " Milton " and the " Southey," the " Pitt " and the " Chatham," the " Addison " and the " Horace Walpole," the " Clive " and the " Hastings," the " Frederick the Great " and the " Madame D'Arblay," the " Restoration Dramatists " and the " Boswell," the " Hallam " and the " Ranke," present with a marvellous consistency the same merits and the same defects. The defects are serious enough. In the first place the system, which Macaulay did not invent, but which he carried to perfection, of regarding the particular book in hand less as a subject of elaborate and minute criticism and exposition than as a mere starting-point from which to pursue the critic's own views of the subject, inevitably leads to unfairness, especially in matters of pure literature. Macaulay's most famous performance in this latter kind, the crushing review of the unlucky Robert Montgomery, though well enough deserved in the particular case, escapes this condemnation only to fall under another, that of looking at the parts rather than at the whole. It is quite certain that, given their plan, the two famous critiques of Tennyson and Keats, in the *Quarterly* and in *Blackwood*, are well enough justified. The critic looks only at the weak parts, and he judges the weak parts only by the stop-watch. But, on his own wide and more apparently generous method, Macaulay was exposed to equal dangers, and succumbed to them less excusably. He had strong prejudices, and it is impossible for any one who reads him with knowledge not to see that the vindication of those prejudices, rather than the exposition and valuation of the subject, was what he had first at heart. He was too well informed (though, especially in the Indian Essays, he was sometimes led astray by his authorities), and he was too honest a man, to be untrustworthy in positive statement. But though he practised little in the courts, he had the born advocate's gift, or drawback, of inclination to *suppressio veri* and *suggestio falsi*, and he has a heavy account to make up under these heads. Even under them perhaps he has less to answer for than on the charge of a general superficiality and shallowness, which is all the more dangerous because of the apparently transparent thoroughness of his handling, and because of the actual clearness and force with which he both sees and puts his view. For a first draft of a subject Macaulay is incomparable, if his readers will only be content to take it for a first draft, and to feel that they must fill up and verify, that they must deepen and widen. But the heights and depths of the subject he never gives, and perhaps he never saw them.

Part of this is no doubt to be set down to the quality of his style ; part to a weakness of his, which was not so much readiness to accept any conclusion that was convenient as a constitutional incapacity for not making up his mind. To leave a thing in half lights, in compromise, to take it, as the legal phrase of the country of his ancestors has it, *ad avizandum*, was to Macaulay abhorrent and impossible. He must "conclude," and he was rather too apt to do so by "quailing, crushing, and quelling" all difficulties of opposing arguments and qualifications. He simply would not have an unsolved problem mystery. Strafford was a "rancorous renegade"; Swift a sort of gifted Judas; Bacon a mean fellow with a great intellect; Dryden again a renegade, though not rancorous ; Marlborough a self-seeking traitor of genius. And all these conclusions were enforced in their own style — the style of *l'homme même*. It was rather teasingly antithetical, "Tom's snip-snap" as the jealous smartness of Brougham called it; it was somewhat mechanical in its arrangement of narrative, set passages of finer writing, cunningly devised summaries of facts, comparisons, contrasts (to show the writer's learning and dazzle the reader with names), exordium, iteration, peroration, and so forth. But it observed a very high standard of classical English, a little intolerant of neologism, but not stiff nor jejune. It had an almost unexampled— a certainly unsurpassed — power (slightly helped by repetition perhaps) of bringing the picture that the writer saw, the argument that he thought, the sentiment that he felt, before the reader's eyes, mind, and feeling. And, as indeed follows from this, it was pre-eminently clear. It is perhaps the clearest style in English that does not, like those of Swift and Cobbett, deliberately or scornfully eschew rhetorical ornament. What Macaulay means you never, being any degree short of an idiot, can fail to understand ; and yet he gives you the sense, equipped with a very considerable amount of preparation and trimming. It would not merely have been ungrateful, it would have been positively wrong, if his audience, specially trained as most of them were to his standpoint of Whig Reformer, had failed to hail him as one of the greatest writers that had ever been known. Nor would it be much less wrong if judges very differently equipped and constituted were to refuse him a high place among great writers.

The characteristics of the *Essays* reproduce themselves on a magnified scale so exactly in the *History* that the foregoing criticism applies with absolute fidelity to the later and larger, as well as to the earlier and more minute work. But it would not be quite fair to say that no new merits appear. There are no new defects ; though the difference of the scope and character of the undertaking intensifies in degree, as well as magnifies in bulk, the faults of advocacy and of partiality which have caused the book to be dismissed, with a flippancy only too well deserved by its own treatment of opponents, as " a Whig pamphlet in four octavo volumes." Yet the width of study and the grasp of results, which, though remarkable, were not exactly extraordinary, in the compass and employed on the subject of a *Reveiw* article, became altogether amazing and little short of miraculous in this enlarged field. One of the earliest and one of the best passages, the view of the state of

England at the death of Charles the Second, may challenge comparison, as a clearly arranged and perfectly mastered collection of innumerable minute facts sifted out of a thousand different sources, with anything in history ancient or modern. The scale of the book is undoubtedly too great; and if it had been carried, as the author originally intended, to a date "within the memory of" his contemporaries, it would have required the life of Old Parr to complete it and the patience of Job to read it through. The necessity of a hero is a necessity felt by all the nobler sort of writers. But the choice of William of Orange for the purpose was, to say the least, unlucky; and the low morality which he had himself, in an earlier work, confessed as to the statesmen of the period imparted an additional stimulus to the historian's natural tendency to be unfair to his political opponents, in the vain hope, by deepening the blacks, to get a sort of whiteness upon the grays. It has further to be confessed that independent examination of separate points is not very favourable to Macaulay's trustworthiness. He never tells a falsehood; but he not seldom contrives to convey one, and he constantly conceals the truth. Still, the general picture is so vivid and stimulating, the mastery of materials is so consummate, and the beauty of occasional passages — the story of Monmouth's Conspiracy, that of James' insane persecution of Magdalen College, that of the Trial of the Seven Bishops, that of the Siege of Londonderry — so seductive, that the most hostile criticism which is not prepared to shut eyes and ears to anything but faults cannot refuse admiration. And it ought not to be omitted that Macaulay was practically the first historian who not merely examined the literature of his subject with unfailing care and attention, but took the trouble to inspect the actual places with the zeal of a topographer or an antiquary. That this added greatly to the vividness and picturesque character of his descriptions need hardly be said; that it often resulted in a distinct gain to historical knowledge is certain. But perhaps not its least merit was the putting down in a practically imperishable form, and in the clearest possible manner, of a vast number of interesting details which time is only too quick to sweep away. The face of England has changed more since Macaulay's time, though a bare generation since, than it had changed in the four or five generations between the day of his theme and his own; and thus he rescued for us at once the present and the past.

It is almost impossible to imagine a greater contrast between two contemporaries of the same nation, both men of letters of the first rank, than that which exists between Thomas Macaulay and Thomas Carlyle. In the subjects to which both had affinity there was a rather remarkable connection. Macaulay's education rather than his sympathies made him something of a master of at least the formal part of poetry, in which Carlyle could do nothing. But essentially they were both writers of prose; they were both men in whom the historico-politico-social interests were much greater than the purely literary, the purely artistic, or the purely scientific — though just as Carlyle was a bad verse-writer or none at all, Macaulay a good one, so Carlyle was a good mathematician, Macaulay a bad one or none at all. But in the point of view from which they regarded the subjects with which they dealt, and in the style in which they treated them, they were poles asunder. Indeed it may be questioned whether " the style is the point of view " would not be a better form of the famous deliverance than that which, in full or truncated form, has obtained currency.

Carlyle was born on the 4th December 1795 at Ecclefechan (the Entepfuhl of the *Sartor*), in Dumfriesshire, being the son of a stone-mason. He was educated first at the parish school, then at that of Annan (the nearest town), and was about fifteen when he was sent, in the usual way of Scotch boys with some wits and no money, to the University of Edinburgh. His destination was equally of course the Church, but he very early developed that dislike to all fixed formularies which characterised him through life, and which perhaps was not his greatest characteristic. To mathematics, on the other hand, he took pretty kindly, though he seems to have early exhausted the fascinations of them. Like most men of no means who have little fancy for any of the regular professions, he attempted teaching; and as a schoolmaster at Annan, Haddington, and Kirkcaldy, or a private tutor (his chief experience in which art was with Charles Buller), he spent no small number of years, doing also some hack-work in the way of translating, writing for Brewster's *Encyclopædia*, and contributing to the *London Magazine*, that short-lived but fertile nurse of genius. The most remarkable of these productions was the *Life of Schiller*, which was published as a volume in 1825, his thirtieth year, at which time he was a resident in London and a frequenter — a not too amiable one — of Coleridge's circle at Highgate and of other literary places.

The most important event in his life took place in 1826, when he married Miss Jane Welsh, a young lady who traced her descent to John Knox, who had some property, who had a genius of her own, and who was all the more determined to marry a man of genius. She had hestitated between Irving and Carlyle, and, whatever came of it, there can be no doubt that she was right in preferring the somewhat uncouth and extremely undeveloped tutor who had taught her several things, — whether love in the proper sense was among them or not will always be a moot point. The *Edinburgh Review* was kind to Carlyle after its fashion, and he wrote for it; but Jeffrey, though very well disposed both to Carlyle and to his wife, could not endure the changes which soon came on his style, and might have addressed the celebrated query which, as mentioned, just at the same time he addressed in delighted surprise to Macaulay, "Where did you get that style," to Carlyle in the identical words but with a very different meaning. Even had it been different, it was impossible that Carlyle should serve anywhere or any one; and his mind, not an early ripening one, was even yet, at the age of thirty-two, in a very unorganised condition. He resolved to retire to his wife's farm of Craigenputtock in Nithsdale; and Mrs. Carlyle had the almost unparalleled heroism to consent to this. For it must be remembered that her husband, with the exception of the revenue of a few essays, was living on her means, that he undertook no professional duties, and that in the farmhouse she had to perform those of a servant as well as those of a wife. Whatever other opinions may be passed on this episode of Carlyle's life, which lasted from 1828 to 1834, there can be no doubt that it "made" him. He did much positive work there, including all his best purely literary essays. There he wrote *Sartor Resartus*, his manifesto and proclamation, a wild book which, to its eternal honour, *Fraser's Magazine* accepted, probably under the influence of Lockhart, with whom, strangely different as they were, Carlyle was always on good, though never on intimate terms. There too was written great part of the earlier form of the *French Revolution*. But the greatest thing that he did at Craigenputtock was the thorough fermentation, clearing, and settling of himself. When he went there, at nearly thirty-three, it was more uncertain what would come of him than it is in the case of many a man when he leaves the University at three and twenty. When he left it, at close on his fortieth year, the drama of his literary life was complete, though only a few lines of it were written.

That drama lasted in actual time for forty-seven years longer ; and for more than the first thirty of them fresh and ever fresh acts and scenes carried it on. For the public his place was taken once and for all by the *History of the French Revolution*, which, after alarming vicissitudes (John Stuart Mill having borrowed the first volume in MS. and lent it to a lady, to be destroyed by her housemaid), appeared in 1837. From at least that time Mrs. Carlyle's aspiration was fulfilled. There were gainsayers of course, — it may almost be said that genius which is not gainsaid is not genius, — there were furious decriers of style, temper, and so forth. But nine out of every ten men at least whose opinion was worth taking knew that a new star of the first magnitude had been added to English literature, however much they might think its rays in some respects baleful.

Lecturing, after the example set chiefly by Coleridge and Hazlitt, was at this time a favourite resource for those men of letters whose line of composition was not of the gainfulest; and Carlyle delivered several courses, some of which are unreported while others survive only in inadequate shapes. But *Heroes and Hero-Worship* was at first delivered orally, though it was not printed till 1841; and about the same time, or rather earlier, appeared the *Miscellaneous Essays* — a collection of his work at its freshest, least mannered, most varied, and in some respects best. *Chartism* (1839) and *Past and Present* (1843) reflected the political problems of the time and Carlyle's interest in them. But it was not till 1845 that a second, in the ordinary sense, great work, *Oliver Cromwell's Letters and Speeches*, was published. Five years passed without anything substantive from him, but in 1850 appeared *Latter-Day Pamphlets*, the most brilliantly satiric, and in 1851 the softest, most finished, and (save theologically) least debatable of all his books, the exquisite biography in miniature called the *Life of Sterling*. Then he engaged, it is difficult to say whether by ill-luck or not, on the last and largest of his great single undertakings, the *History of Frederick the Great*. Fourteen years were passed, as a matter of composition, in "the valley of the shadow of Frederick," as his wife put it: half the time (from 1858 to 1865) saw the actual publication. Shortly after the completion of this, Carlyle visited Edinburgh to receive the Lord Rectorship of his University, and soon after his wife died. He survived her fifteen years, but did nothing more of great importance; indeed, he was seventy-one when this loss happened. Some short things on "John Knox," on "The Early Kings of Norway," and a famous letter on "Shooting Niagara" (the Reform Bill of 1867), with a few more, appeared; but he was chiefly occupied (as far as he was occupied at all) in writing reminiscences, and arranging memorials of Mrs. Carlyle. The publication of these books after his death by the late Mr. Froude led to a violent conflict of opinion both as to the propriety of the publication and as to the character of Carlyle himself.

This conflict fortunately concerns us but little here. It is certain that Carlyle — springing from the lower ranks of society,

educated excellently as far as the intellect was concerned, but
without attention to such trifles as the habit (which his future wife
early remarked in him) of putting bread and butter in his tea, a
martyr from very early years to dyspepsia, fostering a retiring
spirit and not too social temper, thoroughly convinced that the
times were out of joint and not at all thoroughly convinced that
he or any one could set them right, finally possessed of an intensely religious nature which by accident or waywardness had
somehow thrown itself out of gear with religion — was not a happy
man himself or likely to make any one else happy who lived with
him. But it is certain also that both in respect to his wife and
to those men, famous or not famous, of whom he has left too
often unkindly record, his bark was much worse than his bite.
And it is further certain that Mrs. Carlyle was no down-trodden
drudge, but a woman of brains almost as alert as her husband's
and a tongue almost as sharp as his, who had deliberately made
her election of the vocation of being " wife to a man of genius,"
and who received what she had bargained for to the uttermost
farthing. There will always be those who will think that Mr.
Froude, doubtless with the best intentions, made a very great
mistake ; that, at any rate for many years after Carlyle's death, only
a strictly genuine but judicious selection of the Reminiscences
and Memorials should have been published, or else that the
whole should have been worked into a real biography in which
the frame and setting could have given the relief that the text
required. But already, after more than the due voices, there is
some peace on the subject ; and a temporary wave of neglect,
partly occasioned by this very controversy, was to be expected.

That this wave will pass may be asserted with a fulness and
calmness of assurance not to be surpassed in any similar case.
Carlyle's influence during a great part of the second and the
whole of the third quarter of this century was so enormous, his
life was so prolonged, and the general tone of public thought and
public policy which has prevailed since some time before his
death has been so adverse to his temper, that the reaction which

is all but inevitable in all cases was certain to be severe in his. And if this were a history of thought instead of being a history of the verbal expression of thought, it would be possible and interesting to explain this reaction, and to forecast the certain rebound from it. As it is, however, we have to do with Carlyle as a man of letters only ; and if his position as the greatest English man of letters of the century in prose be disputed, it will generally be found that the opposition is due to some not strictly literary cause, while it is certain that any competitor who is set up can be dislodged by a fervent and well-equipped Carlylian without very much difficulty.

He has been classed here as a historian, and though the bulk of his work is very great and its apparent variety considerable, it will be found that history and her sister biography, even when his subjects bore an appearance of difference, always in reality engaged his attention. His three greatest books, containing more than half his work in bulk, — *The French Revolution*, the *Cromwell*, and the *Frederick*, — are all openly and avowedly historical. The *Schiller* and the *Sterling* are biographies; the *Sartor Resartus* a fantastic autobiography. Nearly all the *Essays*, even those which are most literary in subject — all the *Lectures on Heroes*, the greater part of *Past and Present*, *The Early Kings of Norway*, the *John Knox*, are more or less plainly and strictly historical or biographical. Even *Chartism*, the non-antique part of *Past and Present*, and the *Latter-Day Pamphlets*, deal with politics in the sense in which politics are the principal agent in making history, regard them constantly and almost solely in their actual or probable effect on the life-story of the nation, and to no small extent of its individual members. Out of the historic relation of nation or individual Carlyle would very rarely attempt to place, and hardly ever succeeded in placing, any thing or person. He could not in the least judge literature — of which he was so great a practitioner always, and sometimes so great a judge — from the point of view of form : he would have scorned to do so, and did scorn those who did so. His deficiencies in abstract philosophy, whether political, theological, metaphysical, or other, arise directly from this — that he could never contemplate any of these things as abstract, but only in the common conduct of men towards their fellows, towards themselves, and towards God. For Carlyle never " forgot God," though he might speak unadvisedly with his lips of other men's ways of remembering Him. The " human document," as later slang has it, was in effect the only thing that interested him ; and he was content to employ it in constructing human history. More than once he put his idea of this history formally under a formal title. But his entire work is a much better exposition of that idea than these particular essays ; and it is not easy to open any page of it in which the idea itself is not vividly illustrated and enforced upon the reader.

But once more, this is no place for even a summary, much less for a discussion, of the much discussed Carlylian " Gospel of Work " ; of its apostle's less vague, but also less disputable, condemnations of shams and cants ; or of the innumerable applications and uses to which he put these doctrines. The important thing for our purpose is that these applications took form in thirty volumes of the most brilliant, the most stimulating, the most varied, the most original work in English literature. The titles of this work have been given ; to give here any notion of their contents would take the chapter. Carlyle could be — as in the *Cromwell*, where he sets himself and confines himself to the double task of elucidating his hero's rugged or crafty obscurities of speech and writing and of piecing them into a connected history, or where he wrestles with the huge accumulation of documents about Frederick — as practical as the driest of Dry-as-dusts. But others could equal, though few surpass him, in this. Where he stands alone is in a fantastic fertility of divagation and comment which is as much his own as the clear, neat directness of Macaulay is his. Much of it is due to his gospel, or temper, or whatever it is to be called, of earnest suasion to work and scornful denunciation of cant ; something to his wide reading and apt faculty of illustration ; but most to his style.

In the early days of his unpopularity this style used to be abused with heat or dismissed with scorn as mere falsetto, copied to a great extent from Richter. It is certain that in Carlyle's very earliest works there is small trace of it ; and that he writes in a fashion not very startlingly different from that of any well-read and well-taught author of his time. And it is certain also that it was after his special addiction to German studies that the new manner appeared. Yet it is very far indeed from being copied from any single model, or even from any single language ; and a great deal that is in it is not German at all. Something may even be traced to our own more fantastic writers in the seventeenth century, such as Sir Thomas Urquhart in Scotland and Sir Roger L'Estrange in England ; much to a Scottish fervour and quaintness blending itself with and utilising a wider range of reading than had been usual with Scotsmen ; most to the idiosyncrasy of the individual.

Carlyle's style is not seldom spoken of as compact of tricks and manners ; and no doubt these are present in it. Yet a narrow inspection will show that its effect is by no means due so much in reality as in appearance to the retaining of capital letters, the violent breaches and aposiopeses, the omission of pronouns and colourless parts of speech generally, the coining of new words, and the introduction of unusual forms. These things are often there, but they are not always ; and even when they are, there is something else much more important, much more characteristic, but also much harder to put the finger on. There is in Carlyle's fiercer and more serious passages a fiery glow of enthusiasm or indignation, in his lighter ones a quaint felicity of unexpected humour, in his expositions a vividness of presentment, in his arguments a sledge-hammer force, all of which are not to be found together anywhere else, and none of which is to be found anywhere in quite the same form. And despite the savagery, both of his indignation and his laughter, there is no greater master of tenderness. Wherever he is at home, and he seldom wanders far from it, the weapon of Carlyle is like none other, — it is the very sword of Goliath.

And this sword pierces to the joints and marrow as no other of the second division of our authors of the nineteenth century proper pierces, with the exception of that of Tennyson in verse. It is possible to disagree with Carlyle intensely ; perhaps it is not possible to agree with him in any detailed manner, unless the agreer be somewhat destitute of individual taste and judgment. But on his whole aspect and tendency, reserving individual expressions, he is, as few are, great. The *diathesis* is there — the general disposition towards noble and high things. The expression is there — the capacity of putting what is felt and meant in a manner always contemptuous of mediocrity, yet seldom disdainful of common sense. To speak on the best things in an original way, in a distinguished style, is the privilege of the elect in literature ; and none of those who were born within, or closely upon, the beginning of the century has had these gifts in English as have the authors of *The Lotos Eaters* and *Sartor Resartus*.

Only one other writer of history during the century, himself the latest to die of his generation except Mr. Ruskin, deserves, for the union of historical and literary merit, to be placed, if not on a level with Macaulay and Carlyle, yet not far below them ; but a not inconsiderable number of historians and biographers of value who distinguished themselves about or since the middle of the century must be chronicled more or less briefly. Two Scottish scholars of eminence, both in turn Historiographers Royal of Scotland, John Hill Burton and William Forbes Skene, were born in the same year, 1809. Burton, who died in 1881, busied himself with the history of his country at large, beginning with the period since the Revolution, and tackling the earlier and more distinctively national time afterwards. He was not a very good writer, but displayed very great industry and learning with a sound and impartial judgment. Skene, on the other hand, was the greatest authority of his time (he lived till 1892) on "Celtic Scotland," which is the title of his principal book. In the same year (or in 1808) was born Charles Merivale, afterwards

Fellow of St. John's College, Cambridge, and Dean of Ely, who, besides other work, established himself in the same class of historians with Hallam and Milman, Thirlwall and Grote, by his extensive *History of the Romans under the Empire*. On the whole, Merivale (who died in 1894) ranks, both for historical and literary gifts, somewhat below the other members of this remarkable group — a position which is still a very honourable one.

Shortly after these three was born Alexander Kinglake (1811–1891) — a man of very remarkable talents, but something of a "terrible example" in regard to the practice, which has already been noticed as characteristic of the century, of devoting enormously long histories to special subjects and points. Kinglake, who was a native of Somerset, an Eton and Cambridge man, a barrister subsequently, for some years a Member of Parliament, and a man of independent means, first distinguished himself in letters by the very brilliant and popular book of travels in the East called *Eothen* which was published in 1847. That there is something of manner and trick about this is not to be denied; but it must be allowed that the trick and manner have been followed, apparently with success, in travel-writing for about half a century, while it cannot be fairly said that Kinglake himself had any exact models, though he may have owed something to Beckford and a little to Sterne. It is not very easy to say whether Kinglake's literary reputation would have stood higher or lower if he had written nothing else; but as a matter of fact, before many years were over, he attempted a much more ambitious task in the *History of the Crimean War*, the first two volumes of which appeared in 1863, though the book was not finished till twenty years later. That this history shows no small literary faculties no competent judge can deny. The art of word-painting — a dubious and dangerous art — is pushed to almost its furthest limits; the writer has a wonderful gift of combining the minutest and most numerous details into an orderly and intelligible whole; and the quality which the French untranslatably call *d'able au corps*, or, as we more pedantically say, "dæmonic energy," is

R

present everywhere. But the book is monstrously out of proportion, — a single battle has something like an entire volume, and
the events of some two years occupy eight, — and, clear as the
individual pictures are, the panorama is of such endless length
that the mind's eye retains no proper notion of it. In the second
place, the style, though brilliant, is hard and brassy, full of points
that are more suitable to the platform or the newspaper than to
the historic page, — not so much polished as varnished, and after a
short time intolerably fatiguing. In the third, — and this is the
gravest fault of all, — the author's private or patriotic likes or dislikes
pervade the whole performance and reduce too much of it to a
tissue of extravagant advocacy or depreciation, made more disgusting by the repetition of catch phrases and pet labels somewhat
after the manner of Dickens. Sir Stratford Canning, " the great
Eltchi," is one of Kinglake's divinities, Lord Raglan another;
and an acute and energetic, but not quite heaven-born diplomatist, a most honest, modest, and in difficult circumstances steadfast, if not always judicious soldier, become, the one Marlborough
in the council-chamber, the other Marlborough in the field. On
the other hand, for this or that reason, Mr. Kinglake had taken
a violent dislike to the Emperor Napoleon the Third, and affected,
as did some other English Liberals, to consider the *coup d'état*
as not merely a dubious piece of statecraft, but a hideous and
abominable crime. Consequently, he abused all those who took
part in it with tedious virulence, which has probably made not a
few Englishmen look on them with much more leniency than
they deserved. In short, Kinglake, with many of the qualities of
the craftsman in an extraordinary degree, was almost entirely
deficient in those of the artist. He served as a favourite example
to Mr. Matthew Arnold of the deficiency of the British literary
temper in accomplishment and grace, and it cannot be denied
that Mr. Arnold's strictures were here justified to an extent which
was not always the case when he assumed the office of censor.

John Forster, who was born a year later than Kinglake, and
died fifteen years before him, was an industrious writer of bio-

graphies and biographical history, the friend of a good many men of letters, editor for many years of the *Examiner*, and secretary to the Lunacy Commissioners. He paid particular attention to the period of the Rebellion; his *Arrest of the Five Members* being his chief work, among several devoted to it. He wrote a *Life of Goldsmith*, and began one of Swift. In contemporary biography his chief performances were lives of Landor and of Dickens, with both of whom he was extremely intimate. In private life Forster had the character of a bumptious busybody, which character indeed the two books just mentioned, even without the anecdotes abundant in more recent books of biography, abundantly establish. And towards the men of letters with whom he was intimate (Carlyle and Browning may be added to Landor and Dickens) he seems to have behaved like a Boswell-Podsnap, while in the latter half of the character he no doubt sat to Dickens himself. But he was an indefatigable literary inquirer, and seems, in a patronising kind of way, to have been liberal enough of the result of his inquiries. He had a real interest both in history and literature, and he wrote fairly enough.

One of the most curious figures among the historians of this century was Henry Thomas Buckle, who was born near Blackheath in 1823, and privately educated. He had ample means, and was fond of books; and in 1857 he brought out the first volume (which was followed by a second in 1861) of a *History of Civilisation*. He did not nearly complete — in fact he only began — his scheme, in which the European part was ultimately intended to be subordinate to the English, and he died of typhus at Damascus in May 1862. The book attained at once, and for some time kept, an extraordinary popularity, which has been succeeded by a rather unjust depreciation. Both are to be accounted for by the fact that it is in many ways a book rather of the French than of the English type, and displays in fuller measure than almost any of Buckle's contemporaries in France itself, with the possible exception of Taine, could boast, the frank and fearless, some would say the headlong and headstrong, habit

of generalisation — scorning particulars, or merely impressing into
service such as are useful to it and drumming the others out —
on which Frenchmen pride themselves, and for the lack of which
they are apt to pronounce English historians, and indeed English
men of letters of all kinds, plodding and unilluminated craftsmen
rather than artists. In Buckle's reflections on Spain and Scotland,
he accounts for the whole history of both countries and the whole
character of both peoples by local conditions in the first place,
and by forms of civil and ecclesiastical government. In respect
to these last, his views were crude Voltairianism ; but perhaps this
is the best and most characteristic example of his method. He
was extremely prejudiced ; his lack of solid disciplinary education
made him unapt to understand the true force and relative value
of his facts and arguments ; and as his premises are for the most
part capriciously selected facts cemented together with an un-
tempered mortar of theory, his actual conclusions are rarely of
much value. But his style is clear and vigorous ; the aggressive
raiding character of his argument is agreeably stimulating, and
excellent to make his readers clear up their minds on the other
side ; while the dread of over-generalisation, however healthy in
itself, has been so long a dominant force in English letters and
philosophy that a little excess the other way might be decidedly
useful as an alterative. The worst fault of Buckle was the
Voltairianism above referred to, causing or caused by, as is
always the case, a deplorable lack of taste, which is not confined to religious matters.

Edward Augustus Freeman, who was a little younger than
Buckle and survived him for thirty years, had some points in
common with the historian of civilisation, though his education,
interests, and tone in reference to religion were wholly different.
Mr. Freeman, who was not at any public school but was a Fellow
of Trinity College, Oxford, very soon devoted himself to the
study of early English history, and secured a durable position by
his elaborate *History of the Norman Conquest* (1867–76), which,
even though the largest and most important, was only one among

scores of works, ending in an unfinished *History of Sicily*. He was, when he died in 1892, Regius Professor of Modern History at Oxford, and he had for many years been very influential in determining the course of historical study. He was also, for many years of his life, an active journalist, being especially known as a contributor to the *Saturday Review*, and he sometimes took a very busy part in politics. Mr. Freeman was a student of untiring energy, and will always deserve honourable memory as the first historian who recognised and utilised the value of architecture in supplying historical documents and illustrations. His style was at times picturesque but too diffuse, and disfigured by a habit of allusion as teasing as Macaulay's antithesis or Kinglake's stock phrases. That he was apt to pronounce very strong opinions on almost any question with which he dealt, was perhaps a less drawback to his excellence as a historian than the violently controversial tone in which he was wont to deal with those who happened to hold opinions different from his own. Putting defects of manner aside, there is no question that, for his own special period of English history (the eleventh and twelfth centuries), Mr. Freeman did more than any man had done before him, and as much as any man has done for any other period; while in relation to his further subjects of study, his work, though less trustworthy, is full of stimulus and of information.

His chief pupil John Richard Green, who was born in 1837 and died of consumption in 1883, was a native of Oxford, and was educated there at Magdalen College School and Jesus College. Mr. Green, like Mr. Freeman, was a frequent contributor to the *Saturday Review*, and did some clerical duty in the east of London; but he is best known by his historical work on English subjects, especially the famous *Short History of the English People*, perhaps the most popular work of its class and kind ever written. Mr. Green professed, on a principle which had been growing in favour for some time, to extend the usual conception of historical dealing to social, literary, and other matters. These, however, had never as a fact been overlooked by historians, and the popularity of the book was chiefly due to its judicious selection of interesting facts, to the spirit of the narrative, and to the style, based partly on Macaulay, but infused with a modernness which exactly hit the taste of the readers of our time. Mr. Green afterwards expanded this book somewhat; and his early death cut short a series of more extended monographs, *The Making of England, The Conquest of England,* etc., which would have enabled him to display the minute knowledge on which his more summary treatment of the general theme had been based.

Among historians to whom in larger space more extended notice than is here possible would have to be given, perhaps the first place is due to Philip Henry, sixth Earl Stanhope (1805–75), who (chiefly under the title of Lord Mahon, which he bore before his succession to the earldom in 1855) was an active historical writer of great diligence and impartiality, and possessed of a fair though not very distinguished style. The first notable work, — a *History of the War of the Succession in Spain* (1832), — of Lord Stanhope (who was an Oxford man, took some part in politics, and was a devoted Peelite) was reviewed by Macaulay, and he wrote later several other and minor historical books. But his reputation rests on his *History of Europe from the Peace of Utrecht to the Peace of Versailles,* which occupied him for some twenty years, finishing in 1854. Very much less known to the general, but of singular ability, was William Johnson or Cory, who under the earlier name had attracted considerable public attention as an Eton master and as author of a small but remarkable volume of poems called *Ionica.* After his retirement from Eton and the change of his name, Mr. Cory amused himself with the composition of a *History of England,* or rather a long essay thereon, which was very little read and falls completely out of the ordinary conception of such a book, but is distinguished by an exceptionally good and scholarly style, as well as by views and expressions of great originality. Many others must pass wholly unnoticed that we may finish this chapter with one capital name.

One of the greatest historians of the century, except for

one curious and unfortunate defect, and (without any drawback) one of the greatest writers of English prose during that century, was James Anthony Froude, who was born at Dartington near Totnes in 1818, on 23rd April (Shakespeare's birthday and St. George's Day), and died in 1894 at the Molt near Salcombe in his native county. Mr. Froude (the youngest son of the Archdeacon of Totnes and the brother of Richard Hurrell Froude who played so remarkable a part in the Oxford Movement, and of William Froude the distinguished naval engineer) was a Westminster boy, and went to Oriel College, Oxford, afterwards obtaining a fellowship at Exeter. Like his elder brother he engaged in the Tractarian Movement, and was specially under the influence of Newman, taking orders in 1844. The great convulsion, however, of Newman's secession sent him, not as it sent some with Newman, but like Mark Pattison and a few more, into scepticism if not exactly negation, on all religious matters. He put his change of opinions (he had previously written under the pseudonym of "Zeta" a novel called *Shadows of the Clouds*) into a book entitled *The Nemesis of Faith*, published in 1849, resigned his fellowship, gave up or lost (to his great good fortune) a post which had been offered him in Tasmania, and betook himself to literature, being very much, except in point of style, under the influence of Carlyle. He wrote for *Fraser*, the *Westminster*, and other periodicals; but was not content with fugitive compositions, and soon planned a *History of England from the Fall of Wolsey to the Defeat of the Armada*. The first volumes of this appeared in 1856, and it was finished in 1869. Meanwhile Froude from time to time collected his essays into volumes called *Short Studies*, which contain some of his very best writing. His next large work was *The English in Ireland*, which was published in three volumes (1871–74). In 1874–75 Lord Carnarvon sent him on Government missions to the Cape, an importation of a French practice into England which was not very well justified by the particular instance. Between 1881 and 1884 he was occupied as Carlyle's literary executor in issuing his biographical remains.

Later *Oceana* and *The English in the West Indies* contained at once sketches of travel and political reflections; and in 1889 he published an Irish historical romance, *The Two Chiefs of Dunboy*. He was made Regius Professor of Modern History at Oxford in succession to Mr. Freeman, and his two latest works, *Erasmus*, published just before, and *English Seamen* some months after his death, contain in part the results of the appointment.

It is a vulgar observation that the natural element of some men appears to be hot water. No English author of the century justifies this better than Mr. Froude. His early change of faith attracted to him a very considerable share of the obloquy which usually (and perhaps not so unreasonably as is sometimes thought) attaches to violent revolutions of opinion on important points. His *History* was no sooner published than most acrimonious attacks were made upon it, and continued for many years, by a school of historical students with the late Mr. Freeman at their head. His Irish book, coinciding with the rise of " Home Rule " sentiment in Ireland, brought upon him furious enmity from the Irish Nationalist party and from those who, at first or by and by, sympathised with them in England. His colonial visits and criticisms not merely attracted to him the animosity of all those Englishmen who espoused the politics of non-intervention and non-aggrandisement, but aroused lively irritation in the Colonies themselves. About his discharge of his duties as Carlyle's executor, a perfect tempest of indignation arose; it being alleged that he had either carelessly, or through bad taste, or with deliberate treachery, revealed his dead friend's and master's weaknesses and domestic troubles to the public view.

With some of the causes of this odium we are fortunately here dispensed from dealing. Theological and political matters, in so far as they are controversial, are altogether outside of our scope. The question of the dealing with Carlyle's "Remains" is one rather of ethics than of literature proper, and it is perhaps sufficient to make, in reference to it, the warning observation that Lockhart, who is now considered by almost all competent critics as a very pattern of the union of fidelity and good taste towards both his subject and his readers, was accused, at the appearance of his book, of treachery towards Scott.

But it must be confessed that if Mr. Froude's critics were unfair (and they certainly were) he himself gave only too abundant opening to fair criticism. That his first great book (not perhaps any of his others) was planned on an unduly large scale, and indulged in far too extensive dissertation, divagation, and so forth, was rather the fault of his time than of himself. Grote and Macaulay had obtained, the first considerable, the latter immense popularity by similar prolixity; and Carlyle was about, in the *Frederick*, to follow the fashion. But whereas all these three, according to the information open to them, were and are among the most painfully laborious researchers and, with a fair allowance, the most faithful recorders among historians, Mr. Froude displayed an attention to accuracy which his warmest admirers must allow to be sadly, and which enemies asserted to be scandalously insufficient. He has been called by well-affected critics "congenitally inaccurate," and there is warrant for it. Nor did any one of his three great models come short of him in partiality, in advocacy, in the determination to make the reader accept his own view first of all.

He was, in the earlier part of his career at any rate, a very poor man, whereas Macaulay was in easy, and Grote in affluent circumstances, and he had not Carlyle's Scotch thrift. But the carelessness of his dealing with documents had more in it than lack of pence to purchase assistance, or even than lack of dogged resolve to do the drudgery himself. His enemies of course asserted, or hinted, that the added cause was dishonesty at the worst, indifference to truth at the best. As far as dishonesty goes they may be summarily non-suited. The present writer once detected, in a preface of Mr. Froude's to a book with which the introducer was thoroughly in sympathy, repeated errors of quotation or allusion which actually weakened Mr. Froude's own argument — cases where he made his own case worse by miscitation. To the very last, in his *Erasmus* itself, which he had prepared at some pains for the press, his work would always abound in the most astonishing slips of memory, oversights of fact, hastinesses of statement. There is probably no historian of anything like his calibre in the whole history of literature who is so dangerous to trust for mere matters of fact, who gives such bad books of reference, who is so little to be read with implicit confidence in detail. Had his critics confined themselves to pointing this out, and done him justice in his other and real merits, little fault could have been found with them. But it is impossible not to see that these merits were, at least in some cases, part of his crime, in the eyes of those who did not like him; in others were of a kind which their natural abilities did not qualify them to detect.

The first of these merits — the least it may be in some eyes, not so in others — was a steadfast, intense, fiery patriotism, which may remind us of that which Macaulay in a famous passage has ascribed to Chatham in modern times and to Demosthenes of old. This quality differed as much from the flowery and conventional rhetoric not uncommon in writers of some foreign nations, as from the smug self-satisfaction which was so frequent in English speakers and authors of his own earlier time. No one probably of Mr. Froude's day was less blind to English faults than he was; no one more thoroughly grasped and more ardently admired the greatness of England, or more steadfastly did his utmost in his own vocation to keep her great.

His second excellence — an excellence still contested and in a way contestable, but less subject than the first to personal and particular opinion — was his command of the historic grasp, his share of the historic sense. I have seen these terms referred to as if they were chatter or claptrap; while the qualities which they denote are very often confounded with qualities which, sometimes found in connection with them, may exist without either. The historic sense may be roughly described as the power of seizing, and so of portraying, a historic character, incident, or period as if it were alive not dead; in such a manner that the fit reader, whether he is convinced or not that the things ever did happen, sees that they might and probably must have happened. Some of the most estimable and excellent of historians have not had even a glimmering of this sense: they have at best laboriously assembled the materials out of which, sooner or later, some one with the sense will make a live history. But Thucydides and Herodotus had it; Tacitus had it, and even Sallust; it betrays itself in the most artless fashion in Villehardouin and Joinville, less artlessly in Comines; Clarendon had it; Gibbon had it; Carlyle had it as none has had it before or since. And Mr. Froude had it; not much less though more fitfully than Carlyle. It is not in the least necessary to agree with his views; it is possible to regard his facts with the most anxious suspicion. You may think that the case made out for King Henry is pretty weak, and the case made out against Queen Mary is much weaker. But Mr. Froude is among the rare Deucalions of historic literature: he cannot cast a stone but it becomes alive.

Thirdly, and still rising in the scale of incontestability, though even so contested, I believe, by some, is the merit of style. I have sometimes doubted whether Mr. Froude at his best has any superior among the prose writers of the last half of this century. His is not a catching style; and in particular it does not perhaps impress itself upon green tastes. It has neither the popular and slightly brusque appeal of Macaulay or Kinglake, nor the unique magnificence of Mr. Ruskin, nor the fretted and iridescent delicacy of some other writers. It must be frankly confessed that, the bulk of his work being very great and his industry not being untiring, it is unequal, and sometimes not above (it is never below) good journey-work. But at its best it is of a simply wonderful attraction — simply in the pure sense, for it is never very ornate, and does not proceed in point of "tricks" much beyond the best varieties of the latest Georgian form. That strange quality of "liveliness" which has been noticed in reference to its author's view of history, animates it throughout. It is never flat; never merely popular; never merely scholarly; never merely "precious" and eccentric. And at its very best it is excelled by no style in this century, and approached by few in this or any other, as a perfect harmony of unpretentious music, adjusted to the matter that it conveys, and lingering on the ear that it reaches.

NOTE. — As examples of the almost enforced omissions referred to in the text may be mentioned earlier Archdeacon Coxe, the biographer of Marlborough and the historian of the House of Austria; later, Finlay (1799–1875), the valiant successor of Gibbon, and the chronicler of the obscure and thankless fortunes of the country called Greece, after it had ceased to be living. Professor Sir J. R. Seeley, Kingsley's successor at Cambridge (1834–94), equally distinguished in his professional business, and as a lay theologian in a sense rather extra-orthodox than unorthodox; and Sir John Stirling-Maxwell, no mean historian either in the general sense or in the special department of Art. It is open to any one to contend that each and all of these as well deserve notice as not a few dealt with above; yet if they were admitted others still could hardly be excluded.

CHAPTER VI

THE second period of English poetry in the nineteenth century displays a variety and abundance of poetical accomplishment which must rank it very little below either its immediate predecessor, or even the great so-called Elizabethan era. But it is distinguished from both these periods, and, indeed, from almost all others by the extraordinary predominance of a single poet in excellence, in influence, and in duration. There is probably no other instance anywhere of a poet who for more than sixty years wrote better poetry than any one of his contemporaries who were not very old men when he began, and for exactly fifty of those years was recognised by the best judges as the chief poet of his country if not of his time.

Alfred Tennyson was born in 1809 at Somersby, in Lincolnshire, where his father, a member of a good county family, was rector. He was the third son, and his two elder brothers, Frederick and Charles, both possessed considerable poetical gifts, though it cannot be said that the *Poems by Two Brothers* (it seems that it should really have been " three "), which appeared in 1826, display much of this or anything whatever of Alfred's subsequent charm. From the Grammar School of Louth the poet went to Trinity College, Cambridge, where he was contemporary, and in most cases intimate, with an unusually distinguished set of undergraduates, many of whom afterwards figured in the famous Sterling Club (see chapter iv). He also did what not many great future poets have done, he obtained the Chancellor's prize for English verse with a poem on "Timbuctoo," where again his special note is almost, though perhaps not quite, absent: it appears faintly and fitfully in another juvenile poem not formally published till long afterwards, "The Lover's Tale."

It was in 1830 that he made his first substantive appearance with a book of *Poems*. This volume was afterwards subjected to a severe handling by the poet in the way of revision and omission — processes which through life he continued with such perseverance and rigour, that the final critical edition of him, when it appears, will be one of the most complicated of the kind in English literature. So did he also with another which appeared two years (or a little more) later. It is not therefore quite just to judge the criticism which these books received, by the present condition of the poems which figured in them; for though most of the beauties were there then, they were accompanied by many defects which are not there now. Criticism, however, was undoubtedly unfavourable, and even unfair. Although Tennyson was not, either at this time or at any other, a party politician, the two great Tory periodicals, the *Quarterly Review* and *Blackwood's Magazine*, were still animated, the former by a dislike to the Romantic school in poetry, the latter by a dislike to "Cockneys" — though how anybody could have discovered a Cockney in Tennyson may seem marvellous enough. Accordingly Lockhart in the one and Wilson in the other fell foul (though in Wilson's case, at least, not indiscriminately) of work which beyond all question offered very numerous and very convenient handles, in ways which will be mentioned presently, to merely carping criticism. Some attempts at reply were made by the poet's friends, notably A. H. Hallam, but the public did not take to him, and even well-affected and competent older judges, such as Coleridge, expressed very qualified admiration.

But during the next decade, in which he gave himself up silently to the task of perfecting his art, attempting no profession or literary occupation of profit, and living (partly in London, partly

in the country at High Beach and elsewhere) with extreme simplicity and economy on his own small means and a pension which
was provided for him, the leaven of an almost fanatical admiration
was spreading among readers of his own age or a little younger.
And his next publication, a new issue of *Poems* in 1842 — containing the final selection and revision of the others already mentioned,
and a large reinforcement of admirable work — was received, not
indeed with the popular avidity which had been displayed towards
Scott and Byron in the generation before, and which revived in
the case of his own later work, but with an immense enjoyment by
almost all true lovers of poetry.   Even Wordsworth, the most un-
gracious critic of other men's work in his own art of whom the
history of literature gives record, acknowledged Tennyson in the
amplest terms.

This was, as has been hinted above, exactly fifty years before
his death, and though in the first of these five decades the pudding
if not the praise was still rather scanty, his reputation waxed
steadily and never waned.   To keep for the present to chronicle
in biography and bibliography, he published in 1847 the exquisite
"medley" of *The Princess*, his first attempt at a poem of any
length.   1850 was a great year in his career, for in it he published the collection of elegiacs on his friend Arthur Hallam, in
which some have seen his most perfect work, and he became
Poet Laureate.   Three years later he bought a house at Farring-
ford, near Freshwater in the Isle of Wight, which was for
the rest of his life his occasional and, until 1870 (when to avoid
intrusion he built himself another at Aldworth near Haslemere),
his main house.   His poetry now was beginning to bring in some
profit, the editions of it multiplying every year; and during
the last thirty years of his life, if not more, he was probably at
least as richly provided with mere gold as any poet has ever
been.   He was, however, never seduced into hasty writing; and
he never gave himself to any other occupation save poetry, while
during his entire life he was a hater of what is commonly called
society.   In 1855 there appeared *Maud*, the reception of which

seemed at first something of a relapse in welcome, which was in its first form open to some criticism, and which he touched up to one of the finest as a whole, as it was in parts one of the most passionate and melodious of his works. But the *Idylls of the King*, the first and best instalment of which appeared in 1858, completely revived even his popular vogue, and made him indeed popular as no poet had been since Byron. It was said at the time that 17,000 copies of *Enoch Arden*, his next volume (1864), were sold on the morning of publication.

For the rest of his life his issues were pretty frequent, though the individual volumes were never large. A series of dramas beginning with *Queen Mary* in 1875, and continuing through *Harold*, *The Falcon*, *The Cup*, the unlucky *Promise of May*, *Becket*, and *The Foresters*, though fine enough for any other man, could be better spared by his critical admirers than any other portion of his works. But the volumes of poems proper, which appeared between 1864 and his death, *Lucretius*, *Tiresias*, the successive instalments of the *Idylls*, *Locksley Hall Sixty Years After*, *Demeter*, *The Death of Œnone*, and perhaps above all the splendid *Ballads* of 1880, never failed to contain with matter necessarily of varying excellence things altogether incomparable — one of the last, the finest and fortunately also the most popular, being the famous " Crossing the Bar," which appeared in his penultimate, but last not posthumous, volume in 1889. He died at Aldworth in October 1892, and was buried with an unequalled solemnity in Westminster Abbey.

In the case of no English poet is it more important and interesting than in the case of Tennyson, considering the excellence of his own work in the first place, and the altogether unparalleled extent of his influence in the second, to trace the nature and character of his poetical quality. Nor is this difficult, though strange to say it has not always been done. In his very earliest work, so soon as this quality appeared at all, it is to be discovered side by side with other things which are not native. Undoubtedly the tradition which, in the general filiation of

English poetry, connects Tennyson with Keats, is not wholly wrong. In many of the weaker things, and not a few of the better, of the volumes of 1830 and 1832, there is to be seen both the wonderful music which Keats attained by a combination of the classical and romantic appeals — the appeals which in his own case are singly exhibited at their best in the " Grecian Urn " and in " La Belle Dame sans Merci," — and the sometimes faulty and illegitimate means which Keats took to produce this effect. But to any one who compares rationally (and it may be permitted to remark parenthetically, that nothing seems to be more misunderstood than the comparative point of view) the difference between Keats and Tennyson will emerge at once. Both being great poets, there is the inexplicable in both; while as Keats undoubtedly died before he had any chance of applying to his own powers and products the unequalled process of clarifying and self-criticism which went on with Tennyson in the ten years' silence between the second of the volumes just mentioned and his issue of 1842, it is impossible to say that Keats himself could not have done something similar. Nothing that he ever did is worse in point of " gush," of undisciplined fluency, of mistakes in point of taste and of other defects than the notorious piece about " the darling little room," on which the future Poet Laureate's critics were so justly severe ; while in the single point of passion it is very doubtful whether Tennyson ever approached the author of " La Belle Dame sans Merci." There was not perhaps much to choose between the two in their natural power of associating pictorial with musical expression ; while both had that gift of simple humanity, of plain honest healthy understanding of common things, the absence of which gives to Shelley — in some ways a greater poet than either of them — a certain unearthliness and unreality.

But Tennyson had from the first a wider range of interest and capacity than Keats, and he had the enormous advantage of thorough and regular literary training. No poet ever improved his own work as Tennyson did ; nor has any, while never allowing his genius to be daunted by self-comparison with his predecessors,

S

had such a faculty of availing himself of what they had done without copying, of seeing what they had not done and supplying the gap himself. And besides this he had the inexplicable, the incommunicable, the unique, the personal gift. In the very earliest things, in " Claribel," in " Mariana," in the " Recollections of the Arabian Nights," in the " Ode to Memory," in the " Dirge," in the " Dying Swan," in " Oriana," there is even to those who were born long after they were written, even to those who have for years sedulously compared them with almost all things before and with all things since, the unmistakable note of the new, of the new that never can be old. It is there in the rhythms, it is there in the phrase. The poet may take things that had previously existed — the Keatsian and Shelleian lyric, the Wordsworthian attitude to Nature, the Miltonic blank verse ; but inevitably, invariably, each under his hands becomes different, becomes individual and original. The result cannot be accounted for by mannerisms, from which at no time was Tennyson free, and after the thousands and ten thousands of imitations which have been seen since, it stands out untouched, unrivalled.

In the next instalment this quality of intense poetical individuality strengthened and deepened. As we read " The Two Voices," " Œnone," " The Palace of Art," " The Lotos Eaters," " A Dream of Fair Women," it becomes almost incomprehensible how any one who ever read them even in forms less perfect than those that we possess, should have mistaken their incomparable excellence. But the student of literary history knows better. He knows that nearly always the poet has to create his audience, that he sings before the dawn of the day in which he is to be sovereign.

And then with the 1842 book came practically the completion of Tennyson in the sense of the indication of his powers. Edward FitzGerald, as is elsewhere noticed, thought, or at least said, that everything his friend had done after this was more or less a declension. This is a common and not an ignoble Fallacy of Companionship — the delusion of those who have hailed and accompanied a poet or a prophet in his early struggles. It is not even wholly a fallacy, inasmuch as, in the case of the class of poets to which Tennyson belongs, there does come a time when the rest of the products of their genius is so to speak *applied:* it ceases to reveal them in new aspects. They do not repeat themselves; but they chiefly vary. Now came the magnificent " Morte D'Arthur " (the " Idylls of the King " in microcosm, with all their merits and none of their defects), " St. Simeon Stylites," "Ulysses," " Locksley Hall," " St. Agnes' Eve," and other exquisite things; while to this period, as the subsequent arrangement shows, belong not a few, such as " Tithonus " and " The Voyage," which were not actually published till later, and in which keen observers at the time of their publication detected as it were an older ring, a more genuine and unblended vintage.

It is not improper therefore to break off here for a moment and to endeavour to state — leaving out the graces that can never be stated, and are more important than all the others — the points in which this new excellence of Tennyson differed from the excellences of his forerunners. One of them, not the least important, but the least truly original, because something distantly resembling it had been seen before in Keats and Shelley, is the combined application of pictorial and musical handling. Not, of course, that all poets had not endeavoured to depict their subjects vividly and to arrange the picture in a melodious frame of sound, not that the best of them had not also endeavoured to convey, if it were possible, the colours into the sense, the sense into the music. But partly as a result of the natural development and acquired practice of the language, partly for the very reason that the arts both of painting and music had themselves made independent progress, most of all, perhaps, because Tennyson was the first poet in English of the very greatest genius who dared not to attempt work on the great scale, but put into short pieces (admitting, of course, of infinite formal variety) what most of his forerunners would have spun into long poems — the result here is, as a rule, far in advance of those forerunners in this respect, and as an exception on a level with the very best of their exceptions. With Shakespeare there is no comparison ; Shakespeare can send to every poet an "O of Giotto" in his own style to which that poet must bow. But of others only Spenser had hitherto drawn such pictures as those of the " Palace " and the " Dream," and Spenser had done them in far less terse fashion than Tennyson. Only Keats, Shelley, Coleridge, Blake, perhaps Beddoes, and a few Elizabethans had poured into the veins of language the ineffable musical throb of a score of pieces from " Claribel " to " Break ! Break ! " and not one of them had done it in quite the same way. Only Milton, with Thomson as a far distant second, had impressed upon non-dramatic blank verse such a swell and surge as that of " Œnone." And about all these different kinds and others there clung and rang a peculiar dreamy slow music which was heard for the first time, and which has never been reproduced, — a music which in " The Lotos Eaters," impossible as it might have seemed, adds a new charm after the *Faerie Queen*, after the *Castle of Indolence*, after the *Revolt of Islam* to the Spenserian stanza, which makes the stately verses of the " Palace " and the " Dream " tremble and cry with melodious emotion, and which accomplishes the miracle of the poet's own dying swan in a hundred other poems all " flooded over with eddying song."

But there is something more to be noted still. The poet had caught and was utilising the spirit of his time in two ways, one of them almost entirely new. That he constantly sang the subjective view of nature may be set down to the fact that he came after Wordsworth, though the fact that he sang it without the Words-worthian dryness and dulness must be set down to his own credit. But in that sense of the history of former times which is perhaps the chief glory of the nineteenth century in matters of thought he had been anticipated by no one. He might not have attained it without Scott and Byron, but his expression of it was hardly conditioned in the very slightest degree by the expression either of Byron or of Scott. They were not in strictness men of the nineteenth century; he was, and he represented the very best features of his time in attending, from its point of view mainly, to the features of better times.

But if FitzGerald's dictum were taken in the sense that Tennyson's poetical career might, with advantage or with anything but the greatest possible loss, have been closed in 1842, then certainly it would be something more than a crotchet. Nothing perhaps appeared subsequently (with unimportant exceptions such as the plays, and as the dialect pieces of which the "Northern Farmer" was the first and best) the possibility of which could not have been divined from the earlier work. The tree had blossomed; it had almost, to keep up the metaphor, set; but by far the greater part of the fruit was yet to ripen, and very much of it was to be of quality not inferior, of quantity far greater, than anything that had yet been given.

The Princess and *In Memoriam*, the two first-fruits of this later crop, were certainly not the least important. Indeed they may be said to have shown for the first time that the poet was capable of producing, in lighter and severer styles respectively, work not limited to short flights and exemplifying what (perhaps mistakenly) is called "thought," as well as style and feeling, colour and music. *The Princess* is undoubtedly Tennyson's greatest effort, if not exactly in comedy, in a vein verging towards the comic — a side on which he was not so well equipped for offence or for defence as on the other. But it is a masterpiece. Exquisite as its author's verse always is, it was never more exquisite than here, whether in blank verse or in the (superadded) lyrics, while none of his deliberately arranged plays contains characters half so good as those of the Princess herself, of Lady Blanche and Lady Psyche, of Cyril, of the two Kings, and even of one or two others. And that unequalled dream-faculty of his, which has been more than once glanced at, enabled him to carry off whatever was fantastical in the conception with almost unparalleled felicity. It may or may not be agreed that the question of the equality of the sexes is one of the distinguishing

questions of this century; and some of those who would give
it that position may or may not maintain, if they think it worth
while, that it is treated here too lightly, while their opponents
may wish that it had been treated more lightly still. But this
very difference will point the unbiassed critic to the same conclusion, that Tennyson has hit the golden mean; while that,
whatever he has hit or missed in subject, the verse of his essay
is golden, no one who is competent will doubt. Such lyrics as
" The splendour falls " and " Tears, idle tears," such blank verse
as that of the closing passage, would raise to the topmost heights
of poetry whatever subject it was spent upon.

In Memoriam attacked two subjects in the main, — the one
perennial, the other of the time, — just as *The Princess* had done.
The perennial, which is often but another, if not an exclusive,
word for the poetical, was in the first case aspirant and happy
love, in the other mourning friendship. The ephemeral was, in
the latter, the sort of half doubting religiosity which has occupied
so much of the thought of our day. On this latter point, as on
the other just mentioned and on most beside, the attitude of Tennyson was " Liberal-Conservatism " (if political slang may be generalised), inclining always to the Conservative rather than to the
Liberal side, but giving Liberalism a sufficient footing and hearing.
Here again opinions may be divided ; and here again those who
think that in poetry the mere fancies of the moment are nothing
may be disposed to pay little attention to the particular fancies
which have occupied the poet. But here again the manner, as
always with real poets, carries off, dissolves, annihilates the special matter for poetical readers. Tennyson had here taken (not
invented) a remarkable and not frequently used stanza, the iambic dimeter quatrain with the rhymes not alternated, but arranged
a b b a. It is probable that if a well-instructed critic had been
asked beforehand what would be the effect of this employed
with a certain monotone of temper and subject in a book of
some three thousand lines or so, he would have shaken his
head and hinted that the substantive would probably justify

its adjective and the monotone become monotonous.   And if he had been really a deacon in his craft he would have added : " But to a poet there is nothing impossible."   The difficulty was no impossibility to Tennyson.   He has not only, in the rather more than six score poems of this wonderful book, adjusted his medium to a wide range of subjects, all themselves adjusted to the general theme, but he has achieved that poetic miracle, the communication to the same metre and to no very different scheme of phrase of an infinite variety of interior movement. There is scarcely a bad line in *In Memoriam;* there are few lines that do not contain a noble thought, a passionate sentiment, a beautiful picture ; but there is nothing greater about it than the way in which, side by side with the prevailing undertone of the stanza, the individual pieces vary the music and accompany it, so to speak, in duet with a particular melody.   It must have been already obvious to good ears that no greater master of English harmonics — perhaps that none so great — had ever lived ; but *In Memoriam* set the fact finally and irrevocably on record.

Maud was the third, and perhaps it may be said to have been, on a great scale, the last experiment in thus combining the temporal with the eternal.   It was also probably the weakest as a whole, though the poet had never done more poetical things than the passage beginning, " Cold and clear-cut face " ; than the prothalamium, never to have its due sequel, " I have led her home " ; than the incomparable and never-to-be-hackneyed " Come into the garden " ; or than the best of all, " Oh ! that 'twere possible."   It may even be contended that if it were ever allowable to put the finger down and say, " Here is the highest," these, and not the best things of the 1842 volumes, are the absolute summit of the poet's effort, the point which, though he was often near it, he never again quite reached.   But the piece, as a whole, is certainly less of a success, less smooth and finished as it comes from its own lathe, than either *The Princess* or *In Memoriam*.   It looks too like an essay in competition with the " Spasmodic School " of its own day ; it drags in merely casual things — adulteration, popular politics, and ephemera of all kinds — too assiduously, and its characterisations are not happy. There is a tradition that the poet met a critic, and a very accomplished critic too, who was one of his own oldest friends, and said, " What do you mean by calling *Maud* vulgar ? " " I didn't," said the critic, quite truly. " No, but you meant it," growled Tennyson. And there was something of a confession in the growl.

But these slight relapses (and, after all, what sort of a relapse is it which gives us not merely the incomparable things referred to, but others hardly less exquisite ?) never, in the great writers, serve as anything but retreats before an advance ; and certainly, in a sense, the *Idylls of the King* were an advance, though not, perhaps, in all senses. No total so brilliant, so varied within a certain general unity, so perfectly polished in style, so cunningly adjusted to meet the popular without disappointing the critical ear, had ever come from Tennyson's pen as the first quartet of Idylls, *Enid, Vivien, Elaine,* and *Guinevere.* No such book of English blank verse, with the doubtful exception of the *Seasons,* had been seen since Milton. Nothing more adroitly selected than the contrast of the four special pieces — a contrast lost to those who only read them in the completed Arthuriad — has been often attempted or ever achieved. It is true that the inner faithful, the sacred band of Tennysonians, old and young, grumbled a little that polish had been almost too much attended to ; that there was a certain hardish mannerism, glittering but cold, about the style ; that there was noticeable a certain compromise in the appeal, a certain trimming of the sail to the popular breeze. These criticisms were not entirely without foundation, and they were more justified than their authors could know by the later instalments of the poem, which, the latest not published till twenty-seven years afterwards, rounded it off to its present bulk of twelve books, fifteen separate pieces, and over ten thousand lines. Another, more pedantic in appearance, but not entirely destitute of weight, was that which urged that in handling the

Arthurian story the author had, so to speak, "bastardised it," and had given neither mediæval nor modern sentiment or colouring, but a sort of amalgamation of both. Yet the charm of the thing was so great, and the separate passages were so consummate, that even critics were loth to quarrel with such a gift.

The later instalments of the poem — some of them, as has been said, very much later, but still so closely connected as to be best noticed here — were of somewhat less even excellence. It was an inevitable, but certainly an unfortunate thing, that the poet republished the magnificent early fragment above noticed in a setting which, fine as it would have been for any one else, was inferior to this work of the very best time. Some of the lighter passages, as in *Gareth and Lynette*, showed less grace than their forerunners in *The Princess;* and in *Pelleas and Ettarre* and *Balin and Balan* the poet sometimes seemed to be attempting alien moods which younger poets than himself had made their own. But the best passages of some of these later Idylls, notably those of *The Holy Grail* and *The Last Tournament*, were among the finest, not merely of the book, but of the poet. Nowhere has he caught the real, the best, spirit of the legends he followed more happily; nowhere has he written more magnificent verse than in Percivale's account of his constantly baffled quest and of Lancelot's visit to the "enchanted towers of Carbonek."

Far earlier than these, *Enoch Arden* and its companion poems were something more of a return to the scheme of the earlier books — no very long single composition, but a medley of blank verse pieces and lyrics, the former partly expansions of the scheme of the earlier "English Idyll," the latter various and generally beautiful; one or two, such as "In the Valley of Cauterets," of the most beautiful. Here, too, were some interesting translations, with the dialect pieces above referred to; and all the later volumes, except those containing the plays, preserved this mixed manner. Their contents are too numerous for many to be mentioned here. Only in the *Ballads and Other Poems* was something like a distinctly new note struck in the two splendid patriotic pieces on

" The Last Fight of the *Revenge*" and the "Defence of Lucknow,"
which, even more than the poet's earlier " Charge of the Light
Brigade," deserve the title of the best English war-songs since
Campbell; in " Rizpah," an idyll of a sterner and more tragic
kind than anything he had previously attempted; and in the
" Voyage of Maeldune," this last in some respects the most
interesting of the whole. For the marvellous power which great
poets possess of melting, of " founding," so to speak, minor styles
and kinds of poetry to their own image, while not losing a certain
character of the original, has never been shown better than here.
Attention had, even before the date of this poem, been drawn to
the peculiar character of early Celtic poetry, — not the adulterated
style of Ossian, but the genuine method of the old Irish singers.
And, since, a whole band of young and very clever writers have
set themselves, with a mixture of political and poetical enthusiasm,
the task of reviving these notes if possible. They have rarely
succeeded in getting very close to them without mere archaic
pastiche. Tennyson in this poem carried away the whole genius
of the Celtic legend, infused it into his own verse, branded it
with his own seal, and yet left the character of the vintage as
unmistakable as if he had been an Irishman of the tenth century,
instead of an Englishman of the nineteenth. And indeed there
are no times, or countries, or languages in the kingdom of poetry.

A very little more may, perhaps, still be said about this great
poet, — great in the character and variety of his accomplishment, in
the volume of it, and, above all, in the extraordinarily sustained
quality of his genius and the length of time during which it
dominated and pervaded the literature of his country. The
influences of Pope and Dryden were weak in force and merely
external in effect, the influence of Byron was short-lived, that of
Wordsworth was partial and limited, in comparison with the
influence of Tennyson. Of this, as of a mere historical fact,
there can be no dispute among those who care to inform themselves of the facts and to consider them coolly. Of his intrinsic
merit, as opposed to his influential importance, it is not of course

possible to speak so peremptorily. Among the great volume of more or less unfavourable criticism which such a career was sure to call forth, two notes perhaps were the most dominant, the most constant, and (even fervent admirers may admit) the least unjust. He was accused of a somewhat excessive prettiness, a sort of dandyism and coquetry in form, and of a certain want of profundity in matter. The last charge is the more unprofitable in discussion, for it turns mainly on vast and vague questions of previous definition. "What is thought?" "What is profundity?" a by no means jesting demurrer may object, and he will not soon be cleared out of the way. And it will perhaps seem to some that what is called Tennyson's lack of profundity consists only in a disinclination on his part to indulge in what the Germans call the *Schwätzerei*, the endless, aimless talkee-talkee about "thoughtful" things in which the nineteenth century has indulged beyond the record of any since what used to be called the Dark Ages. On the real "great questions" Tennyson was not loth to speak, and spoke gravely enough; even to the ephemeralities, as we have said, he paid rather too much than too little attention. But he did not go into the ins and outs of them as some of his contemporaries did, and as other contemporaries thought fitting. He usually neglected the negligible; and perhaps it would not hurt him with posterity if he had neglected it a little more, though it hurt him a little with contemporaries that he neglected it as much as he did.

The charge of prettiness is to be less completely ruled out; though it shows even greater mistake in those who do more than touch very lightly on it. In the earliest forms of the earlier poems not seldom, and occasionally in even the latest forms of the later, the exquisiteness of the poet's touch in music and in painting, in fancy and in form, did sometimes pass into something like finicalness, into what is called in another language *mignardise*. But this was only the necessary, and, after he was out of his apprenticeship, the minimised effect of his great poetical quality — that very quality of exquisiteness in form, in fancy, in painting, and in music which has just been stated. We have, it must be admitted, had greater poets than Tennyson. Shakespeare, Spenser, Milton, Shelley, undoubtedly deserve this preference to him ; Wordsworth and Keats may deserve it. But we have had none so uniformly, and over such a large mass of work, exquisite. In the lighter fantastic veins he may sometimes be a little unsure in touch and taste; in satire and argument a little heavy, a little empty, a little rhetorical ; in domestic and ethical subjects a little tame. But his handlings of these things form a very small part of his work. And in the rest none of all these faults appears, and their absence is due to the fact that nothing interferes with the exquisite perfection of the form. Some faults have been found with Tennyson's rhymes, though this is generally hypercriticism ; and in his later years he was a little too apt to accumulate tribrachs in his blank verse, a result of a mistaken sense of the true fact that he was better at slow rhythms than at quick, and of an attempt to cheat nature. But in all other respects his versification is by far the most perfect of any English poet, and results in a harmony positively incomparable. So also his colour and outline in conveying the visual image are based on a study of natural fact and a practice in transferring it to words which are equally beyond comparison. Take any one of a myriad of lines of Tennyson, and the mere arrangement of vowels and consonants will be a delight to the ear ; let any one of a thousand of his descriptions body itself before the eye, and the picture will be like the things seen in a dream, but firmer and clearer.

Although, as has been said, the popularity of Lord Tennyson itself was not a plant of very rapid growth, and though but a short time before his position was undisputed it was admitted only by a minority, imposing in quality but far from strong in mere numbers, his chief rival during the latter part of their joint lives was vastly slower in gaining the public ear. It is not quite pleasant to think that the well-merited but comparatively accidental distinction of the Laureateship perhaps did more even for Tennyson in this respect than the intrinsic value of his work. Robert Browning had no such aid, his verse was even more abhorrent than Tennyson's to the tradition of the elders, and until he found a sort of back-way to please, he was even more indifferent to pleasing. So that while Tennyson became in a manner popular soon after 1850, two decades more had to pass before anything that could be called popularity came to Browning. It is, though the actual dates are well enough known to most people, still something of a surprise to remember that at that time he had been writing for very nearly forty years, and that his first book, though a little later than Tennyson's, actually appeared before the death of Coleridge and not more than a few months after that of Scott. Browning, about whose ancestry and parentage a good deal of mostly superfluous ink has been shed, was born, the son of a city man, on 7th May 1812, in the, according to the elder Mr. Weller, exceptional district of Camberwell. He was himself exceptional enough in more ways than one. His parents had means ; but Browning did not receive the ordinary education of a well-to-do Englishman at school and college, and his learning, though sufficiently various, was privately obtained. *Pauline*, his first poem, appeared in 1833, but had been written about two years earlier. He did not reprint it in the first general collection of his verse, nor till after his popularity had been established ; and it cannot be said to be of great intrinsic excellence. But it was distinctly characteristic : — first, in a strongly dramatic tone and strain without regular dramatic form ; secondly, in a peculiar fluency of decasyllabic verse that could not be directly traced to any model ; and, thirdly, in a certain quality of thought, which in later days for a long time received, and never entirely lost from the vulgar, the name of " obscurity," but which perhaps might be more justly termed breathlessness — the expression, if not the conception, of a man who either did not stop at all to pick his words, or was only careful to pick them out of the first choice that presented itself to him of something not commonplace.

In *Pauline*, however, there is little positive beauty. In the next book, *Paracelsus* (1835), there is a great deal. Here the dramatic form was much more definite, though still not attempting acted or actable drama. The poet's appetite for "soul-dissection" was amply shown in the characters not merely of Paracelsus himself, but of his soberer friends Festus and Michal, and of the Italian poet Aprile, a sort of Euphorion pretty evidently suggested by, though greatly enlarged from, the actual Euphorion of the second part of *Faust*, then not long finished. The rapid, breathless blank verse, the crowding rush of simile and illustration, and the positive plethora of meaning, more often glanced and hinted at than fully worked out, were as noteworthy as before in kind, and as much more so in degree as in scale. Here too were lyrics, not antici- pating the full splendour of the poet's later lyrical verse, but again quite original. Here, in fact, to anybody who chose to pay atten- tion, was a real "new poet" pretty plainly announced.

Very few did choose to pay attention; and Browning's next attempt was not of a kind to conciliate halting or hostile opinion, though it might please the initiated. He wrote for his friend Mac- ready a play intended at least to be of the regular acting kind. This play, *Strafford* (1837), contains fine things ; but the involution and unexpectedness of the poet's thought now and always showed themselves least engagingly when they were even imagined as being spoken not read. After yet another three years *Sordello* followed, and here the most peculiar but the least estimable side of the author's genius attained a prominence not elsewhere equalled, till in his latest stage he began to parody himself, and scarcely even then. Although this book does not deserve the disgusted contempt which used to be poured on it, though it contains many noble passages, and as the "story of a soul" is perfectly intelligible to moderate intellects, it must have occasioned some doubts and qualms to intelligent admirers of the poet as to whether he would lose himself in the paths on which he was entering. Such doubts must have been soon set at rest by the curious medley issued in parts, under the general title of *Bells and Pomegranates*, between 1841 and 1846. The plays here, though often striking and showing that the author's disabilities, though never likely to leave, were also not likely to master him, showed also, with the possible exception of the charming nondescript of *Pippa Passes*, no new or positively unexpected faculty. But certain shorter things, lyrical and other, at last made it clear that Browning could sing as well as say : and from this time, 1846 (which also was the year of his marriage with Miss Elizabeth Barrett), he could claim rank as a great poet. He had been hitherto more or less a wanderer, but with headquarters in England ; he now went to Florence, which in turn was his head-quarters till his wife's death in 1861. His publications during the time were only two— *Christmas Eve and Easter Day* in 1850, and *Men and Women* in 1855. But these were both masterpieces. He never did better work, and, with *Bells and Pomegranates* and *Dramatis Personæ*, which appeared in 1864 (when, after Mrs. Browning's death, he had returned to London), they perhaps contain all his very best work.

Up to this time, the thirty-first year from the publication of *Pauline*, Browning's work, though by no means scanty, could hardly be called voluminous as the result of half a life-time of absolute leisure. A little before *Dramatis Personæ* — itself not a long book, though of hardly surpassed quality — the whole of the poems except *Pauline* had been gathered into three small but thick volumes, which undoubtedly did very much to spread the poet's fame — a spread much helped by their immediate successors. The enormous poem of *The Ring and the Book*, originally issued in four volumes and containing more than twenty thousand verses, was published in 1869, and, the public being by this time well prepared for it, received a welcome not below its merits. Having at last gained the public ear, Mr. Browning did not fail to improve the occasion, and of the next fifteen years few passed without a volume, while some saw two, from his pen. These, including translations of the *Alcestis* and the *Agamemnon* (for the poet was at this time seized with a great fancy for Greek, which he rendered with much fluency and a very singular indulgence in a sort of hybrid and pedantic spelling of proper names), were *Balaustion's Adventure* and *Prince Hohenstiel-Schwangau* (1871), *Fifine at the Fair* (1872), *Red Cotton Night-Cap Country* (1873),

Aristophanes' Apology and *The Inn Album* (1875), *Pacchiarotto and how he Worked in Distemper* (1876), *La Saisiaz* (1878), *Dramatic Idylls*, two volumes (1879–80), *Jocoseria* (1883), and *Ferishtah's Fancies* (1884). The five remaining years of Browning's long life were somewhat less fruitful; but *Parleyings with Certain People of Importance* came in 1887, and at the end of 1889, almost simultaneously with his death in Italy, *Asolando*, which some think by far his best volume since *Dramatis Personæ*, a quarter of a century older. These volumes occasionally contained a few, and *Asolando* contained several, of the lovely lyrics above referred to. But the great bulk of them consisted of the curious blank verse, now narrative, now ostensibly dramatic monologue, which the poet had always affected, and which he now seemed to affect more and more. In them, too, from *The Ring and the Book* onwards, there appeared a tendency stronger than ever to an eccentric and almost burlesque phraseology, which at one time threatened to drown all his good qualities, as involution of thought had threatened to drown them in the *Sordello* period. But this danger also was averted at the last.

Critical estimate of Browning's poetry was for years hampered by, and cannot even yet be said to have been quite cleared from, the violent prepossessions of public opinion respecting him. For more than a generation, in the ordinary sense, he was more or less passionately admired by a few devotees, stupidly or blindly ignored by the public in general, and persistently sneered at, lectured, or simply disliked by the majority of academically educated critics. The sharp revulsion of his later years has been noticed; and it amounted almost to this, that while dislike to him in those who had intelligently, if somewhat narrowly, disapproved of his ways was not much affected, a Browning *cultus*, almost as blind as the former pooh-poohing or ignoring, set in, and extended from a considerable circle of ardent worshippers to the public at large. A "Browning Society" was founded in 1881, and received from the poet a kind of countenance which would certainly not have been extended to it by most English men of letters. During

his later years handbooks solemnly addressed to neophytes in
Browningism, as if the cult were a formal science or art, appeared
with some frequency; and there has been even a bulky *Browning
Dictionary*, which not only expounds the more recondite (and, it is
fair to say, tolerably frequent) allusions of the master, but provides
for his disciples something to make up for the ordinary classical
and other dictionaries with which, it seemed to be presumed, their
previous education would have made them little conversant.

This not very wise adulation in its turn not unnaturally excited
a sort of irritation and dislike, to a certain extent renewing the
old prejudice in a new form. To those who could discard extraneous considerations and take Browning simply as he was,
he must, from a period which only very old men can now remember, have always appeared a very great, though also a very far
from perfect poet. His imperfections were always on the surface,
though perhaps they were not always confined to it; and only
uncritical partisanship could at any time have denied them, while
some of them became noticeably worse in the period of rapid composition or publication from 1870 to 1885. A large license of
unconventionality, and even of defiance of convention, may be
claimed by, and should be allowed to, persons of genius such as Mr.
Browning undoubtedly possessed. But it can hardly be denied
that he, like his older contemporary Carlyle, whose example may
not have been without influence upon him, did set at naught not
merely the traditions, but the sound norms and rules of English
phrase to a rather unnecessary extent. A beginning of deliberate
provocation and challenge, passing into an after-period of more or
less involuntary persistence in an exaggeration of the mannerisms
at first more or less deliberately adopted, is apt to be shown by
persons who set themselves in this way to innovate; and it was
shown by Mr. Browning. It is impossible for any intelligent
admirer to maintain, except as a paradox, that his strange modu-
lations, his cacophonies of rhythm and rhyme, his occasional
adoption of the foreshortened language of the telegraph or the
comic stage, and many other peculiarities of his, were not things

T

which a more perfect art would have either absorbed and trans-
formed, or at least have indulged in with far less luxuriance.   Nor
does it seem much more reasonable for anybody to contend that
his fashion of soul-dissection at a hand-gallop, in drama, in monologue, in lay sermon, was not largely, even grossly, abused.   Sometimes the thing was not worth doing at all — there are at least
half a dozen of the books between *The Ring and the Book* and
Asolando from the whole of which a judicious lover of poetry
would not care to save more than the bulk of the smallest of
them should they be menaced with entire destruction.   Even
in the best of these what is good could generally, if not always,
have been put at the length of the shorter *Men and Women* with
no loss, nay, with great advantage.   The obscurity so much
talked of was to some extent from the very first, and to the last
continued to be, in varying degrees, an excuse, or at least an
occasion, for putting at great length thought that was not always
so far from commonplace as it looked into expression which was
very often not so much original as unkempt.   " Less matter with
more art " was the demand which might have been made of Mr.
Browning from first to last, and with increasing instance as he
became more popular.

But though no competent lover of poetry can ever have denied
the truth and cogency of these objections, the admission of them
can never, in any competent lover of poetry, have obscured or
prevented an admiration of Browning none the less intense
because not wholly unreserved.   Even his longer poems, in
which his faults were most apparent, possessed an individuality
of the first order, combined the intellectual with no small
part of the sensual attraction of poetry after a fashion not otherwise paralleled in England since Dryden, and provided an
extraordinary body of poetical exercise and amusement.   The
pathos, the power, at times the humour, of the singular soul-
studies which he was so fond of projecting with little accessory
of background upon his canvas, could not be denied, and have
not often been excelled.   If he was not exactly what is commonly

called orthodox in religion, and if his philosophy was of a distinctly vague order, he was always "on the side of the angels" in theology, in metaphysics, in ethics; and his politics, if exceedingly indistinct and unpractical, were always noble and generous. Further, though he seems to have been utterly destitute of the slightest gift of dramatic construction, he had no mean share of a much rarer gift, that of dramatic character; and in a century of descriptions of nature his, if not the most exquisite, have a freedom and truth, a largeness of outline combined with felicity of colour, not elsewhere to be discovered.

But it is as a lyric poet that Browning ranks highest; and in this highest class it is impossible to refuse him all but the highest rank, in some few cases the very highest. He understood love pretty thoroughly; and when a lyric poet understands love thoroughly there is little doubt of his position. But he understood many other things as well, and could give strange and delightful voice to them. Even his lyrics, still more his short non-lyrical poems, admirable as they often are, and closely as they group with the lyrics proper, are not untouched by his inseparable defect. He cannot be prevented from inserting now and then in the midst of exquisite passages more or fewer of his quirks and cranks of thought and phrase, of his vernacularity or his euphuism, of his outrageous rhymes (which, however, are seldom or never absolutely bad), of those fantastic tricks of his in general which remind one of nothing so much as of dashing a bladder with rattling peas in the reader's face just at the height of the passion or the argument.

Yet the beauty, the charm, the variety, the vigour of these short poems are as wonderful as the number of them. He never lost the secret of them to his latest years. The delicious lines "Never the time and the place, And the loved one all together" are late; and there are half a dozen pieces in *Asolando*, latest of all, which exhibit to the full the almost bewildering beauty of combined sound, thought, and sight, the clash of castanets and the thrill of flutes, the glow of flower and sunset, the subtle appeal for sympathy in feeling or assent in judgment. The song snatches in *Pippa Passes*, " Through the Metidja," "The Lost Leader," " In a Gondola," "Earth's Immortalities," " Mesmerism," " Women and Roses," " Love Among the Ruins," " A Toccata of Galuppis," " Prospice," " Rabbi Ben Ezra," " Porphyria's Lover," " After," with scores of others, and the " Last Ride Together," the poet's most perfect thing, at the head of the list, are such poems as a very few — Shakespeare, Shelley, Burns, Coleridge — may surpass now and then in pure lyrical perfection, as Tennyson may excel in dreamy ecstasy, as some seventeenth century songsters may outgo in quaint and perfect fineness of touch, but such as are nowhere to be surpassed or equalled for a certain volume and variety of appeal, for fulness of life and thought, of action and passion.

Mr. Browning's wife, Elizabeth Barrett, was older than himself by six years, and her period of popularity considerably anticipated his. But except one very juvenile book she published nothing of importance till 1838, when Browning, whom she did not then know, had already manifested his idiosyncrasy. Miss Barrett, whose father's original name was Moulton, was born at Carlton Hall, Durham, on 6th March 1806. The change of name was brought on by succession to estates in the West Indies ; and the family were wealthy. For the greater part of Miss Barrett's youth they lived in Herefordshire at a place, Hope End, which has left great traces on her early poetry ; later her headquarters were in London, with long excursions to Devonshire. These excursions were mainly caused by bad health, from which, as well as from family bereavements, Miss Barrett was a great sufferer. She had read widely ; she began to write as a mere child ; and her studies extended even to Greek, though in a rather amateurish and desultory fashion. Her *Essay on Mind* and other poems appeared in 1825 ; but a considerable interval, as noted above, elapsed before, in *The Seraphim* and other poems, she gave, if not a truer, a more characteristic note. And two more intervals of exactly the same length gave *Poems* 1846 and

Poems 1850, containing most of her best work. Meanwhile she had met Robert Browning, and had married him, rather against the wish of her family, in 1846. The rest of her life was spent mostly at Florence, where, in 1849, the only child of the marriage was born. Two years later appeared *Casa Guidi Windows* and the long " sociological " romance of *Aurora Leigh*. In these, and still more in the *Poems before Congress* (1860), a not unnatural tendency to echo the peculiar form and spirit of her husband's work is observable, not by any means always or frequently to advantage. She died at Florence on 30th June 1861, and next year a volume of *Last Poems* was issued. The most interesting document in regard to her since has been her Letters to R. H. Horne, the author of *Orion*, which were published in 1876.

It has been said that Mrs. Browning's popularity long anticipated her husband's; indeed, years after her death, and on the very eve of the publication of *The Ring and the Book*, it was possible to meet persons, not uncultivated, who were fairly well acquainted with her verse and entirely ignorant of his. The case has since been altered; but it is believed that Mrs. Browning still retains, and it is probable that she will always retain, no small measure of general favour. It has been usual to speak of her as the chief English poetess, which she certainly is if bulk and character of work as distinguished from perfection of workmanship are considered. Otherwise, she must as certainly give place to Miss Christina Rossetti. But Mrs. Browning no doubt combined, in very unusual and interesting manner, the qualities which appeal to what may be called, with no disdainful intention, the crowd of readers of poetry, and those which appeal to the elect. Even the peculiarities which lent themselves so easily to parody — and some of the happiest parodies ever written were devoted to her in *Bon Gaultier* and other books — did not serve her badly with the general, for a parody always in a way attracts attention to the original. Although her expression was not always of the very clearest, its general drift was never easily mistakable; and though she was wont to enshrine her emotions in something of a mist of mysticism, they were in the main simple and human enough. It must also be admitted that pathetic sentiment is almost the surest of popular appeals in poetry; and Miss Barrett — partly through physical suffering, partly through the bereavements above referred to, but very mainly it may be suspected by temperament and preference — was much more a visitant of the House of Mourning than of the House of Mirth. She was, yet again, profoundly and sincerely, if a little vaguely, religious: and her sacred poems, of which the famous and beautiful "Cowper's Grace" is the chief example, secured one portion of the public to her as firmly as the humanitarianism of "The Cry of the Children," chiming in with famous things of Hood and Dickens, did another; "Isobel's Child," a pathetic domesticity, a third; the somewhat gushing and undistinguished Romanticism of "The Duchess May" and "The Brown Rosary," a fourth; and the ethical and political "noble sentiments" of "Lady Geraldine's Courtship," a fifth.

But it would argue gross unfairness in an advocate, and gross incompetence in a critic, to let it be supposed that these popular attractions were the only ones that Mrs. Browning possessed. Despite and besides the faults which will be presently noticed, and which, critically speaking, are very grave faults, she had poetical merits of a very high order. Her metrical faculty, though constantly flawed and imperfect, was very original and full of musical variety. Although her choice of words could by no means always be commended, her supply of them was extraordinary. Before her imprisonment in sick-rooms she had pored on nature with the eagerest and most observant eye, and that imprisonment itself only deepened the intensity of her remembered nature-worship. Her pathos, if it sometimes overflowed into gush, was quite unquestionable in sincerity and most powerful in appeal; her sentiment was always pure and generous; and it is most curious to see how in the noble directness of such a piece as "Lord Walter's Wife," not only her little faults of *sensiblerie*, but her errors of diction, are burnt and smelted out by the fire of the expressed impression. Her verse-pictures — for instance those in the "Vision of Poets" — vie, in beauty if not in clearness of composition and definition, with Tennyson's own. The Romantic pieces already glanced at, obnoxious and obvious as are their defects, unite the pathos and the picturesqueness just assigned to her in a most remarkable manner. And when, especially in the Sonnet, she consented to undergo the limitations of a form which almost automatically restrained her voluble facility, the effect was often simply of the first order. The exquisite "Sonnets from the Portuguese" (which are not from the Portuguese, and are understood to have been addressed to Mr. Browning), especially that glorious one beginning —

> If thou wilt love me, let it be for naught
> Except for love's sake only —

(which is not far below Shakespeare's or the great thing which was published as Drayton's), rank with the noblest efforts of the 16th–17th century in this exquisite form. And if this, instead of having to conform to the requirements of a connected history, were a separate study of Mrs. Browning, it would be necessary to mention scores of separate pieces full of varied beauty.

But in no poet, perhaps not even in Byron, are such great beauties associated with such astonishing defects as in Mrs. Browning; some of these defects being so disgusting as well as so strange that it requires not a little critical detachment to put her, on the whole, as high as she deserves to be put. Like almost all women who have written, she was extremely deficient in self-criticism, and positively pampered and abused her natural tendency towards fluent volubility. There is hardly one of the pieces named above, outside the sonnets, with the exception certainly of "Lord Walter's Wife" and possibly of "Cowper's Grave," which would not be immensely improved by compression and curtailment, "The Rhyme of the Duchess May" being a special example. In other pieces not yet specified, such as "The Romaunt of Margret,"

" Bianca among the Nightingales," and especially "The Poet's Vow," the same defect is painfully felt. That the poetess frequently, and especially in her later poetical work, touches subjects which she does not very well comprehend, and which are very doubtfully suited for poetical treatment at all, is a less important because a more controversial objection; and the merits of such a book as *Aurora Leigh* depend so much upon the arguing out of the gēneral question whether what is practically a modern novel has any business to be written in verse, that they perhaps can receive no adequate treatment here. But as to the fatal fluency of Mrs. Browning there can be no question before any tribunal which knows its own jurisdiction and its own code. And that fluency extends to more than length. The vocabulary is wilfully and tastelessly unusual, — "abele" rhymed "abeel" for "poplar"; American forms such as "human" for "humanity" and "weaken" for a neuter verb; fustianish words like "reboant"; awkward suggestions of phrase, such as "droppings of warm tears."

But all these things, and others put together, are not so fatal as her extraordinary dulness of ear in the matter of rhyme. She endeavoured to defend her practice in this respect in the correspondence with Horne, but it is absolutely indefensible. What is known as assonance, that is to say, vowel rhyme only, as in Old French and in Spanish, is not in itself objectionable, though it is questionably suited to English. But Mrs. Browning's eccentricities do not as a rule, though they sometimes do, lie in the direction of assonance. They are simply bad and vulgar rhymes — rhymes which set the teeth on edge. Thus, when she rhymes "palace" and "chalice," "evermore" and "emperor," "Onora" and "o'er her," or, most appalling of all, "mountain" and "daunting," it is impossible not to remember with a shudder that every omnibus conductor does shout "Pal*lis*," that the common Cockney would pronounce it "Onorer," that the vulgar ear is deaf to the difference between *ore* and *or*, and that it is possible to find persons not always of the costermonger class

who would make of "mountain" something very like "mau-
unting." In other words, Mrs. Browning deliberately, or lazily,
or for want of ear, admits false pronunciation to save her the
trouble of an exact rhyme. Nay, more, despite her Greek, she
will rhyme "idyll" to "middle," and "pyramidal" to "idle,"
though nothing can be longer than the *i* in the first case, and
nothing shorter than the *i* in the second. The positive anguish
which such hideous false notes as these must cause to any one
with a delicate ear, the maddening interruption to the delight of
these really beautiful pieces of poetry, cannot be over-estimated.
It is fair to say that among the later fruit of her poetical tree there
are fewer of these Dead Sea apples, — her husband, who, though
audacious, was not vulgar in his rhymes, may have taught her
better. But to her earlier, more spontaneous, and more characteristic verse they are a most terrible drawback, such as no other
English poet exhibits or suffers.

No poets at all approaching the first class can be said to have
been born within a decade either way of Tennyson and Browning,
though some extremely interesting writers of verse of about the
same date will have to be noticed in the latter part of this chapter.
The next year that produced a poet almost if not quite great,
though one of odd lapses and limitations, was 1822, the birth-
year of Matthew Arnold. When a writer has produced both
prose and verse, or prose of distinctly different kinds in which
one division or kind was very far superior in intrinsic value and
extrinsic importance to the others, it has seemed best here to
notice all his work together. But in the case of Mr. Arnold, as
in some others, this is not possible, the volume, the character,
and the influence of his work in creative verse and critical prose
alike demanding separate treatment for the two sections. He
was the eldest son of Dr. Arnold, the famous headmaster of
Rugby, and was educated first at the two schools, Winchester
and Rugby itself, with which his father was connected as scholar
and master, and then at Balliol, where he obtained a scholarship
in 1840. He took the Newdigate in 1844, and was elected a fellow

of Oriel in 1845. After some work as private secretary, he received an inspectorship of schools, and held it until nearly the time of his death in 1888. He had been Professor of Poetry at Oxford from 1857–67. He published poetry early, and though his fame at this time was never very wide, he was known to those interested in poetry, and especially to Oxford men, for more than twenty years before he acquired popularity as a critic and began the remarkable series of prose works which will be noticed in a later chapter. So early as 1849 he had published, under the initial of his surname only, *The Strayed Reveller, and other Poems;* but his poetical building was not securely founded until 1853, when there appeared, with a very remarkable preface, a collection of *Poems*, which was certainly the best thing that had been produced by any one younger than the two masters already discussed. *Merope*, which followed in 1858, was an attempt at an English-Greek drama, which, with Mr. Swinburne's *Atalanta in Calydon* and *Erechtheus*, is perhaps the best of a somewhat mistaken kind, for Shelley's *Prometheus Unbound* soars far above the kind itself. Official duty first, and the growing vogue of his prose writing later, prevented Mr. Arnold from issuing very many volumes of verse. But his *New Poems* in 1867 made important additions, and in this way and that his poetical production reached by the time of his death no inconsiderable volume — perhaps five hundred pages averaging thirty lines each, or very much more than has made the reputation of some English poets of very high rank. Until late in his own life the general tendency was not to take Mr. Arnold very seriously as a poet; and there are still those who reproach him with too literary a character, who find fault with him as thin and wanting in spontaneity. On the other hand, there are some who not only think him happier in verse than in prose, but consider him likely to take, when the "firm perspective of the past" has dispelled mirages and false estimates, a position very decidedly on the right side of the line which divides the great from the not great.

Family, local, and personal reasons (for Dr. Arnold had a

house in the immediate vicinity of Rydal), as well as the strong
contemporary set in favour of Wordsworth which prevailed in both
universities between 1830 and 1845, caused Mr. Arnold early to
take a distinctly Wordsworthian bent. He was, later, somewhat
outspoken in his criticism of Wordsworth's weaker points ; but it
is impossible for any one to read his own poems without perceiving
that Arnold stands in a line of filiation from Milton, with a slight
deviation by way of Gray, through Wordsworth, though with a
strong personal element in his verse. This personal element,
besides other things, represents perhaps more powerfully than it
represents anything else, and than anything else represents this, a
certain reaction from the ornate and fluent Romanticism of the
school of Keats and Tennyson. Both, especially the latter, influenced Mr. Arnold consciously and unconsciously. But consciously he was striving against both to set up a neo-classic ideal
as against the Romantic ; and unconsciously he was endeavouring to express a very decided, though a perhaps not entirely
genial or masculine, personal temperament. In other words, Mr.
Arnold is on one side a poet of " correctness " — a new correctness
as different from that of Pope as his own time, character, and
cultivation were from Pope's, but still correctness, that is to say
a scheme of literature which picks and chooses according to
standards, precedents, systems, rather than one which, given an
abundant stream of original music and representation, limits the
criticising province in the main to making the thing given the best
possible of its kind. And it is not a little curious that his own
work is by no means always the best of its kind — that it would
often be not a little the better for a stricter application of critical
rules to itself.

But when it is at its best it has a wonderful charm — a charm
nowhere else to be matched among our dead poets of this century.
Coleridge was perhaps, allowing for the fifty years between them,
as good a scholar as Mr. Arnold, and he was a greater poet ; but
save for a limited time he never had his faculties under due
command, or gave the best of his work. Scott, Byron, Keats,

were not scholars at all; Shelley and Tennyson not critical scholars; Rossetti a scholar only in modern languages. And none of these except Coleridge, whatever their mere knowledge or instruction, had the critical vein, the knack of comparing and adjusting, at all strongly developed. Many attempts have been made at a formula of which the following words are certainly not a perfect expression, that a poet without criticism is a failure, and that a critic who is a poet is a miracle. Mr. Arnold is beyond all doubt the writer who has most nearly combined the two gifts. But for the present we are only concerned with his poetry.

This shows itself distinctly enough, and perhaps at not far from its best, in almost his earliest work. Among this earliest is the magnificent sonnet on Shakespeare which perhaps better deserves to be set as an epigraph and introduction to Shakespeare's own work than anything else in the libraries that have been written on him except Dryden's famous sentence; "Mycerinus," a stately blending of well-arranged six-lined stanzas with a splendid finale of blank verse not quite un-Tennysonian, but slightly different from Tennyson's; "The Church of Brou," unequal but beautiful in the close (it is a curious and almost a characteristic thing that Matthew Arnold's finales, his perorations, were always his best); "Requiescat," an exquisite dirge. To this early collection, too, belongs almost the whole of the singular poem or collection of poems called "Switzerland," a collection much rehandled in the successive editions of Mr. Arnold's work, and exceedingly unequal, but containing, in the piece which begins —

Yes! in the sea of life enisled,

one of the noblest poems of its class which the century has produced; the mono-dramatic "Strayed Reveller," which as mentioned above is one of the very earliest of all; and the more fully dramatised and longer "Empedocles on Etna," in regard to which Mr. Arnold showed a singular vacillation, issuing it, withdrawing nearly all of it, and than issuing it again. Its design, like that of the somewhat later "Merope," is not of the happiest, but it contains some lyrical pieces which are among the best-known and the best of their author's work. Early too, if not of the earliest, are certain longer narrative or semi-narrative poems, not seldom varied with or breaking into lyric — " Sohrab and Rustum " with another of the fine closes referred to, perhaps indeed the finest of all; " The Sick King in Bokhara "; " Balder Dead "; "Tristram and Iseult "; " The Scholar-Gipsy," a most admirable "poem of place," being chiefly devoted to the country round Oxford; " Thyrsis " (an elegy on Clough which by some is ranked not far below *Lycidas* and *Adonais*). But perhaps Mr. Arnold's happiest vein, like that of most of the poets of the last two-thirds of the century, lay, not in long poems but in shorter pieces, more or less lyrical in form but not precisely lyrics — in short of the same general class (though differing often widely enough in subject and handling) as those in which the main appeal of Tennyson himself has been said to consist. Such is "The Forsaken Merman," the poet's most original and perhaps most charming if not his deepest or most elaborate thing—a piece of exquisite and passion- ate music modulated with art as touching as it is consummate ; " Dover Beach," where the peculiar religious attitude, with the expression of which so much of Mr. Arnold's prose is concerned, finds a more restrained and a very melodious voice ; the half- satiric, half-meditative " Bacchanalia "; the fine " Summer Night "; the Memorial Verses (Mr. Arnold was a frequent and a skilled attempter of epicedes) on Wordsworth, on Heine, and on the dog *Geist;* with, almost latest of all and not least noble, " Westminster Abbey," the opening passages of which vie in metre (though of a more complicated mould) and in majesty with Milton's " Nativity Ode," and show a wonderful ability to bear this heavy burden of comparison.

Perhaps these last words may not unfairly hint at a defect — if not *the* defect — of this refined, this accomplished, but this often disappointing poetry. Quite early, in the preface before referred to, the poet had run up and nailed to the mast a flag-theory of poetic art to which he always adhered as far as theory went, and which it may be reasonably supposed he always endeavoured to exemplify in practice. According to this "all depends on the subject," and the fault of most modern poetry and of nearly all modern criticism is that the poets strive to produce and the critics expect to receive, not an elaborately planned and adjusted treatment of a great subject, but touches or bursts of more or less beautiful thought and writing. Now of course it need not be said that in the very highest poetry the excellence of the subject, the complete appropriateness of the treatment, and the beauty of patches and passages, all meet together. But it will also happen that this is not so. And then the poet of "the subject" will not only miss the happy "jewels five words long," the gracious puffs and cat's paws of the wind of the spirit, that his less austere brother secures, but will not make so very much of his subjects, of his schemes of treatment themselves. His ambition, as ambition so often does, will over-reach itself, and he will have nothing to show but the unfinished fragments of a poetical Escurial instead of the finished chantries and altar-tombs which a less formal architect is able to boast.

However this may be, two things are certain, the first that the best work of Matthew Arnold in verse bears a somewhat small proportion to the work that is not his best, and that his worst is sometimes strangely unworthy of him; the second, that the best where it appears is of surpassing charm — uniting in a way, of which Andrew Marvell is perhaps the best other example in English lyric, romantic grace, feeling, and music to a classical and austere precision of style, combining nobility of thought with grace of expression, and presenting the most characteristically modern ideas of his own particular day with an almost perfect freedom from the jargon of that day, and in a key always suggesting the great masters, the great thinkers, the great poets of the past. To those who are in sympathy with his own way of thinking he must always possess an extraordinary attraction; perhaps he is not least, though he may be more discriminatingly, admired by those who are very much out of sympathy with him on not a few points of subject, but who are one with him in the Humanities — in the sense and the love of the great things in literature.

The natural and logical line of development, however, from the originators of the Romantic movement through Keats and Tennyson did not lie through Matthew Arnold ; and the time was not yet ripe — it can perhaps hardly be said to be ripe yet — for a reaction in his sense. He was, as has been said, a branch from Wordsworth, only slightly influenced by Tennyson himself, than whom indeed he was not so very much younger. The direct male line of descent lay in another direction ; and its next most important stage was determined by the same causes which almost at the middle of the century or a little before brought about Præ-Raphaelitism in art. Both of these were closely connected with the set of events called the Oxford Movement, about which much has been written, but of which the far-reaching significance, not merely in religion but in literature, politics, art, and almost things in general, has never yet been fully estimated. As far as literature is concerned, and this special part of literature with which we are here dealing, this movement had partly shown and partly shaped the direction of the best minds towards the Middle Ages, which had been begun by Percy's *Reliques* in a vague and blind sort of way, and which had been strengthened, directed, but still not altogether fashioned according to knowledge, by Scott and Coleridge.

This movement which dominates the whole English poetry of the later half of the century with the exception of that produced by a few survivors of the older time, and to which no successor of equal brilliancy and fertility has yet made its appearance, is popularly represented by three writers, two of whom, Mr. William Morris and Mr. Swinburne, are fortunately still alive, and therefore fall out of our province. Rossetti, the eldest of the three, a great influence on both, and as it happens an example unique in all history of combined excellence in poetry and painting, has passed away for some years, and will give us quite sufficient text for explaining the development and illustrating its results without outstripping the limits traced in the preface to this book ; while his sister, and a distinguished junior member of the school, also dead, Mr. Arthur O'Shaughnessy, may profitably be brought in to complete the illustration.

Gabriel Charles Dante Rossetti, generally known as Dante Gabriel Rossetti, was born in London on 12th May 1828. He was the son of an Italian poet and critic of eminence, who, like so many of his countrymen of literary tastes during the early part of the century, had fallen into the Carbonaro movement, and who had to fly first to Malta and then to England. Here he married Miss Polidori, whose mother was an Englishwoman ; and his four children — the two exquisite poets below dealt with, Mr. W. M. Rossetti, a competent critic, and Maria Francesca, the eldest daughter, who wrote an excellent introduction to Dante — all made contributions, and two of them great contributions, to English literature. The father himself, who was Professor of Italian at King's College, London, was an enthusiastic though rather a fantastic Dantist, and somewhat of a visionary generally, with wild notions about mediæval secret societies ; but a man of the greatest honesty and honour, and a brilliant contrast to the various patriot-charlatans, from Ugo Foscolo downwards, who brought discredit on the Italian name in his time in England. These particulars, of a kind seldom given in this book, are not otiose ; for they have much to do with the singular personality of our English Rossetti himself.

He was educated at King's College School ; but his leanings towards art were so strong that at the age of fifteen he began the study of it, leaving school to draw at the Royal Academy and elsewhere. His art career and the formation of the P.R.B. (Præ-Raphaelite Brotherhood) unfortunately fall outside our sphere. It is enough to say that for some twenty years Rossetti, if he was known at all (and he was never known very widely nor did he ever seek notoriety) was known as a painter only, though many who only knew his poems later conceived the most passionate admiration for his painting. Yet he wrote almost as early as he painted, contributing to the famous Præ-Raphaelite magazine, the *Germ*, in 1850, to the remarkable *Oxford and Cambridge Magazine*, which also saw the early work of Mr. Morris, in 1856, and publishing some translations from *The Early Italian Poets* in 1861. He had married the year before this last date and was about to publish *Poems* which he had been writing from an early age. But his wife died in 1862, and in a fit of despair he buried his MSS. in her coffin. They were years afterwards exhumed and the *Poems* appeared in 1870. Eleven years later another volume of *Ballads and Sonnets* was published, and Rossetti, whose health in the interval had been much shattered, and who had unfortunately sought refuge from insomnia in chloral, died next year in April 1882. The last years of his life were not happy, and he was most unnecessarily affected by attacks on the first arrangement of his *Poems*.

These poems had a certain advantage in being presented to a public already acquainted with the work of Mr. Morris and Mr. Swinburne; but Rossetti was not merely older than his two friends, he was also to some extent their master. At the same time the influences which acted on him were naturally diverse from those which, independently of his own influence, acted on them. For the French and English mediæval inspirations of Mr. Morris, for the classical and general study of Mr. Swinburne, he had his ancestral Italians almost for sole teachers; and for their varied interests he had his own art of painting for a continual companion, reminder, and model. Yet the mediæval impulse is almost equally strong on all three, and its intensity shows that it was the real dominant of the moment in English poetry. The opening poem of Rossetti's first book, "The Blessed Damozel," which is understood to have been written very early, though afterwards wrought up by touches both of his love for his wife while living and of his regret for her when dead, is almost a typical example of the whole style and school, though it is individualised by the strong pictorial element rarely absent from his work. The "Blessed Damozel" herself, who

U

" leaned out From the gold Bar of Heaven," is a figure from the *Paradiso*, divested of the excessive abstraction of that part of Dante, and clothed partly in the gayer colours and more fleshly personality of English and French mediævalism, partly in a mystical halo which is peculiar to these nineteenth century re-creations of mediæval thought and feeling. The poem is of extreme beauty, and ornate as is its language in parts there are touches, such as the poet's reflection

> To one it is ten years of years,

which utter the simplest truth and tenderness ; while others, such as the enumeration of the Virgin's handmaidens (over which at the time the hoofs of earless critics danced) —

> With her five handmaidens, whose names
> Are five sweet symphonies —
> Cecily, Gertrude, Magdalen,
> Margaret and Rosalys —

are consummate triumphs of the word-music brought by Tennyson into English poetry. Indeed this couplet of names might be made a sort of text to expound the great appeal to the ear of this kind of poetry, which any one who is deaf to the exceptional and golden harmony of the arrangement need never hope to appreciate. It is perfectly easy to change the order in many ways without affecting the verse ; there is absolutely none of these combinations which approaches the actual one in beauty of sound and suggestion.

" Love's Nocturn " which follows is more of the early Italian school pure and simple ; and " Troy Town," a ballad with burdens, is one of a class of poem much affected by Rossetti and ever since, which has produced some admirable work, but is perhaps a little open to the charge of too deliberate archaism. It is at any rate far inferior to his own " Sister Helen." But "The Burden of Nineveh " which follows is in a quite different style, and besides its intrinsic excellence is noteworthy as showing how very far Rossetti was from being limited in his choice of manners. But to go through the whole contents of this very remarkable volume would be impossible, and we can only particularise the great sonnet-sequence "The House of Life" (which was attacked for want of decency with as little intelligence as "The Blessed Damozel" had been attacked for want of sense), and a set "for pictures." The first, somewhat thorny and obscure in language, is of extreme poetical and philosophical beauty. The latter, beautiful enough, may be said to lend themselves a little to the attacks of those critics who charged Rossetti with, in the Aristotelian phrase, "shifting his ground to another kind" or (to vary the words) of taking the quotation *ut pictura poesis* in too literal a sense. Some songs, especially "Penumbra" and "The Woodspurge," of intense sweetness and sadness, were also included; and the simple directness of "Jenny" showed, like "Nineveh," capacities in the poet not easily to be inferred from the bulk of his poems.

Rossetti's second volume, while it added only too little to the bulk of his work — for much of it consisted of a revised issue of "The House of Life" — added greatly to its enjoyment. But it produced no new kind, unless certain extensions of the ballad-scheme into narrative poems of considerable length — "Rose-Mary," "The White Ship," and "The King's Tragedy" — be counted as such. "Rose-Mary" in particular exhibits the merits and defects of the poet in almost the clearest possible light, and it may be safely said that no English poet, not the very greatest, need have been ashamed of such a stanza as this, where there is no affectation worth speaking of, where the eternal and immortal commonplaces of poetry are touched to newness as only a master touches, and where the turn of the phrase and verse is impeccable and supreme : —

> And lo ! on the ground Rose-Mary lay,
> With a cold brow like the snows ere May,
> With a cold breast like the earth till Spring —
> With such a smile as the June days bring
> When the year grows warm for harvesting.

Here, as elsewhere, it has seemed better to postpone most of the necessary general criticism of schools and groups till the concluding chapter, but in this particular respect the paucity of individuals which our scheme leaves (though Miss Rossetti and Mr. O'Shaughnessy will give valuable assistance presently), may make a few words desirable, even if they be partly repetition and partly anticipation. We find in Rossetti a strong influence of pictorial on poetic art; an overpowering tendency to revert to the forms and figures, the sense and sentiment of the past, especially the mediæval past; and a further tendency to a mysticism which is very often, if not always, poetic in character, as indeed mysticism generally if not always is. We find in point of form a distinct preference for lyric over other kinds, a fancy for archaic language and schemes of verse, a further fancy for elaborate and ornate language (which does not, however, exclude perfect simplicity when the poet chooses), and above all, a predilection for attempting and a faculty for achieving effects of verbal music by cunning adjustment of vowel and consonant sound which, though it had been anticipated partially, and as it were accidentally in the seventeenth century, and had been after the Romantic revival displayed admirably by Coleridge and Keats, and brought to a high pitch by Tennyson, was even further elaborated and polished by the present school. Indeed, they may be said to have absolutely finished this poetical appeal as a distinct and deliberate one. All poets have always attempted, and all poets always will attempt, and when they are great, achieve these enchanting effects of mere sound. But for some considerable time it will not be possible (indeed it will be quite impossible until the structure, the intonation, the phrase of English have taken such turns as will develop physical possibilities as different from those of our language as ours are from those of the seventeenth century) for any poets to get distinctly great effects in the same way. It is proof enough of this that, except the masters, no poet for many years now *has* achieved a great effect by this means, and that the most promising of the newer school, whether they may or may not have found a substitute, are abandoning it.

Rossetti's younger, but very little younger, sister, Christina Georgina, was born in 1830, sat to her brother early for the charming picture of "The Girlhood of Mary Virgin," and is said also to figure in his illustration of the weeping queens in Tennyson's *Morte D'Arthur*. But she lived an exceedingly quiet life, mainly occupied in attention to her mother and in devotion; for she had been brought up, and all her life remained, a member of the Church of England. Her religious feelings more and more coloured her poetical work, which was produced at intervals from 1861 till close upon her death in the winter of 1894-95. It was not hastily written, and latterly formed mainly the embellishment of certain prose books of religious reflection or excerpt. But it was always of an exquisite quality. Its first expression in book form was *Goblin Market, and other Poems* (1861), which, as well as her next volume, *The Prince's Progress* (1866), was illustrated by her brother's pencil. A rather considerable time then passed without anything of importance (a book called *Sing-Song* excepted), till in 1881 *A Pageant, and other Poems* was added. A collection of all these was issued nine years later, but with this the gleanings from the devotional works above mentioned (the chief of which were *Time Flies* and *The Face of the Deep*) have still to be united.

There are those who seriously maintain Miss Rossetti's claim to the highest rank among English poetesses, urging that she excels Mrs. Browning, her only possible competitor, in freedom from blemishes of form and from the liability to fall into silliness and maudlin gush, at least as much as she falls short of her in variety and in power of shaping a poem of considerable bulk. But without attempting a too rigid classification we may certainly say that Miss Rossetti has no superior among Englishwomen who have had the gift of poetry. In the title-piece of her first book the merely quaint side of Præ-Raphaelitism perhaps appears rather too strongly, though very agreeably to some. But "Dreamland," "Winter Rain," "An End," "Echo," the exquisite song for music "When I am dead, my dearest," and the

wonderful devotional pieces called "The Three Enemies" and
"Sleep at Sea," with many charming sonnets, adorned a volume
which, on the whole, showed more of the tendencies of the
school than any which had yet appeared. For it was less
exclusively mediæval than Mr. Morris' *Defence of Guinevere*,
and very much more varied as well as more mature than
Mr. Swinburne's *Queen Mother* and *Rosamond*. *The Prince's
Progress* showed a great advance on *Goblin Market* in dignity
and freedom from mannerism, and the minor poems in general
rivalled those in the earlier collection, though the poetess perhaps never quite equalled "Sleep at Sea." The contents of
A Pageant, and other Poems were at once more serious and lighter
than those of the two former books (for Miss Rossetti, like her
brother, had a strong touch of humour), while the *Collected Poems*
added some excellent pieces. But the note of the whole had
been struck, as is usually the case with good poets who do not
publish too early, at the very first.

The most distinguished members, with the exception of Mr.
and Miss Rossetti, of this school are still alive ; and, as it did not
become fashionable until about five-and-twenty years ago, even
the junior members of it have in but few cases been sent to that
majority of which alone we treat. Mr. John Addington Symonds,
an important writer of prose, began early and never abandoned
the practice of verse, but his accomplishment in it was never
more than an accomplishment. Mr. Philip Bourke Marston, son
of Dr. Westland Marston, the dramatist, was highly reputed as
a poet by his friends, but friendship and compassion (he was
blind) had perhaps more to do with this reputation than strict
criticism. The remarkable talents of Mr. Gerard Manley Hop-
kins, which could never be mistaken by any one who knew him,
and of which some memorials remain in verse, were mainly lost
to English poetry by the fact of his passing the last twenty years
of his life as a Jesuit priest. But the most characteristic figure
now passed away was Arthur O'Shaughnessy (1844–81). He
was an official of the British Museum, and published three

volumes of poetry — *The Epic of Women* (1870), *Lays of France* (1872), and *Music and Moonlight* (1874) — which were completed in the year of his death by a posthumous volume entitled *Songs of a Worker*. Of these the *Lays of France* are merely paraphrases of Marie : great part of the *Songs of a Worker* is occupied with mere translation of modern French verses — poor work for a poet at all times. But *The Epic of Women* and *Music and Moonlight* contain stuff which it is not extravagant to call extraordinary.

It was never widely popular, for O'Shaughnessy pushed the fancy of the Præ-Raphaelites for a dreamy remoteness to its very furthest, and the charge (usually an uncritical one, but usually also explaining with a certain justice a poet's unpopularity) of "lack of human interest" was brought against him. Sometimes, too, either of deliberate conviction or through corrupt following of others, he indulged in expressions of opinion about matters on which the poet is not called upon to express any, in a manner which was always unnecessary and sometimes offensive. But judged as a poet he has the *unum necessarium*, the individual note of song. Like Keats, he was not quite individual — there are echoes, especially of Edgar Poe, in him. But the genuine and authentic contribution is sufficient, and is of the most unmistakable kind. In the first book " Exile," " A Neglected Heart," " Bisclavaret," " The Fountain of Tears," " Barcarolle," make a new mixture of the fair and strange in meaning, a new valuation of the eternal possibilities of language in sound. *Music and Moonlight*—O'Shaughnessy was one of the few poets who have been devoted to music — is almost more remote, and even less popularly beautiful ; but the opening " Ode," some of the lyrics in the title poem (such as " Once in a hundred years "), the song " Has summer come without the rose," and not a few others, renew for those who can receive it the strange attraction, the attraction most happily hinted by the very title of this book itself, which O'Shaughnessy could exercise. That there was not a little that is morbid in him — as perhaps in the school generally — sane criticism cannot deny. But though it is as unwise as it is unsafe to prefer morbidness for itself or to give it too great way, there are undoubted charms in it, and O'Shaughnessy could give poetical form to these as few others could. Two of his own lines —

> Oh! exquisite malady of the soul,
> How hast thou marred me —

put the thing well. Those who have once tasted his poetry return, and probably, though they are never likely to be numerous, always when they have once tasted will return, to the visions and the melodies —

> Of a dreamer who slumbers,
> And a singer who sings no more.

Another poet whose death brings him within our range, and who may be said to belong, with some striking differences of circumstance as well as individual genius, to the same school, was James Thomson, second of the name in English poetry, but a curious and melancholy contrast to that Epicurean animal, the poet of *The Seasons*. He was born at Port-Glasgow on 23rd November 1834, and was the son of a sailor. His parents being in poor circumstances, he obtained, as a child, a place in the Royal Caledonian Asylum, and, after a good education there, became an army schoolmaster — a post which he held for a considerable time. But Thomson's natural character was recalcitrant to discipline and distinguished by a morbid social jealousy. He gradually, under the influence of, or at any rate in company with, the notorious Charles Bradlaugh, adopted atheistic and republican opinions, and in 1862 an act of insubordination led to his dismissal from the army, for which he had long lost, if he ever had, any liking. It is also said that the death of a girl to whom he was passionately attached had much to do with the development of the morbid pessimism by which he became distinguished. For some time Thomson tried various occupations, being by turns a lawyer's clerk, a mining agent, and war correspondent of a newspaper with the Carlists. But even before he

left the army he had, partly with Mr. Bradlaugh's help, obtained
work on the press, and such income as he had during the last
twenty years of his life was chiefly derived from it. He might
undoubtedly have made a comfortable living in this way, for his
abilities were great and his knowledge not small. But in addition
to the specially poetical weakness of disliking "collar-work," he
was hampered by the same intractable and morose temper which
he had shown in the army, by the violence of his religious and
political views, and lastly and most fatally by an increasing slav-
ery to drink and chloral. At last, in 1882, he — after having
been for some time in the very worst health — burst a blood-
vessel while visiting his friend the blind poet Philip Bourke
Marston, and died in University College Hospital on 3rd June.

This melancholy story is to be found sufficiently reflected in
his works. Those in prose, though not contemptible, neither deserve nor are likely to receive long remembrance, being for the
most part critical studies, animated by a real love for literature
and informed by respectable knowledge, but of necessity lacking
in strict scholarship, distinguished by more acuteness than wisdom, and marred by the sectarian violence and narrowness of
a small anti-orthodox clique. They may perhaps be not unfairly
compared to the work of a clever but ill-conditioned schoolboy.
The verse is very different. He began to write it early, and it
chiefly appeared in Mr. Bradlaugh's *National Reformer* with the
signature "B. V.," the initials of "Bysshe Vanolis," a rather characteristic *nom de guerre* which Thomson had taken to express
his admiration for Shelley directly, and for Novalis by anagram.
Some of it, however, emerged into a wider hearing, and attracted
the favourable attention of men like Kingsley and Froude. But
Thomson did nothing of importance till 1874, when "The City of
Dreadful Night" appeared in the *National Reformer*, to the no
small bewilderment probably of its readers. Six years later the
poem was printed with others in a volume, quickly followed by a
second, *Vane's Story, etc.* Thomson's melancholy death attracted
fresh attention to him, and much — perhaps a good deal too much

—of his writings has been republished since. His claims, however, must rest on a comparatively small body of work, which will no doubt one day be selected and issued alone. "The City of Dreadful Night" itself, incomparably the best of the longer poems, is a pessimist and nihilist effusion of the deepest gloom amounting to despair, but couched in stately verse of an absolute sincerity and containing some splendid passages. With this is connected one of the latest pieces, the terrible "Insomnia." Of lighter strain, written when the poet could still be happy, are "Sunday at Hampstead" and "Sunday up the River," "The Naked Goddess," and one or two others ; while other things, such as "The fire that filled my heart of old," must also be cited. Even against these the charge of a monotonous, narrow, and irrational misery has been brought. But what saves Thomson is the perfection with which he expresses the negative and hopeless side of the sense of mystery, of the Unseen; just as Miss Rossetti expresses the positive and hopeful one. No two contemporary poets perhaps ever completed each other in a more curious way than this Bohemian atheist and this devout lady.

So far in this chapter the story of poetry, from Tennyson downwards, has been conducted in regular fashion, and by citing the principal names which represent the chief schools or subschools. But we must now return to notice a very considerable company of other verse-writers, without mention of whom this history would be wofully incomplete. Nor must it by any means be supposed that they are to be regarded invariably as constituting a "second class." On the contrary, some of them are the equals, one or two the superiors, of Thomson or of O'Shaughnessy. But they have been postponed, either because they belong to schools of which the poets already mentioned are masters, to choruses of which others are the leaders, or because they show rather blended influences than a distinct and direct advance in the main poetical line of development. Others again rank here, and not earlier, because they are of the second class, or a lower one.

Of these, though he leaves a name certain to live in English literary history, if not perhaps quite in the way in which its author wished, is Martin Farquhar Tupper, who was born, in 1810, of a very respectable family in the Channel Islands, his father being a surgeon of eminence. Tupper was educated at the Charterhouse and at Christ Church, and was called to the bar. But he gave himself up to literature, especially poetry or verse, of which he wrote an enormous quantity. His most famous book appeared originally in 1839, though it was afterwards continued. It was called *Proverbial Philosophy*, and criticised life in rhythmical rather than metrical lines, with a great deal of orthodoxy. Almost from the first the critics and the wits waged unceasing war against it ; but the public, at least for many years, bought it with avidity, and perhaps read it, so that it went through forty editions and is said to have brought in twenty thousand pounds. Nor is it at all certain that any genuine conception of its pretentious triviality had much to do with the decay which, after many years, it, like other human things, experienced. Mr. Tupper, who did not die till 1889, is understood to have been privately an amiable and rather accomplished person ; and some of his innumerable minor copies of verse attain a very fair standard of minor poetry. But *Proverbial Philosophy* remains as one of the bright and shining examples of the absolute want of connection between literary merit and popular success.

It has been said that Lord Tennyson's first work appeared in *Poems by Two Brothers*, and it is now known that this book was actually by the *three*, — Frederick, Charles, and Alfred. Frederick, the eldest, who, at a great age, is still alive, has never ceased verse-writing. Charles, who afterwards took the name of Turner, and, having been born in 1808, died in 1879, was particularly famous as a sonneteer, producing in this form many good and some excellent examples. Arthur Hallam, whom *In Memoriam* has made immortal, was credited by the partial judgment of his friends with talents which, they would fain think, were actually shown both in verse and prose. A wiser criticism will content itself with saying that in one sense he produced *In Memoriam* itself, and that this is enough connection with literature for any man. His own work has a suspicious absence of faults, without the presence of any great positive merit, — a combination almost certainly indicating precocity, to be followed by sterility. But this consummation he was spared. John Sterling, who has been already referred to, and who stands to Carlyle in what may be called a prose version of the relation between Tennyson and Hallam, wrote some verse which is at least interesting; and Sir Francis Doyle, also elsewhere mentioned, belongs to the brood of the remarkable years 1807–14, having been born in 1810. But his splendid war-songs were written not very early in life.

Of the years just mentioned, the first, 1807, contributed, besides Mr. Frederick Tennyson, the very considerable talent of Archbishop Trench, a Harrow and Trinity (Cambridge) man who had an actual part in the expedition to Spain from which Sterling retreated, took orders, and ended a series of ecclesiastical promotions by the Archbishopric of Dublin, to which he was consecrated in 1864, which he held with great dignity and address during the extremely trying period of Disestablishment, and which he resigned in 1884, dying two years later. Trench wrote always well, and always as a scholar, on a wide range of subjects. He was an interesting philologist, — his *Study of Words* being the most popular of scholarly and the most scholarly of popular works on the subject, — a valuable introducer of the exquisite sacred Latin poetry of the Middle Ages to Englishmen, a sound divine in preaching and teaching. His original English verse was chiefly written before the middle of the century, though perhaps his best known (not his best) verses are on the Battle of the Alma. He was a good sonneteer and an excellent hymn-writer.

1809 contributed three writers of curiously contrasted character. One was Professor Blackie, an eccentric and amiable man, a translator of Æschylus, and a writer of songs of a healthy and spirited kind. The second, Dr. Thomas Gordon Hake, a poet of Parables, has never been popular, and perhaps seldom arrived at that point of projection in which poetical alchemy finally and successfully transmutes the rebel materials of thought and phrase into manifest gold; but he had very high and distinctly rare poetical qualities. Such things as "Old Souls," "The Snake Charmer," "The Palmist," three capital examples of his work, are often, and not quite wrongly, objected to in different forms of some such a phrase as this: "Poetry that is perfect poetry ought never to subject any tolerable intellect to the necessity of search- ing for its meaning. It is not necessary that it should yield up the whole treasures of that meaning at once, but it must carry on the face of it such a competent quantity as will relieve the reader from postponing the poetic enjoyment in order to solve the intellectual riddle." The truth of this in the main, and the demurrers and exceptions to it in part, are pretty clear; nor is this the place to state them at length. It is sufficient to say that in Dr. Hake's verse, especially that part of it published between 1870 and 1880 under the titles *Madeline, Parables and Tales, New Symbols, Legends of the Morrow* and *Maiden Ecstasy,* the reader of some poetical experience will seldom fail to find satis- faction.

It is impossible to imagine a greater contrast than that of this poet with Lord Houghton, earlier known to everybody as Richard Monckton Milnes, who died in 1885. He was of the golden age of Trinity during this century, the age of Tennyson, and throughout life he had an amiable fancy for making the acquaint- ance of everybody who made any name in literature, and of many who made none. A practical and active politician, and a constant figure in society, he was also a very considerable man of letters. His critical work (principally but not wholly collected in *Monographs*) is not great in bulk but is exceedingly good, both in substance and in style. His verse, on the other hand, which was chiefly the produce of the years before he came to middle life, is a little slight, and perhaps appears slighter than it really is. Few poets have ever been more successful with songs for music: the "Brookside" (commonly called from its refrain, "The beating of my own heart"), the famous and really fine "Strangers Yet," are the best

known, but there are many others.   Lord Houghton undoubtedly
had no strong vein of poetry.   But it was always an entire mistake
to represent him as either a fribble or a sentimentalist, while with
more inducements to write he would probably have been one of
the very best critics of his age.

It is necessary once more to approach the unsatisfactory brevity
of a catalogue in order to mention, since it would be wrong to omit,
Sir Samuel Ferguson (1810–86), an Irish writer who produced
some pleasant and spirited work of ordinary kinds, and laboured
very hard to achieve that often tried but seldom achieved adventure,
the rendering into English poetry of Irish Celtic legends and
literature ; Alfred Domett (1811–87), author of the New Zealand
epic of *Ranulf and Amohia* and much other verse, but most
safely grappled to English poetry as Browning's " Waring " ;
W. B. Scott (1812–90), an outlying member of the Præ-Raphaelite School in art and letters, in whom for the most part
execution lagged behind conception both with pen and pencil ;
Charles Mackay (1814–89), an active journalist who wrote a vast
deal in verse and prose, his best things perhaps being the mid-
century " Cholera Chant," the once well-known song of " A good
time coming," and in a sentimental strain the piece called
" O, ye Tears " ; and Mrs. Archer Clive, the author of the remarkable novel of *Paul Ferroll*, whose *IX. Poems by V.* attracted
much attention from competent critics in the doubtful time of
poetry about the middle of the century, and are really
good.

Not many writers, either in prose or poetry, give the impression
of never having done what was in them more than William Edmons-
toune Aytoun, who was born in 1813 and died in 1865.   He was a
son-in-law of " Christopher North," and like him a pillar of *Blackwood's Magazine*, in which some of his best things in prose and verse
appeared.   He divided himself between law and literature, and in
his rather short life rose to a Professorship in the latter and a
Sheriffdom in the former, deserving the credit of admirably stimulating influence in the first capacity and competent performance

in the second. He published poems when he was only seventeen. But his best work consists of the famous *Bon Gaultier Ballads* — a collection of parodies and light poems of all kinds written in conjunction with Sir Theodore Martin, and one of the pleasantest books of the kind that the century has seen — and the more serious *Lays of the Scottish Cavaliers*, both dating from the forties, the satirically curious *Firmilian* (see below), 1854, and some *Blackwood* stories of which the very best perhaps is *The Glenmutchkin Railway*. His long poem of *Bothwell*, 1855, and his novel of *Norman Sinclair*, 1861, are less successful.

The *Lays of the Scottish Cavaliers*, on which his chief serious claim must rest, is an interesting book, if hardly a great one. The style is modelled with extreme closeness upon that of Scott, which even Sir Walter, with all his originality and genius, had not been able always to preserve from flatness. In Aytoun's hands the flats are too frequent, though they are relieved and broken at times by really splendid bursts, the best of which perhaps are "The Island of the Scots" and "The Heart of the Bruce." For Aytoun's poetic vein, except in the lighter kinds, was of no very great strength ; and an ardent patriotism, a genuine and gallant devotion to the Tory cause, and a keen appreciation of the chivalrous and romantic, did not always suffice to supply the want of actual inspiration.

If it had been true, as is commonly said, that the before-mentioned *Firmilian* killed the so-called Spasmodic School, Aytoun's failure to attain the upper regions of poetry would have been a just judgment ; for the persons whom he satirised, though less clever and humorous, were undoubtedly more poetical than himself. But nothing is ever killed in this way, and as a matter of fact the Spasmodic School of the early fifties was little more than one of the periodical outbursts of poetic velleity, more genuine than vigorous and more audacious than organic, which are constantly witnessed. It is, as usual, not very easy to find out who were the supposed scholars in this school. Mr. P. H. Bailey, the author of *Festus*, who still survives, is sometimes classed with them ; but the chief members are admitted to have been Sydney Dobell and Alexander Smith, both remarkable persons, both failures of something which might in each case have been a considerable poet, and both illustrating the "second middle" period of the poetry of the century which corresponds to that illustrated earlier by Darley, Horne, and Beddoes.

Of this pair, Sydney Dobell had some, and Alexander Smith had others, of the excuses which charity not divorced from critical judgment makes for imperfect poets. Dobell, with sufficient leisure for poetical production, had a rather unfortunate education and exceedingly bad health. Smith had something of both of these, and the necessity of writing for bread as well. Dobell, the elder of the two, and the longer lived, though both died comparatively young, was a Kentish man, born at Cranbrook on 5th April 1824. When he was of age his father established himself as a wine-merchant at Cheltenham, and Sydney afterwards exercised the same not unpoetical trade. He went to no school and to no University, privations especially dangerous to a person inclined as he was to a kind of passionate priggishness. He was always ill ; and his wife, to whom he engaged himself while a boy, and whom he married before he had ceased to be one, was always ill likewise. He travelled a good deal, with results more beneficial to his poetry than to his health ; and, the latter becoming ever worse, he died near Cheltenham on 22nd August 1874. His first work, an "Italomaniac" closet drama entitled *The Roman*, was published in 1850; his second, *Balder*, in 1853. This latter has been compared to Ibsen's *Brand :* I do not know whether any one has noticed other odd, though slight, resemblances between *Peer Gynt* and Beddoes' chief work. The Crimean War had a strong influence on Dobell, and besides joining Smith in *Sonnets on the War* (1855), he wrote by himself *England in Time of War*, next year. He did not publish anything else ; but his works were edited shortly after his death by Professor Nichol.

Alexander Smith, like so many of the modern poets of Scotland, was born in quite humble life, and had not even the full advantages open to a Scottish "lad o' pairts." His birthplace, however, was Kilmarnock, a place not alien to the Muses; and before he was twenty-one (his birth year is diversely given as 1829 and 1830) the Rev. George Gilfillan, an amiable and fluent critic of the middle of the century, who loved literature very much and praised its practitioners with more zeal than discrimination, procured the publication of the *Life Drama*. It sold enormously; it is necessary to have been acquainted with those who were young at the time of its appearance to believe in the enthusiasm with which it was received; but a little intelligence and a very little goodwill will enable the critic to understand, if not to share their raptures. For a time Smith was deliberately pitted against Tennyson by "the younger sort" as Dennis says of the faction for Settle against Dryden in his days at Cambridge. The reaction which, mercifully for the chances of literature if not quite pleasantly for the poet, always comes in such cases, was pretty rapid, and Smith, ridiculed in *Firmilian*, was more seriously taxed with crudity (which was just), plagiarism (which was absurd), and want of measure (which, like the crudity, can hardly be denied). Smith, however, was not by any means a weakling except physically; he could even satirise himself sensibly and good-humouredly enough; and his popularity had the solid result of giving him a post in the University of Edinburgh — not lucrative and by no means a sinecure, but not too uncongenial, and allowing him a chance both to read and to write. For some time he stuck to poetry, publishing *City Poems* in 1857 and *Edwin of Deira* in 1861. But the taste for his wares had dwindled: perhaps his own poetic impulse, a true but not very strong one, was waning; and he turned to prose, in which he produced a story or two and some pleasant descriptive work — *Dreamthorpe* (1863), and *A Summer in Skye* (1865). Consumption showed itself, and he died on 8th January 1867.

It has already been said that there is much less of a distinct brotherhood in Dobell and Smith, or of any membership of a larger but special "Spasmodic school," than of the well-known and superficially varying but generally kindred spirit of periods

and persons in which and in whom poetic yearning does not find
organs or opportunities thoroughly suited to satisfy itself. Dobell
is the more unequal, but the better of the two in snatches. His
two most frequently quoted things — "Tommy's Dead" and the
untitled ballad where the refrain —

> Oh, Keith of Ravelston,
> The sorrows of thy line!

occurs at irregular intervals — are for once fair samples of their
author's genius. "Tommy's dead," the lament of a father over
his son, is too long, it has frequent flatnesses, repetitions that do
not add to the effect, bits of mere gush, trivialities. The tragic
and echoing magnificence of the Ravelston refrain is not quite
seconded by the text : both to a certain extent deserve the epithet (which I have repudiated for Beddoes in another place) of
"artificial." And yet both have the fragmentary, not to be analysed, almost uncanny charm and grandeur which have been spoken
of in that place. Nor do this charm, this grandeur, fail to reappear
(always more or less closely accompanied by the faults just mentioned, and also by a kind of flatulent rant which is worse than
any of them) both in Dobell's war-songs, which may be said in a
way to hand the torch on from Campbell to Mr. Kipling, and in
his marvellously unequal blank verse, where the most excellent
thought and phrase alternate with sheer balderdash — a pun which
(it need hardly be said) was not spared by contemporary critics
to the author of *Balder*.

Alexander Smith never rises to the heights nor strikes the distinct notes of Dobell ; but the *Life Drama* is really on the whole
better than either *Balder* or *The Roman*, and is full of what may
be called, from opposite points of view, happy thoughts and quaint
conceits, expressed in a stamp of verse certainly not quite original, but melodious always, and sometimes very striking. He has
not yet had his critical resurrection, and perhaps none such will
ever exalt him to a very high prominent position. He seems to
suffer from the operation of that mysterious but very real law

which decrees that undeserved popularity shall be followed by neglect sometimes even more undeserved. But when he does finally find his level, it will not be a very low one.

To the Spasmodics may be appended yet another list of bards who can claim here but the notice of a sentence or a clause, though by no means uninteresting to the student, and often very interesting indeed to the student-lover of poetry : — the two Joneses — Ernest (1819–69), a rather silly victim of Chartism, for which he went to prison, but a generous person and master of a pretty twitter enough ; and Ebenezer (1820–60), a London clerk, author of *Studies of Sensation and Event*, a rather curious link between the Cockney school of the beginning of the century and some minor poets of our own times, but overpraised by his rediscoverers some years ago ; W. C. Bennett, a popular song-writer ; William Cory (–1892), earlier and better known as Johnson, an Eton master, a scholar, an admirable writer of prose and in *Ionica* of verse slightly effeminate but with a note in it not unworthy of one glance of its punning title ; W. C. Roscoe (1823–59), grandson of the historian, a minor poet in the best sense of the term ; William Allingham (1824–89), sometime editor of *Fraser*, and a writer of verse from whom at one time something might have been expected ; Thomas Woolner, a sculptor of great, and — in *My Beautiful Lady*, *Pygmalion*, etc. — a poet of estimable merit, whose first-named volume attracted rather disproportionate praise at its first appearance. As one thinks of the work of these and others — often enjoyable, sometimes admirable, and long ago or later admired and enjoyed — the unceremoniousness of despatching them so slightly brings a twinge of shame. But it is impossible to do justice to their work, or to the lyrics, merry or sensuous, of Mortimer Collins, who was nearly a real poet of *vers de société*, and had a capital satiric and a winning romantic touch ; the stirring ballads of Walter Thornbury (which, however, would hardly have been written but for Macaulay on the one hand and Barham on the other) and the ill-conditioned but clever Radical railing of Robert Brough at " Gentlemen." But if they cannot be discussed, they shall at least be mentioned. On three others, Frederick Locker, Arthur Hugh Clough, and "Owen Meredith" (Lord Lytton), we must dwell longer.

Clough has been called by persons of distinction a "bad poet"; but this was only a joke, and, with all respect to those who made it, a rather bad joke. The author of "Qua Cursum Ventus," of the marvellous picture of the advancing tide in "Say not the struggle," and of not a few other things, was certainly no bad poet, though it would not be uncritical to call him a thin one. He was born at Liverpool on New Year's Day 1819, spent part of his childhood in America, went to Rugby very young and distinguished himself there greatly, though it may be doubted whether the peculiar system which Arnold had just brought into full play was the healthiest for a self-conscious and rather morbid nature like Clough's. From Rugby he went to Balliol, and was entirely upset, not, as is sometimes most unjustly said, by Newman, but by the influence of W. G. Ward, a genial Puck of Theology, who, himself caring for nothing but mathematics, philosophy, and play-acting, disturbed the consciences of others by metaphysical quibbles, and then took refuge in the Church of Rome. Clough, who had been elected to an Oriel fellowship, threw it up in 1848, turned freethinker, and became the head of an educational institution in London called University Hall. He did not hold this very long, receiving a post in the Education Office, which he held in various forms till his death in 1861 at Florence.

It is not necessary to be biassed by Matthew Arnold's musical epicede of "Thyrsis" in order to admit, nor should any bias against his theological views and his rather restless character be sufficient to induce any one to deny, a distinct vein of poetry in Clough. His earliest and most popular considerable work, *The Bothie of Tober-na-Vuolich* (the title of which was originally rather different, is written in hexameters which do not, like Kingsley's, escape the curse of that "pestilent heresy"; and the later *Amours de Voyage* and *Dipsychus*, though there are fine passages in both, bring him very close to the Spasmodic school, of which in fact he was an unattached and more cultivated member, with fancies directed rather to religiosity than to strict literature. *Ambarvalia* had preceded the *Bothie*, and other things followed. On the whole, Clough is one of the most unsatisfactory products of that well-known form of nineteenth century scepticism which has neither the strength to believe nor the courage to disbelieve " and have done with it." He hankers and looks back, his "two souls" are always warring with each other, and though the clash and con-flict sometimes bring out fine things (as in the two pieces above cited and the still finer poem at Naples with the refrain " Christ is not risen "), though his " Latest Decalogue " has satirical merit, and some of his country poems, written without undercurrent of thought, are fresh and genial, he is on the whole a failure. But he is a failure of a considerable poet, and some fragments of suc-cess chequer him.

Frederick Locker, who on his second marriage took the additional name of Lampson, was born in 1821 of a family long connected with the Navy and with Greenwich Hospital. He himself held for some years a post in the Admiralty ; but he was much more addicted to society and to literature than to official work. His first marriage with Lady Charlotte Bruce strengthened his social position, and his second gave him wealth. He published, as early as 1857, a volume of light verse entitled *London Lyrics*, which, with the work of Prior, Praed, and Mr. Austin Dobson, stands at the head of its kind in English. But — an exceedingly rare thing for amateur as well as for professional writers in our time — he was not tempted either by profit or fame to write copiously. He added during his not short life, which closed in May 1895, a few more poems to *London Lyrics*. He edited in 1867 an anthology of his own kind of verse called *Lyra Elegan-tiarum*, and in 1879 he produced a miscellany of verse and prose, original and selected, called *Patchwork*, in which some have seen his most accomplished and characteristic production. In form it is something like Southey's *Omniana*, partly a commonplace book, partly full of original things ; but the extracts are so choicely made and the original part is so delightful that it is not quite like any book in the language. If Charles Lamb had been of Mr. Locker's time and circumstances he might have made its fellow. "My Guardian Angel," a short prose anecdote, is, as nearly as the present writer knows, unique. Latterly its author was chiefly known as a man of much hospitality and a collector of choice books. He would not do anything bad, and apparently he did not feel inclined to do anything good. And as this is a century when almost everybody must still be doing, and taking the chance of goodness and badness, such an exception to the rule should meet with honour.

No poet of the period, perhaps none of the century, occupies a position less settled by general criticism, or more difficult to settle, than that of Edward Robert, first Earl of Lytton, for a long time known in poetry as "Owen Meredith." The only son of the novelist, he was born on 8th November 1831, and after going to Harrow, but not to either university, entered the diplomatic service at the age of eighteen. In this he filled a great many different offices at a great many different places for nearly thirty years, till, after succeeding to his father's title, he was made First Minister at Lisbon, and then in 1876 Viceroy of India. This post he gave up in 1880, and after the return of the Tory party to power, was sent in 1887 as Ambassador to Paris, where he was very popular, and where he died in 1892.

Despite the fact that his time, save for the interval of 1880-87, was thus uninterruptedly occupied with business, Lord Lytton was an indefatigable writer of verse; while in *The Ring of Amasis* he tried the prose romance. His chief poetical books were *Clytemnestra* (1855); *The Wanderer* (1859), which contains some charming lyrical work; *Lucile* (1860), a verse story; *Songs of Servia* (*Serbski Pesme*) (1861); *Orval, or the Fool of Time* and *Chronicles and Characters* (1869); *Fables in Song* (1874); *Glenaveril,* a very long modern epic (1885); and *After Paradise, or Legends of Exile* (1887). Besides these he collaborated in 1861 with his friend Julian Fane in a poem, *Tannhäuser,* which,

a sufficient organ of expression. Nor did he ever develop this except in *A Little Child's Monument*, where the passionate personal agony injures as much as it helps the poetical result. Mr. Ashe, who was born in 1836, and died in 1889, also a Cambridge man, had a much less ambitious and rather less interesting but somewhat better-organised talent for verse, and his *Sorrows of Hypsipyle*, published in 1866, caused and authorised at the time considerable expectations from him. But his vein was rather the result of classical culture working on a slight original talent than anything better, and he did not rise beyond a pleasant competence in verse which was never that of a poetaster, but hardly ever that of a distinct poet. In which respect he may appear here as the representative of no scanty company dead and living. For even the longest chapter of a book must have an end ; and it is impossible to find room in it for the discussion of the question, whether the friends of Oliver Madox Brown, son of the famous Præ-Raphaelite painter, were or were not wrong in seeing extraordinary promise in his boyish work ; whether the sonnets of Ernest Lefroy (1855–91) were exercises or works of art. A few more remarks on humorous poets and women-poets must close the record.

In the art of merely or mainly humorous singing two names, those of Edward Lear and Charles Stuart Calverley, entirely dominate the rest among dead writers in the last part of the century. Lear, a good deal the elder man of the two, was born in 1813, was a painter by profession, and was the " E. L." of a well-known poem of Tennyson's. It was not till 1861 that his delightful nonsense-verses, known to his friends in private, were first published, and they received various additions at intervals till his death in 1888. The sheer nonsense-verse — the *amphigouri* as the French call it — has been tried in various countries and at various times, but never with such success as in England, and it has seldom, if ever, been cultivated in England with such success as by Lear. His happy concoction of fantastic names, the easy slipping flow of his verse, and above all, the irresistible parody of sense and pathos that he contrived to instil into his rigmarole are unapproachable. In a new and not in the least opprobrious sense he was "within the realms of Nonsense absolute."

Calverley attempted less "uttermost isles" of fun. Born in 1831 of an excellent Yorkshire family, he was educated at Harrow, and — a thing as rare in the nineteenth as common in the seventeenth century — at both universities, gaining at both a great reputation for scholarship, eccentricity, and bodily strength. After some time he married and began to work at the Bar; but an accident on the ice in 1867 brought on concussion of the brain, though he lingered in constantly weakening health till 1884. His *Verses and Translations* twenty-two years earlier had made him the model of all literary undergraduates with a turn for humour; and he was able in spite of his affliction to issue some things later, the chief being *Fly Leaves* in 1872. Calverley, as has been said, was a scholar, and his versions both from and into the classical languages would of themselves have given him a reputation; but his forte lay partly in the easier vein of parody, wherein few excelled him, partly in the more difficult one of original light verse, wherein he had a turn (as in his famous eulogy on tobacco) quite his own. He has never been equalled in this, or even approached, except by James Kenneth Stephen (1859–92), whose premature death deprived his friends of a most amiable personality, and literature, in all probability, of a considerable ornament. As it was, "J. K. S." left next to nothing but two tiny collections of verse, showing an inspiration midway between Calverley and Praed, but with quite sufficient personal note.

Two other writers of less scholarly style, but belonging to the London Bohemian school of the third quarter of the century, W. J. Prowse, "Nicholas" (1836–70), and H. S. Leigh (1837–83), may be noticed. Prowse, whose career was very short, was the author of the charming lines on "The beautiful City of Prague," which have been attributed to others: while Leigh's *Carols of Cockayne* (he was also a play-

wright) vary the note of Hood happily, and now and then with a
real originality.

Except Miss Rossetti, no woman during this time approached
the poetical excellence of Mrs. Barrett Browning. But the
whole period has been unprecedentedly fertile in poetesses,
and whereas we had but five or six to mention in the earlier
chapter devoted to verse, we have here at least a dozen, though
no one who requires very extended notice here. Lady Dufferin
(1807–1867), mother of the well-known diplomatist, a member of
the Sheridan family, and her sister, and junior by a year, Mrs.
Norton (1808–1876), were both writers of facile and elegant verse,
with the Irish note of easy melody. The former was the less
known to the general reader, though a few of her pieces, such as
"The Irish Emigrant" and "Katie's Letter," have always been
favourite numbers for recitation. Mrs. Norton at one time
enjoyed a considerable reputation as a poetess by contributions
to "Annuals" and "Souvenirs," chiefly in the sentimental ballad
style which pleased the second quarter of the century. "The
Outward Bound," "Bingen on the Rhine," and other things are
at least passable, and one of the author's latest and most ambitious
poems, *The Lady of La Garaye*, has a sustained respectability.
To a few fanatical admirers the scanty verse of Emily Brontë
has seemed worthy of such high praise that only mass of work
would appear to be wanting to put her in the first rank of
poetesses if not of poets. Part of this, however, it is to be feared,
is due to admiration of the supposed freedom of thought in her
celebrated "Last Lines," which either in sincerity or bravado
pronounce that "vain are the thousand creeds," and declare for
a sort of vague Pantheism, immanent at once in self and the
world. At thirty, however, a genuine poetess should have produced more than a mere handful of verse, and its best things
should be independent of polemical partisanship either for or
against orthodoxy. As a matter of fact, her exquisite " Remembrance," and the slightly rhetorical but brave and swinging
epigram of "The Old Stoic," give her better claims than the

"Last Lines," and with them and a few others place her as a remarkable though not by any means a supreme figure.

The more prudent admirers of Marian Evans (George Eliot), who wrote a good deal of verse, either admit that her verse was not poetry, or hold up a much-quoted passage, "Oh, may I join the choir invisible," which, like the far superior piece just referred to, is only a hymn on the side which generally dispenses with hymns; and not a very good one, though couched in fair Wordsworthian blank verse. They would no doubt indulge in derisive scorn at the idea of the mild muse of Adelaide Anne Procter, daughter of "Barry Cornwall," receiving praise denied to Miss Brontë and Miss Evans; and it must be admitted that Miss Procter never did anything so good as "Remembrance." On the other hand, she was quite free from the "sawdust" and heaviness which mar George Eliot's verse. Her style was akin to that which has been noticed in speaking of Mrs. Norton, though of a somewhat later fashion, and like those of her father, her songs, especially the famous "Message," had the knack of suiting composers. Menella Bute Stedley and Dora Greenwell, a respectable pair, somewhat older than Miss Procter (she was born in 1825 and died in 1864), considerably outlived her, Miss Stedley's life lasting from 1820 to 1877, and Miss Greenwell's from 1821 to 1882. Both were invalids, and soothed their cares with verse, the latter to the better effect, though both in no despicable strain. Augusta Webster (1840–94) and Emily Pfeiffer (–1890) were later poetesses of the same kind, but lower rank, though both were greatly praised by certain critics. Sarah Williams, a short-lived writer of some sweetness (1841–68), commended herself chiefly to those who enjoy verse religious but "broad"; Constance Naden to those who like pessimist agnosticism; Amy Levy to those who can deplore a sad fate and admire notes few and not soaring, but passionate and genuine.

CHAPTER VII

THE NOVEL SINCE 1850

CERTAIN novelists who were mentioned at the end of chapter iii., though they all lived far into the last half of the century, not only belonged essentially to its first division, but strictly speaking fell out of strict chronological arrangement of any kind, being of the class of more or less eccentric men of genius who may appear at any time and belong to none in particular; and certain others of the earlier time, less eccentric, lived on far towards our own. About 1850 however, a little before or a little after it, there appeared a group of novelists of great talent, and in some cases of genius itself, who were less self-centred, and exemplified to a greater degree the special tendencies of the time. These tendencies were variously connected with the Oxford or Tractarian Movement; the transfer of political power from the upper to the middle classes by the first Reform Bill; the rise of what is for shortness called Science; the greater esteem accorded to and the more general practice of what is, again for shortness, called Art; the extension in a certain sense of education; the re-engagement of England, long severed from continental politics, in those politics by the Crimean war; the enormous development of commerce by the use of steam navigation and of railways; the opening up of Australia and its neighbourhood; the change effected in the East by the removal, gradual for some time, then rapid and complete after the Indian Mutiny, of the power of the East India Company; and the " Liberal " movement generally.

To work and counterwork out the influence of these various causes on separate authors, and the connection of the authors with the causes, would take a volume in itself. But on the scale and within the limits possible here, the names of Charlotte Brontë, Marian Evans (commonly called George Eliot), Charles Kingsley, Anthony Trollope, and Charles Reade will give us such central points as can be most safely utilised. Another, Miss Charlotte Yonge, the chief practitioner of the religious novel, was contemporary with almost the earliest of these, but falls out of this book as still living.

The members of this group were, as happens with a repeated coincidence in literary history too distinct to be altogether neglected, born within a very few years of each other : Reade in 1814, Trollope in 1815, Miss Brontë next year, Kingsley and Miss Evans in 1819 ; but as generally happens likewise, their appearance as authors, or at least as novelists, did not follow in exact sequel. The first-renowned, the shortest-lived, and though by no means the most brilliant or powerful, in a certain way the freshest and most independent, was Charlotte Brontë, the daughter of a Yorkshire clergyman of eccentric and not altogether amiable character and of Irish blood. She was born on 21st April 1816. The origin of the Brontës or Pruntys has, as well as their family history generally, been discussed with the curiously disproportionate minuteness characteristic of our time ; but hardly anything need be said of the results of the investigation, except that they were undoubtedly Irish. Charlotte's mother died soon after the Rev. Patrick Brontë had received the living of Haworth, and Charlotte herself was sent to school at a place called Cowan's Bridge, her experiences at which have in the same way been the subject of endless inquiry into the infinitely little, in connection with the " Lowood " of *Jane Eyre*. After two of her sisters had died, and she herself had been very ill, she was taken away and educated partly at home, partly elsewhere. Her two surviving sisters, who were her juniors, Emily by two years and Anne by four, were both of more or less literary leanings, and as they were all intended to be governesses, the sole profession for poor gentle-women in the middle of the century, Emily and Charlotte were sent to Brussels to qualify. In 1846 the three published a joint volume of *Poems* under the pseudonyms (which kept their initials) of Currer, Ellis, and Acton Bell, and to people over middle age Charlotte Brontë is still perhaps most familiar as Currer Bell. Emily's poems are elsewhere commented upon. The eldest and youngest sister had no poetical vocation, and Anne had not much for prose. But she, like the others, attempted it after the failure of their verse in a triad of novels, *The Professor*, by Charlotte ; *Wuthering Heights* (very much praised by those who look first for unconventionality and force), by Emily, who followed it with *The Tenant of Wildfell Hall;* and *Agnes Grey*, by Anne. But Charlotte could not get *The Professor* published — indeed it is anything but a good book — and set to work at the famous *Jane Eyre*, which after being freely refused by publishers, was accepted by Messrs. Smith and Elder and published in 1847, with the result of violent attacks and very considerable popularity. Death the next year and the year after robbed her of both her sisters and of her brother Patrick, a ne'er-do-weel, who, on the strength of his Bohemianism and his sisters, is sometimes supposed to have had genius. *Shirley* appeared in 1849, and *Villette* in 1852. In 1854 Charlotte married her father's curate, Mr. Nicholls, but died next year, on 31st March 1855.

Perhaps the most interesting way of looking at Charlotte Brontë, who, as has been said, has been violently attacked, and who has also been extravagantly praised (though not so extravagantly as her sister Emily), is to look at her in the light of a precursor or transition-novelist, representing the time when the followers of Scott had wearied the public with second-rate romances, when Thackeray had not arisen, or had only just arisen, and when the modern domestic novel in its various kinds, from the religious to the problematic, was for the most part in embryo, or in very early stages. This latter novel she in fact anticipated in many of its kinds, and partly to the fact of this anticipation, partly to the vividness which her representation of personal experiences gave to her work, may the popularity which it at first had, and such of it as has survived, be assigned. In this latter point, however, lay danger as well as safety. It seems very improbable that if Charlotte Brontë had lived, and if she had continued to write, her stock of experiences would have sufficed her; and it would not appear that she had much else. She is indeed credited with inventing the "ugly hero" in the Mr. Rochester of *Jane Eyre*, but in the long-run ugliness palls almost as much as beauty, perhaps sooner. Except in touches probably due to suggestions from Emily, the "weirdness" of the younger sister was not exhibited by the elder. The more melodramatic parts of the book would not have borne repetition, and its main appeal now lies in the Lowood scenes and the character of Jane herself, which are both admittedly autobiographical. So also Shirley is her sister Emily, the curates who pester her appear to have been almost in case to enter libel actions if they thought proper, and *Villette* is little more than an embroidered version of the Brussels sojourn. How successful an appeal of this kind is, the experience of Byron and many others has shown; how dangerous it is, could not be better shown than by the same experience. It was Charlotte Brontë's good fortune that she died before she had utterly exhausted her vein, though those who fail to regard Paul Emanuel with the affection which he seems to inspire in some, may think that she went perilously near it. But fate was kind to her: some interesting biographies and brilliant essays at different periods have revived and championed her fame: and her books—at least *Jane Eyre* almost as a whole and parts of the others—will always be simply interesting to the novel-reader, and interesting in a more indirect fashion to the critic. For this last will perceive that, thin and crude as they are, they are original, they belong to their own present and future, not to their past, and that so they hold in the history of literature a greater place than many books of greater accomplishment which are simply worked on already projected and accepted lines.

Emily's work, though too small in bulk and too limited in character to be put really high, has this original character in intense equality.

The mantle of Charlotte Brontë fell almost directly from her shoulders on those of another novelist of her sex. The author of *Jane Eyre* died, as has been said, in the spring of 1855. In the autumn of the next year was written, and in the January issue of *Blackwood's Magazine* for 1857 appeared, the first of a series of *Scenes of Clerical Life*. The author, then and for some time afterwards unknown, was Mary Ann or Marian Evans, who took various styles during her life, but wrote habitually under the *nom de guerre* of "George Eliot." Miss Brontë had not been a very precocious novelist; but Miss Evans did not begin to write novels till she was nearly as old as Miss Brontë was when she died. Her time, however, had been by no means wasted. Born on 22nd November 1819, at Arbury in Warwickshire, where her father was land-steward to Mr. Newdigate, she moved, after twenty years' life in the country or at school, with her father into Coventry, and became acquainted with a set of Unitarians who had practically broken all connection with Christianity. She accepted their opinions with the curious docility and reflexiveness which, strong as was her mind in a way, always distinguished her; and as a sign of profession she undertook the translation of Strauss' *Leben Jesu*. In 1849 she went abroad, and stayed for some time at Geneva, studying hard, and not returning to England till next year. Then establishing herself in London, she began to write for the *Westminster Review*, which she helped to edit, and translated Feuerbach's *Wesen des Christenthums*. It is highly probable that she would never have been known except as an essayist and translator, if she had not formed an irregular union with George Henry Lewes, a very clever and versatile journalist, who was almost a philosopher, almost a man of science, and perhaps quite a man of letters of the less creative kind. Under his influence (he had been a novelist himself, though an unsuccessful one, and was an excellent critic) the docility above remarked on

Y

turned itself into the channel of novel-writing, with immediate and amazing success.

Some good judges have thought that Miss Evans never exceeded, in her own special way, the *Scenes of Clerical Life*. But it was far exceeded in popularity by *Adam Bede*, which, oddly enough, was claimed by or at least for an impostor after its triumphant appearance in 1858. The position of the author may be said to have been finally established by *The Mill on the Floss* (1860), though the opening part of *Silas Marner* (1861) is at least equal if not superior to anything she ever did. Her later works were *Romola*, a story of the Italian Renaissance (1863); *Felix Holt, the Radical* (1866); some poems (the *Spanish Gypsy, Jubal*, etc., 1868–74); *Middlemarch* (1871); and *Daniel Deronda* (1876). This last was followed by a volume of essays entitled the *Impressions of Theophrastus Such*. Mr. Lewes having died in 1878, Miss Evans, in May 1880, married Mr. John Cross, and died herself in December of the same year. Her *Life and Letters* were subsequently published by her husband, but the letters proved extremely disappointing to her admirers, and the life was not very illuminative, except as to that docility and capacity for taking colour and pressure from surroundings which have been noticed above.

As a poet George Eliot has been noticed elsewhere. She merely put some of the thoughtful commonplaces of her time and school into wooden verse, occasionally grandiose but never grand, and her purple passages have the purple of plush not of velvet. Nor is she very remarkable as an essayist, though some of her early articles have merit, and though *Theophrastus Such*, appearing at a time when her general hold on the public was loosening, not commending itself in form to her special admirers, and injured in parts by the astonishing pseudo-scientific jargon which she had acquired, was received rather more coldly than it deserved. But as a novelist she is worthy of careful attention. Between 1860 and 1870, a decade in which Thackeray passed away early and during which Dickens did no first-class work, she had some claims to be regarded as the chief English novelist who had given much and from whom more was to be expected; after Dickens' death probably four critics out of five would have given her the place of greatest English novelist without hesitation. Nevertheless, even from the first there were dissidents: while at the time of the issue of *Middlemarch* her fame was at the very highest, the publication of *Daniel Deronda* made it fall rapidly; and a considerable reaction (perhaps to be reversed, perhaps not) has set in against her since her death.

The analysis of George Eliot's genius is indeed exceedingly curious. There are in her two currents or characters which are more or less mingled in all her books, but of which the one dominates in those up to and including *Silas Marner,* while the other is chiefly noticeable in those from *Romola* onward. The first, the more characteristic and infinitely the more healthy and happy, is a quite extraordinary faculty of humorous observation and presentation of the small facts and oddities of (especially provincial) life. The *Scenes of Clerical Life* show this strongly, together with a fund of untheatrical pathos which scarcely appears in so genuine a form afterwards. In *Adam Bede* and *The Mill on the Floss* it combines with a somewhat less successful vein of tragedy to make two admirable, if not faultless, novels; it lends a wonderful charm to the slight and simple study of *Silas Marner.* But, abundant as it is, it would seem that this is observation, not invention, nor that happiest blending of observation and invention which we find in Shakespeare and Scott. The accumulated experiences of her long and passive youth were now poured out with a fortunate result. But in default of invention, and in presence of the scientific or pseudo-scientific spirit which was partly natural to her and partly imbibed from those who surrounded her, she began, after *Silas Marner,* to draw always in part and sometimes mainly upon quite different storehouses. It is probable that the selection of the Italian Renaissance subject of *Romola* was a very disastrous one. She herself said that she " was a young woman when she began the book and an old one when she finished it."

It is a very remarkable *tour de force*, but it is a *tour de force* executed entirely against the grain. It is not alive : it is a work of erudition not of genius, of painful manufacture not of joyous creation or even observation. And this note of labour deepened and became more obvious even when she returned to modern and English subjects, by reason of the increased " purpose" which marked her later works. It has been noted by all critics of any perception as extremely piquant, though not to careful students of life and letters at all surprising, that George Eliot, whose history was always well known, is in almost every one of her books the advocate of the strictest union of love and marriage — no love without marriage and no marriage without love. But she was not satisfied with defending this thesis, beneficial, comparatively simple, and, in the situations which it suggests, not unfriendly to art. In her last book, *Daniel Deronda*, she embarked on a scheme, equally hopeless and gratuitous, of endeavouring to enlist the public sympathies in certain visions of neo-Judaism. In all these books indeed, even in *Deronda*, the old faculty of racy presentation of the humours of life recurred. But it became fainter and less frequent ; and it was latterly obscured, as has been hinted, by a most portentous jargon borrowed from the not very admirable lingo of the philosophers and men of science of the last half of the nineteenth century. All these things together made the later books conspicuously, what even the earlier had been to some extent, lifeless structures. They were constructed no doubt with much art and of material not seldom precious, but they were not lively growths, and they were fatally tinged with evanescent " forms in chalk," fancies of the day and hour, not less ephemeral for being grave in subject and seeming, and almost more jejune or even disgusting to posterity on that account.

Almost as much of the time, though curiously different in the aspect of it which he represented, was Charles Kingsley, who was born in the same year as George Eliot, on the 18th of June 1819. A fanciful critic might indulge in a contrast between the sober though not exactly dull scenery of the Midlands which saw her birth, and that of the most beautiful part of Devonshire (Holne, on the south-eastern fringe of Dartmoor) where, at the vicarage which his father held, Kingsley was born. He was educated at King's College, London, and Magdalene College, Cambridge, took a very good degree, and very soon after his appointment to the curacy of Eversley, in Hampshire, became rector thereof in 1844. He held the living for the rest of his life, dying there on the 23rd January 1875. It was not, however, by any means his only preferment. In 1860 he was made Professor of Modern History at Cambridge, not the most fortunate of appointments; for, with a tendency to small slips in fact at least equal to that of his friend and brother-in-law Mr. Froude, Kingsley, though capable of presenting separate aspects and facets of the past admirably, had not the general historic grasp which redeemed Froude. Nine years later he resigned the post and was made a Canon of Chester, while in 1873 this was exchanged for a Canonry at Westminster and a Chaplaincy to the Queen. Otherwise Kingsley's private life was happy and uneventful, its chief incident being a voyage to the West Indies (which, though unvisited, he had long before so brilliantly described) in 1871.

His literary work was very large, much varied, and of an excellence almost more varied than its kinds. He began, of course, with verse, and his *Saint's Tragedy* (1848), a drama on the story of St. Elizabeth of Hungary, was followed by shorter poems (far too few) at different times, most of them previous to 1858, though the later books contain some charming fragments, and some appeared posthumously. Of all men who have written so little verse during as long a life in our time, Kingsley is probably the best poet. The *Saint's Tragedy* is a little "viewy" and fluent. But in *Andromeda* he has written the very best English hexameters ever produced, and perhaps the only ones in which that alien or rebel takes on at least the semblance of a loyal subject to the English tongue. The rise of the breeze after the passage of the Nereids, the expostulation of Andromeda with Perseus, and the approach of the monster, are simply admirable. "The Last Buccaneer" and "The Red King"—call them "Wardour Street," as some critics may—are among the best of their kind; and scores of songs, snatches, etc., from "The Three Fishers" and "The Starlings" of a very early date to the "When all the world is young" ballad of the *Water Babies* and the posthumous fragment in rhyme of "Lorraine, Lorraine, Lorrèe"—one of the triumphs of that pure poetry which has the mimimum of meaning, yet enough—are of extraordinary vigour, freshness, and charm.

But Kingsley was one of those darlings—perhaps the rarest—of the Muses to whom they grant the gift not only of doing a little poetry exquisitely, but the further gift of abstaining from doing anything ill; and he seems to have recognised almost at once that "the other harmony," that of prose, was the one meant for him to do his day's work in. An enthusiast for the people, and an eager disciple of Carlyle, he produced in the fateful year 1849 two novels, *Alton Locke* and *Yeast*, a little crude, immature, and violent, but of wonderful power and beauty as literature, and putting current ideas of Chartism, the Tractarian movement, the woes of the working classes, and what not, with that most uncommon touch which takes out of the expression all its ephemerality. He had joined Maurice in the "Christian Socialist" movement, and was a frequent newspaper writer in the same sense as that of his novels ; while he soon began to contribute to *Fraser's Magazine* a series of extremely brilliant essays, since collected in various forms, on literature, scenery, sport (he was an ardent fisherman), and things in general. His next novel, *Hypatia*, is still shot with Christian Socialism, but is much less crude ; and a further sobering down without any loss of force appears in the great Elizabethan novel of *Westward Ho!* usually, and perhaps rightly, thought his masterpiece (1855). *Two Years Ago* (1857), the title of which refers to the Crimean War, is much more unequal, and exhibits signs of a certain declension, though to a level still very high. His last novel, *Hereward the Wake* (1866), was and is very variously judged.

But even the poems, the essays, and the novels, do not
by any means fill up the list of the results of Kingsley's
activity. He was a constant, and at his best a very good,
sermon-writer for publication. He produced in the first flush of
the rage for seashore studies (1854) a very pleasant little book
called *Glaucus;* he collected some of his historical lectures in
The Roman and the Teuton; and he wrote in 1863 the delightful
nondescript of *The Water Babies,* part story, part satire, part
Rabelaisian *fatrasie,* but almost all charming, and perhaps the
latest book in which his powers appear at their very best. These
powers, as exhibited in his novels, with a not dissimilar exhibition
in little in his essays, are so remarkable that in certain senses
Kingsley may, with a little kindness, be put in the very first class
of English novelists, and might be put there by the sternest
critical impartiality were it not for his concomitant defects.
These defects are fairly numerous, and they are unfortunately of
a kind not likely to escape attention. He was a rather violent,
though a very generous partisan, and was perpetually going out
of his way to provoke those on the other side by "flings" of this
or that kind. He was extremely fond of arguing, but was a most
poor and unhappy logician. One of the best known and most
unfortunate episodes of his literary life was the controversy into
which he plunged with Newman in 1864. Kingsley had before
on various occasions spoken enthusiastically of Newman's genius
and character : the reference to the peculiar estimate of truth held
by some Roman Catholics, and approved, or supposed to be
approved, by Newman, which was the text for the latter's wrath,
was anything but offensive, and it afterwards became certain,
through the publication of the *Apologia,* that the future Cardinal,
with the inspiration of a born controversialist, had simply made
Kingsley the handle for which he had been waiting. A very little
dialectical skill would have brought Kingsley out of the contest
with honours at least divided ; but, as it was, he played like a
child into Newman's hands, and not only did much to re-establish
that great man in public opinion, but subjected himself at the

time, and to some extent since, to an obloquy at least as unjust
as that which had rested upon Newman. This maladroitness
appears constantly in the novels themselves, and it is accompanied
not merely by the most curious and outrageous blunders in fact
(such as that which represents Marlowe as dying in the time of
James the First, not that of Elizabeth), but by odd lapses of taste
in certain points, and in some (chiefly his later) books by a hap-
hazard and inartistic construction.

We must, of course, allow for these things, which are the more
annoying in that they are simply a case of those which *incuria
fudit*. But when they are allowed for, there will remain such a
gallery of scenes, characters, and incidents, as few English novelists
can show. The best passages of Kingsley's description, from
Alton Locke to *Hereward*, are almost unequalled and certainly
unsurpassed. The shadows of London low life and of working-
class thought in *Alton Locke*, imitated with increasing energy for
half a century, have never been quite reached, and are most
brilliantly contrasted with the lighter Cambridge scenes. *Yeast*,
perhaps the least general favourite among his books, and certainly
the crudest, has a depth of passion and power, a life, an intensity,
the tenth part of which would make the fortune of a novel now ;
and the variety and brilliancy of *Hypatia* are equalled by its
tragedy. Unequal as *Two Years Ago* is, and weak in parts, it
still has admirable passages ; and *Hereward* to some extent recovers
the strange panoramic and phantasmagoric charm of *Hypatia*.
But where *Westward Ho!* deserves the preference, and where
Kingsley vindicates his claim to be the author not merely of
good passages but of a good book, is in the sustained passion of
patriotism, the heroic height of adventure and chivalry, which
pervades it from first to last. Few better historical novels have
ever been written ; and though, with one exception, that of Salva-
tion Yeo, the author has drawn better characters elsewhere, he
has nowhere knitted his incidents into such a consistent whole, or
worked characters and scenes together into such a genuine and
thorough work of art.

Anthony Trollope, one of the most typical novelists of the century, or at least of the half-century, in England, if not one of the greatest, was a member of a literary family whose other members, of more or less distinction, may for convenience' sake best be mentioned here. Little is recorded of his father, who was, however, a barrister, and a Fellow of New College, Oxford. But Anthony's mother, the "Mrs. Trollope" of two generations ago, who was born a Miss Milton in 1780, was herself very well known in print, especially by her novel of *The Widow Barnaby* (1839), which had sequels, and by her very severe *Domestic Manners of the Americans*, which appeared in 1832, after she had qualified herself to write it by a three years' residence in the United States. She wrote a great deal at this period, and survived till 1863 ; but her work hardly survived as long as she did. It has, however, been said, and not without justice, that much of the more vivid if coarser substance of her younger son's humour is to be traced in it. The elder son, Thomas Adolphus, who was born in 1810, and lived from 1841 for some half-century onwards in Italy, was also a prolific novelist, and wrote much on Italian history ; while perhaps his best work was to be found in some short pieces, combining history with a quasi-fictitious interest, which he contributed to the periodicals edited by Dickens.

But neither mother nor elder brother could vie with Anthony, who was born in 1815, was educated at Winchester and Harrow, spent the greater part of his life as an official of the Post Office, and died in December 1882, leaving an enormous number of novels, which at one time were the most popular, or almost the most popular, of their day, and to which rather fastidious judges have found it difficult to refuse all but the highest praise. Almost immediately after Trollope's death appeared an *Autobiography* in which, with praiseworthy but rather indiscreet frankness, he detailed habits of work of a mechanical kind, the confession of which played into the hands of those who had already begun to depreciate him as a mere book-maker. It is difficult to say how many novels he wrote, persevering as he did in composition up to the very time of his death ; and it is certain that the productions of his last decade were, as a rule, very inferior to his best. This best is to be found chiefly, but not entirely, in what is called the " Barsetshire " series, clustering round a county and city which are more or less exactly Hampshire and Win-chester, beginning in 1855 with *The Warden*, a good but rather immature sketch, and continuing through *Barchester Towers* (perhaps his masterpiece), *Doctor Thorne, Framley Parsonage*, and *The Small House at Allington* (the two latter among the early triumphs of the *Cornhill Magazine*), to *The Last Chronicle of Barset* (1867), which runs *Barchester Towers* very hard, if it does not surpass it. Other favourite books of his were *The Three Clerks, Orley Farm, Can You Forgive Her*, and *Phineas Finn* — nor does this by any means exhaust the list even of his good books.

It has been said that Trollope is a typical novelist, and the type is of sufficient importance to receive a little attention, even in space so jealously allotted as ours must be. The novel craved by and provided for the public of this second period (it has also been said) was a novel of more or less ordinary life, ranging from the lower middle to the upper class, correctly observed, diversified by sufficient incident not of an extravagant kind, and furnished with description and conversation not too epigrammatic but natural and fairly clever. This norm Trollope hit with surprising just-ness, and till the demand altered a little or his own hand failed (perhaps there was something of both) he continued to hit it. His interests and experiences were fairly wide ; for, besides being active in his Post Office duties at home and abroad, he was an enthusiastic fox-hunter, fairly fond of society and of club-life, ambitious enough at least to try other paths than those of fiction in his *Thackeray* (a failure), his *Cicero* (a worse failure), and other things. And everything that he saw he could turn into excellent novel-material. No one has touched him in depicting the humours of a public office, few in drawing those of cathedral cities and the hunting-field. If his stories, as stories, are not of enthralling interest or of very artfully constructed plots, their craftsmanship in this respect leaves very little to complain of. And he can sometimes, as in the Stanhope family of *Barchester Towers*, in Mrs. Proudie *passim*, in Madalina Demolines, and in others, draw characters very little removed from those who live with us for ever. It is extremely improbable that there will ever be a much better workman of his own class ; and his books are certainly, at their best, far better than all but one or two that appear, not merely in any given year nowadays, but in any given lustrum. Yet the special kind of their excellence, the facts that they reflect their time without transcending it, and that in the way of merely reflective work each time prefers its own workmen and is never likely to find itself short of them, together with the great volume of Trollope's production, are certainly against him ; and it is hard even for those who enjoyed him most, and who can still enjoy him, to declare positively that there is enough of the permanent and immortal in him to justify the hope of a resurrection.

In Charles Reade, on the other hand, there is undoubtedly something of this permanent or transcendent element, though less perhaps than some fervent admirers of his have claimed. He was born on June 1814 at Ipsden in Oxfordshire, where his family had been some time seated as squires. He had no public school education, but was elected first to a Demyship and then to a Fellowship at Magdalen College, Oxford. He was called to the Bar in 1842 ; but his Fellowship made him independent, and he pursued many crazes — he was one of the most eccentric of those English authors who are noticed in this volume — but no profession. He did not even begin to write very early, and when he did it was drama, not prose or fiction. He was not very successful with the stage, though he never quite gave it up. It was about 1852 when he began to write, or at least to publish, novels ; and between the *Peg Woffington* of that year and his death on 1st April 1884 he produced nearly a score, diversifying the publication with law-suits, eccentric newspaper correspondences, and other things. Indeed he has in more than one of his books introduced mental delusions with such startling subtlety and truth, and was so entirely odd in the ordinary relations of life, that some have not hesitated to insinuate a slight want of sanity.

If there was any madness in him, the hackneyed alliance of great wits was certainly not refused. A novelist of violent likes and dislikes himself, he has found violent partisans and scornful pooh-poohers. Among the former there is perhaps hardly one of his chief books — the quaint and brilliant *Peg Woffington*, the pathetic *Christie Johnstone, Hard Cash, Griffith Gaunt, Put Yourself in his Place, A Terrible Temptation,* and the rest — which has not special sectaries. But catholic criticism would undoubtedly put *It is Never too Late to Mend* (1856) and *The Cloister and the Hearth* (1861) at the head of all. The former is a tale of the moment, based chiefly on some stories which had got abroad of tyranny in gaols, and on the Australian gold fever of a few years earlier. The latter is a pure romance, purporting to tell the adventures of Erasmus' father in the fifteenth century. The contrast of these subjects illustrates admirably a curious combination in Reade's genius which, for the matter of that, might be independently exemplified from either book. On the one side he was one of the earliest and one of the most industrious of those who have been called the " document " or " reporter " novelists — now collecting enormous stores of newspaper cuttings and busying himself with keenest interest in the things of the day ; now, as in *The Cloister and the Hearth*, not disdaining to impart realism and vividness to his pictures by adapting and almost translating whole passages from Erasmus' own *Colloquies*. On the other, he was a poetic seer and dreamer, of the strongest romantic force, and capable of extraordinary flights of power, passion, and pathos. But there was another thing that he was *not*, and that was a critic. His taste and judgment were extremely deficient ; he had no sense of general proportion in his work ; and was quite as likely to be melodramatic as to be tragical, to be coarse as to be strong, to be tedious as to be amusing, to be merely revolting as to purify by pity and terror. Both the books just specially mentioned may be thought too long : it is certain that *The Cloister and the Hearth* is. That a freshness still evident in *Christie Johnstone* has been lost in both (having been killed by "the document") is also true. But still, Reade undoubtedly had genius, and to genius most things can without much trouble be forgiven.

The chief novelist of what is rather loosely called the School of Dickens, was Wilkie Collins, son of the painter of that name, who was born in London on 8th January 1824, and died in 1889. His greatest popularity was in the decade between 1857 and 1866, when *The Dead Secret, The Woman in White, No Name,* and *Armadale,* especially the second, had an immense vogue. Perhaps *The Moonstone,* which is later, is also better than any of these. The strictly literary merit of none could be put high, and the method, that of forwarding the result by a complicated intertwist of letters and narratives, though it took the public fancy for a time, was clumsy ; while the author followed his master in more than one aberration of taste and sentiment. His brother Charles Collins, who had a much shorter life, had a much more delicate style and fancy ; and the *Cruise upon Wheels,* a record of an actual tour slightly embellished and thrown into fictitious form, is one of the books which have, and are not, unless they drop entirely out of sight, likely to lose, a firm following of friends, few perhaps but faithful. Mortimer Collins, a contemporary, but no relation of these, whose poems have already been mentioned, was born in 1827 and died in 1876, the last twenty years of his life having been occupied by various and voluminous literary work. He was one of the last of the so-called Bohemian school in letters and journalism, something of a scholar, a fertile novelist, and a versatile journalist in most of the kinds which make up modern journalism.

Henry Kingsley, younger brother of Charles, was himself a prolific and vigorous novelist ; and though a recent attempt to put him above his brother cannot possibly be allowed by sound criticism, he had perhaps a more various command of fiction, certainly a truer humour, and if a less passionate, perhaps a more thoroughly healthy literary temperament. But his life was not long, and he was unfortunately compelled during most of it to write for a living. Born in 1830, he was educated at King's College, London, and Worcester College, Oxford, on leaving which latter he went to Australia and lived there for five years. Returning in 1859, he wrote the admirable Australian story of *Geoffrey Hamlyn*, which, with *Ravenshoe* two years later, contains most of his work that can be called really first rate. He returned to Australia for his subject in *The Hillyars and the Burtons*, and wrote several other novels before his death in 1876, having been during part of the time a newspaper editor, a newspaper correspondent, and a journalist generally. The absence of composition, which Flaubert deplored in English novels generally, shows at its height in Henry Kingsley, whose *Ravenshoe*, for instance, has scarcely any plot at all, and certainly owes nothing to what it has; while he was a rapid and careless writer. But he had, in a somewhat less elaborate form, all his brother's talents for description of scene and action, and his characters, if more in the way of ordinary life, are also truer to that life. Also he is particularly to be commended for having, without the slightest strait-lacedness, and indeed with a good deal of positive Bohemianism, exhibited the nineteenth century English notion of what constitutes a gentleman perhaps better than any one else. "There are some things a fellow *can't* do"— the chance utterance of his not ungenerous scamp Lord Welter— is a memorable sentence, whereon a great sermon might be preached.

A little older than Henry Kingsley (he died in the same year), much more popular for a time, and the exerter of an influence which has not ceased yet, and has been on the whole distinctly undervalued, was George Henry Lawrence, who was educated at Rugby and Balliol, was called to the Bar, but was generally known in his own time as Major Lawrence from a militia commission which he held. He also fought in, or at least was present during, the war of independence of the southern states of America. Lawrence, who was born in 1827, published in his thirtieth year

a novel, *Guy Livingstone*, which was very popular, and much
denounced as the Gospel of " muscular blackguardism " — a parody
on the phrase " muscular Christianity," which had been applied to
and not unwelcomed by Charles Kingsley. The book exhibited
a very curious blend of divers of the motives and interests which
have been specified as actuating the novel about this time.
Lawrence, who was really a scholar, felt to the full the Præ-Raphaelite influence in art, though by no means in religion, and wrote in a
style which is a sort of transition between the excessive floridness
of the first Lord Lytton and the later Corinthianism of Mr.
Symonds. But he retained also from his prototype, and new modelled, the tendency to take " society " and the manners, especially
the amatory manners, of society very much as his province. And
thus he rather shocked the moralists, not only in *Guy Livingstone*
itself, but in its successors *Sword and Gown, Barren Honour,
Sans Merci*, etc. That Lawrence's total ideal, both in style and
sentiment, was artificial, false, and flawed, may be admitted. But
he has to a great extent been made to bear the blame of exaggera-
tions of his own scheme by others ; and he was really a novelist
and a writer of great talent, which somehow came short, but not
so very far short, of genius.

Mrs. Gaskell was older than most of those hitherto mentioned
in this chapter, having been born in 1810 ; but she did not begin
to write very early. *Mary Barton*, her first and nearly her best
book, appeared in 1848, and its vivid picture of Manchester life,
assisted by its great pathos, naturally attracted attention at that
particular time. *Cranford* (1853), in a very different style, something like a blend of Miss Mitford and Miss Austen, has been the
most permanently popular of her works. *Ruth*, of the same year,
shocked precisians (which it need not have done), but is of much
less literary value than *Mary Barton* or *Cranford*. Mrs. Gaskell,
who was the biographer of Charlotte Brontë, produced novels
regularly till her death in 1865, and never wrote anything bad,
though it may be doubted whether anything but *Cranford* will
retain permanent rank.

The year 1857, which saw *Guy Livingstone*, saw a book as different as possible in ideal, but also one of no common merit, in *John Halifax, Gentleman*. The author of this was Dinah Maria Mulock, who afterwards became Mrs. Craik. She was born at Stoke-upon-Trent in 1826, and had written for nearly ten years when *John Halifax* appeared. She died in 1888, having written a very great deal both in prose and verse ; the former part including many novels, of which the best perhaps is *A Life for a Life*. Mrs. Craik was an example of the influence, so often noticed and to be noticed in the latter part of our period, of the great demand for books on writers of any popularity. Her work was never bad ; but it was to a very great extent work which was, as the French say, the "small change" for what would probably in other circumstances have been a very much smaller quantity of much better work. How this state of things — which has been brought about on the one hand by the printing press, newspapers, and the spread of education, on the other by the disuse of sinecures, patronage, pensions, and easy living generally — is to be prevented from affecting literature very disastrously is not clear. Its negative or rather privative effect cannot but be bad ; if its positive effect is always as good as the works of Mrs. Craik, it will be fortunate.

It is difficult, in a book of this kind, to know how far to attempt the subdivisions of specialist novels which have been common, such as for instance the sporting novel, the practitioners of which have been innumerable. The chief perhaps were Robert Surtees, the author of the facetious series of which " Mr. Jorrocks " is the central and best figure, and Major Whyte-Melville. The former, about the middle of the century, carried out with much knowledge, not inconsiderable wit, and the advantage of admirable illustrations from the pencil of John Leech, something like the original idea of *Pickwick* as a sporting romance, and there is a strong following of Dickens in him. Major Whyte-Melville, born near St. Andrews in 1821 and heir to property there, was educated at Eton, served for some years in the Guards, and with the Turkish Contingent in the Crimean War, and was killed in the hunting-field in 1878. He touched various styles, chiefly those of Lever and Bulwer, while he had a sort of contact with George Lawrence. He was never happier than in depicting his favourite pastime, which figures in most of his novels and inspired him with some capital verse. But in *Holmby House, Sarchedon,* the *Gladiators,* etc., he tried the historical style also.

Nor must the brief life, embittered by physical suffering, but productive of not a little very cheerful work, of Francis Edward Smedley, a relation of the poetess mentioned in the last chapter, be forgotten. He, born in 1818, went to Cambridge, and then became a novelist and journalist, dying in 1864. His best work belongs to exactly the period with which this chapter begins, the early fifties, and had the advantage, like other novels of the time, of illustration by " Phiz." The three chief books are *Frank Fairleigh* (1850), *Lewis Arundel* (1852), and *Harry Coverdale's Courtship* (1854). With a touch of Bulwerian romance, something of the sporting novel, and a good deal of the adventure story, Smedley united plenty of pleasant humour and occasionally not a little real wit.

It will have been observed that more than one of the more distinguished novelists of this time attempted, and that at least one of them achieved, the historical novel; nor was it at all likely that a kind so attractive in itself, illustrated by such remarkable genius, and discovered at last after many centuries of futile endeavour, should immediately or entirely lose its popularity. Yet it is certain that for about a quarter of a century, from 1845 to 1870, not merely the historical novel, but the romance generally, did lose general practice and general attention, while, though about the latter date at least one novel of brilliant quality, Mr. Blackmore's *Lorna Doone,* vindicated romance, and historical romance, it was still something of an exception. Those who are old enough, and who paid sufficient attention to contemporary criticism, will remember that for many years the advent of a historical novel was greeted in reviews with a note not exactly of contempt, but of the sort of surprise with which men greet something out of the way and old fashioned.

z

This was the inevitable result of that popularity of the domestic and usual novel which this chapter has hitherto described, and it was as natural and as inevitable that the domestic and usual novel should in its turn undergo the same law. Not that this, again, was summarily, much less finally displaced; on the contrary, the enormous and ever-increasing demand for fiction — which the establishment of public free libraries, and the custom of printing in cheaper form for sale, has encouraged *pari passu* with the apparent discouragement given to it by the fall of circulating libraries from the absolutely paramount place which they occupied not long ago — maintained the call for this as for other kinds of story. But partly mere love of change, partly the observations of those critics who were not content to follow the fashion merely, and partly also the familiar but inexplicable rise at the same time of divers persons whose talent inclined in a new direction, brought in, about 1880 or later, a demand for romance, for historical romance, and for the short story — three things against which the taste of the circulating-library reader during the generation then expiring had distinctly set itself. The greater part of the results of this change falls out of our subject; but one remarkable name, perhaps the most remarkable of all, is given to us by the Fates.

For one of the pillars of this new building of romance was only too soon removed. Robert Louis Balfour Stevenson (more commonly known to the public by the first two, and to his friends by the second of his Christian names) belonged to the famous family of lighthouse architects who so long carried on the traditions of Smeaton in that department of engineering; and he was to have been an engineer himself. But he was incurably literary; and after school and college at Edinburgh, was called to the Bar, with no more practical results in that profession than in the other. Born on 13th November 1850, he was not extremely precocious in publication; and it was not till nearly the end of the seventies that his essays in the *Cornhill Magazine* and his stories in a periodical called *London*, short lived and not widely circulated, but noteworthy in its way, attracted attention. He followed them up with two volumes of somewhat Sternian travel, *An Inland Voyage* (1878) and *Travels with a Donkey in the Cevennes* (1879); next collecting his *Cornhill Essays* in two other volumes, *Virginibus Puerisque* (1881) and *Familiar Studies of Men and Books* (1882), and his *London* stories in *The New Arabian Nights* (1882). But he did not get hold of the public till a year later than the latest of these dates, with his famous *Treasure Island*, the best boys' story since Marryat, and one of a literary excellence to which Marryat could make no pretensions. The vein of romance which he then struck, and the older and more fanciful one of *The New Arabian Nights*, were followed up alternately or together in an almost annual succession of books — *Prince Otto* (1885), *The Strange Case of Dr. Jekyll and Mr. Hyde* (1886), *Kidnapped* (1886), *The Black Arrow* (a wonderfully good, though not very generally popular, York-and-Lancaster story) (1888), *The Master of Ballantræ* (1889), the exquisite *Catriona* (1893). It also pleased him to write, in collaboration with others, *The Dynamiter*, *The Wrecker*, *The Ebb Tide*, etc., where the tracing of the several shares is not unamusing. Stevenson also attempted poetry, and his *Child's Garden of Verse* (1885) has very warm admirers, who are often more doubtful about *Underwoods* (1887) and *Ballads* (1891). The list of his work is not exhausted, and one of the latest additions to it was *A Footnote to History* (1892), containing an account of the intestine troubles of the island of Samoa, where Mr. Stevenson, long a victim to lung disease, latterly fixed his abode, and where he died suddenly in the winter of 1894.

As has been the case with most of the distinguished writers of recent years, Mr. Stevenson has been praised by some of his contemporaries and juniors with an uncritical fervour which has naturally provoked depreciation from others ; and the charm of his personality was so great that it is extremely difficult for any one who knew him to hold the scales quite even. As the most brilliant and interesting by far, however, of those English writers whose life was comprised in the last half of the century he absolutely demands critical treatment here, and it so happens that his method and results were extremely typical of the literary movement and character of our time. He has left somewhat minute accounts of his own apprenticeship, but they are almost unnecessary : no critic of the slightest competence could fail to divine the facts. Adopting to the full, and something more than the full, the modern doctrine of the all-importance of art, of manner, of style in literature, Mr. Stevenson early made the most elaborate studies in imitative composition. There is no doubt that he at last succeeded in acquiring a style which was quite his own : but it was complained, and with justice, that even to the last he never attained complete ease in this style ; that its mannerism was not only excessive, but bore, as even excessive mannerism by no means always does, the marks of distinct and obvious effort. This was perhaps most noticeable in his essays, which were further marred by the fact that much of them was occupied by criticism, for which, though his taste was original and delicate, Stevenson's knowledge was not quite solid enough, and his range of sympathies a little deficient in width. In his stories, on the other hand, the devil's advocate detected certain weak points, the chief of them being an incapacity to finish, and either a distaste or an incapacity for introducing women. This last charge was finally refuted by *Catriona*, not merely in the heroine, but in the much more charming and lifelike figure of Barbara Grant ; but the other was something of a true bill to the last. It was Stevenson's weakness (as by the way it also was Scott's) to huddle up his stories rather than to wind them off to an orderly conclusion.

But against this allowance — a just but an ample one — for defects, must be set to Stevenson's credit such a combination of literary and story-telling charm as perhaps no writer except Mérimée has ever equalled ; while, if the literary side of him had not the golden perfection, the accomplished ease of the Frenchman, his romance has a more genial, a fresher, a more natural quality. Generally, as in the famous examples of Scott, of Dumas, and of Balzac, the great story-tellers have been a little deficient in mere style ; the fault in Stevenson, if it could be called a fault, was that the style was in excess. But this only set off and enhanced, it did not account for, the magic of his scene and character, from John Silver to Barbara Grant, from " The Suicide Club " to the escapes of Alan Breck. Very early, when most of his critical friends were urging him to cultivate the essay mainly, others discerned the supremacy of his story-telling faculty, and, years before the public fell in love with *Treasure Island*, bade him cultivate that. Fortunately he did so ; and his too short life has left a fairly ample store of work, not always quite equal, seldom quite without a flaw, but charming, stimulating, distinguished as few things in this last quarter of a century have been.

Nearly all of Mr. Stevenson's contemporaries in novel-writing, as well as many distinguished persons far his seniors whose names will occur to every one, lie outside our limits. And in no chapter of this book, perhaps, is it so necessary to turn the back sternly on much interesting performance once famous and popular — not once only of interest to the reader of time and chance but put by this cause or that out of our reach. We cannot talk here of *Emilia Wyndham* or *Paul Ferroll*, both emphatically novels of their day, and that no short one ; and in the latter case, if not in the former, books deserving to be read at intervals by more than the bookworm. The exquisite *Story without an End*, which Sarah Austin half adapted, half translated, and which, with some unusually good translations from Fouqué and others, set a whole fashion fifty years ago, must pass with mere allusion ; the abundant and not seldom excellent fiction of the earlier Hugh Church movement pleads in vain for detailed treatment. For all doors must be shut or open ; and this door must now be shut.

CHAPTER VIII

PHILOSOPHY AND THEOLOGY

IT is the constant difficulty of the literary historian, especially if he is working on no very great scale, that he is confronted with what may be called "applied" literature, in which not only is the matter of superior importance to the form, but the importance of the matter itself disappears to a greater or less extent with time. In these cases it is only possible for him to take notice of those writers who, whatever the subject they handled, would have written literature, and perhaps of those who from the unusual eminence and permanence of their position in their own subjects have attained as it were an honorary position in literature itself.

The literary importance and claim, however, of these applied branches varies considerably; and there have been times when the two divisions whose names stand at the head of this chapter even surpassed — there have been not a few in which they equalled — any section of the purest *belles lettres* in strictly literary attractions. With rare exceptions this has not been the case during the present century; poetry, fiction, history, and essay-writing having drawn off the best hands on the one side, while science has attracted them on the other. But the great Oxford Movement in the second quarter created no small amount of theological or ecclesiastical writing of unusual interest, while there had been earlier, and continued to be till almost the time when the occupation of the field by living writers warns us off, philosophers proper of great excellence. Latterly (indeed till quite recently, when a certain renaissance of philosophical writing not in jargon has taken place with a corresponding depression of the better kind of literary theology) the philosophers of Britain have not held a prominent place in her literature. Whether this was because they have mostly been content to Germanise, or because they have not been provided with sufficient individual talent, it is fortunately unnecessary for us to attempt to determine in this place and at this time.

Among the dead writers of the century who are known wholly or mainly for the cultivation of philosophical studies, Bentham, Mackintosh, John Stuart Mill (to whom some would add his father James), Sir William Hamilton, Dean Mansel, are likely to hold a place in history, while at present many might be disposed to add the name of Mr. T. H. Green, a tutor of Balliol College, who between 1870 and his death propagated in Oxford a sort of neo-Hegelianism much tinctured with political and social Liberalism, and obtained a remarkable personal position. It is however as yet too early to assign a distinct historical place to one whose philosophy was in no sense original, though it was somewhat originally combined and applied, and who exhibited very small literary skill in setting forth. The others are already set " in the firm perspective of the past," and, with yet others who, still living, escape our grasp, have their names clearly marked for a place in an adequate history.

Jeremy Bentham, a curious person who reminds one of a Hobbes without the literary genius, was born in London, near Houndsditch, as far back as 5th February 1748. He was the son of a solicitor who was very well off, and wished his son to take to the superior branch of the law. Jeremy was sent to Westminster, and thence to Queen's College, Oxford, in his thirteenth year. He was a Master of Arts at eighteen, and was called to the Bar six years later ; but he never practised. He must have been very early drawn to the study of the French *philosophes;* much indeed of the doctrine which afterwards made him famous was either taken from, or incidentally anticipated by, Turgot and others of them, and it was a common remark, half in earnest half in gibe, that Bentham's views had made the tour of Europe in the French versions of Dumont before they attained to any attention in England. In 1776 he wrote a *Fragment on Government,* a kind of critique of Blackstone, which is distinguished by acute one-sided deduction from Whig principles; and he became a sort of prophet of the Whigs, who sometimes plagiarised and popularised, some-times neglected, his opinions. He never married, though he would have liked to do so; and lived on his means till 1832, when he died in the eighty-fifth year of his age. His chief books after the *Fragment* had been his *Theory of Punishments and Rewards;* 1787, *Letters on Usury;* 1789, *Introduction to the Principles of Morals and Legislation;* 1813, *Treatise on Evidence;* and 1824, *Fallacies.*

The central pillar and hinge of all Bentham's doctrines in politics, morals, and law is the famous principle of Utility, or to use the cant phrase which he borrowed from Priestley, "the greatest happiness of the greatest number." What the greatest number is — for instance whether in a convict settlement of forty thieves and ten honest men, the thieves are to be consulted — and what happiness means, what is utility, what things have brought existing arrangements about, and what the loss of altering them might be, as well as a vast number of other points, Bentham never deigned to consider. Starting from a few crude phrases such as this, he raised a system remarkable for a sort of apparent consistency and thoroughness, and having the luck or the merit to hit off in parts not a few of the popular desires and fads of the age of the French Revolution and its sequel. But he was a political theorist rather than a political philosopher, his neglect of all the nobler elements of thought and feeling was complete, and latterly at least he wrote atrocious English, clumsy in composition and crammed with technical jargon. The brilliant fashion in which Sydney Smith has compressed and spirited his *Fallacies* into the famous "Noodle's Oration" is an example of the kind of treatment which Bentham requires in order to be made tolerable in form; and even then he remains one-sided in fact.

Sir James Mackintosh has been mentioned before, and is less of a philosopher pure and simple than any person included in this list — indeed his philosophical reputation rests almost wholly upon his brilliant, though rather slight, *Dissertation on Ethics* for the *Encyclopædia Britannica*. The greater part by far of his by no means short life (1765–1832) was occupied in practising medicine and law, in defending the French Revolution against Burke (*Vindiciæ Gallicæ*, 1791); in defending the French Royalists in the person of Peltier against Bonaparte, 1803; in acting as Recorder and Judge in India, 1804–1811; and in political and literary work at home for the last twenty years, his literature being chiefly history, and contributions to the *Edinburgh Review*. But there has been a certain tendency, both in his own time and since, to regard Mackintosh as a sort of philosopher thrown away. If he was so, he would probably have made his mark rather in the history of philosophy than in philosophy itself, for there are no signs in him of much original depth. But he wrote very well, and was a sound and on the whole a fair critic.

Of the two Mills, the elder, James, was like Mackintosh only an *interim* philosopher : his son John belongs wholly to our present subject. James was the son of a farmer, was born near Montrose in 1773, and intended to enter the ministry, but became a journalist instead. In the ten years or so after 1806, he composed a *History of British India*, which was long regarded as authoritative, but on which the gravest suspicions have recently been cast. Mill, in fact, was a violent politician of the Radical type, and his opinions of ethics were so peculiar that it is uncertain how far he might have carried them in dealing with historical characters. His book, however, gained him a high post in the East India Company, the Directors of which just at that time were animated by a wish to secure distinguished men of letters as servants. He nevertheless continued to write a good deal both in periodicals and in book form, the chief examples of the latter being his *Political Economy*, his *Analysis of the Human Mind*, and his *Fragment on Mackintosh*. James Mill, of whom most people have conceived a rather unfavourable idea since the appearance of his son's *Autobiography*, was an early disciple of Bentham, and to a certain extent resembled him in hard clearness and superficial consistency.

His son John Stuart was born in London on 20th May 1806, and educated by his father in the unnatural fashion which he has himself recorded. Intellectually, however, he was not neglected, and after some years, spent mainly in France, he was, through his father's influence, appointed at seventeen to a clerkship in the India House, which gave him a competence for the rest of his life and a main occupation for thirty-four years of it. He was early brought into contact (by his father's friendship with Grote and others) with the Philosophical Radicals, as well as with many men of letters, especially Carlyle, of the destruction of the first version of whose *French Revolution* Mill (having lent it to his friend Mrs. Taylor) was the innocent cause. To this Mrs. Taylor, whom he afterwards married, Mill was fanatically attached, the attachment being the cause of some curious flights in his later work. His character was very amiable, and the immense influence which, especially in the later years of his life, he exercised, was partly helped by his personal friendships. But it was unfortunate for him that in 1865 he was returned to Parliament. His political views, though it was the eve of the triumph of what might be called his party, were *doctrinaire* and out of date, and his life had given him no practical hold of affairs, so that he more than fulfilled the usual prophecy of failure in the case of men of thought who are brought late in life into action. Fortunately for him he was defeated in 1868, and passed the rest of his life mostly in France, dying at Avignon on 8th May 1873.

Brought up in an atmosphere of discussion and of books, Mill soon took to periodical writing, and in early middle life was for some years editor of the *London and Westminster Review ;* but his literary ambition, which directed itself not to pure literature but to philosophical and political discussion, was not content with periodical writing as an exercise, and his circumstances enabled

him to do without it as a business. In 1843 he published what
is undoubtedly his chief work, *A System of Logic, Ratiocinative and
Inductive*, five years later a companion treatise on *Political
Economy* which may perhaps rank second. In 1859 his essay on
Liberty, a short but very attractive exposition of his political
principles, appeared; next year a collection of essays entitled
Dissertations and Discussions. After lesser works on *Utilitarianism* and on Comte, of whom he had been a supporter in more
senses than one, but whose later eccentricities revolted him, he
issued in 1865 his *Examination of Sir William Hamilton's Philosophy*, which ranks as the third of his chief works, and completes
his system, as far as a system so negative can be said to be completed, on the side of theology and metaphysics. Among his
smaller works may be mentioned *Representative Government*, and
(very late) the fanatical and curious *Subjection of Women*. His
Autobiography, an interesting but melancholy book, appeared
shortly after his death.

Mill must be accounted on the whole by good judges, even if
they are utterly opposed to his whole system of philosophy, the
chief philosophical *writer* of England in this century; and the
enormous though not permanent influence which he attained
about its middle was deserved, partly by qualities purely literary,
but partly also by some purely philosophical. He had inherited
from his father not merely the theoretical exaltation of liberty
(except in the philosophical sense) which characterised eighteenth
century philosophers, but also that arrogant and pragmatical impatience of the supernatural which was to a still greater extent
that century's characteristic. The arrogance and the pragmati-
cality changed in John Stuart Mill's milder nature to a sort of
nervous dread of admitting even the possibility of things not
numerable, ponderable, and measurable; and it may be observed
with amusement that for the usual division of logic into Deductive
and Inductive he substituted *Ratiocinative* for the first member,
so as not even by implication to admit the possibility of deduction
from any principles not inductively given. So, too, later, in his

Examination of Sir William Hamilton, between the opposing spectres of Realism and Idealism, he was driven to take refuge in what he called "permanent possibilities" of Sensation, though logicians vainly asked how he assured himself of the permanence, and jesters rudely observed that to call a bottle of gin a "permanent possibility of drunkenness" was an unnecessary complication of language for a very small end or meaning. His great philosophical weapon (borrowed from though of course not invented by his father) was the Association of Ideas, just as his clue in political economy was in the main though not exclusively *laissez-faire,* in ethics a modified utilitarianism, and in politics an absolute deference to, tempered by a resigned distrust of, the majority. The defect in a higher and more architectonic theory of the world with which he has been charged is not quite justly chargeable, for from his point of view no such theory was possible.

Even those, however, who, as the present writer acknowledges in his own case, are totally opposed to the whole Millian conception of logic and politics, of metaphysics and morality, must, unless prejudiced, admit his great merits of method and treatment. He not only very seldom smuggles in sophistry into the middle of his arguments, but even paralogisms are not common with him; it is with his premises, not with his conclusions, that you must deal if you wish to upset him. Unlike most contemners of formal logic, he is not in much danger, as far as his merely dialectic processes go, from formal logic itself; and it is in the arbitrary and partial character of his preliminary admissions, assumptions, and exclusions that the weak points of his system are to be found.

His style has also very considerable merits. It is not brilliant or charming; it has neither great strength nor great stateliness. But it is perfectly clear, it is impossible to mistake its meaning, and its simplicity is unattended by any of the down-at-heel neglect of neatness and elegance which is to be found, for instance, in Locke. Little scholastic as he was in most ways, Mill had far outgrown the ignorant eighteenth century contempt of the School-

men, and had learnt from them an exact precision of statement
and argument, while he had managed to keep (without its concomitant looseness and vulgarity) much of the eighteenth century's
wholesome aversion to jargon and to excess of terminology.   In
presenting complicated statements of detail, as in the *Political
Economy*, the *Representative Government*, and elsewhere, he has
as much lucidity as Macaulay, with an almost total freedom from
Macaulay's misleading and delusive suppression of material details.
And besides his usual kind of calm and measured argument, he
can occasionally, as in divers passages of the *Sir William Hamilton* and the political books, rise or sink from the logical and
rhetorical points of view respectively to an impassioned advocacy,
which, though it may be rarely proof against criticism, is very
agreeable so far as it goes.   That Mill wholly escaped the defects
of the popular philosopher, I do not suppose that even those who
sympathise with his views would contend ; though they might
not admit, as others would, that these defects were inseparable
from his philosophy in itself.   But it may be doubtful whether,
all things considered, a better *literary* type of the popular
philosopher exists in modern English ; and it certainly is not
surprising that, falling in as he did with the current mode of
thought, and providing it with a defence specious in reasoning
and attractive in language, he should have attained an influence
perhaps greater than that of which any English philosophical
writer has been able during his lifetime to boast.

The convenience of noticing the Mills together, and of putting
Sir William Hamilton next to his most famous disciples, seems
to justify a certain departure from strict chronological order.
Hamilton was indeed considerably the senior of his critic, having
been born on 8th March 1788.   His father and grandfather, both
professors at the University of Glasgow, had been plain " Dr.
Hamilton."   But they inherited, and Sir William made good, the
claim to a baronetcy which had been in abeyance since the days
of Robert Hamilton, the Covenanting leader.   He himself proceeded from Glasgow, with a Snell Exhibition, to Balliol in 1809.

He was called to the Scottish Bar, but never practised, though some business came to him as Crown solicitor in the Court of Teinds (tithes). He competed in 1820 for the Chair of Moral Philosophy, which Wilson, with far inferior claims, obtained; but it is fair to say that at the time the one candidate had given no more public proofs of fitness than the other. Soon, however, he began to make his mark as a contributor of philosophical articles to the *Edinburgh Review*, and in 1836 he obtained a professorship in the University for which he was even better fitted — that of Logic and Metaphysics. His lectures became celebrated, but he never published them; indeed his only publication of any importance during his lifetime was a collection of his articles under the title of *Dissertations*, with the exception of his monumental edition of Reid, on which he spent, and on which it has sometimes been held that he wasted, most of his time. He died in 1856, and his lectures were published after his death by his successor, Professor Veitch (himself an enthusiastic devotee of literature, especially Border literature, as well as of philosophy), and his greatest disciple, Mansel, between 1859 and 1861. And this was how Mill's *Examination* came to be posthumous. The " Philosophy of the Conditioned," as Hamilton's is for shortness called, could not be described in any brief, and perhaps not with propriety in any, space of the present volume. It is enough to say that it was an attempt to reinforce the so-called " Scotch Philosophy " of Reid against Hume by the help of Kant, as well as at once to continue and evade the latter without resorting either to Transcendentalism or to the experience-philosophy popular in England. In logic, Hamilton was a great and justly honoured defender of the formal view of the science which had been in persistent disrepute during the eighteenth century; but some of the warmest lovers of logic doubt whether his technical inventions or discoveries, such as the famous Quantification of the Predicate, are more than " pretty " in the sense of mathematicians and wine-merchants. This part of his doctrine, by the way, attracted special attention, and was carefully elaborated by another disciple, Professor Thomas Spencer Baynes (1823–1887), who, after chequering philosophy with journalism, became editor of the *Encyclopædia Britannica*, and a careful Shakespearian student. Yet another disciple, and the most distinguished save one, was James Frederick Ferrier, nephew of Susan Ferrier, to whom we owe three most brilliant novels, who was born in 1808 and died in 1864 at St. Andrews, where he had for nearly twenty years been Professor of Moral Philosophy, after previously holding for a short time a History Professorship at Edinburgh. Of this latter University Ferrier had been an alumnus, as well as of Oxford. He edited his father-in-law Wilson's works, and was a contributor to *Blackwood's Magazine*, but his chief book was his *Institutes of Metaphysic*, published in 1854. Too strong a Hamiltonian influence (not in style but in some other ways), and an attempt at an almost Spinosian rigidity of method, have sometimes been held to have marred Ferrier's philosophical performance ; but it is certain that he had the makings of a great metaphysician, and that he was actually no small one.

The great merit of Hamilton was that he, in a somewhat irregular and informal way (for, as has been said, he was ostensibly more a commentator and critic than an independent theorist), introduced German speculation into England after a fashion far more thorough than the earlier but dilettante and haphazard attempts of De Quincey and Coleridge, and contributed vastly to the lifting of the whole tone and strain of English philosophic disputation from the slovenly commonsense into which it had fallen. In fact, he restored metaphysics proper as a part of English current thought ; and helped (though here he was not alone) to restore logic. His defects were, in the first place, that he was at once too systematic and two piecemeal in theory, and worse still, that his philosophical style was one of the very worst existing, or that could exist. That this may have been in some degree a designed reaction from ostentatious popularity is probable ; and that it was in great part caught from his studious frequentation of that Hercynian forest, which takes the place of the groves

of Academe in German philosophical writing, is certain. But
the hideousness of his dialect is a melancholy fact; and it may
be said to have contributed at least as much to the decadence of
his philosophical vogue as any defects in the philosophy itself.
He was, in fact, at the antipodes from Mill in attractiveness of
form as well as in character of doctrine.

There are some who think that Henry Longueville Mansel was
actually in more than one respect, and might, with some slight
changes of accidental circumstance, have been indisputably, the
greatest philosopher of Britain in the nineteenth century. Of the
opinion entertained by contemporaries of great intellectual gifts,
that of Mark Pattison, a bitter political and academical opponent,
and the most acrimonious critic of his time, that Mansel was,
though according to Pattison's view, an " arch-jobber," an " acute
thinker, and a metaphysician " seems pretty conclusive. But
Mansel died in middle age, he was much occupied in various
kinds of University business, and he is said by those who knew
him to have been personally rather indolent. He was born in
Northamptonshire on 6th October 1820, and after schooldays at
Merchant Taylors' passed in the then natural course to St. John's
College, Oxford, of which he became fellow. He was an active
opponent of the first University Commission, in reference to which
he wrote the most brilliant satire of the kind proper to University
wits which this century has produced — the Aristophanic parody
entitled *Phrontisterion*. But the Commission returned him good
for evil, insomuch as he became the first Waynflete Professor of
Moral and Metaphysical Philosophy, a post created in consequence
of it. In 1859 he was Bampton Lecturer, and his sermons in
this office again attained the first excellence in style, though they
were made the subject of severe criticism not merely by the
disciples of Liberal philosophy, but by some timid defenders of
orthodoxy, for their bold application of the philosophy of the conditioned, on scholastic lines, to the problems of theodicy. Mansel
was not a more frequent lecturer than the somewhat indulgent
conditions of the English Universities, especially Oxford, even

after the Commission, required; but his deliverances were of exceptional importance, both in conception and expression. At the death of Milman, his political friends being in power, he was made Dean of St. Paul's, but enjoyed the dignity only a short time, and died in 1870. Besides *Phrontisterion* and his *Bampton Lectures*, which bring him under both the divisions of this chapter, he had published in his lifetime an excellent edition of Aldrich's "Logic," *Prolegomena Logica* (the principal work of the Hamiltonian school, though quite independent in main points), and an enlarged edition of an Encyclopædia dissertation on *Metaphysics*. His essays, chiefly from the *Quarterly Review*, were published after his death, with *Phrontisterion* and other things.

It will appear from this brief summary that Mansel was a many-sided man; and it may be added that he possessed an exceptionally keen wit, by no means confined to professional subjects, and was altogether far more of a man of the world than is usual in a philosopher. But though this man-of-the-worldliness may have affected the extent and quantity of his philosophical work, it did not touch the quality of it. It may be contended that Mansel was on the whole rather intended for a critic or historian of philosophy than for an independent philosophical teacher; and in this he would but have exhibited a tendency of his century. Yet he was very far from mere slavish following even of Hamilton, while the copying, with a little travesty and adjustment of German originals, on which so much philosophical repute has been founded in England, was entirely foreign to his nature and thought. In Mill's *Examination of Hamilton*, the *Bampton Lectures*, above referred to, came in for the most vehement protest, for Mill, less blind than the orthodox objectors, perceived that their drift was to steer clear of some of the commonest and most dangerous reefs and shoals on which the orthodoxy of intelligent but not far-sighted minds has for some generations past been wrecked. But Mansel's rejoinder, written at a time when he was more than ever distracted by avocations, and hampered

2 A

certainly by the necessity of speaking for his master as well as for himself, and probably by considerations of expediency in respect to the duller of the faithful, was not his happiest work. In fact he was too clear and profound a thinker to be first-rate in controversy — a function which requires either unusual dishonesty or one-sidedness in an unusual degree. He may sometimes have been a very little of a sophist — it is perhaps impossible to be a great philosopher without some such touch. But of paralogism — of that sincere advancing of false argument which from the time of Plato has been justly regarded as the most fatal of philosophic drawbacks — there is no trace in Mansel. His natural genius, moreover, assisted by his practice in miscellaneous writing, which though much less in amount of result than Mill's was even more various in kind, equipped him with a most admirable philosophical style, hitting the exact mean between the over-popular and the over-technical, endowing even the *Prolegomena Logica* with a perfect readableness, and in the *Metaphysics* and large parts of the editorial matter of the *Aldrich* showing capacities which make it deeply to be regretted that he never undertook a regular history of philosophy.

The place which might have been thus filled, was accepted but partially and with no capital success by divers writers. Frederick Denison Maurice, who will be mentioned again in this chapter, wrote on *Moral and Metaphysical Philosophy*, but the book, though like all his work attractively written, does not show very wide or very profound knowledge of the subject. The *Lectures on the History of Ancient Philosophy*, by William Archer Butler, a Dublin professor, who died prematurely, would probably, had the author lived, have formed the best history of the subject in English, and even in their fragmentary condition make an admirable book, free from jargon, not unduly popular, but at once sound and literary. The most ambitious attempt at the whole subject was that of George Henry Lewes, the companion of George Eliot, a versatile man of letters of great ability, who brought out on a small scale in 1845, and afterwards on a much larger one, a *Biographical History of Philosophy*. This, though occasionally superficial, and too much tinged with a sort of second-hand Positivism, had, as the qualities of these defects, an excellent though sometimes a rather treacherous clearness, and a unity of vision which is perhaps more valuable for fairly intelligent readers than desultory profundity. But it can hardly take rank as a book of philosophical scholarship, though it is almost a brilliant specimen of popular philosophical literature.

Philosophy, science, and perhaps theology may dispute between them two remarkable figures, nearly contemporary, the one an Oxford and the other a Cambridge man — Whately and Whewell. Besides the differences which their respective universities impress upon nearly all strong characters, there were others between them, Whately being the better bred, the more accomplished writer, and the more original, Whewell the more widely informed, and perhaps the more thoroughgoing. But both were curiously English in a sort of knock-me-down Johnsonian dogmatism; and both were in consequence extremely intolerant. For Whately's so-called impartiality consisted in being equally biassed against Evangelicals and Tractarians; and both were accused by their unfriends of being a little addicted to the encouragement of flatterers and toadies. Richard Whately, the elder, was born in London in 1787, his father being a clergyman in the enjoyment of several pluralities. He went to Oriel, gained a fellowship there in 1811, and was with intervals a resident in Oxford for some twenty years, being latterly Principal of St. Alban Hall (where he made Newman his Vice-Principal), and in 1829 Professor of Political Economy. In 1831 the Whigs made him Archbishop of Dublin, which difficult post he held for more than thirty years till his death in 1863. His work is not very extensive, but it is remarkable. His *Historic Doubts relative to Napoleon Bonaparte* was an exceedingly clever "skit" on the Rationalist position in regard to miracles and biblical criticism generally; though Whately's orthodoxy was none of the strictest. His Bampton Lectures on *Party Feeling in Religion* preceded rather curiously the greatest outburst of the said party feeling which had been seen in England since the seventeenth century. But the books by which he is or was most widely known are his *Logic* and *Rhetoric*, expansions of Encyclopædia articles (1826 and 1828) intentionally popular and perhaps almost unnecessarily exoteric, but extremely stimulating and clear. Whately, who had some points in common with Sydney Smith, was, like him, in part the victim of the extreme want of accuracy and range in the Oxford education of his youth ; but his mental and literary powers were great.

William Whewell, the son of a carpenter, showed talent for mathematics early, and obtaining an exhibition at Trinity, Cambridge, became fellow, tutor, and Master of his College. He had the advantage, which his special studies gave, of more thorough training, and extended his attention from pure and applied mathematics to science and a kind of philosophy. His chief works were *The History* (1837) and *The Philosophy* (1840) *of the Inductive Sciences*, his Bridgewater Treatise on *Astronomy and Physic in Reference to Natural Philosophy* (1833) and his *Plurality of Worlds* (1853) being also famous in their day ; but he wrote voluminously in various kinds. He was rather a bully, and his work has no extraordinary merit of style, but it is interesting as being among the latest in which science permitted her votaries not to specialise very much, and rather to apply the ancient education to the new subjects than to be wholly theirs.

If the difficulty of deciding on rejection or admission be great in the case of philosophers proper, much greater is it in the numerous subdivisions which are themselves applied philosophy as philosophy is applied literature. The two chief of these perhaps are Jurisprudence and Political Economy. Under the head of the first, three remarkable writers at least absolutely demand notice — Austin, Maine, and Stephen. The first of these was in respect of influence, if not also of actual accomplishment, one of the most noteworthy Englishmen of the century. Born in 1790, he died in 1859, having begun life in the Army which he exchanged for the Bar not long after Waterloo. He was made Professor of Jurisprudence in the new University College of London in 1827. He held this post for five years only; but it resulted in his famous *Province of Jurisprudence Determined*, a book standing more or less alone in English. He did not publish much else, though he did some official work; and his *Lectures on Jurisprudence* were posthumously edited by his wife, a Miss Taylor of Norwich, who has been referred to as translator of the *Story without an End*, and who did much other good work. Austin (whose younger brother Charles (1799–1874) left little if anything in print but accumulated a great fortune at the Parliamentary Bar, and left a greater, though vague, conversational reputation) had bad health almost throughout his life, and his work is not large in bulk. At first pooh-poohed and neglected, almost extravagantly prized later, and later still, according to the usual round, a little cavilled at, it presents Utilitarian theory at its best in the intellectual way; and its disciplinary value, if it is not taken for gospel, can hardly be overrated. But its extreme clearness, closeness, and logical precision carry with them the almost inevitable defects of hardness, narrowness, and want of "play," as well as of that most fatal of intellectual attitudes which takes for granted that everything is explicable. Still, these were the defects of Austin's school and time; his merits were individual, and indeed very nearly unique.

Sir Henry James Summer Maine was born in 1822, and educated first as a Blue Coat boy and then at Pembroke College, Cambridge. After a quite exceptional career as an undergraduate, he became fellow of Trinity Hall, of which he died Master in 1888. But he had only held this latter post for eleven years, and the midmost of his career was occupied with quite different work. He had been made Professor of Civil Law in his University in 1847, at a very early age, when he had not even been called to the Bar; but he supplied this omission three years later, and a little later still exchanged his Cambridge Professorship for a Readership at Lincoln's Inn. In 1862 he obtained the appointment, famous from its connection with letters, of Legal Member of the

Viceroy's Council in India. On quitting it after seven years he was transferred to the Council at Home, and became Professor of Comparative Jurisprudence at Oxford. Besides his work as a reviewer, which was considerable, Maine wrote — in an admirable style, and with a scholarship and sense which, in the recrudescence of more barbaric thought, have brought down socialist and other curses on his head — many works on the philosophy of law, politics, and history, the chief of which were his famous *Ancient Law* (1861), *Village Communities* (1871), *Early Law and Custom* (1883), with a severe criticism on Democracy called *Popular Government* (1885). Few writers of our time could claim the phrase *mitis sapentia* as Maine could, though it is possible that he was a little too much given to theorise. But his influence in checking that of Austin was admirable.

A colleague of Maine's on the *Saturday Review*, his successor in his Indian post, like him a *malleus demagogorum*, but in some ways no small contrast, was Sir James Fitzjames Stephen (1829–94), the most distinguished member of a family unusually distinguished during the past century in the public service and in literature. His father, Sir James Stephen, was himself well known as a reviewer, as a civil servant, as Professor of Modern History at Cambridge, and as author of *Essays in Ecclesiastical History* and *Lectures on the History of France* (1849 and 1851). The second Sir James was born at Kensington in 1829, went to Eton, thence to King's College, London, and thence to Trinity, Cambridge, and was called to the Bar in 1854. His legal career was brilliant and varied, and led him to the Bench, which he resigned shortly before his death. Sir James Stephen published some works of capital importance on his own subject, the chief relating the Criminal Law, collected both earlier and later a good deal of his *Saturday* work, discussed a famous passage of Indian History in the *Story of Neocomar* (1885), and wrote not a little criticism — political, theological, and other — of a somewhat negative but admirably clear-headed kind — the chief expression of which is *Liberty, Equality, and Fraternity* (1873).

Even less room can be given to the Political Economists than to the "Jurisprudents," partly because the best writers of them, such as J. S. Mill, have figured or will figure elsewhere ; partly because, from Ricardo to Jevons and Cliffe Leslie, though they have often displayed no mean literary power, the necessities or supposed necessities of their subject have usually kept their books further away from *belles lettres* than the documents of any other department of what is widely called philosophy. But a paragraph must at least be given to one of the earliest and one of the most famous of them.

If a prize were offered to the best-abused person in English literature, few competitors would have much chance with Thomas Robert Malthus, author of the *Essay on the Principles of Population* (1798), and of divers works on Political Economy, of which he was Professor in the East India College at Haileybury. To judge from the references which for many years used to be, and to some extent still are, made to Malthus, still more from the way in which the term " Malthusian " is still often used, he might be supposed to have been a reprobate anarchist and revolutionary, who had before his eyes neither the fear of God, nor the love of man, nor the respect of morality and public opinion. As a matter of fact Malthus was a most respectable and amiable clergyman, orthodox I believe in religion, Tory I believe in politics, who incurred odium chiefly by his inculcation of the most disagreeable lessons of the new and cheerless science which he professed. Born on 24th February 1766 near Dorking, of a very respectable family, he went to Cambridge, took honours, a fellowship at his college (Jesus), and orders, obtained a benefice, and spent most of the last thirty years of his life in the Professorship above referred to, dying in 1854. His *Essay* was one of the numerous counter-blasts to Godwin's anarchic perfectibilism, and its general drift was simply to show that the increase of population, unless counter-acted by individual and moral self-restraint, must reduce humanity to misery. The special formula that " population increases in a geometrical, food in a arithmetical ratio," is overstrained and a little absurd ; the general principle is sound beyond all question, and not only consistent with, but absolutely deducible from, the purest Christian doctrines. Malthus wrote well, he knew thoroughly what he was writing about, and he suffers only from the inevitable drawback to all writers on such subjects who have not positive genius of form, that a time comes when their contentions appear self-evident to all who are not ignorant or prejudiced.

The greatest *theological* interest of the century belongs to what is diversely called the Oxford and the Tractarian Movement ; while, even if this statement be challenged on non-literary grounds, it will scarcely be so by any one on grounds literary. For the present purpose, of course, nothing like a full account of the Movement can be attempted. It is enough to say that it arose partly in reaction from the Evangelical tendency which had dominated the more active section of the Church of England for many years, partly in protest against the Liberalising and Latitudinarian tendency in matters both temporal and spiritual. In contradistinction to its predecessor (for the Evangelicals had been the reverse of literary), it was from the first — *i.e.* about 1830, or earlier if we take *The Christian Year* as a harbinger of it — a very literary movement both in verse and prose. Of its three leaders, Pusey — whose name, given to it in derision and sometimes contested by sympathisers as unappropriate, unquestionably ranks of right as that of its greatest theologian, its most steadfast character, and the most of a born leader engaged in it — was something less of a pure man of letters than either Keble or Newman. But he was a man of letters ; and perhaps a greater one than is usually thought.

Edward Bouverie Pusey, who belonged to the family of Lord Folkestone by blood, his father having become by bequest the representative of the very old Berkshire house of Pusey, was born at the seat of this family in 1800. He went to Eton and to Christ Church, and became a fellow of Oriel, studied theology and oriental languages in Germany, and was made Professor of Hebrew at the early age of twenty-seven. He was a thorough scholar, and even in the times of his greatest unpopularity no charge of want of competence for his post was brought against him by any one who knew. It is, however, somewhat comic that charges of Rationalism were brought against his first book, a study of contemporary German theology. In or soon after 1833 he joined Newman and Keble in the famous *Tracts for the Times*, at the same time urging the return to a more primitive and catholic theology in his sermons, and by means of the great enterprise in translation called the *Oxford Library of the Fathers*, of which he executed part and sedulously edited others. Pusey first came before general public notice outside Oxford in 1843, in consequence of a very high-handed exertion of power by the authorities of the University, who, without allowing him a hearing, suspended him for a sermon on the Eucharist from preaching for three years. His mouth was thus closed at the very moment when Newman "went over"; and when some of the enemies of the movement declared that Pusey would go too. Others were equally certain that if he stayed it was either from base motives of self-interest, or, still more basely, in order to do underhand damage to the Church. But all who unite knowledge and fairness now admit, not only his perfect loyalty, but the almost unexampled heroism and steadfastness with which for some ten or fifteen years after Newman's secession, against popular obloquy, against something very like persecution from the authorities of the Church and the University, and against the constant and repeated discouragement given by the desertion of friends and colleagues, he upheld his cause and made the despised and reproached "Puseyites" of his middle life what he lived to see them — the greatest and almost the dominant party in the Anglican Church. He was less fortunate in his opposition to the secularising of the Universities, and in his attempts (which ill-willers did not fail to liken to the attempts made to stifle his own teaching) to check by legal means the spread of Rationalism. But he was nearly as full of honours as of years when he died on 16th September 1882.

Many of the constituents of this remarkable and perhaps unexampled success — Pusey's personal saintliness, his unselfish use
of his considerable income, his unwearied benevolence in other
than pecuniary ways — do not concern us here. But his works,
which are numerous, and the most literary of which are his
Sermons and his *Eirenicon*, contributed not a little to it. Pusey's
style was accused by some of bareness and by others of obscurity;
but these accusations may be safely dismissed as due merely to
the prevalent fancy for florid expression, and to the impatience of
somewhat scholastically arranged argument which has also distinguished our times.

The second of this remarkable trio, John Keble, was the eldest,
having been born on 24th April 1792, at Fairford, in Gloucester-
shire, with which county his family had for some centuries been
connected. Keble's father was a clergyman, and there was a
clerical feeling and tradition in the whole family. John went to
no public school, but was very carefully educated at home,
obtained an open scholarship at Corpus Christi College, Oxford,
when he was only fourteen, and went into residence next year —
for just at this time extremely early entrance at the University
was much commoner than a little earlier or later. He had only
just entered his nineteenth year when he took a double first, and
had not concluded it when he was elected, at the same time with
Whately, to an Oriel fellowship. He followed this up by winning
both the Chancellor's Essays, English and Latin, and established
his reputation as the most brilliant man of his day. He was
ordained as soon as he could be, and served the usual offices of
tutor in his College and examiner in the University. But even
such semi-public life as this was distasteful to him, and he soon
gave up his Oriel tutorship for a country curacy and private pupils.
Indeed the note, some would say the fault, of Keble's whole life
was an almost morbid retiringness, which made him in 1827 refuse
even to compete with Hawkins for the Provostship of Oriel. It
is possible that he would not have been elected, for oddly enough
his two future colleagues in the triumvirate, both Fellows, were

both in favour of his rival; but his shunning the contest has been deeply deplored, and by some even blamed as a *gran rifiuto*. The publication of *The Christian Year*, however, which immediately followed, probably did more for the Movement and for the spiritual life of England than any office-holding could have done; and in 1831, Keble, being elected Professor of Poetry, distinguished himself almost as much in criticism as he had already done in poetry. He obtained, and was contented with, the living of Hursley, in Hampshire, where he resided till his death on 29th March 1866.

Keble's very generally granted character as one of the holiest persons of modern times, and even his influence on the Oxford Movement, concern us less here than his literary work, which was of almost the first importance merely as literature. The reaction from an enormous popularity of nearly seventy years' date, and the growth of anti-dogmatic opinions, have brought about a sort of tendency in some quarters to belittle, if not positively to sneer at, *The Christian Year*, which, with the *Lyra Innocentium* and a collection of *Miscellaneous Poems*, contains Keble's poetical work. There never was anything more uncritical. The famous reference which Thackeray— the least ecclesiastically inclined, if by no means the least religious, of English men of letters of genius in this century — makes to its appearance in *Pendennis*, shows what the thoughts of unbiassed contemporaries were. And no very different judgment can be formed by unbiassed posterity. With Herbert and Miss Rossetti, Keble ranks as the greatest of English writers in sacred verse, the irregular and unequal efforts of Vaughan and Crashaw sometimes transcending, oftener sinking below the three. If Keble has not the exquisite poetical mysticism of Christina Rossetti he is more copious and more strictly scholarly, while he escapes the quaint triviality, or the triviality sometimes not even quaint, which mars Herbert. The influence of Wordsworth is strongly shown, but it is rendered and redirected in an entirely original manner. The lack of taste which mars so much religious poetry never shows itself even for a moment in Keble; yet the correctness of his diction, like the orthodoxy of his thought, is never frigid or tame. There are few poets who so well deserve the nickname of a Christian Horace, though the phrase may seem to have something of the parodox of "prose Shakespeare." The careful melody of the versification and the exact felicity of the diction exclude, it may be, those highest flights which create most enthusiasm, at any rate in this century. But for measure, proportion, successful attainment of the proposed end, Keble has few superiors.

It would indeed be surprising if he had many, for, with his gift of verse, he was also one of the most accomplished of critics. His *Prælectiones Academicæ*, written, as the rule then was, in Latin, is unfortunately a sealed book to too many persons whom modern practice calls and strives to consider "educated"; but he did not confine himself even in these to classical subjects, and he wrote not a few reviews in English dealing with modern poetry. His æsthetics are of course deeply tinged with ethic; but he does not in the least allow moral prepossessions to twist his poetic theory, which may be generally described as the Aristotelian teaching on the subject, supplied and assisted by the aid of a wide study of the literatures not open to Aristotle. There can be no doubt that if Keble's mind had not been more and more absorbed by religious subjects he would have been one of the very greatest of English critics of literature; and he is not far from being a great one as it is. He did not publish many sermons, though one of his, the Assize Sermon at Oxford in 1833, is considered to have started the Movement; and opinions as to his pulpit powers have varied. But it is certainly not too much to say that it was impossible for Keble not to make everything that he wrote, whether in verse or prose, literature of the most perfect academic kind, informed by the spirit of scholarship and strengthened by individual talent.

John Henry Newman was the eldest son of a man of business of some means (who came of a family of Cambridgeshire yeomen) and of a lady of Huguenot descent. He was born in London on 21st February 1801, was educated privately at Ealing, imbibed strong evangelical principles, and went up to Oxford (Trinity College) so early that he went in for "Greats" (in which he only obtained a third class) before he was nineteen. He continued, however, to reside at Trinity, where he held a scholarship, and more than made up for his mishap in the schools by winning an Oriel fellowship in 1823. In three successive years he took orders and a curacy in the first, the Vice-Principalship of St. Alban's Hall under Whately in the second, and an Oriel tutorship in the third; while in 1827 he succeeded Hawkins, who became Provost, in the Vicarage of St. Mary's, the most important post of the kind — to a man who chose to make it important — in Oxford.

Newman did so choose, and his sermons — not those to the University, though these also are notable, but those nominally "Parochial," really addressed to the undergraduates who soon flocked to hear him — were the foundation and mainstay of his influence, constitute the largest single division of his printed work, and perhaps present that work in the best and fairest light. His history for the next sixteen years cannot be attempted here; it is the history of the famous thing called the Oxford Movement, which changed the intellectual as well as the ecclesiastical face of England, on which libraries have been written, and which, even yet, has not been satisfactorily or finally judged. His travels with Hurrell Froude in the Mediterranean during 1832-33 seem to have been the special turning-point of his career. After ten years, perhaps of "development," certainly of hard fighting, he resigned St. Mary's in 1843, and after two years more of halting between two opinions he was received into the Church of Rome in October 1845. He left Oxford, never to return to it as a residence, and not to visit it for thirty-two years, in the following February.

His first public appearance after this was in the once famous Achilli trial for libel, in which the plaintiff, an anti-Roman lecturer, recovered damages from Newman for an utterly damning description of Achilli's career in the Roman Church itself. Impartial judges generally thought and think that the verdict was against the weight of evidence. At any rate it produced a decided revulsion in Newman's favour, of which he was both too convinced of his own position and too astute not to take advantage. He had hitherto since his secession resided (he had been re-ordained in Rome) at Birmingham, London, and Dublin, but he now took up his abode, practically for the rest of his life, at Birmingham or rather Edgbaston. In 1864 the great opportunity, presented by Kingsley's unguarded words (*vide supra*), occurred, and he availed himself of it at once. Most of those who read the *Apologia pro Vitâ Suâ* were not familiar with Newman's masterly English, and his competent, if not supreme, dialectic and sophistic. They were not, as a former generation had been, prejudiced against him; the untiring work of those of his former friends who remained faithful to the Church of England had of itself secured him a fair hearing. During the remaining twenty-five years of his life he had never again to complain of ostracism or unfair prejudice. The controversy as to the Vatican Council brought him once more forward, and into collision with Mr. Gladstone, but into no odium of any kind. Indeed he was considerably less popular at Rome than at home, the more supple and less English character of Manning finding greater favour with Pius IX. The late seventies, however, were a time of triumph for Newman. In 1877 he was elected an Honorary Fellow of his own College, Trinity, and next year paid what may be called a visit of restoration to Oxford, while in 1879 the new Pope Leo XIII., a man of great abilities and wide piety, raised Newman to the cardinalate. He visited Rome on the occasion, but returned to Birmingham, where the Edgbaston Oratory was still his home for the remaining years of his life. This did not end till 11th August 1890, when almost all men spoke almost all good things over his grave, though some did not spare to interpose a sober criticism. The books composed during this long and eventful career, especially in the first half of it, were very numerous, Cardinal Newman's works at the time of his death, and before the addition of Letters, etc., extending to nearly forty volumes. Much of the matter of these is still *cinis dolosissimus*, not to be trodden on save in the most gingerly manner in such a book as this. Yet there are probably few qualified and impartial judges who would refuse Newman, all things considered, the title of the greatest theological writer in English during this century; and there are some who uphold him for one of the very greatest of English prose writers. It is therefore impossible not to give him a place, and no mean place, here.

Although his chief work, indeed all but a very small part of it, was in prose, he was a good verse writer. The beautiful poem or hymn usually called from its first words "Lead, kindly Light," but entitled by its author "The Pillar of Cloud," is not merely as widely known as any piece of sacred verse written during the century, but may challenge anything of that class (out of the work of Miss Christina Rossetti) for really poetical decoction and concoction of religious ideas. It was written, with much else, during a voyage in a sailing ship from Sicily to Marseilles at the close (June 1833) of that continental tour which was of such moment in Newman's life; and the whole batch ferments with spiritual excitement. Earlier, and indeed later, Newman, besides plenty of serious verse, contributed to the *Lyra Apostolica* or written independently, was a graceful writer of verse trifles; but his largest and best poetical work, *The Dream of Gerontius*, was not produced till he was approaching old age, and had long passed the crisis of his career. Possibly the new ferment of soul into which the composition of the *Apologia* had thrown him, may have been responsible for this, which is dated a year later. It is the recital in lyrical-dramatic form of an anticipatory vision, just before death, of the Last Things, and unites dignity and melody in a remarkable manner. The only other parts of his work to which Newman himself attached the title "literature" were the prose romances of *Callista* and *Loss and Gain*. They display his power over language, but are exposed on one side to the charges usually incurred by novels with a purpose, and on the other to a suspicion of bad taste, incurred in the effort to be popular.

By far the larger bulk of the works, however, belongs to theology. This includes twelve volumes of Sermons, all but a small part delivered before Newman's change of creed, and eight of them the *Parochial and Plain Sermons*, preached in the pulpit of St. Mary's but not to the University ; four of treatises, including the most famous and characteristic of Newman's works except the *Apologia*, *The Grammar of Assent*, and *The Development of Christian Doctrine ;* four of Essays ; three of Historical Sketches ; four theological, chiefly on Arianism, and translations of St. Athanasius; and six Polemical, which culminate in the *Apologia*. With respect to the substance of this work it is soon easy, putting controversial matters as much as possible apart, to discover where Newman's strength and weakness respectively lay. He was distinctly deficient in the historic sense ; and in the *Apologia* itself he threw curious light on this deficiency, and startled even friends and fellow-converts, by speaking contemptuously of " antiquarian arguments." The same defect is quaintly illustrated by a naïf and evidently sincere complaint that he should have been complained of for (in his own words) " attributing to the middle of the third century what is certainly to be found in the fourth." And it is understood that he was not regarded either by Anglican or by Roman Catholic experts as a very deep theologian in either of his stages. The special characteristic — the *ethos* as his own contemporaries and immediate successors at Oxford would have said — of Newman seems to have been strangely combined. He was perhaps the last of the very great preachers in English — of those who combined a thoroughly classical training, a scholarly form, with the incommunicable and almost inexplicable power to move audiences and readers. And he was one of the first of that class of journalists who in the new age have succeeded the preachers, whether for good or ill, as the prophets of the illiterate. It may seem strange to speak of Newman as a journalist ; but if

any one will read his essays, his *Apologia*, above all the curious set
of articles called *The Tamworth Reading-Room*, he will see what a
journalist was lost, or only partly developed, in this cardinal. He
had the conviction, which is far more necessary to a journalist
than is generally thought; and yet his convictions were not of
that extremely systematic and far-reaching kind which no doubt
often stands in the journalist's way. He had the faculty of mixing
bad and good argument, which is far more effective with mixed
audiences than unbated logic. And, little as he is thought of as
sympathising with the common people, he was entirely free from
that contempt of them which always prevents a man from gaining
their ear unless he is a consummately clever scoundrel.

It may however be retorted that if Newman was a born
journalist, sermons and theology must be a much better school
of style in journalism than articles and politics. And it is quite
true that his writing at its best is of extraordinary charm, while
that charm is not, as in the case of some of his contemporaries
and successors, derived from dubiously legitimate ornament and
flourish, but observes the purest classical limitations of proportion
and form. It has perhaps sometimes been a little overvalued,
either by those who in this way or that — out of love for what he
joined or hate to what he left — were in uncritical sympathy with
Newman, or by others it may be from pure ignorance of the fact
that much of this charm is the common property of the more
scholarly writers of the time, and is only eminently, not specially,
present in him. But of the fact of it there is no doubt. In such
a sermon for instance as that on " The Individuality of the Soul,"
a thought or series of thoughts, in itself poetically grandiose
enough for Taylor or even for Donne, is presented in the simplest
but in the most marvellously impressive language. The sentences
are neither volleying in their shortness, nor do they roll
thundrously; the cadences though perfect are not engineered
with elaborate musical art; there are in proportion very few
adjectives; the writer exercises the most extreme continence in
metaphor, simile, illustration, all the tricks and frounces of literary

art. Yet Taylor, though he might have attained more sweetness or more grandeur, could hardly have been more beautiful; and though Donne might have been so, it would have been at the expense of clearness. Newman is so clear that he has often been accused of being, and sometimes is, a little hard; but this is not always or often the case: it is especially not so when he is dealing with things which, as in the sermon just referred to and that other on "The Intermediate State," admit the diffusion of religious awe. The presence of that awe, and of a constant sense and dread of Sin, have been said, and probably with truth, to be keynotes of Newman's religious ideas, and of his religious history; but they did not harden, as in thinkers of another temper has often been the case, his style or his thought. On the contrary, they softened both; and it is when he is least under the influence of them that unction chiefly deserts him. Yet he by no means often sought to excite his hearers. He held, as he himself somewhere says, that "impassioned thoughts and sublime imaginings have no strength in them." And this conviction of his can hardly be strange to the fact that few writers indulge so little as Newman in what is called fine writing. He has "organ passages," but they are such as the wind blowing as it lists draws from him, not such as are produced by deliberate playing on himself.

In a wider space it would be interesting to comment on numerous other exponents of the Movement. Archdeacon afterwards Cardinal Manning (1808–93), the successful rival of Newman among those Anglican clergymen who joined the Church of Rome, was less a man of letters than a very astute man of business; but his sermons before he left the Church had merit, and he afterwards wrote a good deal. Richard Hurrell Froude (1803–36), elder brother of the historian, had a very great and not perhaps a very beneficent influence on Newman, and through Newman on others; but he died too soon to leave much work. His chief distinguishing note was a vigorous and daring humour allied to a strong reactionary sentiment. Isaac Williams, the second poet of the Movement (1802–65), was in

most respects, as well as in poetry, a minor Keble. W. G.
Ward, commonly called "Ideal" Ward from his famous, very
ill-written, very ill-digested, but important *Ideal of a Christian
Church*, which was the alarm-bell for the flight to Rome, was a
curiously constituted person of whom something has been said in
reference to Clough. He had little connection with pure letters,
and after his secession to Rome and his succession to a large
fortune he finally devoted himself to metaphysics of a kind.
His acuteness was great, and he had a scholastic subtlety and
logical deftness which made him very formidable to the loose
thinkers and reasoners of Utilitarianism and anti-Supernaturalism.
One of the latest important survivors was Dean Church (1815–91),
who, as Proctor, had arrested the persecution of the Tractarians,
with which it was sought to complete the condemnation of
Ward's *Ideal*, and who afterwards, both in a country cure and
as Dean of St. Paul's, acquired very high literary rank by work
on Dante, Anselm, Spenser, and other subjects, leaving also
the best though unfortunately an incomplete history of the
Movement itself; while the two Mozleys, the one a considerable
theologian, the other an active journalist, brothers-in-law of
Newman, also deserve mention. Last of all perhaps we must
notice Henry Parry Liddon (1829–90), of a younger generation,
but the right-hand man of Pusey in his later day, and his
biographer afterwards — a popular and pleasing, though rather
rhetorical than argumentative or original, preacher, and a man
very much affected by his friends. Even this list is nothing like
complete, but it is impossible to enlarge it.

Midway between the Movement and its enemies, a partial
sympathiser in early days, almost an enemy when the popular
tide turned against it, almost a leader when public favour once
more set in in its favour, was Samuel Wilberforce, Bishop of Oxford
and Winchester (1805–73). The third son of the celebrated
emancipationist and evangelical, he had brothers who were more
attracted than himself by the centripetal force of Roman doctrine,
and succumbed to it. Worldly perhaps as much as spiritual

motives kept him steadier. He did invaluable work as a bishop; and at all times of his life he was in literature a distinct supporter of the High Church cause, though with declensions and defections of Erastian and evangelical backsliding. He was a very admirable preacher, though his sermons do not read as well as they "heard"; some of his devotional manuals are of great excellence; and in the heyday of High Church allegory (an interesting by-walk of literature which can only be glanced at here, but which was trodden by some estimable and even some eminent writers) he produced the well hit-off tale of *Agathos* (1839). But it may be that he will, as a writer, chiefly survive in the remarkable letters and diaries in his *Life*, which are not only most valuable for the political and ecclesiastical history of the time, but precious always as human documents and sometimes as literary compositions.

Three remarkable persons must be mentioned among the opponents of (and in one case harsh judgment might say the deserters of) the Movement. These were Arthur Penrhyn Stanley, Mark Pattison, and Benjamin Jowett. Stanley, born in 1815, was the son of the (afterwards) Bishop of Norwich and a nephew of the first Lord Stanley of Alderley, and was brought up very much under the influence of Arnold, whose biographer he became. But he went further than Arnold in Broad Church ways. His career at Rugby and at Oxford was distinguished, and after being fellow and tutor of University College for some ten years, he became successively Canon of Canterbury, Canon of Christ Church, and Professor of Ecclesiastical History at Oxford, and Dean of Westminster, in which last post he had almost greater opportunities than any bishop, and used them to the full. He also wrote busily, devoting himself especially to the geography of Palestine and the history of the Eastern Church, which he handled in a florid and popular style, though not with much accuracy or scholarship. Personally, Stanley was much liked, though his conception of his duties as a sworn servant of the Church has seemed strange to some. He died in July 1881.

Mark Pattison (1813–84), Fellow and Rector of Lincoln
College, had a less amiable character than Stanley's, but a
greater intellect and far nicer, profounder, and wider scholarship,
though he actually did very little.   He fell under the influence
of Newman early, and was one of that leader's closest associates
in his monastic retreat at Littlemore.   But when Newman "went
over," the wave swept Pattison neither to Rome nor safely on to
higher English ground, but into a religious scepticism, the exact
extent of which was nowhere definitely announced, but which
was regarded by some as nearly total.   He did not nominally
leave the Church, but he acted always with the extreme Liberal
party in the University, and he was one of the famous Seven who
contributed to *Essays and Reviews*.[1]   The shock of his religious
revolution was completed by a secular disappointment — his
defeat for the office of Rector, which he actually attained much
later ; and a temper always morbid, appears, to judge from his
painful but extraordinarily interesting and characteristic *Memoirs*,
to have been permanently soured.   Even active study became
difficult to him, and though he was understood to have a more
extensive acquaintance with the humanists of the late Renaissance
than any man of his day, his knowledge took little written form
except a volume on Isaac Casaubon.   He also wrote an admirable
little book on *Milton* for the *English Men of Letters*, edited
parts of Milton and Pope, and contributed a not inconsiderable
number of essays and articles to the *Quarterly* and *Saturday
Reviews*, and other papers.   The autobiography mentioned was
published after his death.

Despite Pattison's peculiar temper he had warm and devoted
friends, and it was impossible for any one, whether personally liking him or not, to deny him the possession of most
unusual gifts.   Whether his small performance was due to the

[1] This famous book, published in 1860, was a collection of papers by six
clergymen and a layman, some of which undoubtedly were, and the rest of which
were by association thought to be, unorthodox.   It was condemned by Convoca-
tion, and actual legal proceedings were taken against two of the writers, but without final effect.

shocks just referred to, to genuine fastidiousness and resolve to do nothing but the best, or to these things mixed with a strong dash of downright indolence and want of energy, is hard to say. But it would be entirely unjust to regard him as merely a man who was "going to do something." His actual work though not large is admirable, and his style is the perfection of academic correctness, not destitute of either vigour or grace.

There were some resemblances between Pattison and Jowett (1817–94) ; but the latter, unlike Pattison, had never had any sympathies with the religious renaissance of his time. Like Pattison he passed his entire life (after he obtained a Balliol fellowship) in his College, and like him became head of it ; while he was a much more prominent member of the Liberal party in Oxford. His position as Regius Professor of Greek gave him considerable influence even beyond Balliol. He, too, was an *Essayist and Reviewer*, and he exercised a quiet but pervading influence in University matters. He even acquired no mean name in literature, though his work, after an early *Commentary* on some Epistles of St. Paul, was almost entirely confined to translations, especially of Plato, and though in these translations he was much assisted by pupils. He wrote well, but with much less distinction and elegance than Pattison, nor had he by any means the same taste for literature and erudition in it. But, as an influence on the class of persons from whom men of letters are drawn, no one has exceeded him in his day.

The dramatic catastrophe of the Disruption of the Scotch Kirk, which, by a strange coincidence, was nearly contemporary with the crisis of the Oxford Movement, set the final seal upon the reputation of Thomas Chalmers, who headed the seceders. But this reputation had been made long before, and indeed Chalmers died 30th May 1847, only four years after he "went out." He was a much older man than the Oxford leaders, having been born in 1780, and after having for some years, though a minister, devoted himself chiefly to secular studies, he became famous as a preacher at the Tron Church, Glasgow. In 1823 he was appointed Professor of Moral Philosophy at St. Andrews, and (shortly afterwards) of Theology in Edinburgh. He was one of the Bridgewater treatise writers — a group of distinguished persons endowed to produce tractates on Natural Theology — and his work, *The Adaptation of External Nature to the Moral and Intellectual Constitution of Man*, was one of the most famous of that set, procuring for him a correspondence-membership from the French Institute and a D.C.L. from Oxford. Chalmers' works are extremely voluminous ; the testimony as to the effect of his preaching is tolerably uniform ; he was a man of very wide range of thought, and of remarkable faculty of popularisation ; and there is no doubt that he was a born leader of men. But as literature his works have hardly maintained the reputation which they once had, and even those who revere him, unless they let reverence stifle criticism, are apt to acknowledge that there is more rhetoric than logic in him, and that the rhetoric itself is not of the finest.

Edward Irving, at one time an assistant to Chalmers, and an early friend of Carlyle, was twelve years the junior of Chalmers himself, and died thirteen years before him. But at nearly the time when Chalmers was at the height of his reputation as a preacher in Glasgow, Irving was drawing crowds to the unfashionable quarter of Hatton Garden, London, by sermons of extraordinary brilliancy. Later he developed eccentricities of doctrine which do not concern us, and his preaching has not worn much better than that of his old superior. Irving, however, had more strictly literary affinities than Chalmers ; he came under the influence of Coleridge (which probably had not a little to do both with his eloquence and with his vagaries) ; and he may be regarded as having been much more of a man of letters who had lost his way and strayed into theology than as a theologian proper.

To what extent this great and famous influence of Coleridge actually worked upon Frederick Denison Maurice has been debated. It is however generally stated that he, like his friend Sterling, was induced to take orders in the Church of England by this influence. He was not a very young man when in 1834, the year of Irving's death, he did this, for he had been born in 1805, and had been educated at Cambridge, though being then a Unitarian he did not take a degree. He afterwards went to Oxford and took an M.A. degree there, and he was regarded for a time as a sort of outlying sympathiser with the Tractarian Movement. But his opinions took a very different line of development not merely from those of Newman, but from those of Keble and Pusey. He indeed never left the Church, in which he held divers preferments; and though his views on eternal punishment lost him a professorship in King's College, London, he met with no formal ecclesiastical censure. But he came to be regarded as a champion of the Broad Church school, and upheld eloquently and vehemently, if not always with a sufficiency either of logic or of learning, a curious conglomerate of "advanced" views, ranging from Christian Socialism to something like the views of the Atonement attributed to Origen, and from deprecation of dogma to deprecation of the then fashionable political economy. He was made Professor of Moral Philosophy at Cambridge in 1866, and died in 1872. Maurice's sermons were effective, and his other works numerous. A very generous and amiable person with a deficient sense of history, Maurice in his writing is a sort of elder, less gifted, and more exclusively theological Charles Kingsley, on whom he exercised great and rather unfortunate influence. But his looseness of thought, wayward eclecticism of system, and want of accurate learning, were not remedied by Kingsley's splendid pictorial faculty, his creative imagination, or his brilliant style.

Somewhat akin to Maurice, but of a more feminine and less robust temperament, was Frederick Robertson, generally called "Robertson of Brighton," from the place of his last cure. Robertson, who was the son of a soldier, was born in London on 3rd February 1816. After a rather eccentric education and some vacillations about a profession, he went, rather late, to Oxford, and was ordained in 1840. He had very bad health, but did duty, chiefly at

Cheltenham and at Brighton, pretty valiantly, and died on August 1853. He published next to nothing in his lifetime, but after his death there appeared several volumes of sermons which gained great popularity, and were followed by other posthumous works. Robertson's preaching is not very easy to judge, because the published sermons are admittedly not what was actually delivered, but after-reminiscences or summaries, and the judgment is not rendered easier by the injudicious and gushing laudation of which he has been made the subject. He certainly possessed a happy gift of phrase now and then, and remarkable earnestness.

NOTE. — In no chapter, perhaps, has there been greater difficulty as to inclusion and exclusion than in the present. The names of Bishop Christopher Wordsworth, of Dean Alford, of Bishop Lightfoot for England, of Bishop Charles Wordsworth, of Dean Ramsay, of Drs. Candlish, Guthrie, and Macleod for Scotland, may seem to clamour among orthodox theologians, those of W. R. Greg, of James Hinton, of W. K. Clifford among not always orthodox lay dealers with the problems of philosophy, or of theology, or both. With less tyrannous limits of space Principal Tulloch, who was noteworthy in both these and in pure literature as well (he was the last editor of *Fraser*), must have received at least brief notice in this chapter, as must his brother Principal, J. C. Shairp (an amiable poet, an agreeable critic, and Professor of Poetry at Oxford), in others.

CHAPTER IX

LATER JOURNALISM AND CRITICISM IN ART AND LETTERS

In a former chapter we conducted the history of criticism, especially literary criticism, and that chiefly as displayed in the periodicals which were reorganized and refreshed in the early years of the century, to about 1850. We have now to take it up at that point and conduct it — subject to the limitations of our plan as regards living authors, and in one extremely important case taking the license of outstepping these limits — to the present or almost the present day. We shall have to consider the rise and performances of two great individual writers, one of whom entirely recreated, if he may not almost be said to have created, the criticism of art in England, while the other gave a new temper, if not exactly a new direction, to the criticism of literature ; and we shall have, in regard to periodicals, to observe the rise, in the first place of the weekly newspaper, and then of the daily, as competitors in strictly critical and literary work with the quarterly and monthly reviews, as well as some changes in these latter.

For just as we found that the first development of nineteenth century criticism coincided with or followed upon a new departure or development in periodicals, so we shall find that a similar change accompanied or caused changes in the middle of the century. Although the popularity of the quarterly and monthly reviews and magazines which had been headed respectively by the *Edinburgh* and *Blackwood* did not exactly wane, and though some of the most brilliant work of the middle of the century —

George Eliot's novels, Kingsley's and Froude's essays, and the like — appeared in them, the ever fickle appetite of readers seemed to desire something else in shape, something different in price, style, and form. Why this sort of change, which is perpetually recurring, should usually bring with it a corresponding change, and sometimes a corresponding improvement, of literary production, is more than any one can say, but the fact is not easily disputable.

On the present occasion the change took three successive forms — first, the raising, or rather restoring, of the weekly sixpenny critical newspaper to a higher pitch of popularity than it had ever held ; secondly, the cheapening and multiplying of the monthly magazines ; thirdly, the establishment of new monthly reviews, somewhat more resembling the old quarterlies than anything else, but with signed instead of anonymous articles.

The uprising of the weekly newspaper took shape in two remarkably different forms, represented respectively by *Household Words*, which Dickens started early in the fifties, and by the *Saturday Review*, which came a little later. The former might best be described as a monthly of the *Blackwood* and *London* kind cheapened, made more frequent in issue, and adjusted to a considerably lower and more popular standard of interest and culture — politics, moreover, being ostensibly though not quite really excluded. Dickens contributed to it largely himself. He received contributions from writers of established repute like Bulwer and Lever ; but he made his chief mark with the paper by breeding up a school of younger writers who wrote to his own pattern in fiction, miscellaneous essay, and other things. Wilkie Collins was the chief of these, but there were many others. In particular the periodical developed a sort of popular, jocular, and picturesque-descriptive manner of treating places, travels, ceremonies, and what not, which took the public fancy immensely. It was not quite original (for Leigh Hunt, Wainewright the murderer-miscellanist of the *London*, some of the *Blackwood* men, and others, had anticipated it to a certain extent), and it was vulgarised as regards all its models; but it was distinct and remarkable. The æsthetic and literary tone of *Household Words*, and of its successor *All the Year Round* to a somewhat less extent, was distinctly what is called Philistine; and though Dickens always had a moral purpose, he did not aim much higher than amusement that should not be morbid, and instruction of the middle-class diffusion-of-knowledge kind. But there was very little harm and much good to be said of *Household Words;* and if some of the imitations of it were far from being happy, its own popularity and that of its successor were very fairly deserved.

The aims, the character, and the success of the *Saturday Review* were of the most widely different character. It was less novel in form, for the weekly review was an established thing, and had at least two very respectable examples — the *Examiner*, which (under the Hunts, under Fonblanque, under Forster, and under the late Mr. Minto) had a brilliant, if never an extremely prosperous, career for three-quarters of the century, and the *Spectator*, which attained a reputation for unswerving honesty under the editorship of Mr. Rentoul, and has increased it under that of its present conductors. But both these were Liberal papers first of all; the *Saturday Review*, at first and accidentally Peelite, was really (throughout the nearly forty years during which it remained in the possession of the same family and was directed by a succession of editors each of whom had been trained under his predecessor) Independent Tory, or (to use a rather unhappy and now half-forgotten name) Liberal-Conservative. It never tied itself to party chariot-wheels, and from the first to the last of the period just referred to very distinguished writers of Liberal and Radical opinions contributed to it. But the general attitude of the paper during this time expressed that peculiar tone of mainly Conservative persiflage which has distinguished in literature the great line of writers beginning with Aristophanes. Its staff was, as a rule, recruited from the two Universities (though there was no kind of exclusion for the unmatriculated; as a matter of fact, neither of its first two editors was a son either of Oxford or

Cambridge), and it always insisted on the necessity of classical culture. It eschewed the private personality which had been too apt to disfigure newspapers of a satirical kind during the first half of the century; but it claimed and exercised to the full the privilege of commenting on every public writing, utterance, or record of the subjects of its criticism. It observed, for perhaps a longer time than any other paper, the salutary principles of anonymity (real as well as ostensible) in regard to the authorship of particular articles; and those who knew were constantly amused at the public mistakes on this subject.

Applying this kind of criticism, — perfectly fearless, on the whole fairly impartial, informed, human errors excepted, by a rather exceptionally high degree of intelligence and education, and above all keeping before it the motto, framed by its "sweet enemy" Thackeray, of being written "by gentlemen for gentlemen," — the *Saturday Review* quickly attained, and for many years held, the very highest place in English critical journalism as regards literature, in a somewhat less degree politics, and in a degree even greater the farrago of social and miscellaneous matters. By consent too general and too unbiassed to be questioned, it gave and maintained a certain tone of comment which prevailed for the seventh, eighth, and ninth decades of the century, and of which the general note may be said to have been a coolly scornful intolerance of ignorance and folly. There were those who accused it even in its palmiest days of being insufficiently positive and constructive; but on the negative side it was generally sound in intention, and in execution admirably thorough. It may sometimes have mishandled an honest man, it may sometimes have forgiven a knave; but it always hated a fool, and struck at him with might and with main.

The second change began with the establishment of the *Cornhill* and *Macmillan's Magazine*, two or three years later. There was no perceptible difference in the general scheme of these periodicals from that of the earlier ones, of which *Blackwood* and *Fraser* were the most famous; but their price was lowered from half a crown to a shilling, and the principle of signed articles and of long novels by famous names was adopted. The editorship of Thackeray in the *Cornhill*, with the contributions of Matthew Arnold and others, quickly gave a character to it; while *Macmillan's* could boast contributions from the Kingsleys, Henry and Charles, as well as from many others. From this time the monthly magazine, with the exception of *Blackwood*, found a shilling, which attempts have been recently made to lower to sixpence, its almost necessary tariff, while the equal necessity of addressing the largest possible audience made pure politics, with occasional exceptions, unwelcome in it. It is to the credit of the English magazines of this class, however, that they have never relinquished the tradition of serious literary studies. Many of the essays of Mr. Arnold appeared first either in one or the other of the two just mentioned; the *Cornhill* even ventured upon Mr. Ruskin's *Unto this Last;* and other famous books of a permanent character saw the light in these, in *Temple Bar,* started by Mr. Bentley, in the rather short-lived *St. Paul's,* of which Anthony Trollope was editor, and in others.

Whether the starting of the monthly " Review" as distinguished from the " Magazine," which came again a little later towards the middle or end of the sixties, be traceable to a parallel popularisation of the quarterly ideal — to the need for the political and "heavy" articles which the lightened monthlies had extruded — or to a mere imitation of the famous French *Revue des Deux Mondes,* is an academic question. The first of these new Reviews was the *Fortnightly,* which found the exact French model unsuitable to the meridian of Greenwich, and dropped the fortnightly issue, while retaining the title. It was followed by the *Contemporary,* the *Nineteenth Century,* and others. The exclusion of fiction in these was not invariable — the *Fortnightly,* in particular, has published many of Mr. Meredith's novels. But, as a rule, these reviews have busied themselves with more or less serious subjects, and have encouraged signed publication.

It would, of course, be impossible here to go through all, or even all the most noteworthy, of the periodicals of the century. We are dealing with classes, not individuals, and the only class yet to be noticed — daily newspapers falling out of our ken almost entirely — are those weekly newspapers which have eschewed politics altogether. The oldest and most famous of these is the *Athenæum*, which still flourishes after a life of nearly seventy years, while between forty and fifty years later the *Academy* was founded on the same general principles. But the *Athenæum* has always cleaved, as far as its main articles went, to the unsigned system, while the *Academy* started at a period which leant the other way. Of late years, too, criticism proper, that is to say, of letters and art, has played a larger and larger part in daily newspapers, some of which attempt a complete review of books as they appear, while others give reviews of selected works as full as those of the weeklies. If any distinct setting of example is necessary to be attributed in this case, the credit is perhaps mainly due to the original *Pall Mall Gazette*, an evening newspaper started in 1864 with one of the most brilliant staffs ever known, including many of the original *Saturday* writers and others.

The result of this combined opportunity and stimulus in so many forms has been that almost the whole of the critical work of the latter part of the century has passed through periodicals — that, except as regards Mr. Ruskin, a writer always indocile to editing, every one who will shortly be mentioned in this chapter has either won his spurs or exercised them in this kind, and that of the others, mentioned in other chapters and in connection with other subjects, a very small proportion can be said to have been entirely disdainful of periodical publication. At the very middle of the century, and later, the older Quarterlies were supported by men like John Wilson Croker, a survival of their first generation Nassau W. Senior, and Abraham Hayward, the last a famous talker and "diner-out." Other chief critics and essayists, besides Kingsley and Froude, were George Brimley, Librarian of Trinity College, Cambridge ; Henry Lancaster, a Balliol man and a Scotch barrister ; and Walter Bagehot, a banker, and not a member of either University. Brimley has left us what is perhaps the best appreciation of Tennyson in the time between the days when that poet was flouted or doubted by the usual critic, and those when he was accepted as a matter of course or cavilled at as a matter of paradox ; and Lancaster occupies pretty much the same position with regard to Thackeray. It is not so easy to single out any particular and distinguishing critical effort of Bagehot's, who wrote on all subjects, from Lombard Street to Tennyson, and from the *Coup d'État* (which he saw) to Browning. But his distinction of the poetical art of Wordsworth and that of these other poets as " pure, ornate, and grotesque " will suffice to show his standpoint, which was a sort of middle place between the classical and the Romantic. Bagehot wrote well, and possessed a most keen intelligence. Also to be classed here are Dr. John Brown of Edinburgh, the very agreeable author of *Horæ Subsecivæ*, and James Hannay, a brilliant journalist, a novelist of some merit and an essayist of more, and author of *A Course of English Literature* which, though a little popular and desultory, is full of sense and stimulus.

Most popular of all at the time was Sir Arthur Helps (1813–75), a country gentleman of some means and of the usual education, who took to a mixed life of official and literary work, did some useful work in regard to Spanish-American history, but acquired most popularity by a series of dialogues, mostly occupied by ethical and æsthetic criticism, called *Friends in Council*. This contains plenty of knowledge of books, touches of wit and humour, a satisfactory standard of morals and manners, a certain effort at philosophy, but suffers from the limitations of its date. In different ways enough — for he was as quiet as the other was showy — Helps was the counterpart of Kinglake, as exhibiting a certain stage in the progress of English culture during the middle of the century — a stage in which the Briton was considerably more alive to foreign things than he had been, had enlarged his sphere in many ways, and was at least striving to be cosmopolitan, but had lost insular strength without acquiring Continental suppleness.

Of the literary critic who attracted most public attention during this period, — the late Mr. Matthew Arnold, — considerable mention has already been made in dealing with his poetry, and biographical details must be looked for there. It will be remembered that Mr. Arnold was not very early a popular writer either as poet or prose-man, that his poetical exercises preceded by a good deal his prose, and that these latter were, if not determined, largely influenced by his appointment to the Professorship of Poetry at Oxford. He began, however, towards the end of the fifties and the beginning of the sixties, to be much noticed, not merely as the deliverer of lectures, but as the contributor of essays of an exceedingly novel, piquant, and provocative kind; and in 1865 these, or some of them, were collected and published under the title of *Essays in Criticism*. These *Essays* — nine in number, besides a character-istic preface — dealt ostensibly for the most part, if not wholly, with literary subjects, — "The Function of Criticism," "The Literary Influence of Academies," "The Guérins" (brother and sister), "Heine," "Pagan and Mediæval Religious Sentiment," "Joubert," "Spinoza," and "Marcus Aurelius," — but they extended the pur-port of the title of the first of them in the widest possible way. Mr. Arnold did not meddle with art, but he extended the province of literature outside of it even more widely than Mr. Ruskin did, and was, under a guise of pleasant scepticism, as dogmatic within the literary province as Mr. Ruskin in the artistic. It might almost be said that Mr. Arnold put himself forth, with a becoming attempt at modesty of manner, but with very uncompromising in-tentions, as "Socrates in London," questioning, probing, rebuking with ironical faithfulness, the British Philistine — a German term which he, though not the first to import it, made first popular — in literature, in newspapers, in manners, in politics, in philosophy. Foreign, and specially French, ways were sometimes directly, sometimes obliquely, held up as examples for our improvement; and the want of "ideas," the want of "light," the want of "culture," was dwelt on with a mixture of sorrow and satire. All this was couched in a very peculiar and (till its mannerism

2 C

became irritating) a very captivating style, which cannot be assigned to any single original, but which is a sort of compound or eclectic outcome of the old Oxford academic style as it may be seen at times in Newman, of French persiflage, and of some elements peculiar to Mr. Arnold himself. The strongest, though the most dangerous, of these elements was a trick of iterating words and phrases, sometimes exactly, sometimes with a very slight variation, which inevitably arrested attention, and perhaps at first produced conviction, on the principle formulated by a satirist (also of Oxford) a little later in the words —

What I tell you three times is true.

But besides and underneath all this flourish, all this wide-ranging scatter of sometimes rather hap-hazard arrows, there was a solid literary value in Mr. Arnold's method. As has been noticed earlier in this chapter, the literary essay of the best kind had somewhat gone off in England during the middle of the century, and the short, crisp criticisms which had appeared to take its place in weekly papers were almost necessarily exposed to grave faults and inadequacies. It was Mr. Arnold's great merit that by holding up Sainte-Beuve, from whom he had learnt much, and other French critics, and by urging successfully the revival of the practice of " introducing " editions of classics by a sound biographical and critical essay from the pen of some contemporary, he did much to cure this state of things. So that, whereas the *corpus* of English essay-criticism between 1800 and 1835 or thereabouts is admirable, and that of 1835 to 1865 rather thin and scanty, the last third of the century is not on such very bad terms as regards the first. And he gave example as well as precept, showing — though his subjects, as in the case of the Guérins, were sometimes most eccentrically selected — a great deal of critical acuteness, coupled, it may be, with something of critical " will-worship," with a capricious and unargued preference of this and rejection of that, but exhibiting wide if not extraordinarily deep reading, an honest enthusiasm for the best things, and above all a fascinating rhetoric.

The immediate effect of this remarkable book was good almost unmixedly on two of the three parties concerned. It was more than time for the flower of middle-class complacency, which horticulturists of all degrees, from Macaulay downwards, had successively striven to cultivate, and which was already overblown, to drop from its stalk ; and the whiff of pleasant scorn which Mr. Arnold directed at it was just the thing to puff it off. So the public, upon which he was never likely to produce too much effect, had reason to thank him for the effect that he did produce, or helped to produce. And on the critics too his effect, or the effect of which he was the symptom and voice, was also good, recalling them on the one hand from the dulness of the long reviews of the period, and on the other from the flippancy of the short, while inculcating a wider if not always a sounder comparison. Practically German poetry had nothing left to do in Mr. Arnold's day, and French had much : he thought just the other way, and reserved his encomium of France for its prose, in which it was drooping and failing. But this did not matter : it is the general scope of the critic's advice which is valuable in such cases, and the general scope of Mr. Arnold's was sound. On the third party, however, — himself, — the effect was a little disastrous. The reception which, after long waiting, he had attained, encouraged him not so much to continue in his proper sphere of literary criticism as to embark on a wide and far-ranging enterprise of general censure, which narrowed itself pretty rapidly to an attempt to establish undogmatic on the ruins of dogmatic Christianity. It would be very improper to discuss such an undertaking on the merits here ; or to criticise narrowly the series of singular treatises which absorbed (with exceptions, no doubt, such as the quaint sally of *Friendship's Garland* on the occasion of the Franco-German War) Mr. Arnold's energies for some fifteen or sixteen years. The titles — *Culture and Anarchy, God and the Bible, St. Paul and Protestantism, Literature and Dogma,* etc. — are well known. Of the contents it is enough to say that, apart from the popular audacity of their wit and the interesting spectacle of a pure man of letters confidently attacking thorny questions without any apparatus of special knowledge and study, they have not been generally thought quite worthy of their author. There are many brilliant passages in these books as writing, just as there are some astonishing lapses of taste and logic ; but the real fault of the whole set is that they are popular, that they undergo the very curse, of speaking without qualification and without true culture, which Mr. Arnold had himself so freely pronounced.

Fortunately, however, he never quite abandoned the old ways ; and in his last years he returned to them almost wholly. Nothing better of the kind (individual crotchets always excepted) has ever been written than his introductions to selected lives from Johnson's *Poets*, to Byron, to Shelley (the most crotchety and unsound of all), to Wordsworth (incomparably the best). He aided others ; and a collection of his purely or mainly literary work is still eagerly expected. Even this would be extremely unequal and open to exception here and there. But it would contain some of the very best things to be found in any English critic. And this after all, if not the absolutely highest, is one of the highest things that can be said of a critic, and one of the rarest. Undoubtedly the influence of Mr. Arnold did not make for good entirely. He discouraged — without in the least meaning to do so, and indeed meaning quite the contrary — seriousness, thoroughness, scholarship in criticism. He discouraged — without in the least meaning to do so, and indeed meaning quite the contrary — simplicity and unaffectedness in style. But he was a most powerful stimulus, and in some ways, if not in all, a great example. Some at least of the things he said were in the very greatest need of saying, and some of the ways in which he said them were inimitably charming. .

Contemporary with Mr. Arnold, and his complement in critical influence, was John Ruskin, the sole living author of whom it has seemed proper to treat here at length, and, since the death of Mr. Froude, the sole surviving man of letters of the first class who had published before the middle of the century. He was born in

1819 : he has given copious accounts of his family, of his youth at Denmark Hill, and so forth, and all the world knows that his father was a sherry merchant who, though he lived rather plainly, was able to give his son an early and plentiful indulgence in that Continental travel which had so much to do with developing his genius. Mr. Ruskin's education was oddly combined ; for, after going to no school, he was sent to Christ Church as a gentleman-commoner and took his degree in 1842, having gained the Newdigate three years earlier. He wrote a good deal of other verse in his early years, — and he made himself a not inconsiderable draughtsman. But his real vocation was as little the practice of art as it was the practice of poetry. As early as 1843 there appeared, by "a Graduate of Oxford," the first volume of the famous *Modern Painters*, which ran to five large volumes, which covered seventeen years in its original period of publication, and which was very largely altered and remodelled by the author during and after this period. But Mr. Ruskin by no means confined his energies before 1860 to this extensive task. The *Seven Lamps of Architecture* (1849), and (between 1851 and 1853) the larger *Stones of Venice*, did for architecture what the companion work did for painting. The Præ-Raphaelite move-ment of the middle of the century found in Mr. Ruskin an ardent encomiast and literary apostle, and between 1850 and 1860 he delivered divers lectures, the text of which — *Architect-ure and Painting* (1854), *Political Economy of Art* (1858) — was subsequently published in as elaborately magnificent a style as his other works. As *Modern Painters* drew to its close he became prolific of more numerous and shorter works, generally with some-what fantastic but agreeable titles — *Unto this Last* (1861), *Munera Pulveris* (1862), *Sesame and Lilies* (1865), *The Cestus of Aglaia* (1865), *The Ethics of the Dust* (1866), *The Crown of Wild Olive* (1866), *Time and Tide by Wear and Tyne* (1867), *The Queen of the Air* (1869), *Aratra Pentelici* and *The Eagle's Nest* (1872), *Ariadne Florentina* (1873), *Proserpina* and *Deucalion* (1875 *seq.*), *St. Mark's Rest* and *Præterita* (1885). Not a few of these were issued in parts and numbers, but Mr. Ruskin's bulkiest and most characteristic venture in this kind was *Fors Clavigera*, which was published at irregular intervals from 1871 to 1884. He has written many other things even in book form, besides innumerable essays and letters, some of which have been collected in two gatherings — *Arrows of the Chace* and *On the Old Road*.

Two things are mainly perceptible in this immense and at first sight rather bewildering production. The first, the most disputable and probably the least important, though the most at the author's heart, is a vast, fluctuating, but on the whole pretty coherent body of doctrine in reference to Art. Up to Mr. Ruskin's day, æsthetics had been little cultivated in England, and such handlings of the subject as existed — Burke's, Adam Smith's, Alison's, and a few others — were of a jejune and academic character. Even writers of distinct literary genius and of great taste for the matter, who had not resided abroad long, such as Hazlitt, much more such as Charles Lamb and Hartley Coleridge, betray the want of range and practice in examples. Even the valuable and interesting work of Mrs. Jameson (1794–1860) was more occupied with careful arrangement and attractive illustration than with original theory; and, well as she wrote, her *Characteristics of Shakespeare's Women* (1832) is perhaps more important as literature than the series of volumes — *Sacred and Legendary Art*, etc. — which she executed between 1845 and her death. The sense of the endless and priceless illustration of the best art which was provided by Gothic domestic and ecclesiastical architecture was only wakening; as for painting, the examples publicly visible in England were very few, and even private collections were mostly limited to one or two fashionable schools — Raphael and his successors, the later Low Country schools, the French painters in the grand style, and a few Spaniards.

Strongly impressed by the Romantic revival (he has all his life been the staunchest of Sir Walter's devotees), a passionate lover of Gothic architecture both at home and abroad, and early drawn both to the romantic nature-painting of Turner and the gorgeous

colouring of the early Italian schools, Mr. Ruskin heralded Art
with a passion of which eighteenth century " gusto " had had no
notion. But he was by no means satisfied with heralding Art
alone. Anathematising at once the doctrine that utility is beauty
— that beauty is utility he would always have cheerfully admitted
— and the doctrine that the beautiful is not necessarily connected
either with utility, with goodness, or with truth, he from the first
and to the last has endeavoured to work ethics and æsthetics into
a sort of single texture of warp and woof respectively, pushing his
endeavours into the most multiform, the most curious, and it must
be owned sometimes the most grotesque ramifications and ex-
tremities. But he was not satisfied with this bold attempt at the
marriage of two things sometimes deemed hostile to, and generally
held to be independent of, one another. He must needs be bolder
still, and actually attempt to ally with Art, if not to subject to her,
the youngest, the most rebellious, and, as it might seem, the most
matter-of-fact and utilitarian of all the sciences — that of Political
Economy. As we have seen, he had brought the subjects together
in lectures pretty early in his career, and he developed the combination further in the eccentric book called *Unto this Last*,
originally published in the *Cornhill Magazine* as noted above. In
this Æsthetics and Economics combined took a distinctly Socialist
turn ; and as England was under the very fullest dominion of the
Liberal middle-class regime, with its belief in *laissez-faire* and in
supply-and-demand, Mr. Ruskin was not a little pooh-poohed. It
would be improper here to attack or to defend his views, but it is
part of the historian's duty to say that, for good or for ill, they
have, though in forms different from his and doubtless by no means
always meeting his approval, made constant headway, and that
much legislation and still more agitation on the extreme Liberal
side, and not there only, may be said to represent, with very slight
transformation, Ruskinian doctrine applied, now and then, to very
anti-Ruskinian purposes.

With regard to æsthetics proper, it might be contended, without too much rashness, that the history of Ruskinism has not been

different ; but to some observers it seems to have described rather
a curve than a steady ascent. After being, between 1840 and 1860,
laughed at, despised, attacked all at once, Mr. Ruskin found his
influence as an art teacher rise steadily during the seventh decade
of the century, and attain its highest point about the close
thereof, when he was made Slade Professor in his own university,
and caused young Oxford to do many fantastic things. But, as
always happens, the hour of triumph was the hour, not, perhaps,
of downfall, but of opposition and renegation. Side by side with
Mr. Ruskin's own theories had risen the doctrine of Art-for-Art's
sake, which, itself as usual half truth and half nonsense, cut at
the very root of Ruskinism. On the other hand, the practical
centre of art-schools had shifted from Italy and Germany to
Paris and its neighbourhood, where morality has seldom been able
to make anything like a home ; and the younger painters and
sculptors, full of realism, impressionism, and what not, would
have none of the doctrines which, as a matter of fact, stood in
immediate relationship of antecedence to their own. Lastly, it
must be admitted that the extreme dogmatism on all the subjects of the encyclopedia in which Mr. Ruskin had seen fit to
indulge, was certain to provoke a revolt. But with the substance
of Ruskinism, further than is necessary for comprehension, we are
not concerned.

Yet there are not many things in the English nineteenth
century with which a historian is more concerned than with the
style of the deliverance of these ideas. We have noticed in
former chapters — we shall have to notice yet more in the conclusion — the attempts made in the years just preceding and
immediately following Mr. Ruskin's birth, by Landor, by De
Quincey, by Wilson, and by others in the direction of ornate, of —
as some call it — *flamboyant* English prose. All the tendencies
thus enumerated found their crown and flower in Mr. Ruskin
himself. That later the crowns and the flowers were, so to speak,
divided, varied, and multiplied by later practitioners, some of
whom will presently be noticed, while more are still alive, is quite

true. But in 1895 it is not very unsafe to prophesy that the *flamboyant* style of the nineteenth century will be found by posterity to have reached its highest exposition in prose with Mr. Ruskin himself.

Like all great prose styles — and the difference between prose and poetry here is very remarkable — this was born nearly full grown. The instances of comparison in those who have tried both harmonies are rare; those in poets only are delusive and uncertain. But with the three greatest poets of England who have also been great prose writers, Milton, Dryden, Shelley, the assertion that the distinctive quality of their prose developed itself earlier than the distinctive quality of their verse is only disputable in the case of Milton. And Milton, as it happened, wrote prose and verse in manners more nearly approaching each other than any one on record. Mr. Ruskin has not been a poet, except in extreme minority; but he has been a great prose writer from the first. It is almost inconceivable that good judges can ever have had any doubt about him. It is perfectly — it is, indeed, childishly easy to pick faults, even if matter be kept wholly out of sight. In Mr. Ruskin's later books a certain tendency to conversational familiarity sometimes mocks those, and not those only, who hold to the tradition of dignified and *ex cathedra* pronouncement; in his earlier, and in all, it is possible for Momus to note an undue floridness, an inclination to blank verse in prose, tricks and manners of this or that kind unduly exuberant and protuberant.

But when all these things have been allowed for to the very fullest, what an enormous advance there is on anything that had gone before ! The ornate prose writers of the seventeenth century had too frequently regarded their libraries only ; they had seldom looked abroad to the vast field of nature, and of art other than literary art. The ornate writers of the eighteenth, great as they were, had been as afraid of introspection as of looking outwards, and had spun their webs, so far as style and ornament were concerned, of words only. Those of the early nineteenth had been conscious of revolt, and, like all conscious revolters, had not possessed their souls in sufficient quietness and confidence. Landor, half a classic and half a Romantic, had been too much the slave of phrase, — though of a great phrase. Wilson, impatient in everything, had fluctuated between grandeur and *galimatias*, bathos and bad taste; De Quincey, at times supreme, had at others simply succumbed to "rigmarole." Mr. Ruskin had a gift of expression equal to the best of these men; and, unlike them, he had an immense, a steady, a uniform group of models before him. Indulge as he might in extravagance, there were always before him, as on a vastly extended dais set before the student, the glories of nature and of art, the great personalities and productions of the great artists. He had seen, and he could see (which is a different thing), the perennial beauties of mountain and cloud, of tree, and sea, and river; the beauties long, if not perennial, of architecture and painting. A man may say foolish things, — Mr. Ruskin has said plenty; but when he has Venice and Amiens and Salisbury, the Alps and the Jura and the Rhine, Scott and Wordsworth, Turner and Lionardo, always silently present before his mind's eye, he can never, if he is a man of genius, go wholly wrong. And he can never go more than a little wrong when he is furnished by his genius with such a gift of expression as Mr. Ruskin has had.

For this gift of expression was such as had never been seen before, and such as, for all the copying and vulgarising of it, has never been seen since. It is a commonplace of literary history that description, as such, is not common or far advanced in the earlier English prose. We find Gray, far on in the eighteenth century, trying to describe a sunrise, and evidently vexed at the little "figure it makes on paper." Then the tourists and the travellers of the end of that age made valiant but not always well directed efforts to induce "it" to make a figure on paper. Then came the experts or student-interpreters in ornate prose who have been mentioned. And then came Mr. Ruskin. "Never so before and never quite so since," must be the repeated verdict. The first sprightly runnings in these, as in other kinds, are never surpassed. Kingsley, an almost contemporary, Mr. Swinburne, a younger rival, have come near; others have done creditably in imitation; none have equalled, and certainly none have surpassed. Let the reader read the "Wave Studies" in the first volume of *Modern Painters*, more than fifty years old; the "Pine Forest in the Jura," almost forty; the "Angel of the Sea," fully thirty-five, and say, if he has any knowledge of English literature, whether there had been anything like any of these before. Shelley, perhaps, in some of his prose had gone near it. Shelley was almost as great a prose writer as he was a poet. No one else could even be mentioned.

Nor was it mere description, great as Mr. Ruskin is in that, which differentiated him so strongly. He is a bad arguer; but his arguments are couched in rhetoric so persuasive that the very critics who detect his fallacies would almost consent to forfeit the power of detecting, if they could acquire that of constructing, such delightful paralogisms. His crotchets of all sorts are sometimes merely childish, and not even always or very often original; for, like all fertile minds, he never could receive any seed of thought from another but it bore plant and fruit at once. But the statement of them is at its best so captivating that weaklings may pardonably accept, and strong men may justly tolerate, the worthless kernel for the sake of the exquisite husk. Few men have less of the true spirit of criticism than Mr. Ruskin, for in his enthusiasm he will compass sea and land to exalt his favourite, often for reasons which are perfectly invalid; and in his appreciation he is not to be trusted at all, having a feminine rather than a masculine faculty of unreasoned dislike. But praise or blame, argue or paralogise as he may, the golden beauty of his form redeems his matter in the eyes of all but those who are unhappy enough not to see it.

That his influence has been wholly good no one can say. There is scarcely a page of him that can be safely accepted on the whole as matter, and the unwary have accepted whole volumes;

his form is peculiarly liable to abuse in the way of imitation, and it has actually been abused to nausea and to ridicule. But this is not his fault. There is so little subtlety about Mr. Ruskin that he can hardly deceive even an intelligent child when he goes wrong. There is so much genius about him that the most practised student of English can never have done with admiration at the effects that he produces, after all these centuries, with the old material and the old tools. He is constantly provocative of adverse, even of severe criticism ; of half the heresies from which he has suffered — not only that of impressionism — he was himself the unconscious heresiarch. And yet the more one reads him the more one feels inclined almost to let him go uncriticised, to vote him the primacy in nineteenth-century prose by simple acclamation.

Richard (or as his full name ran), John Richard Jefferies, occupies, though an infinitely smaller and a considerably lower place than Mr. Ruskin's, yet one almost as distinctly isolated in a particular department of æsthetic description. The son of a farmer at Coate, in North Wiltshire, and born in November 1848, he began journalism at eighteen, and was a contributor to the *North Wilts Herald* till he was nearly thirty. Then he went to London, and in 1878 published some sketches (previously contributed to the *Pall Mall Gazette*) under the title of *The Game-Keeper at Home*. These, though not much bought, were very much admired ; and Jefferies was encouraged to devote himself to work of the same kind, which he varied with curious and not very vigorous semi-philosophic speculations and attempts at downright novels (a kind which he had also tried in his youth). Unfortunately the peculiar sort of descriptive writing in which he excelled was not very widely called for, could hardly under the most favourable circumstances have brought in any great sums of money, and was peculiarly liable to depreciate when written to order. It does not appear that Jefferies had the rare though sometimes recorded power of accommodating himself to ordinary newspaper hack-work, while reserving himself for better things now and then; and finally, he had not been long in London before painful and ultimately fatal disease added to his troubles. He died in August 1887, being not yet forty. A burst of popularity followed; his books, *The Game-Keeper at Home, Wild Life in a Southern Country, The Amateur Poacher, Round about a Great Estate*, etc., none of which had been printed in large numbers, were sold at four or five times their published price; and, worst of all, cheap imitations of his style began to flood the newspapers. Nay, the yet later results of this imitation was that another reaction set in, and even Jefferies' own work was once more pooh-poohed.

The neglect, the over-valuation, and the shift back to injustice, were all examples of the evils which beset literature at the present time, and which the much-blamed critic is almost powerless to cause or cure. In other days Jefferies was quite as likely to have been insufficiently rewarded at first by the public; but he would then have had no temptation to over-write himself, or try alien tasks, and he would have stood a very good chance of a pension, or a sinecure, or an easy office in church or state, on one or other of which he might have lived at ease and written at leisure. Nothing else could really have been of service to him, for his talent, though rare and exquisite, was neither rich nor versatile. It consisted in a power of observing nature more than Wordsworthian in delicacy, and almost Wordsworthian in the presence of a sentimental philosophic background of thought. Unluckily for Jefferies, his philosophic background was not like Wordsworth's, clear and cheerful, but wholly vague and partly gloomy. Writing, too, in prose not verse, and after Mr. Ruskin, he attempted an exceedingly florid style, which at its happiest was happy enough, but which was not always at that point, and which when it was not was apt to become trivial or tawdry, or both. It is therefore certain that his importance for posterity will dwindle, if it has not already dwindled, to that given by a bundle of descriptive selections. But these will occupy a foremost place on their particular shelf, the shelf at the head of which stand Gilbert White and Gray.

Mr. Arnold, it has been said, abstained almost entirely from dealing with art. Mr. Ruskin, who has abstained from dealing with nothing, did not abstain from criticism of literature, but his utterances in it have been more than usually *obiter dicta*. Yet we must take the two together if we are to understand the most powerful influence and the most flourishing school of criticism, literary and other, which has existed for the last thirty years. This school may be said to halt in a way between purely literary and generally æsthetic handling, and when it can to mix the two. Most of its scholars — men obviously under the influence both of Arnold and of Ruskin, either in submission or in revolt, are alive, and we reason not of them. But, as it happens, the two most famous, one of whom was a prose writer, pure and simple, the other a copious artist in prose and verse, have died recently and call for judgment. These were Walter Horatio Pater and John Addington Symonds.

The first-named was born in 1839, and went to Oxford, where he was elected to a fellowship at Brasenose. He spent the whole of the rest of his life either at that college or in London, practising no profession, competing for no preferment, and for many years at least producing literature itself with extreme sparingness. It was in 1873 that Mr. Pater first collected a volume of *Studies in the History of Renaissance*, which attracted the keenest attention both as to its manner and as to its matter. The point of view, which was that of an exceedingly refined and carefully guarded Hedonism, was in a way and at least in its formulation novel. Mr. Pater did not meddle with any question of religion; he did not (though there were some who scented immorality in his attitude) offend directly any ethical prejudice or principle. But he laid it down explicitly in some places, implicitly throughout, that the object of life should be to extract to the utmost the pleasure of living in the more refined way, and expressly and especially the pleasure to be derived from education and art. The indebtedness of this both to the Arnoldian and Ruskinian creeds, its advance (in the

main a legitimate advance) on the former, and its heretical deviation from the development of the latter, require no comment.
But this propaganda, if so violent a word may be used, of Mr.
Pater's placid creed, called to aid a most remarkable style — a style
of the new kind, lavish of adjective and the *mot de lumière*, but
not exceedingly florid, and aiming especially at such an arrangement of the clause, the sentence, and the paragraph, such a
concerted harmony of cadence and symphony, as had not been
deliberately tried before in prose. The effects which it produced
on different tastes were themselves sufficiently different. Some
found the purport too distasteful to give a dispassionate attention
to the presentment ; others disliked the manner itself as formal,
effeminate, and " precious." But there were others who, while
recognising the danger of excess in this direction, thought and
think that a distinct and remarkable experiment had been made
in English prose, and that the best examples of it deserved a place
with the best examples of the ornater styles at any previous time
and in any other kind.

Mr. Pater was not tempted by such popularity as his book
received to hasten publication ; indeed it was understood that
after beginning to print a second collection of Essays, he became
dissatisfied with them, and caused the type to be broken up.
But the advance of so-called Æstheticism was too strong an
invitation, and prepared for him too large and eager an audience,
so that the last decade of his life saw several books, *Marius the Epicurean, Imaginary Portraits, Appreciations,* while others appeared
posthumously. Of these the first-named is unquestionably the
best and most important. Although Greek had been the indispensable — almost the cardinal — principle in Mr. Pater's own
literary development, he had been so strongly affected by modern
thought and taste, that he could hardly recover a dispassionate
view of the older classics. *Imaginary Portraits,* an attempt at
constructive rather than critical art, required qualities which
he did not possess, and even made him temporarily forget his
impeccable style : *Appreciations,* good in itself, was inferior to

the first book. But *Marius the Epicurean* far excelled all these. It, too, took the form of fiction, but the story went for so little in it that deficiencies therein were not felt. The book was in effect a reconstruction, partly imaginative, but still more critical, of a period with which Mr. Pater was probably more in sympathy than with any other, even the Renaissance itself, to wit the extremely interesting and strangely modern period when classicism and modernity, Christianity and Paganism, touched and blended in the second century after Christ after the fashion revealed to us in the works of Apuleius most of all, of Lucian to some extent, and of a few others. Mr. Pater indeed actually introduced the philosopher-novelist of Madaura in the book, though he was not the hero; and his own peculiar style proved itself admirably suited to the period and subject, whether in description and conversation, or in such translation or paraphrase as that of the famous and exquisite *Pervigilium Veneris*.

For this style, however, in perfection we must still go back to the *Studies of the Renaissance*, which is what Mr. Arnold liked to call a *point de repère*. The style, less exuberant, less far-reaching and versatile, and, if any one pleases to say so, less healthy than Mr. Ruskin's, is much more chastened, finished, and exquisite. It never at its best neglects the difference between the rhythm of prose and the metre of verse; if it is sometimes, and indeed usually, wanting in simplicity, it is never overloaded or gaudy. The words are picked; but they are seldom or never, as has been the case with others, not only picked but wrenched, not only adjusted to a somewhat unusual society and use, but deliberately forced into uses and societies wholly different from those to which readers are accustomed. Above all, no one, it must be repeated, has ever surpassed, and scarcely any one has ever equalled Mr. Pater in deliberate and successful architecture of the prose-paragraph — in what may, for the sake of a necessary difference, be called the scriptorial in opposition to the oratorical manner. He may fall short of the poetic grandeur of Sir Thomas Browne, of the phantasmagoric charm of

De Quincey at his rare best, of the gorgeous panoramas of Mr. Ruskin. But his happiest paragraphs are like *flamboyant* chantries, not imposing, not quite supreme in quality, but in their own kind showing wonderful perfection of craftsmanship.

Of the same school, though a less exact and careful practitioner in it, was John Addington Symonds, who was born in Bristol on the 5th of October 1840, and died at Rome on 19th April 1893. He was the son of a famous doctor whose name figures often in literary history, inasmuch as he made Clifton a frequent resort for persons of consumptive tendencies. Mr. Symonds himself lived there for a great part of his life. Unfortunately the disease which his father had combated revenged itself upon him ; and it was only by spending the greater part of his later years at Davos that he staved it off as long as he did. Educated at Harrow and at Balliol, a Fellow of Magdalen, and succeeding tolerably young to an affluent fortune, Mr. Symonds was able to indulge his tastes, literary and other, pretty much as he chose. The result was fortunate in one way, unfortunate in another. He could hardly have made a living by literature, in which though an eager worker he was a thorough dilettante. But if he had been at less liberty to write what and howsoever he pleased, he might or rather would have been obliged to compress and chasten the extreme prolixity and efflorescence of his style.

His largest work, the *History of the Renaissance in Italy*, is actually one of great value in information, thought, and style ; but its extreme redundance cannot be denied, and has indeed already necessitated a sort of boiling down into an abstract. Both in prose essays (which he wrote in great numbers, chiefly on Greek or Renaissance subjects) and in verse (where he was not so successful as in prose) Mr. Symonds was one of the most characteristic and copious members of the rather foolishly named "æsthetic" school of the last third of the century, the school which, originally deriving more or less from Mr. Ruskin, more and more rejected the ethical side of his teaching. But Mr. Symonds, who had been very much under the influence of Professor Jowett, had philosophical

velleities, which have become more generally known than they
once were through the interesting biography published after his
death by Mr. Horatio Brown. But for the redundance above
mentioned, which is all pervading with him both in thought and
style, and which once suggested to a not unfriendly critic the remark that he should like " to squeeze him like a sponge," Symonds
would probably or rather certainly occupy a much higher place than
he has held or ever will hold. For his appreciation both of books
and of nature was intense, and his faculty of description abundant.
But the *ventosa et enormis loquacitas* of his style was everywhere,
so that even selection would be hard put to it to present him really
at his best.

William Minto, who was born in 1846 and died in 1893,
Professor of Logic and English Literature at Aberdeen, showed
fewer marks of the joint direction of " æsthetic " criticism to
art and letters than these two, and had less distinct and
original literary talent. He had his education mainly at
Aberdeen itself, where he was born and died; but he made
a short visit to Oxford. Subsequently taking to journalism,
he became editor of the *Examiner*, and considerably raised the
standard of literary criticism in that periodical, while after quitting
it he wrote for some time on the *Daily News*. His appointment
to the professorship enabled him to devote himself entirely to
literature, and he produced some novels, the best of which was
The Crack of Doom. He had much earlier executed two extremely
creditable books, one on *English Prose*, and one on part of the History of English verse, the only drawbacks to which were a rather
pedagogic and stiff arrangement; he was a frequent contributor
to the *Encyclopædia Britannica*, and after his death some of his
professorial Lectures on the Georgian era were published, but
without his final revision. The strongest side of Minto's criticism
lay in his combination of sufficiently sound and wide knowledge
of the past with a distinct and rather unusual sympathy with the
latest schools of literature as they rose. He was untainted by
the florid style of his day, but wrote solidly and well. If it were

necessary to look for defects in his work they would probably be found in a slight deficiency of comparative estimate, and in a tendency to look at things rather from the point of view of modern than from that of universal criticism. But this tendency was not in him, as it so often is, associated with ignorance or presumptuous judgment.

CHAPTER X

THE remarks which were made at the beginning of the chapter on Philosophy and Theology apply with increasing force to the present chapter; indeed, they need to be restated in a much more stringent and exclusive form. To give some history of English philosophy and theology in the nineteenth century, by noticing its literary expression, was possible, though it had to be done, so to speak, in shorthand. To do the same thing with science, or even with what is technically called scholarship, would be simply impossible. Much of their expression is hardly susceptible of literary form at all, hardly any ever receives such form, while the subdivision of the branches of physical science is now so great and their shadow so wide that no systematic sketch of them is to be thought of. It is only possible to mention a few distinguished writers, writers who would have been distinguished whatever their subject, but who happen to have devoted themselves, solely or mainly, to scientific writing, or to classical criticism and philology.

A curious independent study might be made of the literary gradations of classical scholarship. In the Middle Ages, though the complete ignorance of the classics, once imagined as prevailing, has been shown to be a figment, scarcely anybody could claim to be a scholar. During the Renaissance almost every man of letters had necessarily some tinge of scholarship, and some of the greatest in its earlier period, such as Erasmus, were scholars first of all. The growth of vernacular literature, the constant increase and subdivision of subjects, and the advance in minute study of the Greek and Latin languages, brought about an inevitable cleavage, and from the seventeenth century onwards scholarship became an independent profession or vocation. For some considerable time, however, it was the almost indispensable novitiate of a literary career, and the tradition that a scholar must be first applied to, for no matter what literary work, was still potent in the times of Salmasius, and cannot be said to have been discredited in those of Bentley, who would undoubtedly have been as formidable in purely political or general controversy as he was on *Phalaris* or on his own private interests. The eighteenth century, however, saw the divorce nearly completed, and by the period of our present volume it was an accomplished fact.

Even then, however, though for men of letters it was not customary to turn first to scholars, scholars had not ceased to be men of letters, and philology (or the mere study of language, as apart from literature) had not absorbed them.

During that part of our period which is still concerned with the last century, there were many excellent scholars in England, but perhaps only three — two of whom as scholars were of no great account — who make much figure in purely literary history. Jacob Bryant (1715–1804), an odd person of uncritical judgment but great learning, who belongs more to the last volume than to the present, devoted himself chiefly to mythology, a subject which had not yet attracted general interest, and which was treated by him and others in a somewhat unhistorical manner. Gilbert Wakefield (1756–1801) was one of the characteristic figures of the Revolutionary time. He was a Cambridge man, and took orders, but left the church, became a violent Jacobin, and went to prison for a seditious libel. He was one of those not very uncommon men who, personally amiable, become merely vixenish when they write : and his erudition was much more extensive than sound. But he edited several classical authors, not wholly without intelligence and scholarship, and his *Silva Critica*, a sort of *variorum* commentary from profane literature on the Bible, was the forerunner, at least in scheme, of a great deal of work which has been seen since.

A very different person from these in scholarly attainments, in natural gifts, and (it must unfortunately be added) in personal respectability, was Richard Porson, who is generally bracketed with Bentley as the greatest of English scholars, not of our own day, and who might have been one of the most brilliant of men of letters. He was born in Norfolk on Christmas Day 1759, of low station, but was well educated by the parson of the parish, and sent to Eton by a neighbouring squire. In 1779 he went to Trinity College, Cambridge, obtained a scholarship, did brilliantly in University contests and became fellow in 1782. Although he was almost a boy the genius of his papers in scholarship attracted notice at home and abroad, and he made some excursions into general literature wherein, as in his recorded conversations, he showed epigrammatic wit of the first rank. He lost his fellowship because he would not take orders; but was made Regius Professor of Greek, an appointment which unluckily was then, in both Universities, almost honorary as regards income. The Whig party accepted his partisanship, but had no opportunity of rewarding it, and after receiving the Librarianship of the London Institution in Moorfields, he died of apoplexy in 1808. He possessed in almost the highest degree that power of divination, based on accurate knowledge, which distinguishes the scholar, and it is, as has been said, nearly certain that he would have been a brilliant writer in English on any subject he chose to take up. But he was a hopeless drunkard, an offensive sloven, rude and aggressive in society — in short a survival of the Grub Street pattern of the century of his birth. This period, which was that of Burney, Elmsley, Gaisford, and other scholars, robust but not very literary (except in the case of Elmsley, who was a contributor both to the *Edinburgh* and the *Quarterly Reviews*), was succeeded by one in which the English Universities did not greatly distinguish themselves in this department. Gaisford indeed lived till 1855 at

Oxford, and Cambridge produced among other respectable scholars the already mentioned Malden and George Long (1800–79), a Lancashire man, who went to Trinity, distinguished himself greatly, but found such preferment as he met with outside his university, in America, at University College, London, and elsewhere. Long was a great diffusion-of-useful-knowledge man, and edited the *Penny Cyclopædia*: but he did more germane work later in editing the *Bibliotheca Classica*, an unequal but at its best excellent series of classics, and in dealing with the great stoics Marcus Aurelius and Epictetus. He was also one of the mainstays of the most important enterprise of the middle of the century in classical scholarship, the *Classical Dictionaries* edited by the late Sir William Smith and published by Mr. Murray ; and he wrote an extensive but not extraordinarily valuable *Decline of the Roman Republic*. Long appears to have been one of those men who, with great ability, vast knowledge, and untiring industry, somehow or other miss their proper place, whether by fault or fate it is hard to say.

About 1860 three remarkable persons illustrated scholarship in the Universities of Oxford, Cambridge, and Edinburgh respectively, with a combination of literary and linguistic knowledge which had been growing rarer up to their time, and which has grown rarer still since.

The Oxford representative was John Conington, who was born at Boston on 10th August 1825. He went to Rugby and to Magdalen College, Oxford, whence he migrated to University College, and there obtained a fellowship, making nearly a clean sweep of the chief University prizes meanwhile. He became in 1854 the first Professor of Latin, and held the post till his death in 1869. He edited Virgil, Æschylus (part) and Persius, translated Horace, Homer, and Virgil, and did a certain amount of miscellaneous literary work. He was neither a very exact nor a very great scholar : his scholarship indeed took rather the character of that of foreign nations, other than Germany, than the dogged minuteness of German, or the large but solid strength of English study of the classics. But he was an exceedingly stimulating professor ; and coming at the time when it did, his work was valuable as a reminder that the classics are live literature, and not so much dead material for science.

Hugh Andrew Johnstone Munro, a native of Elgin, where he was born in 1819, a Shrewsbury boy and a scholar and fellow of Trinity College, Cambridge, who became Professor of Latin there in 1869 and died in 1882, was an incomparably greater verbal scholar than Conington, and may fairly be said to have taken up the torch of Bentley and Porson. His great edition (with a less great translation) of Lucretius, his work on Horace and Catullus, and his scattered papers, all come up to a very high standard ; and in the delightful art of Greek and Latin composition in verse, where England has long stood paramount, and which, since she has abandoned it, remains uncultivated throughout Europe, he was almost supreme. But Munro, though he never surrendered wholly to the philological heresy, was affected thereby ; and some of his Lucretian readings were charged with a deficiency in ear such as that with which he justly reproached his German predecessors.

The most strictly literary of the three has yet to be mentioned. William Young Sellar, born near Golspie in the same year as Conington, was educated at the Edinburgh Academy, at the University of Glasgow, and (as a Snell exhibitioner) at Balliol. After holding an Oriel fellowship for some years, and doing professorial or assistant-professorial work at Durham and St. Andrews, he became in 1863 Professor of Humanity at Edinburgh, and remained so till his death in 1890. In the year of his election to the professorship appeared his *Roman Poets of the Republic*, quite the best book of its kind existing in English ; and this was followed up by others on Virgil, Horace, Tibullus, and Propertius — good, but less good, the mannered correctness of the Augustans evidently appealing to the author less than the more strictly poetic excellence of Lucretius and Catullus. Attempts, too few but noteworthy, have since been made to handle classical

literature in the style of the *Roman Poets of the Republic*, but
it has never been surpassed, and it has very seldom been
equalled.

On another scheme and in other circumstances names like
those of Kennedy and Shilleto, of Linwood and Burges, of Monk
and Blomfield, would cry for admission here, but as it is they
must be ruled out. And it is not possible to widen the scope
much, so as to take in some eminent students who have given
not unliterary expression to the study of languages and subjects
other than the classical. It has indeed been a constantly increasing feature of the century that fresh studies — Ægyptology,
the study of the Semitic languages, the study of the older forms
not merely of English but of the other modern tongues, the
enormous range of knowledge opened to Englishmen, and as
it were forced on them by our possession of India and our commerce and connection with other nations of the East, as well as
the newer subjects of comparative mythology, folk-lore, and the
like, all more or less offshoots of what may be generally termed
scholarship, have been added to the outer range of the Humanities.
Some of these appeal to very few, none of them to more than
few persons ; and literature, in its best description if not exactly
definition, is that which does or should appeal to all persons
of liberal education and sympathies. Yet one exponent of these
studies (and of more than one of them) must have a place
here, as well for the more than professionally encyclopædic
character of his knowledge as for his intellectual vigour and his
services to letters.

William Robertson Smith was born in 1846, and died in
1894. A native of Aberdeenshire, the son of a Free Kirk
minister, and educated at Aberdeen and elsewhere, he became
Professor of Hebrew in the Free Church College of that city, and
for some years discussed his subject, in the manner of the
Germans, without hindrance. His articles in the *Encyclopædia
Britannica*, however, gave offence, and after much controversy he
was deprived of his chair in 1881. Two years later, however, he

was made Lord Almoner's Professor of Arabic at Cambridge, where he also became Fellow of Christ's and University Librarian. And from a contributor he proceeded to be first assistant-editor and then editor in chief of the *Encyclopædia*. His health, never very strong, became worse and worse, and he finally succumbed to a complication of diseases. It was understood that the theological scandal connected with his name was anything but a pleasure to him, and the justice of it does not concern us; but his repute as an Orientalist is uncontested. Besides works directly bearing on the Bible, he wrote two important books on *Kinship and Marriage in Early Arabia* and on *The Religion of the Semites*. He was at least as remarkable for general as for special learning, and if not actually a great man of letters, had a knowledge of literature rivalled by few of his contemporaries.

To turn to physical science, Sir Humphry Davy, a great chemist and no mean writer, was born at Penzance in December 1778. His father was a wood-carver, but he himself was apprenticed to a surgeon-apothecary, and betook himself seriously to chemistry. Fortunately for him, Dr. Beddoes, the father of the poet, a physician of great repute at Clifton, took him to be his assistant there, and Davy, in his twentieth year, not only had much improved opportunities of study, but made valuable friends, both among the persons of rank who then frequented Clifton for health, and among the literary society of which Coleridge and Southey were then the ornaments in Bristol. This part of his sojourn was noteworthy for his experiments with nitrous oxide ("laughing gas"). These attracted a great deal of attention, and in 1801, being then barely twenty-three, he was appointed to a lectureship in the Royal Institution, London. His appointment was the beginning of a series of brilliant lectures in the same place during almost the whole of the century, first by Davy himself, then by his assistant Faraday, and then by Faraday's assistant Tyndall. He was knighted in 1812, and soon afterwards married Mrs. Apreece, a lively, pretty, and wealthy widow. His later years were occupied, first by the investigations which

led to the perfecting of his famous safety-lamp for coal-mines
(these brought him a handsome testimonial and a baronetcy), and
later by electrical researches. He had not reached middle age
when his health began to fail, and he died in 1829, aged little
more than fifty. In connection with literary science or scientific
literature Davy was perhaps more remarkable as a lecturer than
as a writer, but his accomplishments as the latter were considerable, and in his later years he wrote two non-scientific books,
Salmonia and *Consolations in Travel.* These (though the former
was attacked as the work of an amateur and a milksop by
Christopher North) were very popular in their day. Davy always
kept up his friendship with men of letters, especially the Lake
Poets and Scott (who was a connection of his wife's), and he was
no very small man of letters himself.

A contemporary (though very much longer lived) of Davy's
and the most famous Englishwoman who has ever written on
scientific subjects, was Mary Fairfax, better known from the name
of her second husband as Mrs. Somerville. She was born at
Jedburgh on 26th December 1780, and when twenty-four married
her cousin, Captain Greig, a member of a family of Scotchmen
who had settled in the Russian navy. Her first husband died
two years afterwards, and six years later she married Dr. William
Somerville, also her cousin. She had already devoted much
attention, especially during her widowhood, to mathematics and
astronomy ; and after her second marriage she had no difficulty
in pursuing these studies. She adapted Laplace's *Mécanique
Céleste* in 1823, and followed it up by more original work on
physics, astronomy, and physical geography. Her life was prolonged till 1872, and an interesting autobiography appeared a
year later. It is possible that Mrs. Somerville profited somewhat
in reputation by her concidence with the period of "diffusion of
useful knowledge." But she had real scientific knowledge and
real literary gifts ; and she made good use of both.

Of at least respectable literary merit, though hardly of enough to
justify the devoting of much space to them here, were Sir David

Brewster (1781–1868), Sir John Herschel (1792–1871), Sir Charles Lyell (1797–1875), Sir Roderick Murchison (1792–1871), the first a mathematician and physicist, the second an astronomer, the third and fourth geologists, and all more or less copious writers on their several subjects. John Tyndall (1820–1893), a younger man than any of these, had perhaps a more distinctly literary talent. Born in Ireland, and for some time a railway engineer, he gave himself up about 1847 to the study and teaching of physics, was remarkable for the effect of his lecturing, and held several Government appointments. His Presidential Address to the British Association at Belfast in 1874 was not less noteworthy for materialism in substance than for a brilliant if somewhat brassy style.

But the chief Englishmen of science who were men of letters during our period were Charles Darwin and Thomas Huxley. The opinions of the first of these, their origin, the circumstances of their first expression, and the probabilities of their future, have been the subject of about as much controversy as in a given time has been bestowed upon any subject, certainly on any similar subject. But we enjoy here the privilege of neglecting this almost entirely. Darwin is to the literary historian a very interesting subject, for he was the grandson of Erasmus Darwin, who himself, besides being the capital example of the polished mediocrity of eighteenth century verse when all freshness had gone out of it, was a man of science and an evolutionist in his way. Charles (who was also christened Robert) was the son of yet another Dr. Darwin, an F.R.S. He was born on 12th February 1809 at Shrewsbury, and his mother was (as was afterwards his wife) a daughter of the Wedgwoods of Etruria. After passing through the famous school of his native town, Darwin went to Edinburgh for some years and then entered Christ's College, Cambridge, in 1828. Here he devoted himself to physical science, and after taking his degree was, in 1831, appointed to the *Beagle*, which was starting on a scientific cruise. He spent five years in the South Seas and did not return to England till late in 1836 — a voyage which perhaps prejudicially affected his health, but established his knowledge of nature. After his return he settled down to scientific work, alone and in the scientific societies, married in 1839, and was busy for many years afterwards in publishing the results of the voyage. He possessed considerable means, and for the last forty years of his life lived at his ease at Down near Beckenham, experimenting in crossing species and maturing his views. These took form, under circumstances interesting but foreign to our theme, in the famous *Origin of Species*, published in 1859, and this was followed by a great number of other books, the most noteworthy of which, if not the scientifically soundest, was *The Descent of Man* (1871). Darwin died after many years of continuous ill-health on 19th April 1882.

Late in life he is said to have confessed that his relish for Shakespeare and for pure literature generally, which had in earlier days been keen, had entirely vanished. But there was perhaps nothing very surprising in this, seeing that he had for half a century given himself up with extraordinary and ever-increasing thoroughness to a class of investigations the most remote possible from literature, and yet not, as pure mathematical study not seldom induces its votaries, inducing men to cultivate letters by mere contrast. Yet the ancestral literary tendency had only fallen dormant in him then ; and earlier it had been active. It can indeed hardly be said that either his contribution to the *Voyage of the Beagle*, or *The Origin of Species*, or *The Descent of Man*, or any of the others, is absolutely remarkable for style in the ordinary sense of that phrase. The style of Darwin attempts no ornateness, and on the other hand it is not of those extremely simple styles which are independent of ornament and to which ornament would be simply a defacement. But it is very clear ; it is not in the least slovenly ; and there is about it the indefinable sense that the writer might have been a much greater writer, simply as such, than he is, if he had cared to take the trouble, and had not been almost solely intent upon his matter. Such writers are not so common that they should be neglected, and they may at least stand in the Court of the Gentiles, the " provincial band " of literature.

A very remarkable book which was in a way Darwinism before Darwin, which attracted much attention and violent opposition in 1844, the year of its publication, and which for a long time remained unowned, was the *Vestiges of Creation*, subsequently known to be the work of Robert Chambers, the younger of two brothers who did great things in the popular publishing trade at Edinburgh, and who founded a house which has always been foremost in the diffusion of sound and cheap literature, information, and amusement. Robert was born at Peebles in 1802 and died at St. Andrews in 1871, having been, besides his publishing labours, a voluminous author and compiler. Nothing he did was quite equal to the *Vestiges*, a book rather literary than scientific, and treating the still crude evolution theory rather from the point of view of popular philosophy than from that of strict biological investigation ; but curiously stimulating and enthusiastic, with a touch of poetry in it not often to be found in such books, and attractive as showing the way in which doctrines which are about to take a strong hold of the general mind not infrequently communicate themselves, in an unfinished but inspiring form, to persons who, except general literary culture and interest, do not seem to offer any specially favourable soil for their germination. Purely scientific men have usually rather pooh-poohed the *Vestiges*, but there is the Platonic quality in it.

The *Vestiges*, like its more famous successor, was violently attacked as irreligious. One of its opponents, from a point of view half orthodox and half scientific, was Hugh Miller, a man of sterling excellence, of an interesting and in its close melancholy career, of real importance as a geologist, and possessed of an extremely agreeable literary faculty. Miller was born at Cromarty in 1802, and though more than fairly educated, held till he was past thirty no higher position than that of a stone-mason. He had begun to write, however, earlier than this, and, engaging in particular in the two rather dissimilar subjects of geology and

" Free Kirk " polemic, he was made editor of the *Witness*, a news-paper started in the interest of the new principles. After nearly twenty busy years of journalism and authorship he shot himself in December 1856, as it is supposed in a fit of insanity brought on by overwork. Miller was a very careful observer, and his *Old Red Sandstone* (1841) made a great addition to the knowledge of fossils. He followed this up by a great number of other works, some merely polemical, others descriptive of his own life and travels. In all the better parts of Hugh Miller's writings there is a remarkable style, extremely popular and unpretentious but never trivial or slipshod, which is not far below the best styles of the century for its special purpose, though in some respects it smacks more of the eighteenth, and has a certain relation with that of White of Selborne.

The most considerable literary gifts of the century among men of science probably belonged to a man more than twenty years younger than Miller, and more than fifteen younger than Darwin, who died so recently that until the greater part of this book was written it seemed that he would have no place in it. Thomas Henry Huxley, born in May 1825, at Ealing, studied medicine, and becoming a navy doctor, executed like Darwin a voyage to the South Seas. His scientific work, though early distinguished, met with no great encouragement from the Admiralty, and he left the service, though he held many public appointments in later life. He became F.R.S. at six-and-twenty, and from that time onwards till his sixtieth year he was a busy professor, lecturer, member of commissions, and (for a time) inspector of fisheries. In the ever greater and greater specialising of science which has taken place, Huxley was chiefly a morphologist. But outside the range of special studies he was chiefly known as a vigorous champion of Darwinism and a something more than vigorous aggressor in the cause of Agnosticism (a word which he himself did much to spread), attacking supernaturalism of every kind, and (though disclaiming materialism and not choosing to call himself an atheist) unceasingly demanding that all things should submit themselves to naturalist criticism. A great number of brilliant essays and lectures were composed by him on different parts of what may be called the debateable land between science, philosophy, and theology. And one of his most characteristic and masterly single studies was a little book on Hume, contributed to the series of " English Men of Letters " in 1879.

This varied, copious, and brilliant polemic may or may not have been open in substance to the charge which the bolder and more thoroughgoing defenders of orthodoxy brought against it, that it committed the logical error of demanding submission on the part of supernaturalism to laws and limits to which, by its very essence, supernaturalism disclaimed allegiance. But the form of it was excellent. Mr. Huxley had read much, and had borrowed weapons and armour from more than one Schoolman and Father as well as from purely profane authors. He had an admirable style, free alike from the great faults of his contemporaries, " preciousness " and slipshodness, and a knack of crisp but not too mannered phrase recalling that of Swift or, still more, of Bentley. It has been said, with some truth as well as with some paradox, that a literary critic of the very first class was lost in him, at the salvage only of some scientific monographs, which like all their kind will be antiquated some day, and of some polemics which must suffer equally from the touch of time.

CHAPTER XI

DRAMA

AT no period, probably, in the history of English literature, from the sixteenth century until that with which we are now dealing, would it have been possible to compress the history of the drama during a hundred years into the space which it is here proposed to give it. If we were dealing with the works of living men the historian might be justly charged with arrogant incompetence in not taking more notice of them. But, fortunately, that is not the case; and the brevity of the treatment is equally compatible with a belief that the plays of the present day are masterpieces, and with a suspicion that they are not. As to the past we have, with the exception of a few protesters, general consent that the English drama of the nineteenth century has displayed one curious and disastrous characteristic. The plays, as a rule, which have been good literature have either never been acted or have seldom succeeded as plays; the plays that have been acted and have been successful have seldom been good literature.

The best idea of the state of the drama between 1790 and 1810 may perhaps be obtained by any one who cares to look through — it would require a monomania, a desert island, or at least a succession of wet days in a country inn to enable any one to *read* through — the ten volumes of Mrs. Inchbald's *Modern British Theatre*, printed in 1811 "from the prompt-books of the Theatres Royal." This publication, supplementing the larger

British Theatre of the same editor, contains more than two volumes of the works of Frederick Reynolds, a prolific playwright who was responsible for the English version of *Werther* in drama; another of Mrs. Inchbald's own writing and adaptation; one of Holcroft's later works; one of Cumberland's; and the other five made up of lesser pieces by Colman the younger, Dibdin, and others, serious plays in blank verse such as Hannah More's *Percy*, and the Honourable John St. John's *Mary Queen of Scots*, etc. More than one of these was a person of talent, more than one a person even of very great talent; while Holcroft and Colman, if not others, had displayed special ability for drama. Yet there is, perhaps, in the fifty plays of the ten volumes only one that can be called a good play, only one which is readable, and that is the *Trip to Scarborough*, which Sheridan simply adapted, which he did little more than edit, from Vanbrugh's *Relapse*. Outside these volumes the acting drama of the period may be best studied in the other and better work of the pair just mentioned, and in O'Keefe.

John O'Keefe, or O'Keeffe (for the name is spelt both ways), was a very long-lived man, who was born at Dublin in 1748 and died at Southampton in 1833. But in the later years of his life he suffered from blindness; and the period of his greatest dramatic activity almost exactly coincided with that of our first chapter. He is said to have written some fifty pieces, of various kinds, between 1781 and 1798; and in the latter year he published a collection of about thirty, referring in the preface to others which "an inconsiderate disposal of the copyright" prevented him from including. O'Keefe was to a certain extent a follower of Foote; but his pieces—though he was a practised actor—depended less upon his own powers of exposition than Foote's. They range from rather farcical comedies to pure farces and comediettas much interspersed with songs for music; and their strictly literary merit is not often great, while for sheer extravagance they require the utmost license of the boards to excuse them. There is, however, something much more taking in them than in most of the dramatic work of the time. For instance, the " wild farce " (referred to but not named by Lamb in his paper on Munden) of *The Merry Mourners*, though as " improbable " as Mrs. Barbauld thought *The Ancient Mariner* to be, has a singular hustle and bustle of sustained interest, and not a few shrewd strokes such as the following, which perhaps does not only apply to the end of the *eighteenth* century. " Your London ladies are so mannified with their switch rattans and coats, and watch-chain nibbities, and their tip-top hats and their cauliflower cravats, that, ecod ! there's no mark of their being women except the petticoat." *The Castle of Andalusia* (1782) is an early and capital example of the bandit drama, and *The Poor Soldier* of the Irish comic opera. *Wild Oats* supplied favourite parts to the actors of the time in Rover and Ephraim Smooth ; and, with a little good will, one may read even slight things like *A Beggar on Horseback* and *The Doldrum* with some amusement. But O'Keefe has few gifts beyond knowledge of the stage, Irish shrewdness, Irish rattle, and an honest, straightforward simplicity ; and that one turns to him from other dramatists of the period with some relief, is even more to their discredit than to his credit.

A curious and early fruit of this gradual divorce between drama and literature was Joanna Baillie, a lady whose virtues, amiability, and in a way talents, caused her to be spoken of by her own contemporaries with an admiration which posterity has found it hard to echo as concerns her strictly literary position in drama — some of her shorter poems were good. She was born in 1762 at Bothwell, of a good Scotch family, and her mother was a sister of the great surgeon Hunter. This gift descended to her elder brother Matthew, who was very famous in his own day as an anatomist and physician. Partly to be near him, Joanna and her sister Agnes established themselves at Hampstead, where she often entertained Scott and other great people, and where she lived till 23rd February 1851. In 1798 she published the first of a series of *Plays on the Passions*, in which the eighteenth century theory of the ruling passion was carried out to the uncompromising and even

whimsical extent of supplying a brace of dramas, a tragedy and a
comedy, on each of the stronger passions, Hatred, Fear, Love, etc.
The first volume, which opened with the rather striking closet drama
of *Basil*, sometimes spoken of as *Count Basil*, was prefaced by
an introductory discourse of considerable ability. The book, coming at a dead season of literature, was well received. It reached
its third edition in the second year from its appearance, and one of
its plays, *De Montfort*, was acted, with Kemble in the title part, not
without success. A second volume followed in 1802, and a third in
1812. In 1804 one of *Miscellaneous Plays* had been issued, while
others and some poems were added later. Joanna's plays in general,
it was admitted, would not act (though the Ettrick Shepherd in
the *Noctes Ambrosianæ* denies this), and it requires some effort to
read them. The blank verse of the tragedies, though respectable,
is uninspired ; the local and historical colour, whether of Byzantine,
Saxon, or Renaissance times, is of that fatal " property " character
which has been noticed in the novel before Scott ; and the passion-
scheme is obviously inartistic. The comedies are sometimes gen-
uinely funny ; but they do not display either the direct and fresh
observation of manners, or the genial creation of character, which
alone can make comedy last. In short Miss Baillie was fortunate
in the moment of her appearance, but she cannot be called either
a great dramatist or a good one.

The school of Artificial Tragedy — the phrase, though not a
consecrated one, is as legitimate as that of artificial comedy —
which sprung up soon after the beginning of this century, and
which continued during its first half or thereabouts, if not later,
is a curious phenomenon in English history, and has hardly yet
received the attention it deserves. The tragedy of the eighteenth
century is almost beneath contempt, being for the most part
pale French echo or else transpontine melodrama, with a few
plaster-cast attempts to reproduce an entirely misunderstood
Shakespeare. It was impossible that the Romantic movement in
itself, and the study of the Elizabethan drama which it induced,
should not lead to the practice of tragedy, while the existence of

the Kembles as players and managers, might be thought to promise well for the tragic stage.

Yet there has always been something out of joint with English nineteenth century tragedy. Of Lamb's *John Woodvil* and Godwin's *Antonio* mention has been made. Byron's tragedies are indeed by no means the worst part of his work; but they also shared the defects of that work as poetry, and they were not eminently distinguished for acting qualities. Scott had no dramatic faculty; Shelley's *Cenci*, despite its splendid poetry, is not actable; indeed the only one of the great English nineteenth century *Pléiade* who was successful on the stage was Coleridge; and *Remorse* and *Zapolya* are not masterpieces.

Yet the fascination of the theatre, or at least of the drama, seemed to continue unaltered, and the attempts on or in it varied from the wild fantasy pieces of Beddoes (which no stage but the Elizabethan — if even that — could ever have welcomed) to the curious academic drama of which types extend not merely from Milman's *Fazio* in 1815 to Talfourd's *Ion* twenty years later, but further still. Of Milman notice has been taken in his far truer vocation as historian. Talfourd was a good lawyer, a worthy man, and as noted above, the friend and editor of Lamb. But his tragedies are very cold, and it is difficult to believe that *Ion* can have had any other attraction besides the popularity and skill of Macready, who indeed was greatly responsible for the appearance both of this and of better plays. In particular he stood usher to divers productions of Browning's which have been mentioned, such as the rather involved and impossible *Strafford*, and the intensely pathetic but not wholly straightforward *Blot in the 'Scutcheon*. This last is the one play of the century which — with a certain unsubstantiality of matter, a defect almost total in character, and a constant provocation to the fatal question, "Why are all these people behaving in this way?" — has the actual tragic *vis* in its central point.

The character, however, and the condemnation of the English drama of the first half of this century from the literary point of

view, are summed up in the single statement that its most prominent and successful dramatist was James Sheridan Knowles. Born
in 1784, and son of the great Sheridan's cousin at Cork, Knowles
was introduced to London literary society pretty early. He tried
soldiering (at least the militia) and medicine; but his bent towards
the stage was too strong, and he became an actor, though never
a very successful one, and a teacher of acting, though never a
manager. He was about thirty when he turned dramatist, and
though his plays justify the theatrical maxim that no one who
has not practical knowledge of the stage can write a good acting
play, they also justify the maxim of the study that in his day
literary excellence had in some mysterious way obtained or suffered a divorce from dramatic merit. Not that these plays are
exactly contemptible as literature, but that as literature they are
not in the least remarkable. The most famous of his tragedies
is *Virginius*, which dates, as performed in London at least, from
1820. It was preceded and followed by others, of which the
best are perhaps *Caius Gracchus* (1815), and *William Tell*
(1834). His comedies have worn better, and *The Hunchback*
(1832), and the *Love Chase* (1836), are still interesting examples
of last-century artificial comedy slightly refreshed. Independently
of his technical knowledge, Knowles really had that knowledge of
human nature without which drama is impossible, and he could
write very respectable English. But the fatal thing about him
is that he is content to dwell in decencies for ever. There is
no inspiration in him; his style, his verse, his theme, his character, his treatment are all emphatically mediocre, and his technique as a dramatist deserves only a little, though a little, warmer
praise.

Better as literature, and at least as good as drama, are the best
plays of the first Lord Lytton, another of the eminent hands of
Macready, who undoubtedly counted for something in the success of *The Lady of Lyons*, *Richelieu*, and *Money*, the two first
produced in 1838, and the last in 1840. *Richelieu* is the nearest
to Knowles in competence without excellence, the other two

perhaps excel if not positively yet relatively.   Many spectators
quite recently, while unable to check laughter at the grandiloquent
sentimentality and the stock situations of *The Lady of Lyons*, have
been unable to avoid being touched by its real though ordinary
pathos, and moved by its astonishing cleverness ; while *Money* is
probably the very best comic example of the hybrid kind above
referred to, the modernised artificial comedy.   But Bulwer's other
plays, though the unsuccessful *Duchesse de la Vallière* is not bad
reading, were less fortunate, and one of them is the subject of
perhaps the most successful of Thackeray's early reviews in the
grotesque style, preserved in the *Yellowplush Papers*.

It will be observed that, with the single and not very notable
exception of Sheridan Knowles, almost all the names already
mentioned are those of persons to whom drama was a mere by-
work.   Another exception may be found in James R. Planché
(1796–1880), a man of no very exalted birth or elaborate education, but an archæologist of some merit, and from 1854 onwards
an official representative of the honourable though discredited
science of Heraldry as Rouge Croix Pursuivant and Somerset
Herald.   From 1818 onward Planché was the author, adapter,
translator, and what not, of innumerable — they certainly run to
hundreds — dramatic pieces of every possible sort from regular
plays to sheer extravaganzas.   He was happiest perhaps in the
lighter and freer kinds, having a pleasant and never vulgar style
of jocularity, a fair lyrical gift, and the indefinable knowledge of
what is a play.   But he stands only on the verge of literature
proper, and the propriety, indeed the necessity, of including him
here is the strongest possible evidence of the poverty of dramatic
literature in our period.   It would indeed only be possible to extend
this chapter much by including men who have no real claim to
appear, and who would too forcibly suggest the hired guests of
story, introduced in order to avoid a too obtrusive confession of
the absence of guests entitled to be present.

The greater and more strictly literary names of those who
have tried the stage in the intervals of happier studies, from Miss

Mitford and R. H. Horne to Tennyson, have been mentioned elsewhere; and there is no need to return to them. Dr. James Westland Marston (1820–90) was once much praised, and was an author of Macready's. Miss Isabella Harwood, daughter of the second editor of the *Saturday Review*, produced under the pseudonym of "Ross Neil" a series of closet-dramas of excellent composition and really poetical fancy, but wanting the one thing needful. Perhaps a few other writers might with pains be added; and of course every reviewer knows that the flow of five-act tragedies, though less abundant than of old, has continued. But, on the whole, the sentence already put in more than one form remains true and firm — that in this period the dramatic work of those who have been really men and women of letters is generally far inferior to their other work, and that, with the rarest exceptions, the dramatic work of those who have not excelled in other kinds of literature is not literature at all.

CHAPTER XII

CONCLUSION

A CONCLUSION which avows that it might almost as well have presented itself as a preface may seem to be self-condemned; it must be the business of the following pages to justify it. In summing up on such a great matter as this it is desirable — it is indeed necessary — to indicate, in broader lines than at the mere outset would have seemed appropriate or indeed possible, the general course of thought and of speech, of literary matter and literary form, during the century and more which is submitted to the view. We can thus place individuals in their position to each other and to the whole more boldly and with less reserve; we can sketch the general character of existing movements, the movers in which have been exempt from individual consideration by virtue of their life and work being incomplete; we can at once record accomplishment and indicate tendency.

The period dealt with in the first chapter of this book illustrates the differences in appeal of such periods to the merely dilettante and "tasting" critic, and to the student of literature in the historical and comparative fashion. To the former it is one of the most ungrateful of all such sub-periods or sub-divisions in English literature. He finds in it none, or at most Boswell's *Johnson*, Burns, and the *Lyrical Ballads* (this last at its extreme end), of the chief and principal things on which alone he delights to fix his attention. Its better poetry, such as that of Cowper and Crabbe, he regards at best with a forced

425

esteem; its worse is almost below his disgust. Its fiction is preposterous and childish; it contributes nothing even to the less "bellettristic" departments of literature that is worth his attention; it is a tedious dead season about which there is nothing tolerable except the prospect of getting rid of it before very long.

To the latter — to the historical and comparative student — on the other hand, it has an interest of an absolutely unique kind. As was observed in a former volume of this history, the other great blossoming time of English literature — that which we call Elizabethan, and by which we mean the last five and twenty years of the Queen's reign and the fifty or sixty after her death — was preceded by no certain signs except those of restless seeking. Here, on the contrary, with no greater advantage of looking back, we can see the old fruit dropping off and the new forming, in a dozen different kinds and a hundred different ways. Extravagance on one side always provokes extravagance on the other; and because the impatient revolt of Coleridge and some others of the actual leaders into the Promised Land chose to present the eighteenth century as a mere wilderness in respect of poetry, enjoyment of nature, and so forth, there have been of late years critics who maintained that the poetical decadence of that century is all a delusion; in other words (it may be supposed) that Akenside and Mason are the poetical equals of Herrick and Donne. The *via media*, as almost always, is here also the *via veritatis*. The poets of the eighteenth century were poets; but the poetical stream did not, as a rule, run very high or strong in their channels, and they were tempted to make up for the sluggishness and shallowness of the water by playing rather artificial and rococo tricks with the banks. The fiction of the eighteenth century was, at its greatest, equal to the greatest ever seen; but it was as yet advancing with uncertain steps, and had not nearly explored its own domain. The history of the eighteenth century had returned to the true sense of history, and was endeavouring to be accurate; but it only once attained — it is true that with Gibbon it probably attained once for all — a perfect combination of diligence and range, of matter and of style.

In all these respects the list might, if it were proper, be extended to much greater length. The twenty years from 1780 to 1800 show us in the most fascinating manner the turn of the tide, not as yet coming in three feet abreast, rather creeping up by tortuous channels and chance depressions, but rising and forcing a way wherever it could. In the poets, major and minor, of the period, omitting, and even not wholly omitting, Burns and Blake — who are of no time intrinsically, but who, as it happens, belong accidentally to this time as exponents, the one of the refreshing influence of dialect and freedom from literary convention, the other of the refreshing influence of sympathy with old models and mystical dreaming — all the restlessness of the approaching crisis is seen. Nothing in literature is more interesting than to watch the effect of the half-unconscious aims and desires of Cowper and Crabbe, to see how they try to put the new wine in the old bottles, to compare them with Goldsmith and Thomson on the one hand, with Wordsworth and Coleridge on the other. Hayley perhaps alone, or almost alone, is rebel to the comparative method. Hayley is one of these hopeless creatures who abound at all periods, and whose native cast of nothingness takes a faint fashion from the time. But even in the verse of "Monk" Lewis we see the itch for new measures, the craving for lyric movement; even in the day-flies of the Della Crusca group the desire to be "something different." And then in Bowles, with his sonnets of places, in Sayers, with his rhymeless Pindarics, we come upon the actual guides to the right way, guides the oddest, the blindest, the most stumbling, but still — as not merely chronology but the positive testimony and the still more positive practice of those who followed them show — real guides and no misleaders.

Least studied, perhaps, because of its want of positive savour in comparison with their later achievements, but more interesting than all of these, is the early work of Southey, Coleridge, and Wordsworth themselves, and the work, not merely early but later, of men like Rogers and Campbell. Here the spectacle already presented in Crabbe and Cowper is repeated; but the process is in a further stage, and the fermentation is determining, according to the nature of the fermenting material. On Rogers it is nearly powerless; in Campbell only in his lyrics does it succeed in breaking up and dissolving the old crust; in Southey the effect is never quite complete; in Coleridge and Wordsworth, but especially in Coleridge, the leaven changes all the latter lump. Thenceforward the process is reversed. Instead of instances of advance amid a mass of inertia or aimless wandering we have instances of reaction amid a mass of advance. The work of the revolutionary time is done; the scholar, contrary to Goethe's dictum, has now not merely to exercise himself but to perfect.

The phenomena of the time in fiction are of the same character, but they lead as yet to no such distinct turn. The tale-telling of Beckford is like the singing of Burns, not uncoloured by the time, but still in the main purely individual; the purpose of the novels of Holcroft, Godwin, and Bage is groping in the dark; the Radcliffian romance and its exaggeration by Lewis exhibit the same uncertainty, the same application of the Rule of False. And there is for once a more philosophical and less cowardly explanation — that Scott, the Joshua in this instance, as Coleridge and Wordsworth were in the other, was occupied elsewhere before he sought the Palestine of the novel. For it must be remembered that prose fiction, though it had been cultivated in a scattered and tentative way for thousands of years, was up to this time the most inorganic of literary kinds. Poets, when they chose to give themselves up to poetry and to turn their backs on convention, were almost as well off then as now. They had but to open the great Greeks of the fifth and fourth centuries before Christ, the Latins such as Lucretius and Catullus, the great mediæval, the great Renaissance examples of their own art, to see, as soon as they chose to see, where and how to go right. The adventurer in fiction was destitute of any such assistance. Only a few examples of much real excellence in his art were before him ; many of those existing (including most of the mediæval instances) were hardly before him at all ; and none of these, with the exception of the eighteenth century novel of manners and character (which, in the nature of the case, was at that special time the last thing he wanted to imitate), and the short tale of France and Italy, could be said to have been brought to anything like perfection. Hence the wanderings and the stumblings here were far greater, the touch of the groping hands far feebler and less sure than even in poetry ; but the crying for the light was there too, and it was to be heard in time. Even as it was, before the century closed, Miss Edgeworth had given important new lines to fiction, and was on the eve of opening the most fertile of all its seams or veins, that of national or provincial character ; the purpose-novel just referred to was full of future, though it might be a future of a perilous and disputable kind ; the terror-romance, subdued to saner limits and informed with greater knowledge and greater genius, was not soon to cease out of the land ; and, a detail not to be neglected, the ever increasing popularity of the novel was making it more and more certain that it would number good intellects sooner or later.

In all other directions, with the single exception of drama, in which there was neither performance nor promise, so far as literature was concerned, to any great extent, the same restlessness of effort, and not always the same incompetence of result was seen. The fact of the revolutionary war abroad and the coercive policy thereby necessitated at home may have somewhat postponed the appearance of the new kind of periodical, in all shapes from quarterly to daily, which was to be so great a feature of the next age ; but the same causes increased the desire for it and prepared not a few of its constituents. It is impossible for any tolerably careful reader not to notice how much more "modern," to use an unphilosophical but indispensable term, is the political satire both in verse and prose, which has been noticed in the first chapter of this book, than the things of more or less the same kind that immediately preceded it. It was an accident, no doubt, that made the *Anti-Jacobin* ridicule Darwin's caricature of eighteenth century style in poetry; yet that ridicule did far more to put this particular convention out of fashion than all the attacks of the same paper on innovators like Coleridge (who at that time had hardly attempted their literary innovations) could do harm. The very interest in foreign affairs, brought about by the most universal war that had ever been known, helped to introduce the foreign element which was to play so large a part in literature; and little affection as the critic may have for the principles of Godwin or of Paine, he cannot deny that the spirit of inquiry, the rally and shock of attack and defence, are things a great deal better for literature than a placid contentment with accepted conventions.

Theology indeed may share with drama the reproach of having very little that is good to show from this time, or indeed for a long time to come. For the non-conformist sects and the Low Church party, which had resulted from the Evangelical movement in the earlier eighteenth century, were, the Unitarians excepted, for the most part illiterate. The Deist controversy had ceased, or, as conducted against Paine, required no literary skill; and the High Church movement had not begun. Philosophy, not productive of very much, was more active; and the intensely alien and novel styles of German thought were certain in time to produce their effect, while their working was in exact line with all the other tendencies we have been surveying.

In short, during these twenty years, literature in almost all its parts was being thoroughly " boxed about." The hands that stirred it were not of the strongest as yet, they were absolutely unskilled, and for the most part they had not even any very clear conception of what they wanted to do. But almost everybody felt that something had to be done, and was anxious — even childishly anxious — to do something. It by no means always happens that such anxiety is rewarded or is a good sign; but it is always a noteworthy one, and in this instance there is no doubt about either the fact of the reward or its goodness.

The subsequent history of poetry during the century divides itself in an exceedingly interesting way, which has not perhaps yet been subjected to full critical comment. There are in it five pretty sharply marked periods of some ten or fifteen years each, which are distinguished, the first, third, and fifth, by the appearance in more or less numbers of poets of very high merit, and of characteristics more or less distinctly original; the second and fourth by poetic growths, not indeed scanty in amount and sometimes exquisite in quality, but tentative, fragmentary, and undecided. It will of course be understood that in this, as in all literary classifications, mathematical accuracy must not be expected, and that the lives of many of the poets mentioned necessarily extend long before and after the periods which their poetical production specially distinguishes. In fact the life of Wordsworth covers as nearly as possible the whole five sub-periods mentioned, reckoning from his own birth-year to that of almost the youngest of the poets, of whom we shall here take account. And perhaps there are few better ways of realising the extraordinary eminence of English nineteenth century poetry than by observing, that during these eighty years there was never a single one at which more or fewer persons were not in existence, who had produced or were to produce poetry of the first class. And the more the five-fold division indicated is examined and analysed the more curious and interesting will its phenomena appear.

The divisions or batches of birth-years are worth indicating separately: the first comprises the eighth and ninth decades of the eighteenth century, from the birth of Scott and the Lakers to that of Shelley, with Keats as a belated and so to speak posthumous but most genuine child of it; the second covers about fifteen years from the birth of George Darley, who was of the same year (1795) with Keats, to the eve of that of Tennyson; the third goes from 1810 or thereabouts, throwing back to include the elder Tennysons and Mrs. Browning; the fourth extends from about 1825 to 1836; the fifth from the birth of Mr. Morris (throwing back as before to admit Rossetti) to the end.

In the first of these we see the Romantic revolt or renaissance, whichever word may be preferred, growing up under the joint influences of the opening of mediæval and foreign literature; of the excitement of the wars of the French Revolution; of the more hidden but perhaps more potent force of simple ebb-and-flow which governs the world in all things, though some fondly call it Progress ; and of the even more mysterious chance or choice, which from time to time brings into the world, generally in groups, persons suited to effect the necessary changes. The " Return to Nature," or to be less question-begging let us say the taking up of a new standpoint in regard to nature, made half unconsciously by men like Cowper and Crabbe, assisted without intending it by men like Burns and Blake, effected in intention if not in full achievement by feeble but lucky pioneers like Bowles, asserts itself once for all in the *Lyrical Ballads*, and then works itself out in different — in almost all possibly different — ways through the varying administration of the same spirit by Wordsworth and Coleridge, Shelley and Keats, in the highest and primary rank, by Scott and Byron in the next, by Southey, Campbell, Leigh Hunt, Moore, and others in the third. And it is again most interesting to watch how the exertion of influence and the character of it are by no means in proportion to the exact poetical strength of the agent. Scott and Byron, certainly inferior as poets to the first four mentioned, have probably had a greater bulk of poetical influence and poetical action on mankind at large certainly, and a vastly earlier, more immediate and more sweeping influence on other poets than their betters. Leigh Hunt, a poet quite of the third rank, exercised directly and indirectly, through Shelley and Keats, an influence on the form of poetry, on metre, cadence, phrase, greater than any of the others, save Wordsworth and Byron, and perhaps more than these. In all ways, however, by this channel and that, in straightforward or stealthy fashion, the poetic flood comes up, and by the death of Byron, Shelley and Keats having still more prematurely gone before, it is at its very highest spring. Six and twenty years passed, from 1798 to 1824, from the time when the *Lyrical*

Ballads were brought out to take their chance to the time when Mr. Beddoes, Mr. Procter, and somebody else clubbed to publish Shelley's posthumous poems at their own expense or at least guarantee, and justly objected to paying for more than 250 copies, because more were not likely to be sold. In these six and twenty years such an addition had been made to English poetry as five times the space had not previously seen, as perhaps was not far from equalling the glorious gains of a not very different though somewhat longer space of time between the appearance of the *Shepherd's Calendar* and the death of Shakespeare.

But the sequel of this abnormally high tide is hardly less interesting than itself. We generally expect at such moments in literature either a decided falling off, or else a period of decent imitation, of "school work." It would be absurd to say that there is no contrast, no falling off, and no imitation in the group of poets noticed at the end of the second chapter in this volume. But they are not utterly decadent, and they are by no means purely or merely imitative. On the contrary, their note is quite different from that of mere school work, and in a sort of eccentric and spasmodic fashion they attain to singular excellence. Hood, Praed, Macaulay, Taylor, Darley, Beddoes, Hartley Coleridge, Horne, are not to Wordsworth or Coleridge, to Byron or to Shelley, what the later so-called Elizabethan playwrights are to Jonson and Fletcher, the later poets of the same time to Spenser and Donne. But they almost all, perhaps all, seem forced to turn into some bye-way or backwater of poetry, to be unable or unwilling to keep the crown of the causeway, the flood of the tide. Hood and Praed — the former after actually attempting great poetry, and coming nearer to it than some great poets come in their first attempts — wander into the special borderland of humorous and grotesque verse, achieving in different parts of it something not unlike absolute and unsurpassed success. Beddoes, and to some extent Darley, adopt fantastic varieties, grim in the former's hands, playful chiefly in the latter's, but alike remote from everyday interests and broad appeals ; while the incompar-

2 F

able lyrics of Beddoes are of no special time or school, their very Elizabethanism being somewhat delusive. Taylor and Horne attempt the serious moral play with hardly any stage purposes or possibilities, and Horne in *Orion* tries an eccentric kind of ethical or satirical epic. Macaulay — the most prominent of all, and the most popular in his tastes and aims — is perhaps the nearest to a " schoolman," adapting Scott as he does in his *Lays;* yet even here there is no mere imitation.

Thus the people of this minor transition exhibit — in a most interesting way, rendered even more interesting by the repetition of it which, as we have seen and shall see, came about twenty years later — the mixed phenomena of an after-piece and a *lever de rideau*, of precursorship and what we must for want of a better word call decadence. They were not strong enough in themselves, or were not favourably enough circumstanced, entirely to refresh or redirect the main current of poetry ; so they deviated from it. But hardly in the least of them is there absent the sign and symptom of the poetic spirit being still about, of the poetic craft still in full working order. And their occasional efforts, their experiments in the half-kinds they affected, have a curious charm. English poetry would be undeniably poorer without the unearthly snatches of Beddoes, the exquisitely urbane verse-of-society of Praed, the pathetic-grotesque of Hood, even the stately tirades of Horne and Taylor. Some of them, if not all, may at this or that time have been exaggerated in value, by caprice, by reaction, by mere personal sympathy. But no universal critic will refuse admiration to them in and for themselves.

In the next stage we are again face to face, not with half-talents, uncertain of their direction, but with whole genius, inevitably working on its predestined lines. Nothing quite like the poetical career and the poetical conception of Alfred Tennyson and of Robert Browning, so different in all respects, except that of duration and coincidence in time, meets us in English, perhaps nothing similar meets us in any literature. It is easy to overestimate both ; and both have been overestimated. It is still easier

to depreciate both; and both have been depreciated.   Both wrote
constantly, and at frequent intervals, for some sixty years — the
same sixty years — and, with not more than fair allowance for the
effects of time, both wrote at the end better than at the beginning,
and nearly as well as at the best time of each.   Wordsworth, it is
true, wrote for nearly as long, but no one can assert the same
duration of equality in his production.

In a certain sense, no doubt, neither can claim the same
distinct individuality, the same unmistakable and elementary
quality, as that which distinguishes Chaucer, Spenser, Shakespeare, Wordsworth, Shelley.   The work of each is always at once
recognisable by any tolerably competent judge; but the signs of
identity are more composite than atomic, more derived and
literary than essentially native.   Browning's unconventional mannerisms, and his wide range of subject, have made him seem
even less of a mere scholar than Tennyson; but, as a fact, each is
independent enough to a certain extent and to a certain extent
only.   In both appears, perhaps for the first time, certainly for
the first time in combination with distinct original genius, that
indebtedness to the past, that relapse upon it in the very act of
forming vast schemes for the future, which is more the note of the
nineteenth century than anything else.   They not merely have all
literature and all history behind them; but they know it.   Yet
this knowledge does not weigh on them.   They do not exactly
neglect it as Wordsworth and Shelley were still able to do, but
they keep it under.   It is the attendant fiend for which they must
find work, but which they never, as too many of their contemporaries and followers have done, allow to become their master.
And so they two, as it seems to me, do actually win their way to
the first class, not perhaps to the absolutely first division of it, but
to a first class still pretty rigidly limited.

It is not the object of this Conclusion to deal with the performances of individuals at any length, and therefore I must refer back
to the text for a detailed indication of the position of Keats as the
summer-up of the tradition of the first of the groups or periods here

noticed, and the begetter, master, and teacher of the third, as well as for descriptions of the different manners in which Tennyson and Browning respectively shared and distributed between themselves that catholic curiosity in poetical subject, that exploration of all history and art and literature, which is the main characteristic of strictly nineteenth century poetry. But it is very pertinent here to point out the remarkable way in which these two poets, from the unexampled combination of length and potency in their poetical period of influence, governed all the poetry that has followed them. We shall now see that under their shadow at least two well-marked groups arose, each of magnitude and individuality sufficient to justify the assignment to it of a separate position. Yet it was in their shadow that these rose and flourished, and though the trees themselves have at length fallen, the shadow of their names is almost as great as ever.

The first of these two groups, the fourth of our present classification, renews, as has been said before, the features of its twenty or thirty years older forerunner, the group between Keats and Tennyson, in a most curious and attractive fashion. Once more we find the notes of uncertainty, of straying into paths, — not always quite blind-alleys, but bye-paths certainly, — the presence of isolated burst and flash, of effort unsuccessful or unequal as a whole. But here we find, what in the earlier chapter or section we do not find, distinct imitativeness and positive school-following. This imitation, attempting Shelley at times with little success (for, let it be repeated, Shelley is not imitable), selected in regular chronological order, three masters, Wordsworth, Tennyson, and Browning, though in each stage the master of the preceding rather shared than yielded his chair. It has been said in a famous passage that Wordsworth was more read about sixty years ago than at any time before or since, and this may perhaps be true. But his influence on writers has not depended on his popularity with readers, and from Sir Aubrey de Vere, who was born more than a century ago, to verse-writers who have only just published, his unmistakable tone, the tone which, so far as we can see, would never have been if Wordsworth had never existed, shows itself. The writing influence of Tennyson did not begin till the issue of the *Poems* of 1842, but it began almost immediately then, and has remained in full force to the present day. It is an influence somewhat more external and technical than Wordsworth's, but for that reason even more unmistakable, and some of its results are among the most curious of school-copies in literature. As for Browning, imitation there tried both the outside and the inside, not very often with happy results, but, of course, with results even more obvious to the most uncritical eye than the results of the imitation of Tennyson itself.

The attempts to be original and to break away from these and their imitations — the principal of them being that of the so-called Spasmodic school, which flourished at the dead waist and middle of the century — were not particularly happy, and those who incline to gloomy views may say that the imitation was less happy still. In Mr. Matthew Arnold, a recalcitrant but unmistakable Wordsworthian, sharing a partly reluctant allegiance between Wordsworth, the ancients, Goethe, and Tennyson himself, it is impossible not to think that a freer attitude, a more independent and less literary aim, might have strengthened his elegance, supplied his curious mixture of stiffness and grace, and even made him less unequal than he actually is. And yet he is much the greatest poet of the period. Its effect was more disastrous still upon the second Lord Lytton, who was content to employ an excellent lyrical vein, and a gift of verse satire of the fantastic kind so distinct and fascinating, that it approaches the merit of fantasists in other kinds of the former group, like Beddoes and Darley, to far too great an extent on echoes. The fact is, that by this time, to speak conceitedly, the obsession of the book was getting oppressive. Men could hardly sing for remembering, or, at least, without remembering, what others had sung before them, and became either slavishly imitative or wilfully recalcitrant to imitation. The great leaders indeed continued to sing each in his own way, and, though with perfect knowledge of their forerunners, not in the least hampered by that knowledge. But something else was needed to freshen the middle regions of song.

It was found in that remarkable completion of the English Romantic movement, which is in relation to art called præ-Raphaelitism, and which is represented in literature, to mention only the greatest names, by Rossetti, his sister, Mr. Morris, and Mr. Swinburne. The death of the two former, and the fact that the movement itself, still active in art, has in a manner rounded itself off, though it is not necessarily finished, in literature, enable us to discuss it here as a whole, though its two chief poets are luckily still alive.

The first thing of interest in general history which strikes us, in regard to this delightful chapter of English poetry, is its illustration — a common one in life and letters — of the fact that there is a false as well as a true side to the question quoted by Aristotle : " If water chokes you, what are you to drink on the top of it ? " " Wine," one kind of humourist might answer ; " More water," another : and both rightly. It has been said that the group which preceded this suffered from the pressure of too constant, wide, and various reminiscence, literary, artistic, and other. The præ-Raphaelites refreshed themselves and the world by applying still more strenuously to the particular kind and period of such reminiscence which had been hitherto, despite the mediæval excursions of many from Percy to Tennyson, imperfectly utilised. The literary practitioners of the school (with whom alone we are concerned) were not indeed by any means purely mediæval in their choice of subject, in their founts of inspiration, or in their method of treatment. English poetry has known few if any more accomplished scholars both in the classics and in the modern languages than Mr. Swinburne, for instance ; and something similar might be said of others. But, on the whole, the return of this school — for all new things in literature are returns — was to a mediævalism different from the tentative and scrappy mediævalism of Percy, from the genial but slightly superficial mediævalism of Scott, and even from the more exact but narrow and distinctly conventionalised mediævalism of Tennyson. They had other appeals, but this was their chief.

It may seem that mere or main archaism is not a very charming or powerful thing, and in weaker hands it would not have been either one or the other ; but it so happened that these hands were very strong indeed. Mr. Rossetti had one of the most astonishing combinations ever known of artistically separate gifts, as well as a singular blend of passion and humour. His sister was one of the great religious poets of the world. Mr. Swinburne has never been surpassed, if he has ever been equalled, by any poet in any language for command of the more rushing and flowing forms of verse. Mr. Morris has few equals in any time or country for narrative at once decorative and musical. Moreover, though it may seem whimsical or extravagant to say so, these poets added to the very charm of mediæval literature which they thus revived a subtle something which differentiates it from — which to our perhaps blind sight seems to be wanting in — mediæval literature itself. It is constantly complained (and some of those who cannot go all the way with the complainants can see what they mean) that the graceful and labyrinthine stories, the sweet snatches of song, the quaint drama and legend of the Middle Ages lack — to us — life ; that they are shadowy, unreal, tapestry on the wall, not alive even as living pageants are. By the strong touch of modernness which these poets and the best of their followers introduced into their work, they have given the vivification required.

Beyond them we must not go, nor inquire whether the poets who have not come to forty years represent a new school of the masterful and supreme kind, or one of the experimental and striving sort, or something a good deal worse than this, a period of sheer interval and suspense, unenlivened even by considerable attempt. Not only our scheme, not only common prudence and politeness, but most of all the conditions of critical necessity insist on the curtain being here dropped. It is possible that a critic may be able to isolate and project himself sufficiently to judge, as posterity will judge them, the actually accomplished work of his own contemporaries and juniors. But even such a skilful and fortunate person cannot judge the work which they have not yet produced, and which may in all cases, and must in some, modify their position and alter their rank.

But what has been has been, and on this mass (not in the actual case "vulgar" by any means) of things done it is possible to pronounce securely. And with security it may be said that for total amount, total merit, total claims of freshness and distinctness, no period of poetical literature can much, if at all, exceed the ninety years of English verse from *The Ancient Mariner* to *Crossing the Bar*. The world has had few poets better than the best of ours during this time in degree; it has had none like Shelley, perhaps none exactly like Wordsworth, in kind. The secret of long narrative poems that should interest has been recovered; the sonnet, one of the smallest but one of the most perfect of poetic forms, has been recovered likewise. Attempts to recover the poetic drama have been mostly failures; and serious satire has hardly reappeared. But lighter satire, with other "applied" poetry, has shown variety and excellence. Above all lyric, the most poetic kind of poetry, has attained a perfection never known before, except once in England and once in Greece. It has been impossible hitherto to make a full and free anthology of the lyric poets from Burns and Blake to Tennyson and Browning to match the anthologies often made of those from Surrey or Sidney to Herrick or Vaughan. But when it can be done it is a question whether the later volume will not even excel the earlier in intensity and variety, if not perhaps in freshness of charm.

And then it is needful once more to insist, even at the risk of disgusting, on the additional interest given by the subtle and delicate, but still distinctly traceable gradations, the swell and sinking, the flow and ebb, of poetical production and character during the time. As no other flourishing time of any poetry has lasted so long, so none has had the chance of developing these mutations in so extensive and attractive a manner; in none has it been possible to feel the pulse of poetry, so to speak, in so connected and considerable a succession of experiment. Poetical criticism can never be scientific; but it can seldom have had an opportunity of going nearer to a scientific process than here, owing to the volume, the connection, the duration, the accessibility of the phenomena submitted to the critic. The actual secret as usual escapes; but we can hunt the fugitive by a closer trail than usual through the chambers of her flight.

Of the highest poetry, however, as of other highest things, Goethe's famous axiom *Über allen Gipfeln ist Ruh* holds good. Although there is a difference between the expressions of this highest poetry in the fifth and fourth centuries before Christ, in the fourteenth, seventeenth, and nineteenth after Christ there is also a certain quiet sameness, not indiscernibility but still identity. The lower kinds of literature admit of more apparent and striking freshness of exterior. And perhaps the most strikingly fresh, some might even say the distinctive, product of the nineteenth century, is its prose fiction.

This, as has been shown in detail, is much later in date than the poetry in anything like a characteristic and fully developed state. Although it was busily produced during the last twenty years of the eighteenth century and the first fifteen of the nineteenth, the very best work of the time, except such purely isolated things as *Vathek*, are experiments, and all but the very best — the novels of Miss Edgeworth, those written but not till quite the end of the time published by Miss Austen, and a very few others — are experiments of singular lameness and ill success.

With Scott's change from verse to prose, the modern romance admittedly, and to a greater extent than is generally thought the modern novel, came into being; and neither has gone out of being since. In the two chapters which have been devoted to the subject we have seen how the overpowering success of *Waverley* bred a whole generation of historical novels; how side by side with this the older novel of manners, slightly altered, continued to be issued, with comic deviations chiefly, as in the hands of Theodore Hook ; how Bulwer attempted a sort of cross between the two ; how about the middle of the century the historical novel either ceased or changed, to revive later after a middle period illustrated by the brilliant romances of Kingsley ; how about the same time the strictly modern novel of manners came into being in the hands of Thackeray, Miss Brontë, George Eliot, and Anthony Trollope, Dickens overlapping both periods in a fantastic and nondescript style of his own ; and how more recently still both romance and novel have spread out and ramified into endless subdivisions.

There is, however, this broad line of demarcation between poetry and the novel, that they are written for different ends and from different motives. It is natural to man to write poetry ; it does not appear to be by any means so certainly or unvaryingly necessary to him to read it. Except at rare periods and for short times, poetry has never offered the slightest chance of livelihood to any considerable number of persons ; and it is tolerably certain that if the aggregate number of poets since the foundation of the world had had nothing to live on but their aggregate gains as poets, starvation would have been the commonplace rule, instead of the dramatic exception, among the sons of Apollo.

On the other hand, it is no doubt also natural to man to tell prose stories, and it seems, though it was a late-discovered aptitude, that it is not unnatural to him to read them ; but the writing of them does not seem to be at all an innate or widely disseminated need. Until some hundred or two hundred years ago very few were written at all ; the instances of persons who do but write novels because they must are exceedingly rare, and it is as certain as anything can be that of the enormous production of the last three-quarters of a century not 5, perhaps not 1 per cent would have been produced if the producing had not led, during the whole of that time, in most cases but those of hopeless incompetence to some sort of a livelihood, in many to very comfortable income, and in some to positive wealth and fame.

In other words, poetry is the creation of supply and novel-writing of demand ; poetry can hardly ever be a trade and in very rare cases a profession, while novel-writing is commonly a very respectable profession, and unfortunately sometimes a rather disreputable trade.

Like other professions, however, it enlists genius sometimes, talent often ; and the several and successive ways in which this genius and this talent show themselves are of more than sufficient interest. But the steady demand, and the inevitable answer to it, work adversely to such spontaneous and interesting fluctuations of production as those which we have traced in reference to poetry. There have been times, particularly that between the cessation of Sir Walter's best work and the perfecting of that of Thackeray, in which the average value of even the best novels was much lower than at other times. But even in these the average volume maintained itself very well, and, indeed, steadily increased.

It is this which, with another to be mentioned shortly, will, so far as it is possible for a contemporary to judge, be noted in the literary history of the future as the distinguishing crop or field of the nineteenth century. Sermons, essays, plays, no doubt, continue to be written ; but the novel has supplanted the sermon, the essay, the play in the place which each at different times held as the *popular* form of literature. It may be added, or repeated, that it has in part at least achieved this result by trespassing upon the provinces of all these three forms and of many others. This is true, but is of somewhat less importance than might be thought. The fable has an old trick of adjusting itself to almost every possible kind of literary use, and the novel is only an enlarged and more fully organised fable. It does not, no doubt, do best when it abuses this privilege of its ancestor, and saturates itself overmuch with " purpose," but it has at least an ancestral right to do so.

There is no doubt also that the popularity of the novel has been very directly connected with a cause which has had all manner of effects fathered upon it — often with no just causation or filiation whatever — to wit, the spread of education. In the proper sense of course the spread of education must always be strictly limited. The number of educable persons probably bears a pretty constant ratio to the population, and when the education reaches the level of the individual's containing power, it simply runs over and is lost. But it is possible to teach nearly everybody reading and writing; and it is a curious but exact observation that a very large proportion of those who have been taught reading require something to read. Now the older departments of literature do not lend themselves with any facility to constant reading by the average man or woman, whose requirements may be said to be amusement rather than positive delight, occupation much rather than intellectual exertion, and above all, something to pass time. For these requirements, or this compound requirement, the hearing of some new thing has been of old recognised as the surest and most generally useful specific. And the novel holds itself out, not indeed always quite truly, as being new or nothing by name and nature. Accordingly the demand for novels has gone on ever increasing, and the supply has never failed to keep up with it.

Nor would it be just to say that the quality has sunk appreciably. The absolutely palmy day of the English nineteenth century in novel-writing was no doubt some thirty-five or forty years ago. Not even the contemporary France of that date can show such a " galaxy-gallery " as the British novelists — Dickens, Thackeray, Miss Brontë, George Eliot, Trollope, Kingsley, Bulwer, Disraeli, Lever, Mr. Meredith, and others — who all wrote in the fifties. But at the beginning of the period the towering genius of Scott and the perfect art of Miss Austen, if we add to them Miss Edgeworth's genial talent, did not find very much of even good second-rate matter to back them; there was, as has been said, a positively barren time succeeding this first stage and preceding the " fifty " period; and twenty years or a little more ago, when Thackeray and Dickens were dead, Trollope and George

Eliot past their best, Kingsley and Bulwer moribund, Mr. Meredith writing sparely and unnoticed, the new romantic school not
arisen, and no recruit of distinction except Mr. Blackmore firmly
set, things were apparently a great deal worse with us in point of
novel-writing than they are at present.   Whether, with a return of
promise and an increase of performance, with a variation of styles
and an abundance of experiment, there has also been a relapse
into the extravagances which we have had in this very book to
chronicle as characterising the fiction of exactly a century ago, —
whether we have had over-luxuriant and non-natural style, attempts
to attract by loose morality, novels of purpose, novels of problem,
and so forth, — and whether the coming age will dismiss much of
our most modern work as not superior in literary and inferior in
other appeal to the work of Godwin and Lewis, Holcroft and
Bage, it is not necessary distinctly to say.   But our best is certainly better than the best of that time, our worst is perhaps not
worse ; and the novel occupies a far higher place in general estimation than it did then.   Indeed it has been observed by the
sarcastic that to some readers of novels, and even to some writers
of them, "novel" and "book" seem to be synonymous terms, and
that when such persons speak of "literature," they mean and
pretty distinctly indicate that they mean novel-writing, and novel-
writing only.   This at least shows that the seed which Scott sowed,
or the plant which he grafted, has not lost its vitality.

Certainly not less, perhaps even more, distinctive of the time
in history must be that development and transformation of what
is broadly called the newspaper, of which the facts and details
have occupied two more of these chapters.   It is true that at times
considerably earlier than even the earliest that here concerns us,
periodical writing had been something of a power in England as
regards politics, had enlisted eminent hands, and had even served
once or twice as the means of introduction of considerable works
in *belles lettres*.   But the Addisonian Essay had been something
of an accident ; Swift's participation in the *Examiner* was another ;
Defoe's abundant journalism brought him more discredit than

profit or praise ; and though Pulteney and the Opposition worked the press against Walpole, the process brought little benefit to the persons concerned. Reviewing was meagrely done and wretchedly paid ; the examples of *Robinson Crusoe* earlier and *Sir Launcelot Greaves* later are exceptions which prove the rule that the *feuilleton* was not in demand ; in fact before our present period newspaper-writing was rather dangerous, was more than rather disreputable, and offered exceedingly little encouragement to any one to make it the occasion of work in pure literature, or even to employ it as a means of livelihood, while attempting other and higher, though less paying kinds.

The period of the French Revolution, if not the French Revolution itself, changed all this, assisted no doubt by the natural and inevitable effects of the spread of reading and the multiplication of books. People wanted to see the news ; papers sprang up in competition to enable them to see the news ; and the competitors strove to make themselves more agreeable than their rivals by adding new attractions. Again, the activity of the Jacobin party, which early and of course directed itself to the press, necessitated activity on the other side. The keenest intellects, the best-trained wits of the nation, sometimes under some disguise, sometimes openly, took to journalism, and it became simply absurd to regard the journalist as a disreputable garreteer when Windham and Canning were journalists. The larger sale of books and the formation of a regular system of " pushing " them also developed reviews — too frequently, no doubt, in the direction of mere puffing, but even thus with the beneficent result that other reviews came into existence which were not mere puff-engines.

Even these causes and others will not entirely explain the extraordinary development of periodicals of all kinds from quarterly to daily, of which the *Edinburgh*, *Blackwood*, the *Examiner*, and the *Times* were respectively the most remarkable examples and pioneers in the earlier years of the century, though as a literary organ the *Morning Post* had at first rather the advantage of the *Times*. But, as has been said here constantly, you can never explain everything in literary history ; and it would be extremely dull if you could. The newspaper press had, for good or for ill, to come ; external events to some obvious extent helped its coming ; individual talents and aptitudes helped it likewise ; but the main determining force was the force of hidden destiny.

There is, however, no mistake possible about the results. It is but a slight exaggeration to say that the periodical rapidly swallowed up all other forms of literature, to this extent and in this sense, that there is hardly a single one of these forms capital performance in which has not at one time or another formed part of the stuff of periodicals, and has not by them been first introduced to the world. Not a little of our poetry ; probably the major part of our best fiction ; all but a very small part of our essay-writing, critical, meditative, and miscellaneous ; and a portion, much larger than would at one time have seemed conceivable, of serious writing in history, philosophy, theology, science, and scholarship, have passed through the mint or mill of the newspaper press before presenting themselves in book form. A certain appreciable, though small part of the best, with much of the worst, has never got beyond that form.

To attempt to collect the result of this change is to attempt something not at all easy, something perhaps which may be regarded as not particularly valuable. The distinction between literature and journalism which is so often heard is, like most such things, a fallacy, or at least capable of being made fallacious. Put as it usually is when the intention is disobliging to the journalist, it comes to this : — that the *Essays of Elia*, that Southey's *Life of Nelson*, that some of the best work of Carlyle, Tennyson, Thackeray, and others the list of whom might be prolonged at pleasure, is not literature. Put as it sometimes is by extremely foolish people, it would go to the extent that anything which has *not* been published in a daily, weekly, monthly, or quarterly publication is literature.

There is probably no subject on which it is more necessary to clear the mind of cant than this. Of course there is journalism in the sense opposed to literature, though not necessarily opposed in any bad sense. No wise man intends, and no wise man will ever suffer, articles which are in the strict sense articles, which are intended to comment on merely passing events, and to produce a merely immediate effect, to be extracted from journals and put on record as books. Not only is the treatment unsuitable for such record, but it may almost be said that the treatment suitable for things so to be recorded is actually unsuitable for things ephemeral. But there is a very large amount of writing to which this does not in the least apply, and in which it can make no kind of real difference whether the result appears by itself in a bound cloth volume as a whole, or in parts with other things in a pamphlet, covered with paper, or not covered at all. The grain of truth which the fallacy carries is really this : — that the habit of treating some subjects in the peculiar fashion most effective in journalism may spread disastrously to the treatment of other subjects which ought to be treated as literature. This is a truth, but not a large one. There have been at all times, at least since the invention of printing and probably before it, persons who, though they may be guiltless of having ever written an article in their lives, have turned out more or less ponderous library volumes in which the very worst sins of the worst kind of journalist are rampant.

There are, however, more thoughtful reasons for regarding the development of periodicals as not an unmixed boon to letters. The more evanescent kinds of writing are, putting fiction out of the question, so much the more profitable in journalism that it certainly may tempt — that it certainly has tempted — men who could produce, and would otherwise have produced, solid literature. And there is so much more room in it for light things than for things which the average reader regards as heavy, that the heavy contributor is apt to be at a discount, and the light at a premium. But all this is exceedingly obvious. And it may be met on the other side by the equally obvious consideration already referred to, that periodicals have made the literary life possible in a vast number of cases where it was not possible before ; that whereas " toil, envy, want, the patron, and the gaol " was not a very exaggerated description of its prospects little more than a hundred years ago, the patron has become superfluous, want and the gaol rather unlikely, except in cases of extreme misconduct, incompetence, or ill-luck, while if toil and envy remain unvanquished, they are not specially fated to the literary lot. Indeed the more paradoxical of Devil's Advocates against the press usually urge that it has made the literary life too easy, has tempted too many into it, and has thereby increased the flood of mediocrity.

The most serious objection of all perhaps, though even this is rather idle in face of accomplished facts, is that the perpetual mincing up and boiling down of the constituents of the diet of reading have produced, in the appetite and digestive faculties of the modern reader, an inability to cope with a really solid meal of perhaps slightly tough matter, and that periodicals not merely eschew the provision of this solid stuff themselves, but do their best to make things worse by manipulating the contents of books that do contain it.

The fact, however, once more, concerns us much more than moralisings about the fact ; and the fact of the prominence, the extraordinary prominence, of the periodical press in the nineteenth century, is as little open to dispute as the prominence in that century's later mechanical history of discoveries in electricity, or in its earlier of experiments with steam. Occasionally one may hear enthusiasts of one kind or another announcing with joy or horror that the periodical is killing the book. But if it is, it is very impartially engaged in begetting it at the same time that it kills ; and it may be very seriously doubted whether this killing of a book is an easy act of murder to commit. With the printing press to produce, the curiosity of man to demand, and his vanity and greed — if not also his genius and ambition — to supply, the book is in all probability pretty safe. In the forms and varieties of this periodical publication we have seen some interesting changes.

2 G

As might have been expected, the tendency has been for the intervals of publication to be shortened — for the quarterly to give way as the fashionable form to the monthly, the monthly to the weekly, the weekly to the daily. Many years ago Macaulay, in a mild protest against having his articles altered by Macvey Napier, suggested in effect that the bloom might be left on poor things destined to be read only for a month or so. The duration of an article now may be measured rather by hours than by weeks. Still many of these changes are more apparent than real ; and just as the institution of the graver monthly reviews twenty years ago simply reintroduced the quarterly article in a scarcely altered form after it had been pushed out of favour by the slighter magazine, so other introductions have been in fact reintroductions.

One point, however, of real importance in literary history remains to be noticed, and that is the conflict between signed and anonymous writing. Partly from the causes above enumerated as having conduced to the keeping of journalism in a condition of discredit and danger, partly owing to national idiosyncrasies, the habit of anonymous writing was almost universal in the English press at the beginning of the century. It may have been perfectly well known that such and such an article in the *Quarterly* was by Southey or Croker, such another in the *Edinburgh* by Sydney Smith or Macaulay, but the knowledge was, so to speak, unofficial. The question of the identity of "Zeta" in *Blackwood* cost a man's life ; and the system resulted (in daily papers especially) in so much editorial intermixture and refashioning, that sometimes it would really have been impossible to assign a single and authentic paternity. Even about the editorship of the great periodicals a sort of coquetry of veiling was preserved, and editors' names, though in most cases perfectly well known, seldom or never appeared.

It is difficult to say exactly when or how this system began to be infringed. But there is no doubt that the prominence given in *Household Words* to the name and personality of Dickens, who was not unfriendly to self-advertisement, had a good deal to do with it ; and when, a little later, the cheap shilling magazines appeared, writing with names became the rule, without them the exception. Criticism, however, for obvious reasons still held back ; and it was not till about five and twenty years ago that the example, taken more or less directly from the French, of signed reviews was set by the *Academy* among weekly papers, and the *Fortnightly* among monthly reviews. It has been very largely followed even in daily newspapers, and the *Saturday Review* was probably the last newspaper of mark that maintained an absolutely rigid system of anonymity. It should, however, be observed that the change, while not even yet complete — leading articles being still very rarely signed — has by no means united all suffrages, and has even lost some that it had. Mr. John Morley, for instance, who had espoused it warmly as editor of the *Fortnightly*, and had, perhaps, done more than any other man to spread it, has avowed in a very interesting paper grave doubts about the result. Still it undoubtedly has increased, and is increasing, and in such cases it is much easier to express an opinion that things ought to be dimin- ished, than either to expect that they will, or to devise any means whereby the diminution is to be effected. As for what is desir- able as distinguished from what is likely, the weight of opinion may be thought to be in favour of the absence of signature. Anonymous criticism, if abused, may no doubt be abused to a graver extent than is possible with signed criticism. But such a hackneyed maxim as *corruptio optimi* shows that this is of itself no argument. On the other hand, signed criticism diminishes both the responsibility and the authority of the editor ; it adds either an unhealthy gag or an unhealthy stimulus to the tongue and pen of the contributor ; it lessens the general weight of the verdict ; and it provokes the worst fault of criticism, the aim at showing off the critic's cleverness rather than at exhibiting the real value and character of the thing criticised. And perhaps some may think the most serious objection of all to be that it encourages the employment of critics, and the reception of what they say, rather for their names than for their competence.

In that very important department of literature which stands midway between Belles Lettres and Science, the department of History, the century cannot indeed claim such striking and popularly effective innovations as in the departments of prose fiction and of periodical writing. Yet it may be questioned whether the change of this old kind is not in itself almost as noteworthy as in the other cases is the practical introduction of a new. What the change is was epigrammatically, if somewhat paradoxically, summed up recently by a great authority, Lord Acton. "History," the Cambridge Professor of that art or science said in his inaugural lecture, "has become independent of the historian."

It is possible to demur to the fact, but it is not difficult to explain the meaning. From the necessity of the case, the earliest history, at least in the West, is almost independent of documents and records. Thucydides and Herodotus wrote, the one from what he had actually seen and heard of contemporary events, the other partly from the same sources and partly from tradition of short date. Somewhat later historians of course had their predecessors before them, and in a few cases a certain amount of document, but never a large amount. When history, vernacular or Latin, began to be written again in the dark and middle ages, the absence of documents was complicated (except in the case of those early chroniclers, English and Irish chiefly, who merely put down local events) by that more peculiar and unaccountable, though possibly kindred, absence of critical spirit, which, of the many things more or less fancifully attributed to the mediæval mind, is perhaps the most certain. It is a constant puzzle to modern readers how to account exactly for the fashion in which men, evidently of great intellectual ability, managed to be without any sense of the value of evidence, or any faculty of distinguishing palpable and undoubted fiction from what either was, or reasonably might be held to be, history. But by degrees this sense came into being side by side with the multiplication of the document itself. Even then, however, it was very long before the average historian either could or would regard himself as bound first to consult all the documents available, and then to sift and adjust them in accordance rather with the laws of evidence and the teachings of the philosophy of history than with his own predilections, or with the necessities of an agreeable narrative. But the patient industry of the French school of historical scholars, at the end of the seventeenth and the beginning of the eighteenth century, founded this new tradition; the magnificent genius of Gibbon showed how the observance of it might not be incompatible with history-writing of the most literary kind; the national and natural tendency of German study adopted it; and shortly after Gibbon's own day the school of historians, which is nothing if not documentary, began gradually to oust that of which the picturesque, if not strictly historical, legend about the Abbé Vertot and his " Mon siège est fait " is the anecdotic *locus classicus* of characterisation.

It has been shown, in the chapter devoted to the subject, how this school of documentary historians grew and flourished in England itself, from the days of Turner and Palgrave to those of Froude and Freeman. Certainly there could not, at least for some time, be said to be any very sensible tendency in history to dispense with the historian, or, in other and perhaps rather more intelligible words, of history ceasing to be literary. No historians have been more omnilegent, more careful of the document, than Carlyle and Macaulay, much as they differed in other respects, and in no histories has the " historian " — that is to say, the personal writer as opposed to the mere " diplomatist " — been more evident than he is in theirs. Nor is it very easy to see why the mere study of the document, still less why the mere accumulation of the document, should ever render superfluous the intelligent shaping which the historian alone can give. In the first place, documents are contradictory and want shifting and harmonising; in the second they want grasping and interpreting; in the third (and most important of all) they need to be made alive.

Nevertheless Lord Acton's somewhat enigmatic utterance points, however vaguely, to real dangers, and it would be idle to say that these dangers have not been exemplified in the period and department we are considering. In the first place, the ever-increasing burden of the documents to be consulted is more and more crushing, and more and more likely to induce any one but a mere drudge either to relinquish the task in despair, or to perform it with a constant fear before his eyes, which prevents freedom and breadth of work. In the second it leads, on the one hand, to enormous extension of the scale of histories, on the other to an undue restraining and limiting of their subjects. Macaulay took four large volumes to do, nominally at least, not more than a dozen years; Froude twelve to cover fifty or sixty; Grote as many to deal with the important, but neither long nor richly documented, period of Greek, or rather Athenian, flourishing. To this has to be added the very serious drawback that when examination of documents is ranked before everything, even the slightest questioning of that examination becomes fatal, and a historian is discredited because some one of his critics has found a document unknown to him, or a flaw, possibly of the slightest importance, in his interpretation of the texts.

Nevertheless it is necessary to lay our account with this new style of history, and it is fortunately possible to admit that the gains of it have not been small. Thanks to its practitioners, we know infinitely more than our fathers did, though it may not be so certain that we make as good a use of our knowledge. And the evil of multiplication of particulars, like other evils, brings its own cure. The work of mere rough-hewing, of examination into the brute facts, is being done — has to no small extent actually been done — as it never was done before. The " inedited " has ceased to be inedited — is put on record for anybody to examine with little trouble. The mere loss of valuable material, which has gone on in former ages to an extent only partially compensated by the welcome destruction of material that has no value at all, has been stopped. The pioneers of the historical summer (to borrow a decorative phrase from Charles of Orleans) have been very widely abroad, and there is no particular reason why the summer itself should not come.

When it does it will perhaps discard some ways and fashions which have been lately in vogue ; but it will assuredly profit by much that has been done during the period we survey, no less in form than in matter. The methods have been to a certain extent improved, the examples have been multiplied, the historical sense has certainly taken a wider and deeper hold of mankind. Very little is wanting but some one *ausus contemnere vana ;* and when the future Thucydides or the future Carlyle sets to work, he will be freed, by the labour of others, alike from the paucity of materials that a little weakened Thucydides, and from the brute mass of them that embittered the life of Carlyle.

Not so much is to be said of the remaining divisions or departments individually. If the drama of the century is not, in so far as acting drama is concerned, almost a blank from the point of view of literature, the literary drama of the century is almost a blank as regards acting qualities. It is true that there have been at times attempts to obtain restitution of conjugal rights on one side or on the other. In the second and third decades, perhaps a little later, a strong effort was made to give vogue to, and some vogue was obtained for, the scholarly if pale attempts of Milman and Talfourd, and the respectable work of others. Bulwer, his natural genius assisted by the stage-craft of Macready, brought the acting and the literary play perhaps nearer together than any one else did. Much later still, the mighty authority of Tennyson, taking to dramatic writing at the time when he was the unquestioned head of English poetry and English literature, and assisted by the active efforts of the most popular actor and manager of the day, succeeded in holding the stage fairly well with plays which are not very dramatic among dramas, and which are certainly not very poetical among their author's poems. With more recent times we have luckily nothing to do, and the assertions of some authors that they themselves or others have brought back literature to the stage may be left confronted with the assertions of not a few actors that, for reasons which they do not themselves profess entirely to comprehend, a modern drama is almost bound not to be literary if it is to act, and not to act if it is literary. Some have boldly solved the difficulty by hinting, if not declaring, that the drama is an outworn form except as mere spectacle or entertainment; others have exhausted themselves in solutions of a less trenchant kind; none, it may safely be said, has really solved it. And though it is quite true that what has happened was predicted sixty or seventy years ago, as a result of the breach of the monopoly of Covent Garden and Drury Lane, it is fair to say that the condition of the drama of at least a quarter of a century earlier had been little if at all better than it has been since. It is a simple fact that since Sheridan we have had no dramatist who combined very high acting with very high literary merit.

Of what have been called the applied departments of literature, a somewhat less melancholy account has to be given; but, except in their enormous multiplication of quantity, they present few opportunities for remarks of a general character.

Very great names have been added to the list of theological writers, but these names on the whole belong to the earlier rather than to the later portion of the period, and even then something of a change has been observable in the kinds of their writing. The sermon, that is to say the literary sermon, has become more and more uncommon; and the popular ear which calls upon itself to hear sermons at all prefers usually what are styled practical discourses, often deviating very considerably from the sermon norm, or else extremely florid addresses modelled on later Continental patterns, and having as a rule few good literary qualities. So, too, the elaborate theological treatise has gone out of fashion, and it may be doubted whether, at least for the last half century, a single book of the kind has been added to the first class of Anglican theological writing. This writing has thus taken the form either of discourses of the older kind, maintained in existence by endowment or by old prescription, such as the Bampton Lectures, or of rather popular polemics, or of what may be called without disrespect theological journalism of various kinds. The general historical energy of the century, moreover, has not displayed itself least in the theological department, and valuable additions have been made, not merely to general church history, but to a vast body of biography and journal-history, as well as to a certain amount of Biblical scholarship. In this latter direction English scholars have distinguished themselves by somewhat less violation of the rules of criticism in general than their foreign brethren and masters. But it cannot be said that the nineteenth century is ever likely to rank high in the history of English theology. Even its greatest names — Irving, Chalmers, the Oxford leaders, and others, with perhaps the single exception of Newman — are important much more personally and as influences than as literary figures ; while the rank and file, putting history aside, have been distinctly less noteworthy than in any of the three preceding centuries.

The " handmaid of theology " has received, at any rate during the first half of the period, or even the first three-quarters, more distinguished attentions than her mistress ; and the additions made to the list headed by Erigena and Anselm, if we allow Latin to count, by Bacon and Hobbes, if we stick to the vernacular, have been many and great. Yet it would not be unreasonable laudation of times past to say that there hardly, after Hume's death, arose any philosopher who combined the originality, the acuteness, and the literary skill of Hume during the first half of this century, while certainly, at least till within a period forbidden to our scheme, the latter part of the time has not seen any writer who could vie even with those of the earlier. To a certain extent the historical and critical tendencies so often noticed have here been unfortunate, inasmuch as they have diverted philosophical students from original writing — or at least from writing as original as the somewhat narrow and self-repeating paths of philosophy admit — to historical and critical exercises. But there is also no doubt that the immense authority which the too long neglected writers of Germany attained, a little before the middle of the century, has been unfortunate in at least one respect, if not also in others. The ignorant contempt of technicalities, and the determination to refer all things to common sense employing common language, which distinguished the eighteenth century with us, was certain to provoke a reaction ; and this reaction, assisted by imitation of the Germans, produced in the decades from 1840 onwards an ever-increasing tendency among English philosophers or students of philosophy to employ a jargon often as merely technical as the language of the schoolmen, and not seldom far emptier of any real argument. It is not too much to say that if the rough methods of Hobbes with a terminology far less fallacious, were employed with this jargon, it would look much poorer than Bramhall's scholasticisms look in the hands of the redoubtable Nominalist. Fortunately of late there have been more signs than one of yet another turn of tide, and of a fresh appeal to the *communis sensus*, not it may be hoped of the obstinately and deafly exoteric character of the eighteenth century, but such as will refuse to pay itself with words, and will exercise a judicious criticism in a language understanded of all educated people. Then, and not till then, we may expect to meet philosophy that is literature and literature that is philosophic.

Science, that is to say physical science, which has sometimes openly boasted itself as about to take, and has much more commonly made silent preparations for taking, the place both of philosophy and of theology, will hardly be said by the hardiest of her adherents to have done very much to justify these claims to seats not yet quite vacant from the point of view of the purely literary critic. We have had some excellent scientific writers, from Bishop Watson to Professor Huxley ; and some of the books of the century which would deserve remembrance and reading, whatever their subject matter, have been books of science. Yet it is scarcely rash to assert that the essential characteristics of science and the essential characteristics of literature are, if not so diametrically opposed as some have thought, at any rate very far apart from one another. Literature can never be scientific ; and though science may be literary, yet it is rather in the fashion in which a man borrows some alien vesture in order to present himself, in compliance with decency and custom, at a foreign court. Mathematics give us the example — perhaps the only example — of pure science, of what all science would be if it could, and of what it approaches, ever more nearly, as far as it can. It is needless to say that the perfect presentation of mathematics is in pure symbols, divested of all form and colour, of all personal tincture and bias. And it should be equally superfluous to add that it is in form and colour, in suggestion of sound rather than in precise expression and sense, in personal bias and personal tincture, that not merely the attraction but the very essence of literature consists.

By so much as verbal science or scholarship, which would seem to be more especially bound to be literature, claims to be and endeavours to be strictly scientific, by so much also necessarily does it divorce itself from the literature which it studies. This, if not an enormously great, is certainly rather a sore evil; and it is one of the most considerable and characteristic signs of the period we are discussing. The older scholarship, though sufficiently minute, still clung to the literary side proper : it was even, in the technical dialect of one of the universities, opposed to " science," which word indeed was itself used in a rather technical way. The invention of comparative philology, with its even more recent off-shoot phonetics, has changed all this, and we now find " linguistic " and " literary " used by common consent as things not merely different but hostile, with a further tendency on the part of linguistics to claim the term " scholarship " exclusively for itself.

This could hardly in any case be healthy. What may be the abstract value of the science, or group of sciences, called philology, it is perhaps not necessary here to inquire. It is sufficient to say that it clearly has nothing to do with literature except in accidental and remote applications, that it stands thereto much as geology does to architecture. Unfortunately, while the scientific side of scholarship is thus becoming, if it has not become, wholly unliterary, the æsthetic side has shown signs of becoming, to far too great an extent, unscientific in the bad and baneful sense. With some honourable exceptions, we find critics of literature too often divided into linguists who seem neither to think nor to be capable of thinking of the meaning or the melody, of the individual and technical mastery, of an author, a book, or a passage, and into loose æsthetic rhetoricians who will sometimes discourse on Æschylus without knowing a second aorist from an Attic perfect, and pronounce eulogies or depreciations on Virgil without having the faintest idea whether there is or is not any authority for *quamvis* with one mood rather than another. Nor is it possible to see what eirenicon is likely to present itself between two parties, of whom the extremists on the one side may justly point to such things as have here been quoted, while the extremists on the other feel it a duty to pronounce phonetics the merest " hariolation," and a very large part of what goes by the name of philology ingenious guesswork, some of which may possibly not be false, but hardly any of which can on principles of sound general criticism be demonstrated to be true. It is not wonderful, though it is in the highest degree unhealthy, that the stricter scholars should be more or less scornfully relinquishing the province of literary criticism altogether, while the looser æsthetics consider themselves entitled to neglect scholarship in any proper sense with a similarly scornful indifference.

It is, however, impossible that offences of this sort should not come now and then in the history of literature, and fortunately, in that history, they disappear as they appear. For the present purpose it is more important to conclude this conclusion with a few general remarks on the past, fewer on the present, and fewest of all on the future.

On this last head, indeed, no words were perhaps even better than even fewest ; though something of the sort may be expected. Rash as prophecy always is, it is never quite so rash as in literature ; and though we can sometimes, looking backward, say — perhaps even then with some rashness — that such and such a change might or ought to have been expected, it is very seldom that we can, when deprived of this illegitimate advantage, vaticinate on such subjects with any safety. Yet the study of the present always, so to speak, includes and overlaps something of the future, and by comparison at least of other presents we can discern what it is at least not improbable that the future may be. What, then, is the present of literature in England?

It can be described with the greater freedom that, as constantly repeated, we are not merely at liberty *ex hypothesi* to omit references to individuals, but are *ex hypothesi* bound to exclude them. And no writer, as it happens rather curiously, of anything like great promise or performance who was born later than the beginning of the fifties has died as yet, though the century is so near its close. Yet again, all the greatest men of the first quarter of the century, with the single exception of Mr. Ruskin, are gone ; and not many of the second remain. By putting these simple and unmistakable facts together it will be seen, in a fashion equally free from liability to cavil and from disobliging glances towards persons, that the present is at best a stationary state in our literary history. Were we distinctly on the mounting hand, it is, on the general calculation of the liabilities of human life, certain that we must have had our Shelley or our Keats side by side with our Wordsworth and our Coleridge. That we have much excellent work is certain; that we have much of the absolutely first class not so. And if we examine even the good work of our younger writers we shall find in much of it two notes or symptoms — one of imitation or exaggeration, the other of uncertain and eccentric quest for novelty — which have been already noted above as signs of decadence or transition.

Whether it is to be transition or decadence, that is the question. For the solution of it we can only advance with safety a few considerations, such as that in no literary history have periods of fresh and first-rate production ever continued longer than — that they have seldom continued so long as — the period now under notice, and that it is reasonable, it is almost certain, that, though by no means an absolutely dead season, yet a period of comparatively faint life and illustration should follow. To this it may be added as a consideration not without philosophical weight that the motives, the thoughts, the hopes, the fears, perhaps even the manners, which have defrayed the expense of the literary production of this generation, together with the literary forms in which, according to custom, they have embodied and ensconced themselves, have been treated with unexampled, certainly with unsurpassed, thoroughness, and must now be near exhaustion; while it is by no means clear that any fresh set is ready to take their place. It is on this last point, no doubt, that the more sanguine prophets would like to fight the battle, urging that new social ideas, and so forth, *are* in possession of the ground. But this is not the field for that battle.

In dealing with what has been, with the secular hour that we have actually and securely had, we are on far safer, if not on positively safe ground. Here the sheaves are actually reaped and brought home; and if the teller of them makes a mistake, his judgment, and his judgment only, need be at fault. Not all ways of such telling are of equal value. It may be tempting, for instance, but can hardly be very profitable, to attempt to strike an exact balance between the production of the century from 1780 to 1880 with that of the other great English literary century from 1580 to 1680. Dear as the exercise is to some literary accountants, there is perhaps no satisfactory system of book-keeping by which we can really set the assets and the liabilities of the period from the appearance of Spenser to the death of Browne against the assets and liabilities of that from the appearance of Burns to the death of Tennyson, and say which has the greater sum to its credit. Still more vague and futile would it be to attempt to set with any exactness this balance-sheet against that of the other great literary periods of other countries, languages, and times. Here again, most emphatically, accuracy of this kind is *not* to be expected.

But what we can say with confidence and profit is that the nineteenth century in England and English is of these great periods, and of the greatest of them; that it has taken its place finally and certainly, with a right never likely to be seriously challenged, and in a rank never likely to be much surpassed.

The period which lisped its numbers in Burns and Blake and Cowper, which broke out into full song with Wordsworth, Coleridge, Scott, Byron, Shelley, and Keats, which, not to mention scores of minor singers, took up the tale with Tennyson and Browning and passed it on to Arnold, Rossetti, Mr. Morris, and Mr. Swinburne, need fear no comparisons in the matter of poetry. In prose fiction, as we have seen, it stands alone. It is almost a century of origins as regards the most important kinds; it is quite a century of capital and classical performance in them. In "making"—prose or verse—no time leaves record of performance more distinguished or more various.

That in one great literary kind, drama, it exhibits lamentable deficiency, that indeed in that kind it hardly counts at all, has been admitted; and it is not probable that in any of the serious prose kinds, except history, it will ever rank very high when compared with others. Its theology has, as far as literature is concerned, been a little wanting in dignity, in finish, and even in fervour, its philosophy either commonplace or jargonish, its exercises in science and scholarship ever divorcing themselves further from literary ideals. But in the quality of its miscellaneous writing, as well as in the facilities given to such writing by its special growth—some would say its special fungus—of the periodical, it again rises to the first class. Hardly the period of Montaigne and Bacon, certainly not that of Dryden, Cowley, and Temple, nor that of Addison and Steele, nor that of Johnson and Goldsmith, can vie with the century of Charles Lamb and William Hazlitt, of Leigh Hunt and Thomas de Quincey, of Macaulay and Thackeray and Carlyle, of Arnold and Mr. Ruskin. Miscellaneous we have been,—perhaps too much so,—but we should be a little saved by the excellence of some of our miscellanists.

Pessimists would probably say that the distinguishing and not altogether favourable notes of the century are a somewhat vagabond curiosity in matter and a tormented unrest of style. The former concerns us little, and is chiefly noticeable here because of the effect which it has had on the great transformation of historical writing so often noticed ; the latter concerns us intimately. And no doubt there is hardly a single feature — not even the growth of the novel, not even the development of the newspaper — which will so distinctly and permanently distinguish this century in English literary history as the great changes which have come over style, and especially prose style. There has been less opportunity to notice these collectively in any of the former chapters than there has been to notice some other changes : nor was this of much importance, for the present is the right place for gathering up the fragments.

The change of style in prose is undoubtedly as much the leading feature of the century as is in poetry the change of thought and outlook, on which latter enough perhaps has been said elsewhere ; the whole of our two long chapters on poetry being indeed, with great part of this conclusion, a continuous exposition of it. But the change in prose was neither confined to, nor specially connected with, any single department of literature. Indirectly indeed, and distantly, it may be said to have been connected with the growth of the essay and the popularity of periodicals ; and yet it is not quite certain that this was anything more than a coincidence due to the actual fact that the first extensive practitioners of ornate prose, Wilson and De Quincey, were in a way journalists.

That the sudden ornateness, in part a mere ordinary reaction, was also in part due to a reflection of the greater gorgeousness of poetry, though it was in itself less a matter of thought than of style, is true. But literary reactions are always in part at least literary developments ; and after the prose of Burke and Gibbon, even after that of Johnson, it was certain that the excessive plainness reached in the mid-eighteenth century would be exchanged for something else. But it could not possibly have been anticipated that the change would exhibit the extent or the variety that it has actually shown.

That it has enriched English literature with a great deal of admirable matter is certain; that it has not merely produced a great deal of sad stuff, but has perhaps inflicted some permanent or at least lasting damage on the purity, the simplicity, and in the best sense the strength of style, is at least equally certain. It is less easy to say whether it is, as a movement, near its close, or with what sort of reaction it is likely to be followed. On the one hand the indication of particular follies and excesses may not seem decisive; for there is little doubt that in all the stages of this *flamboyant* movement—from De Quincey to Carlyle, from Carlyle to Mr. Ruskin, from Mr. Ruskin to persons whom it is unnecessary to mention—the advocates of the sober styles thought and said that the force of extravagance could no further go, and that the last outrages had been committed on the dignity and simplicity of English. On the other hand there are signs, which are very unlikely to deceive the practised critic, tending to show that the mode is likely to change. When actual frippery is seen hanging up in Monmouth Street or Monmouth Street's successors, when cheap imitations of fashionable garments crowd the shop windows and decorate the bodies of the vulgar—then the wise know that this fashion will shortly change. And certainly something similar may be observed in literature to-day. Cacophony jostles preciousness in novel and newspaper; attempts at contorted epigram appear side by side with slips showing that the writer has not the slightest knowledge of the classics in the old sense, and knows exceedingly little of anything that can be called classic in the widest possible acceptation of the term. Tyrannies cease when the cobblers begin to fear them; fashions, especially literary fashions, when the cobblers take them up.

Yet the production of what must or may be called literature is now so large, and in consequence of the spread of what is called education the appetite so largely exceeds the taste for it, that it is not so easy as it would once have been to forecast the extent and validity of any reaction that may take place.

If, without undue praising of times past, without pleading

2 H

guilty to the prejudices sometimes attributed to an academic education, and also without trespassing beyond the proper limits of this book, it may be permitted to express an opinion on the present state of English literature, that opinion, while it need not be very gloomy, can hardly be very sanguine. And one ground for discouragement, which very especially concerns us, lies in the fact that on the whole we are now *too* "literary." Not, as has been said, that the general taste is too refined, but that there is a too indiscriminate appetite in the general; not that the actual original force of our writers is, with rare exceptions, at all alarming, but that a certain amount of literary craftsmanship, a certain knowledge of the past and present of literature, is with us in a rather inconvenient degree. The public demands quantity, not quality; and it is ready, for a time at any rate, to pay for its quantity with almost unheard of returns, both, as the homely old phrase goes, in praise and in pudding. And the writer, though seldom hampered by too exact an education in form, has had books, as a rule, too much with him. Sometimes he simply copies, and knows that he copies; oftener, without knowing it, he follows and imitates, while he thinks that he is doing original work.

And worse than all this, the abundance of reading has created an altogether artificial habit — a habit quite as artificial as any that can ever have prevailed at other periods — of regarding the main stuff and substance of literature. Much reading of novels, which are to the ordinary reader his books, and his only books, has induced him to take their standards as the standards of both nature and life. And this is all the more dangerous because in all probability the writers of these very novels have themselves acquired their knowledge, formed their standards, in a manner little if at all more first-hand. We have nature, not as Jones or Brown saw it for himself, but as he saw it through the spectacles of Mr. Ruskin or of Jefferies; art, not as he saw it himself, but as he saw it through those of Mr. Ruskin again or of Mr. Pater; literary criticism as he learnt it from Mr. Arnold or from Sainte-

Beuve ; criticism of life as he took it from Thackeray or from Mr. Meredith.

Something like this has occurred at least three times before in the history of European literature. It happened in late Græco-Roman times, and all the world knows what the cure was then, and how the much-discussed barbarian cleared the mind of Europe of its literary cant by very nearly clearing out all the literature as well. It happened on a much smaller scale, and with a less tremendous purgation, at the close of the Middle Ages, when the world suddenly, as it were, shut up one library and opened another ; and at the end of the seventeenth and beginning of the eighteenth century, when it shut both of these or the greater part of them, and took to a small bookshelf of " classics," a slender stock of carefully observed formulæ and — common sense.

What it will take to now, nobody can say ; but that it will in one fashion or another change most of its recent wear, shut most of its recent books, and perhaps give itself something of a holiday from literature, except in scholastic shapes, may be not quite impossible. Another *Lyrical Ballads* may be coming for this decade, as it came a hundred years ago : all we can say is that it apparently has not come yet. But whether it does come or does not, the moment is certainly no bad one, even if chronology did not make it inviting, for setting in order the actual, the certain, the past and registered production of the century since the dawn of the great change which ended its vigil. The historian, as he closes his record, is only too conscious of the objections to omission that may probably be brought against him, and of those of too liberal admission which certainly will be brought. It is possible that for some tastes even this chapter may not contain enough of *Tendenz*-discussion, that they may miss the broader sweeps and more confident generalisations of another school of criticism. But the old objection to fighting with armour which you have not proved has always seemed a sound one, and has seldom failed to be justified of those who set it at nought. Careful arrangement of detail and premiss, cautious drawing of conclusions, and constant subjection of these conclusions to that process of literary comparison which I believe to be the strongest, the safest, the best engine of literary criticism altogether — these are the things which I have endeavoured to observe here. It might have shown greater strength of mind to reject a large number of the authors here named, and so bring the matter into case for more extended treatment of interesting individuals. But there is something, as it seems to me, a little presumptuous in a too peremptory anticipation of the operations of Time the Scavenger. The critic may pretty well foresee the operations of the wallet-bearer, but he is not to dictate to him the particular "alms for oblivion" which he shall give. As it used to be the custom for a dramatic author, even though damned, to have his entrées at the theatre, so those who have once made an actual figure on the literary stage are entitled, until some considerable time has elapsed, to book-room. They lose it gradually and almost automatically; and as I have left out many writers of the end of last century whom, if I had been writing sixty years since, I should doubtless have put in, many of the first half of it whom I should have admitted if I had been writing thirty years since, so in another generation others will no doubt exercise a similar thinning on my own passed or pressed men.

But few, however, I think, appear here without more or less right of admission to the mind-map of the century's literature which a well-furnished mind should at this moment contain. That such a mind-map, quite irrespective of examinations and lecture-courses, and of literary bread-study generally, is a valuable thing, I have no doubt. And I think, without wishing to magnify mine office, that the general possession of it might do something to counteract these disastrous influences which have been referred to a little earlier. A man should surely be a little less apt to take the pinchbeck poetry of his own day for gold when he remembers the Della Cruscans and Sentimentalists, the Montgomerys and the Tuppers; the terror-novel and the Minerva Press should surely be useful skeletons to him at his feast of fiction in kinds which it would be beyond my province to describe more particularly.   He will not clamour, as I have known very excellent persons clamour, for the " raising of English to a new power " when he has before him the long procession of ingenious jargonists whose jargon has been in its turn hailed as a revelation and dismissed as an old song. And he will neither overexalt the dignity of literature, nor be a self-tormentor and a tormentor of others about its approaching decline and fall, when he sees how constantly, how incessantly, the kissed mouth has renewed its freshness, the apparently dying flower has shed seed and shot suckers for a new growth.

INDEX

(It has been endeavoured in this Index to include the name (with dates) of every author, and the title of every book, discussed in detail. But in order to avoid unnecessary bulk, books and authors merely referred to, as well as parts of books, are not usually given.)

THE HISTORY

OF

EARLY ENGLISH LITERATURE.

Being the History of English Poetry from its Beginnings to the Accession of King Ælfred.

BY THE

REV. STOPFORD A. BROOKE.

WITH MAPS.

Large 12mo.   Gilt top. $2.50.

NOTICES.

" I had been eagerly awaiting it, and find it on examination distinctly the best treatise on its subject."— PROF. CHARLES F. RICHARDSON, *Dartmouth College.*

" I know of no literary estimate of Anglo-Saxon poetry that in breadth of view and sympathetic appreciation can be compared with this."— PROF. W. E. MEAD, *Wesleyan University.*

" In this work we have the view of a real lover of literature, and we have its utterance in a diction graceful enough to make the reading an intellectual pleasure in itself."— *The Christian Union.*

" No other book exists in English from which a reader unacquainted with Anglo-Saxon may gain so vivid a sense of the literary quality of our earliest poetry."
— *The Dial.*

" A delightful exposition of the poetic spirit and achievement of the eighth century."— *Chicago Tribune.*

" In Mr. Stopford Brooke's monumental work he strives with rare skill and insight to present our earliest national poetry as a living literature, and not as a mere material for research."— *London Times.*

" It is a monument of scholarship and learning, while it furnishes an authentic history of English literature at a period when little before was known respecting it."
— *Public Opinion.*

" It is a comprehensive critical account of Anglo-Saxon poetry from its beginnings to the accession of King Alfred.   A thorough knowledge of the Anglo-Saxon language was needed by the man who undertook such a weighty enterprise, and this knowledge is possessed by Mr. Brooke in a degree probably unsurpassed by any living scholar."— *Evening Bulletin.*

MACMILLAN & CO.,

66 FIFTH AVENUE, NEW YORK.

A HISTORY

ELIZABETHAN LITERATURE.

BY

GEORGE SAINTSBURY.

Price, $1.00, net.

NOTICES.

"The work has been most judiciously done and in a literary style and perfection which, alas, the present era has furnished too few examples." — *Christian at Work*.

"Mr. Saintsbury has produced a most useful, first-hand survey — comprehensive, compendious, and spirited — of that unique period of literary history when 'all the muses still were in their prime.' One knows not where else to look for so well-proportioned and well-ordered conspectus of the astonishingly varied and rich products of the turning English mind during the century that begins with Tortel's Miscellany and the birth of Bacon, and closes with the restoration." — *The Dial*.

"Regarding Mr. Saintsbury's work we know not where else to find so compact, yet comprehensive, so judicious, weighty, and well written a review and critique of Elizabethan literature. But the analysis generally is eminently distinguished by insight, delicacy, and sound judgment, and that applies quite as much to the esti-mates of prose writers as to those of the poets and dramatists. . . . A work which deserves to be styled admirable." — *New York Tribune*

MACMILLAN & CO.,

66 FIFTH AVENUE, NEW YORK.

A HISTORY

OF

EIGHTEENTH CENTURY LITERATURE.

(1660-1780.)

BY

EDMUND GOSSE, M.A.,

Clark Lecturer in English Literature at Trinity College, Cambridge.

Price, $1.00, net.

NOTICES.

" Mr. Gosse's book is one for the student because of its fulness, its trustworthiness, and its thorough soundness of criticisms; and one for the general reader because of its pleasantness and interest. It is a book, indeed, not easy to put down or to part with." — OSWALD CRAWFURD, in *London Academy.*

" Mr. Gosse has in a sense preëmpted the eighteenth century. He is the most obvious person to write the history of its literature, and this attractive volume ought to be the final and standard work on his chosen theme." — *The Literary World.*

" We have never had a more useful record of this period."
— *Boston Evening Traveler.*

" A brilliant addition to critical exposition. Written in a finished and elegant style, which gives enchantment even to the parts of the narrative of a biographical and statistical character, the work illumines obscure writings and literature and brings new interest to famous ones. One of its great excellences is the easy transition made from one style of writing to another. The plan is distinct and well-preserved, but the continuity between parts is so close that unity and coherence mark the work in a material degree." — *Boston Journal.*

MACMILLAN & CO.,

66 FIFTH AVENUE, NEW YORK.